ISBN 978-1-331-82539-5
PIBN 10095459

1 MONTH OF
FREE
READING

at

www.ForgottenBooks.com

By purchasing this book you are
eligible for one month membership to
ForgottenBooks.com, giving you
unlimited access to our entire
collection of over 1,000,000 titles via
our web site and mobile apps.

To claim your free month visit:

www.forgottenbooks.com/free95459

English
Français
Deutsche
Italiano
Español
Português

www.forgottenbooks.com

Mythology Photography **Fiction**
Fishing Christianity **Art** Cooking
Essays Buddhism Freemasonry
Medicine **Biology** Music **Ancient
Egypt** Evolution Carpentry Physics
Dance Geology **Mathematics** Fitness
Shakespeare **Folklore** Yoga Marketing
Confidence Immortality Biographies
Poetry **Psychology** Witchcraft
Electronics Chemistry History **Law**
Accounting **Philosophy** Anthropology
Alchemy Drama Quantum Mechanics
Atheism Sexual Health **Ancient History**
Entrepreneurship Languages Sport
Paleontology Needlework Islam
Metaphysics Investment Archaeology
Parenting Statistics Criminology
Motivational

DAI NIPPON

THE BRITAIN OF THE EAST

A STUDY IN NATIONAL EVOLUTION

BY

HENRY DYER, C.E., M.A., D.Sc.

EMERITUS PROFESSOR, IMPERIAL UNIVERSITY OF TOKYO
FORMERLY PRINCIPAL OF AND PROFESSOR OF ENGINEERING IN THE IMPERIAL COLLEGE
OF ENGINEERING, TOKYO
LIFE GOVERNOR, GLASGOW AND WEST OF SCOTLAND TECHNICAL COLLEGE
ETC., ETC.

LONDON
BLACKIE & SON, LIMITED, 50 OLD BAILEY, E.C.
GLASGOW AND DUBLIN
1904

I DEDICATE THIS BOOK

TO THE STUDENTS OF THE KOBU-DAIGAKKO

WHO HAVE DONE SO MUCH TO MAKE

MODERN JAPAN

Not only as a memorial of past work, but also in the hope
that they may find it helpful in the solution of the problems
which lie before their country in the future.

PREFACE

MY object in the following pages has not been to give a history of modern Japan or detailed statistics of recent developments—to do that adequately would require at least a volume for the treatment of each of the main subjects mentioned in the different chapters—it has rather been to indicate the forces which have been at work in bringing about what is admitted to be the wonder of the latter half of the nineteenth century ; namely, the rise of Japan as a member of the comity of nations, and to note some of the chief results. Historical details are therefore omitted and the use of statistics has been limited to such figures as seemed necessary in order that a fairly complete picture might be given of the different aspects of national life which have gone to make modern Japan. As one who took an active part in the educational and engineering works which have been among the main factors in producing the great changes that have taken place, I have naturally given special attention to these and to their direct results on the national life, but at the same time I have endeavoured to take a wider view of the subject, and have at least indicated, I admit imperfectly, the inner forces which, after all, have been most powerful. It is well to remember that "cause" means the sum of the conditions which produce a phenomenon. I have noted what have seemed to me to be the chief conditions which have brought about the great developments that have taken place in Japan, but national evolution is such a complex phenomenon that it is difficult either to state exactly the nature of the conditions or to estimate their relative importance. One thing, however, is clear, and that is, the fact that the impulse came from within accounts in great part for the rapid progress which Japan has made in Western methods.

In Japan, as in other countries, the developments of industry and commerce have started forces which are causing many serious problems, not only of an economic but also of a social and moral nature, which will require very careful consideration. Lovers of Japan are somewhat dismayed at the disintegration of taste and ideals which is coming about in consequence of modern competition, and which is having very serious effects not only on the national life but also on international relations. My satisfaction at the great success which has attended the work of the students of the Imperial College of Engineering has been damped when I ponder over the problems which lie before Japan, but my consolation has come when I recognise that without that work Japan as a separate nationality would probably have disappeared under the aggression of Foreign Powers. The world cannot afford to lose such a unique nationality, not only because of its special qualities but also because it is the chief progressive force in the Far East. Although she is confronted with many difficult problems, Japan is now strong and determined not only to maintain her independence but to be a very important factor in the evolution which is rapidly transforming economic and political conditions in the Pacific area.

Without attempting the *rôle* of a prophet, I have in

the concluding chapters glanced at some of the political, economic, and social results of modern developments, and have indicated some of the problems which I believe lie before Japan. On these subjects there will of course be great differences of opinion, and what I have said must be taken only for what it is worth; but having a fairly intimate knowledge of the affairs of the country during the whole of the period of modern development, I venture to hope that I have at least suggested points which are worthy of the attention of all who are interested in the future of Japan. My own ideas with regard to that future are decidedly optimistic, and I believe that in material, intellectual, and moral influence Japan will fully justify her claim to be called the Britain of the East.

Instead of burdening the pages of the book with numerous notes and references to authorities, I have, at the end of each chapter, given the names of the most important books and documents I have consulted on the subjects of that chapter, and in the Appendix I have added a list of books and other publications which will be useful to those who wish detailed information on the important developments in Japan of which I have been able to give only a broad outline. I owe so much to my numerous friends in Japan, that it is impossible to name them all, but there are two who must be specially mentioned. Dr. Sakatani, the Vice-Minister of Finance, has kept me supplied with all the most important Government publications, and to him I am very grateful. The files of the *Japan Daily Mail*, of which my old colleague Captain Brinkley is the editor, are mines of information not only for the details of current history but also for able and important discussions on all things Japanese. I receive the journal weekly from Japan, and it has been of great service to me. Captain Brinkley's monumental book on *Japan and China* should be carefully studied by all who wish to know Japan. It deals with history, manners and customs, religion, art, politics and modern conditions, and gives full information on many points which I have been able only to touch. I have repeatedly quoted Captain Brinkley when dealing with subjects on which he is a special authority. My students in all parts of the country have not only kept me informed with regard to their work but have also discussed with me many of the questions on which I have touched in this book. Its plan renders necessary a certain amount of repetition of some of the main facts of modern Japanese history, so that my readers may understand their connection with the subjects directly under discussion, and logical arrangement has, to a certain extent, been sacrificed to the convenience of general readers.

DOWANHILL, GLASGOW,
September 1904.

CONTENTS

CHAPTER I

INTRODUCTORY

CHAPTER II

FALL OF FEUDALISM

CHAPTER III

THE JAPANESE MIND

CHAPTER VIII

INDUSTRIAL DEVELOPMENTS

CHAPTER IX

ART INDUSTRIES

CHAPTER X

COMMERCE

CHAPTER XI

Food Supply

CHAPTER XII

Colonisation and Emigration

CHAPTER XIII

Constitutional Government

CHAPTER XIV

Administration

CHAPTER XV

FINANCE

CHAPTER XVI

INTERNATIONAL RELATIONS

CHAPTER XVII

FOREIGN POLITICS

CHAPTER XVIII

SOCIAL RESULTS

CHAPTER XIX

THE FUTURE

CHAPTER XX

RECENT EVENTS

APPENDICES

APPENDIX A

APPENDIX B

APPENDIX C

CHAPTER I

INTRODUCTORY

IN my preface I have briefly indicated the object of this book, but in order that my readers may understand my point of view and the trend of thought which runs through its pages, it is desirable that I should give a few preliminary explanations which will help to bring them, to a certain extent, within the sphere of my mental environment. The writing of even the simplest history necessitates rethinking it, and in that process the introduction of the personal equation is inevitable. A study of national evolution is much more complicated than a mere record of facts, and when an attempt is made to estimate the chief forces which have been at work, and not only to state their results in the past but also to indicate what they are likely to be in the future, it is evident that the value of the opinions expressed must depend, to a very large extent, on the personal experience of the writer. I have no intention, at present, of attempting to write my own natural history, and in making a short statement of some of the facts of my experience I do not put it forward as an apology for any of my shortcomings in my treatment of the subjects discussed in the book. I shall be content if it be accepted as an explanation.

When the embassy from Japan of which Iwakura, the Junior Prime Minister, was the head, came to Britain at the end of 1872, I was offered, through Professor Rankine of Glasgow University and Mr. H. M. Matheson, the agent of the Public Works Department of Japan in London, the position of Principal of the Engineering College which

The Imperial College of Engineering.

it was proposed to found in Tokyo. Mr. Ito (now Marquis Ito), one of the ambassadors, was Vice-Minister of Public Works, and it was his wish that a College should be organised which would train men who would be able to design and superintend the works which were necessary for Japan to carry on if she adopted Western methods. Fortunately, for some time previously I had made a special study of all the chief methods of scientific and engineering study in the different countries of the world and of the organisation of some of the most important institutions, with the intention of devoting myself to the advancement of engineering education in Britain, so that I had fairly definite ideas both as to what was desirable and what was possible. I little thought that my first experiments would be made in far Japan, a country which, at that time, was almost unknown to foreigners, but which is now leading the way not only in education but also in many of the arts of peace and war.

Mr. Ito was kind enough to arrange that his private secretary, Mr. Hayashi (now Viscount Hayashi, Japanese Minister in London), should accompany me to Japan, and we sailed from Southampton early in April 1873. My time on the voyage was chiefly occupied in writing a draft of the Calendar of the proposed College, and on my arrival in Tokyo I was able to present it complete to the Acting Vice-Minister of Public Works, and it was accepted by the Government without change of any kind.

I was pleasantly surprised to recognise in Mr. Yamao, the Acting Vice-Minister of Public Works, a man whom I had seen as a student in the evening classes of Anderson's College, Glasgow (now incorporated in the Glasgow and West of Scotland Technical College), when he was learning the practice of shipbuilding in Napier's yard. I did not make his personal acquaintance during his stay in Glasgow, but his connection with that city gave us much in common.

I wish to bear testimony to the whole-hearted support which he gave to all my proposals for the education of engineers, and to his personal kindness on every possible occasion. To his efforts much of the success of the College was due. Mr. Hayashi became Chief Commissioner of the College, representing the Department of Public Works and managing the finances and the administrative staff, while I, as Principal, was responsible for the educational arrangements. After seeing the College fairly started and rendering it most effective service, Mr. Hayashi entered the wider administrative departments of the Government and became Governor of one of the southern provinces. Later on, he became a member of the diplomatic service. After representing his country for several years in China, he acted as Vice-Minister for Foreign Affairs during the war with China, and for his special services he was raised to the peerage under the title of Baron Hayashi. He next went to St. Petersburg as Minister Plenipotentiary for Japan; he is now, as Viscount Hayashi, in a similar position in London, and he will be remembered in history as the diplomatist who carried on the final negotiations which resulted in the alliance between Great Britain and Japan.

While fully recognising the services of the representatives of the Japanese Government and the liberal support of the Government itself, it must of course be admitted that the success which attended the work of the College was chiefly due to the enthusiastic manner in which the various members of the staff entered on their duties. We were, for the most part, young men without much experience, and in looking back I now recognise the risks which were run in placing us in such responsible positions. No doubt we made mistakes, but even our most severe critics admit that the College was the most successful educational institution in Japan. The subsequent careers of the members of the staff have proved the wisdom which was shown in their selection. The original professors of the College were W. E. Ayrton, Natural Philosophy; D. H.

Marshall, M.A., Mathematics; Edward Divers, M.D., Chemistry; Edmund F. Mondy, A.R.S.M., Drawing ; and William Craigie, M.A., English Language and Literature ; while George Cawley, Robert Clark, and Archibald King took charge of the practical parts of the instruction in engineering. Almost all these names are now well known in the world of science and education, and the bearers of them have not only distinguished themselves by their researches, but from their experience in Japan they have been able to exercise great influence in moulding the conditions of scientific and engineering education in this country.

Additions were made to the staff of the College as its work developed. John Milne, F.G.S., became Professor of Geology and Mining and made himself a world-wide reputation by his investigations in seismology ; John Perry, B.E., A. W. Thomson, B.Sc., Thomas Gray, B.Sc., and Thomas Alexander, C.E., as Professors in the Engineering Department, developed the methods of instruction and began the researches which have made them famous ; and Josiah Conder, A.R.I.B.A., became Professor of Architecture and still remains in Japan in the practice of the profession by which he has done so much to meet the modern requirements of the country. Captain Brinkley, R.A., the distinguished Japanese scholar and authority on everything Japanese, was for some time Professor of Mathematics. To Captain Brinkley's writings I am specially indebted for information on many of the points discussed in the following pages. Our first Professor of English, Mr. Craigie, was compelled to return to Scotland after a few years on account of his health, and his colleagues received the news of his death shortly afterwards, with great sorrow. He was succeeded by W. Gray Dixon, M.A., and he in turn by his brother, James M. Dixon, M.A., both of whom did excellent work in their own department. We soon gathered round the foreign staff of the College a number of Japanese assistants, who in a comparatively short time were able to render very efficient service.

With such an able staff, all enthusiastic in the work, the

College was certain to be a success if all the other conditions were favourable. The Japanese authorities did all in their power to bring about that success. Within five years from its institution, handsome and commodious buildings had been erected and the most improved appliances of all kinds supplied for teaching purposes. The general arrangements which I made for the course of training were such as to meet the requirements of the country. It extended over six years, the first and second of which were devoted to the general training required for all depart- Courses of study. ments of engineering. At the beginning of the third year the students selected the special departments which they wished to follow. The technical courses were—(*a*) Civil Engineering, (*b*) Mechanical Engineering, (*c*) Telegraphy, (*d*) Architecture, (*e*) Practical Chemistry, (*f*) Mining, (*g*) Metallurgy. Naval Architecture was added a few years later. One-half of the third and fourth years was spent at College, and the other half at practical work. The last two years of the course were spent entirely at practical work.

In this way the students obtained a fair introduction to the theory and the practice of their profession, and there can be no doubt that the success which has attended their work has been, in great part, due to the method adopted in their training. In the College itself mere book-work was made of secondary importance, and by means of drawing offices, laboratories, and practical engineering works the students were taught the relations between theory and practice, and trained in habits of observation and original thought. The College being in the Department of Public Works, the students had the run of all the engineering establishments and public works under its control, and in this way they had exceptional advantages. I do not propose to enter into further details of the work of the College, my present object being simply to give a general sketch of the methods employed.

Some of our first graduates were sent over to Universities and Colleges in Britain, and without exception they distinguished themselves in their classes, not infrequently taking the first place. The best proof, however, of the

Success of students. value of the training which they received is the excellent work which the students have done since they left College, as there are few engineering or industrial works in Japan in which they are not to be found taking an active part in the management.

Having been about ten years in Japan and seen the College firmly established, for personal and family reasons

Departure from Japan. I resigned my position, and on my suggestion Dr. Edward Divers was appointed Principal of the College, and instructions were sent to the agents in London to select a man who would take up my work as Professor of Engineering. Charles Dickenson West, M.A., University of Dublin, was appointed, and he still continues to occupy the Professorship of Mechanical Engineering in the Engineering College of Tokyo University. As marks of appreciation of my services the Emperor bestowed on me the Order of the Rising Sun (Third Class), the highest honour of the kind given to any foreign employé up to that time, and the Government conferred on me the title of Honorary Principal of the College. Since the Engineering College was made a College of the University of Tokyo, I have been appointed Emeritus Professor of that institution. My students have taken an active part in the formation and carrying on of many associations and societies in connection with engineering and science, and they have elected me an Honorary Member of the most important of these, and I receive frequent communications from them informing me of their work. The former students of the Imperial College of Engineering (Kobu-Daigakko) are now to be found not only in all the most important engineering and industrial undertakings in Japan, but a considerable number of them are actively engaged in China and Korea; so that the College has been a most important factor in bringing about the changes in Japan and in influencing conditions in the Far East generally.

The extent of these changes and the amount of that influence will be indicated very plainly in the following pages, and I might quote from contemporary Results of work of College. journals and subsequent observers to show the place which the College took in the national evolution of Japan, but space will allow me to mention the opinions only of a few who were able to judge of the actual results. On the occasion of his last visit to Britain, Marquis Ito was unable to visit Scotland as he had expected to do, as events called him back to Japan, but Viscount Hayashi wrote stating that the Marquis had expressed his high appreciation of my services in Japan, saying, " That Japan can boast to-day of being able to undertake such industrial works as the construction of railways, telegraphs, telephones, shipbuilding, working of mines, and other manufacturing works entirely by the hands of Japanese engineers is mainly attributable to the College so ably established and set in motion by you." The Marquis had previously expressed similar opinions to Mr. Alfred Stead, who records that in the course of an interview with him he said, " When I was in London, engaged in my work of preparing the Japanese Constitution, I was approached on the subject of forming a special Engineering College in Japan. It was pointed out that the advantages would be very great for the country, and that such a scheme of engineering education had never been carried out in any other country. Accordingly I established the College, and brought many foreign Professors to Japan for that purpose. The Japanese engineers who are now running the most important concerns in Japan were trained in the College and can dispense altogether with foreign aid." [1] The opinions of the Marquis have been confirmed by many of the leading men in Japan and by others who have had opportunities of judging.

In his interesting and valuable book, *Japan in Transition*, Mr. Stafford Ransome, M.Inst.C.E., who spent considerable time in Japan as the special commissioner of the well-known

[1] Stead, *Japan, Our New Ally*, p. 57.

journal, *The Engineer*, says : " Although the higher branches of modern technical training had been experimented with in Japan at a somewhat earlier period, it was not until 1873, when Mr. Henry Dyer was engaged by the Japanese Government, that a solid system of technical education was inaugurated."　In his review of the circumstances which led to " Japan's Accession to the Comity of Nations," Baron Alexander von Siebold says : " After the Restoration of the monarchy the first attempts were made with the help of English and American teachers, to introduce something like unity into the system of public instruction.　Of these endeavours the immediate result was the establishment of the ' Imperial College of Engineering,' which had reached a flourishing state by the year 1875.　The founding of this Polytechnical College was a particularly happy idea of the Japanese Government, aiming, as it did, simultaneously with the introduction of railways and telegraphs, and the training of a native staff of experts to work them.　That institution has already borne rich fruit.　The whole of Japan is now covered with a network of railways, which are being constantly extended."

Many of the scientific and technical journals contained descriptions of the work of the College and its results, but meantime it would be out of place to enter into these, although a full account may be published in the future. The only other opinions to which I will refer are those of Dr. Edward Divers, F.R.S., who was Professor of Chemistry in the Imperial College of Engineering from its foundation, and who succeeded me as Principal.　A discussion had arisen in *The Engineer* in connection with a series of articles which had been written by Mr. Stafford Ransome, the special correspondent already referred to, who had been sent to Japan to give an account of the development of engineering in that country.　In such matters differences of opinion are certain to exist, and I would prefer not to enter into the discussion at all, but as a matter of history it cannot be ignored. A very fair statement of the facts of the case were given by

Dr. Divers in a letter to *The Engineer,*[1] and to this I would refer for details. Meantime I shall quote only a few sentences. After sketching the early history of the Imperial College of Engineering, Dr. Divers says : "While, as will have become plain, there are many engineers who may claim to have each done something in Japanese training—and, in individual cases, sometimes very much—there is, it may truly be said, one to whom, almost alone, Japan owes its well-organised and elaborated system of engineering education, namely, Dr. Henry Dyer of Glasgow, one of the Governors of the Glasgow and West of Scotland Technical College, whose latest act in connection with it has been the selection this year of a Professor of Naval Architecture as colleague to Mr. Miyoshi, Professor of the same subject. Dr. Dyer came to Japan in 1873, not as a Professor of Engineering only, but to found and organise in all its details, large and small, an institution for the education of engineers in Japan. He was given a salary proportional to his double duties, and an extent of power in the control of affairs quite exceptional for a foreigner in the Japanese service, whether then or since. The result of his work was the College of Engineering, the first school of engineering of any kind in the country, and such as could hardly have been developed under less favourable circumstances. Its magnitude of plan and completeness of execution soon made it far and away the most prominent educational institution in Japan. It attracted, too, the particular notice of the foreign—British and other— community in Tokyo and the Treaty port of Yokohama, some of whom dubbed it 'Dyer's' College, and in conjunction with some wealthy Japanese notables endowed it with a very respectable fund to provide annual prizes for the cadets."

Dr. Divers enters at some length into the changes in the administration which took place (and which will be noticed in a following chapter), and then says : "There is only left me, in order to complete this long account of the foundation

---

[1] May 6, 1898.

and growth of engineering education in Japan, to show in what estimation Japanese engineers and the Imperial University hold the services of Dr. Dyer.   With the one exception of the Geographical Society, the Engineering Society of Japan is the most influential learned society in the country.   It has a journal of its own, and a very long roll of members, of which only three are foreigners.   Of these three, again, but one is an engineer, and he is Dr. Dyer. Again in the 'Historical Summary'—Chronology would be more correct—of the Imperial University contained in its 'Calendar' no one is mentioned at all except its successive Presidents and Mr. Henry Dyer, the first Principal of the College of Engineering.   It is not customary in Japan to refer to individuals in official-so-called histories of institutions. The honour to Dr. Dyer is therefore especially great that he is not only named but the value of his services acknowledged." As the fact connected with my departure from Japan has already been noted it is not necessary to quote Dr. Divers further.

In the years immediately following the Restoration, it must be admitted that there was in Japan a certain amount of overlapping in the work of the different Departments of Government.   The Minister of Public Works was anxious to train men who would be useful in carrying out engineering works, and he therefore arranged that the Imperial College of Engineering should be in his Department, so that the students might have the advantage of experience on practical works.   On the other hand, the authorities of the Education Department were anxious to have all the educational institutions in the country under their control, and when they could not manage this they sometimes started duplicate courses of their own ; but the connection of the Imperial College of Engineering with the Public Works Department gave it a great advantage, and the majority of engineering students attended it.   Some years after I left Japan the Public Works Department was absorbed in some of the other Government Departments and the Engineering College became a College of the Imperial University of Tokyo, but this and other facts will be noted when we are dealing with education in Japan.

Meantime, therefore, it is not necessary to enter into further details of the history of the Imperial College of Engineering, my present object being, as I have said, to bring Observations on my readers within the sphere of my mental the Continent environment and thus help to explain my point and in Britain. of view in the following pages, but a very imperfect idea of that would be given if I did not briefly indicate my experience since I left Japan. The greater part of the first year after my return was spent on the Continent of Europe in the study of educational institutions and the inspection of engineering works. Hitherto my attention had been chiefly confined to the scientific aspect of my work, but personal knowledge of social and economic conditions in Europe soon showed me that engineering education was only a small part of the problem of education, and indeed that undue attention to it might help to intensify social problems.

A very active share in the organisation and management of educational institutions in Glasgow of all grades, and an increasing interest in social problems, have kept me in close touch with the actual conditions, and this has been supplemented by the study of reports of all kinds from all parts of the world. An interesting fact in the history of education is to be found in the organisation of the Glasgow and West of Scotland Technical College. When that College was formed by the amalgamation of existing scientific institutions in Glasgow, I was able to transfer from Japan the programme of studies of the Imperial College of Engineering to the Glasgow institution which is the successor of the College in which the Vice-Minister of Public Works and I studied as apprentices in the evening classes.

There can be no doubt that a lengthened absence from Britain enables one, on his return, to observe British social conditions from a detached and comparative Social problems point of view which was not before possible, in Britain. and he finds much in these conditions to excite the most painful anxiety, which may result either in deadly pessimism or in an active determination to devote himself to efforts which tend to improvement.   The ever-widening extremes of poverty and wealth, the conditions of life of our poorest classes, the production on a large scale of degenerates who are physically, mentally, and morally unfit for a fair share of the duties of citizenship, the uncertainty of employment, the growth of monopoly which is placing the conditions of the people at the mercy of a comparatively small number of capitalists, and the immense armaments which are sucking the life-blood of the nations, are all factors which give rise to very serious thought.   The brutal materialism which pervades all classes of the community makes true art almost impossible, while the soul-destroying ennui of the leisured on the one hand and the restlessness of the middle and poorer classes render their intellects, their hearts, and their consciences almost inaccessible.   An increasing number of all classes do not even make a profession of religion, but content themselves with the pursuit of self-centred individualism and refined sensualism which blinds them to the importance of the great social problems with which every industrial country in the world is now confronted.

Those who return from Japan, especially if they have known it under the old regime, may well doubt whether the Social problems importation of Western civilisation is likely in Japan.   to be an unmixed blessing to the people, although they will admit that it was necessary to save Japan from foreign aggression.   Fortunately, the most thoughtful among the Japanese are recognising these facts, and they are becoming more and more impressed with the necessity for attention being paid to the social and economic conditions of the people and to the problems arising therefrom.   My friends in Japan keep me ·supplied with many of the more important journals and official reports, and long conversations with those who visit this country prove to me that the most thoughtful minds in Japan fully recognise the difficulty of the problems with which they are confronted. ,They see that the engineer is the real revolutionist; for his work changes social and economic conditions and brings forces into action which are more powerful than anything which can be done by mere legislation. The students of the Imperial College of Engineering are the men who, to a large extent, have been the means of developing engineering and industry in Japan, and it seems appropriate that a study of that remarkable evolution which has made that country a world Power should be preceded by an outline of the circumstances in which the College was founded and an indication given of the results which have followed from that evolution. Some of these results have no doubt diminished the charm which Old Japan had for lovers of nature and art, but it cannot be doubted that if the Japanese had not taken advantage of Western science and methods for the development of their resources, in order that their country might become strong, it would probably ere this have been dominated by a Western Power. The problem of the future is :—How best to take full advantage of all that is good in Western civilisation while retaining the special characteristics of Japan and bringing them into organic harmony with those of other nations. On the solution of that problem depends the welfare of Japan.

BIBLIOGRAPHICAL NOTE

For details of the institutions referred to in this chapter, reference should be made to the Calendar of the Imperial College of Engineering, Tokyo, Japan, 1873-1888, and to the Reports of the same College. For recent developments the Calendar of the Imperial University of Tokyo should be consulted. The Calendar of the Glasgow and West of Scotland Technical College shows the application of the experience of Japan to a Scottish College. Existing social and economic conditions in Britain should be studied in such books as Booth's *Life and Labour of the People in London* and Rowntree's *Poverty, a Study of Town Life*, and in other countries in similar books. The literature which has been published in recent years on industrial, social, economic, and political subjects is very extensive, and reference should be made to special catalogues.

CHAPTER II

FALL OF FEUDALISM

NOTWITHSTANDING all that has been written about Japan in recent years, a very common impression in Europe and America seems to be that feudalism was put an end to in Japan by a stroke of the pen of the Emperor, and that the cause of the change was the advent of foreigners in the Land of the Rising Sun. Although there is an element of truth in the impression, it is so imperfect that it is desirable to indicate, in outline, the causes leading to the revolution which inaugurated the great developments that have taken place in Japan during the latter half of the nineteenth century, so that these developments may be better understood. To do so completely would involve a study of Old Japan in its many aspects; all that we can attempt is a sketch which will indicate the chief forces which were at work.

It is not necessary to enter into an examination of the origins of Japanese history. It is sufficient for our purpose
Early Japanese to say that the Emperors (Mikados) of the
history. present dynasty have been the *de jure* sovereigns of Japan since the legendary era, the first Mikado, Jimmu Tenno, dating from 660 B.C., but according to recent historical researches the first date to be considered trustworthy in Japanese historical annals is A.D. 461. The earliest records show that the sway of the Emperors was absolute over the whole empire, and that its influence in the government of the country was limited only by the defective state of the means of communication, which necessarily left

a good deal of discretionary powers in the hands of the local chiefs. The amount of these powers in the various cases would depend to a large extent on geographical position and local circumstances, and no doubt also on the individualities of the persons concerned, but it can easily be seen that this state of affairs contained the germs of the feudalism which grew to perfection in after-years, when the local chiefs became for many purposes practically independent. The work of the engineer, by annihilating distances, not only welds countries together, but for economic purposes makes the whole world one, and, as we shall see, it did much to hasten the course of events in Japan.

Towards the end of the seventh century the hereditary Ministers of State, the Fujiwara families, began to encroach upon the power of the Emperors, and from that time up till the revolution in 1868 the Emperors reigned but did not rule. The conversion of the nation to Buddhism in the sixth and seventh centuries was the most important event in Japanese history. For a century or two before that, Chinese civilisation had been slowly gaining ground in Japan, but when the Buddhist missionaries crossed the water all Chinese institutions followed them with a rush. Science, of a kind, began to be cultivated and books began to be written, so that Chinese thought had a great influence on the Japanese mind. The custom of abdicating the throne in order to spend old age in prayer was adopted, a custom which, more than anything else, led to the effacement of the Mikado's authority during the Middle Ages.

The Fujiwara family engrossed the power of the State from A.D. 670 to 1050, and monopolised all the great posts of the Government. Discontent arose from this state of affairs, and civil war ensued in consequence of the abuses which had arisen, and the Fujiwara family lost the influence and power which it had so long enjoyed. A successful soldier, Yoritomo, while nominally supporting the Emperor, ousted the families of the hereditary Ministers from their positions and aggrandised himself. Instead of restoring the real power to the Emperor he caused himself to be appointed the head of the feudal families and generalissimo (Shogun) of the Empire; a fact which was remembered in the revolution of 1868, when it was thought by the supporters of the Shogun of that time that the action of the larger clans was due not to loyalty to the Emperor but to jealousy of the Shogun.

It is easy to understand how the state of affairs which existed led to the belief among foreigners that there were two Emperors in Japan, one who attended to spiritual matters and the other to the administration of the country. This belief was entirely wrong, as the Emperor remained the source of all power and honour, while the Shogun utilised his position as commander-in-chief to concentrate the affairs of the nation under his control. Discontent, however, frequently arose among the feudal chiefs, who understood the real position of the Shogun; and when abuses became oppressive, civil wars ensued and several changes took place in the Shogun family, the position being seized from time to time by a new military chief who had the ability to arrogate the power to himself and his family. In this way one family succeeded another until that of Tokugawa assumed power in 1603 and retained it until the revolution in 1868.

The point to be distinctly remembered is, that in all these changes the position of the Emperor was never called

The Emperor always the source of power and honour.

in question, and in fact when the Shoguns abused their power the plea put forward by those who wished to displace them was that they were supporting the cause of the Emperor against the presumptuous arrogance of the man who wrongly had assumed a great part of his power. They did this not only because it was politic to do so, but also because, no doubt, they believed it to be a duty which they owed to loyalty. For not only is the very antiquity of the Imperial line the cause of the awe and veneration entertained for the Emperor by his people; but the fact that, while he was looked upon as the source of all power in the State, he yet confined his activity to the bestowal of titles and honours, brought it about that, while he thus did not give the slightest cause for complaint, at the same time he earned a great deal of gratitude from what human vanity holds most dear. The Emperors, therefore, were held in most loyal adoration in all ages throughout the Empire. The maintenance of the Emperor was essential to the power of the Shoguns, and, his sovereignty acknowledged, the very aloofness made it easy for them to appear not the usurpers, as they in fact were, but as trustees of the throne. It is easy to understand how the Shogun came to be described by the representatives of other nations who came in contact with Japan in the seventeenth and eighteenth centuries as the real sovereign of the realm, and how that, in modern times, he was described in British treaties (the Convention, for example, of October 1854) as " His Imperial Highness the Emperor," in the British treaty of August 1858 as " His Majesty the Tycoon," and also in the Prussian treaty of 1861 as " Seine *Majestät der Taikun.*" As a matter of fact, " Tycoon " was not a Japanese title at all, but was probably adopted from the Chinese when the treaties were being arranged to mask the defective political status of the Shogun.

The three political orders in the State were the Kugé or nobles of the Emperor's Court, who were chiefly offshoots of the Imperial Family ; the Daimyos, or feudal chiefs; and the Samurai, their two-sworded re- Orders in the State. tainers, who formed the military strength of the nation and were at the same time its most educated class. They con- sequently came to the front, in the affairs of the nation, after the revolution. The first of these orders numbered about 150 families, the second 268, and the third about 400,000 households. Below them was the agricultural, artisan, and merchant population, numbering over thirty millions and called Heimin ; who were without political status, but who nevertheless were allowed considerable freedom in the management of their own affairs. So

far as the details of administration were concerned, the
territorial extent over which the powers of the Government of the Shogunate were operative was limited to the
domains under the direct sway of the Shogun himself.
The territories under the control of the Daimyos enjoyed
almost complete autonomy. Such measures as were
necessary to control the feudal lords and to prevent them
from acquiring dangerous independence were enforced by
indirect methods rather than openly, but otherwise they
enjoyed in their respective domains the rights and prerogatives of independent sovereignty. They could not
declare war, conclude peace, or coin money, but they
exercised autonomous control in almost all other important
matters pertaining to the executive power of a State. This
system of semi-independence extended also to other classes
of the population. The predominant influence acquired in
the course of time by the military order became a very
marked feature in Japan, but with it all, the farmer, the
merchant, the craftsman, and others of the common people
enjoyed under the law, rights and privileges, lesser in degree
and in extent, but equally well recognised and respected.
The commercial and municipal systems established from
early days afford an example of this. Within certain limits
the people of the cities, towns, villages, and rural neighbour-
hoods controlled their own local affairs, and while there
were no rich men in the modern sense, there was little
actual poverty and no degradation such as is to be seen in
modern industrial towns in all parts of the world.

The line of the Tokugawa Shoguns held their power
for a period of nearly two hundred and seventy years, and
Forces causing during that time the country was at peace and
downfall of the dual form of government seemed to be
Shogunate. fixed on a stable basis. As Japan was self-
contained as regards resources, and commerce and industry
in the modern sense were unknown, and also because the
people seemed to be united in religion, the forces which
undermined feudalism in Europe were absent, but notwith-

standing the apparent calm there grew up a strong current of discontent with the existing state of affairs, and this increased with every blunder made by the Government of the Shogun.

Sir Ernest Satow has expressed the opinion that the real author of the movement which culminated in the revolution of 1868 was the second Prince of Mito, who was born in 1622 and died in 1700. With the help of a number of the most distinguished scholars in Japan he wrote the *Dai Nihon Shi* or "History of Japan," a work which fills two hundred and forty-three volumes. It, however, remained in manuscript, copied from hand to hand by eager students, until 1851, when the wide demand for it caused it to be published. The tendency of this book, as well as of others which appeared, was to direct the minds of the people to the Mikado as the true and only source of authority, and to make clear the historical fact that the Shogun was in fact a usurper. All this caused an increasing wish on the part, not only of serious students of history, but also of others to whom they had communicated their knowledge, that the Mikado should be restored to his ancient authority, and this would in itself have brought about a revolution in due time. Events, however, were hastened by the demands which the representatives of foreign countries were making upon the Japanese for the conclusion of treaties of trade and commerce between Japan and the countries which they represented. Before, however, dwelling on these comparatively recent events, it will be useful to note some of the earlier relations of Japan with foreigners.

So far as is known, Mendez Pinto, a Portuguese adventurer, seems to have been the first European who landed on Japanese soil, and the wonderful Early relations stories which he told about the country excited with foreigners. a great amount of curiosity ; hundreds of Portuguese of all classes were attracted to Japan, where they received a ready welcome from the people and from the feudal chiefs, who wished to take advantage of their knowledge and appliances and especially of the foreign implements of war. Merchants were followed by missionaries, among whom was St. Francis Xavier, whose preaching was attended with such success that it is said that in 1581 there were two hundred churches and one hundred and fifty thousand native Christians. Towards the end of the sixteenth and the beginning of the seventeenth century the political intrigues of the Jesuit missionaries and their interference in the affairs of the country became so audacious and obnoxious to the authorities that they determined that a policy of exclusion from the outside world was the only way of avoiding impending dangers; accordingly all the missionaries and converts were either expelled from the country or executed, and all intercourse with foreigners was prohibited under pain of death. So thoroughly was the work supposed to be done that Christianity was said to have been extirpated in Japan, but after the revolution of 1868 it was found by the French missionaries that there were villages in which numbers of the people retained fragments of the beliefs which had been implanted by the Jesuits.

The only exceptions to foreign intercourse were in favour of the Dutch and Chinese, who were allowed to carry on trade at Nagasaki under the strict surveillance of the Government. Preference was shown to the Dutch because they were not of the same religion as the Spaniards and the Portuguese; at least, it was thought that their form of Christianity was not likely to cause them to take part in political intrigues. Nagasaki, however, seemed to have a fascination for foreigners of different nationalities; no doubt in great part due to the mystery which surrounded the Japanese nation, and the desire not only to gain information but also to share in the reputed wealth of the country, of which fabulous accounts were given. On the other hand, many Japanese were eager to extract as much information as possible from the foreigners; so that in course of time many European ideas filtered from Nagasaki throughout the country and an elementary and somewhat debased knowledge of Western science was propagated. The Dutch physicians especially imparted to a considerable number of Japanese a knowledge of European medical theory and practice.

During the fifth Tokugawa Shogunate, Arai Hakuseki (Chikugo-no-Kami), one of the greatest scholars Japan has ever produced, was so impressed with the necessity for a wider education on the part of his countrymen that he made the acquisition of Western knowledge the pursuit of his life, and he gained the confidence of the sixth Shogun and induced him to endeavour to realise some of his political ideals. He continued to be influential in the time of the seventh Shogun, who was a minor, but retired when his successor came into power. He was a voluminous writer, and his historical works were much read and esteemed and were a source of inspiration to many thinkers and men of action in subsequent times.

Some Japanese educators.

Arai was also a diligent collector of information from the Dutch who were in Nagasaki, some of whom periodically visited Yedo, and his influence was no doubt great in obtaining the withdrawal of the prohibition of the study of Dutch books and of other scientific and technical works. Several Shoguns, in succession, appointed to honourable posts those who had a knowledge of the arts and sciences, such as astronomy, medicine, mathematics, and gunnery. The Dutch language was studied by considerable numbers so that they might be able to make themselves acquainted with the most recent publications. The want of teachers and the difficulty of obtaining foreign books prevented much progress being made. European ideas, however, began to make themselves felt on political subjects to such an extent that the Shogun's Government took steps to repress them, as no doubt those in power foresaw that their development would render their positions impossible.

The memory of some of the men who took a leading part in the education of public opinion is now held in venera-

tion by their countrymen.   Among them one of the most
notable was Sakuma Shozan, a samurai of the province of
Shinano, who was influential in introducing several branches
of Western science, especially those relating to military
practice and tactics.   In 1848, five years before Commodore
Perry came to Uraga, he gave instruction in gunnery
according to Western methods, and from accounts in a Dutch
book he constructed artillery and otherwise did much to
pave the way for the introduction of Western culture and
ideas in general.

Probably, however, the most popular hero of the time was
Yoshida Shoin, a Choshu samurai, who by his work as an
educator had great moral and spiritual influence on the
young men of his clan, and from among his disciples came
many of the leaders who brought about the abolition of the
feudal system and the establishment of the new government
on a firm basis.   A popular although not very exact account
of this remarkable man has been given by R. L. Stevenson
in his *Familiar Studies of Men and Books*, who describes him
under the name of Yoshida Torajiro, the Japanese pro-name
being subject to change during the lifetime of the bearer.
Yoshida paid for his zeal for reform with his life, and the
story of his career is still an inspiration to his countrymen.
His last scene was of a piece with his career, and fitly
crowned it.   When being examined before the Court, " he
seized on the opportunity of a public audience, confessed and
gloried in his design, and reading his auditors a lesson in the
history of their country, told at length the illegality of the
Shogun's power and the crimes by which its exercise was
sullied.   So, having said his say for once, he was led forth
and executed, thirty-one years old."

It is evident that the influx of Western ideas was not by
any means the chief cause of the fall of the feudal system.
That had its origin in a return to the old ideal when the
Emperor was not only the source of power, but also the
head of the actual Government, and in a strong desire for
national unity.   The feudal system and the authority of the

Shogun were opposed to this ideal, and their overthrow became a necessity before the nation could be consolidated under a strong centralised Government, which would be able to take advantage of the Western ideas taught by Arai, Sakuma, Yoshida, and others.

Some of the most powerful feudal chiefs in the south of the Empire, notably those of Satsuma and Choshu, were not slow to perceive the advantage which Western arms and science would give them in any struggle they might have with the Shogun, and Conditions on the arrival of foreigners in Japan. had been long making preparations for an armed conflict, and only wanted the opportunity and the excuse for striking. This they found in the negotiations which the Shogun had entered into with the foreign representatives, who came with the demand that the country should be opened to them, and which they had backed with a force which he knew he could not resist. When Commodore Perry of the American Navy steamed into the Bay of Yedo in 1853 he found a Government tottering to its fall; although no doubt many of those who were opposed to it cared less for the rights of the Mikado than for the opportunity of aggrandising themselves at the expense of the Shogun.

The Shogun yielded to the demands of Perry and of the representatives of the other foreign Powers, Britain, France, and Russia, who quickly followed him, and consented to open Yokohama, Hakodate, and certain of the other ports for trade and commerce (1857-59). In order to gain time and collect information he sent embassies to the United States and to Europe in 1860 and 1861; for even with their very limited knowledge of the resources of the foreign Powers the Shogun and his advisers had come to the conclusion that it were vain to refuse what they claimed. The advisers of the Mikado, however, had practically no knowledge on the subject, and they determined that the "land of the gods" would not be polluted by outsiders, and that at all hazards the ports would be closed. Some of the rash adherents of the anti-foreign party attempted to give effect to the policy which they advocated by firing on foreign ships and by assassinating foreigners. When matters were in a critical position they were brought to a crisis by the Prince of Choshu causing some ships belonging to France, Holland, and the United States to be fired upon by the forts at Shimonoseki, and this led to the bombardment of that place by the combined fleets of those countries at that time in Eastern waters, together with that of Great Britain, which espoused their cause on the ground of the solidarity of all foreign interests in Japan, and an indemnity of 3,000,000 dollars was exacted. The resistance which the Choshu clan offered to the assault of the foreign Powers, and the offensive action which it took against the Shogun, proved that for years it had been taking advantage of foreign arms and methods of war, and preparing for the struggle which had now come. The Shogun attempted to punish Choshu for the humiliation which had been brought on Japan, but his forces were defeated, and shortly afterwards he himself died. A few months later the Mikado also died, on the 3rd of February 1867, his son Matsuhito, then in his fifteenth year, succeeded him, and is now the reigning Emperor, the one hundred and twenty-first of the line. The Court of Kyoto, prompted by the great Daimyos of Choshu and Fall of the Satsuma, suddenly decided on the abolition of Shogunate. the Shogunate, and the new Shogun submitted to the decree which was issued. Some of his followers offered an ineffectual resistance, but after a short time they capitulated.

The government of the country was reorganised during 1867-68, and was nominally an absolute monarchy, with the Mikado as the sole source of authority, both legislative and executive, and the dreams of the literary party were realised. The Shogunate which had made treaties with the hated foreigners had been swept away, and they hoped that Japan would go back to the conditions of primitive ages, when it was really the "land of the gods," but they little reckoned with the forces which had been called into action in the conflict. Western ideas, methods, and arms had over-thrown the Shogunate, and now, in turn, they were to con-vert the followers of the Mikado. These wished to ignore the existence of foreigners and drive them from the country, but some of the leaders of the southern clans, prompted by younger men who had been to England and knew something of the resources of the foreign Powers, did all in their power to oppose these proposals which they knew would be futile, and they were successful in convincing the advisers of the Mikado that it was desirable to come to terms with the foreigners.

The story of the young men who were able to exercise influence in the manner indicated is one of the most romantic in the history of Japan, and a short space may Young men who be devoted to a sketch of it. Soon after the became leaders. Shogun had concluded the treaty of peace, friendship, and commerce with Lord Elgin, the Daimyo of Choshu expressed a great desire to send some of his young men to England in order that they might study the science and industries of the West with a view to the advancement of their country. It being still illegal for any one to leave Japan, he arranged that five young men from his province should be quietly put on board a vessel belonging to Jardine, Matheson, and Co., and that through that firm the necessary funds should be supplied for their support in Britain. On their arrival in London they were placed under the care of Mr. H. M. Matheson, who made arrangements for their education. Their names were Ito, Side, Yamao, Nomura, and Endo. About two years after their arrival Ito and Side asked leave to return to Japan, as they knew that stirring events were going on, and they were able to influence affairs to a considerable extent. Endo's health was not good, and he returned shortly after. The two who remained, Yamao and Nomura, made good progress in the study of the principles of science and also obtained some practice in their industrial applications. Yamao came to Napier's shipbuilding yard, and, as I have mentioned, attended the evening classes in Anderson's College, Glasgow,

at the time when I was a student in them, and on my arrival
in Japan I found him Acting Vice-Minister of Public Works.
He is now Viscount Yamao, Controller of an Imperial
Household and President of the Institution of Engineers
of Japan. Ito is now Marquis Ito, several times Prime
Minister and the most distinguished statesman in Japan.
Side is Count Inouye, who has held several Ministerial
portfolios and is also a very distinguished statesman.
Nomura is Viscount Inouye, late Director-General of Imperial
Railways in Japan, while Endo became Master of the Mint,
but died some time ago. A year or two later other
young Japanese began to come to Britain, as well as to the
Continent of Europe and to America, and the stream has
gone on ever since. Foreign travel or residence is now
looked upon as an essential part of the education of every
Japanese who is ambitious of taking an active part in public
affairs in Japan.

As a result of the influence which was brought to bear
on the advisers of the Mikado, an embassy with an Imperial
Embassy to Prince at its head was sent to give the Mikado's
foreign countries. consent to the treaties which had been made with
the representatives of the foreign Powers. It has been con-
tended that neither constitutional law nor practice prohibited
the Shogun from entering into treaty relations with other
Powers, but it is probable that there was no law on the subject
as such an event was not anticipated, while if certain events
in practice seemed to justify the contention, they only proved
that the Shoguns had successfully kept the Mikados in the
background in any such arrangements. There can be no
doubt that in preparing and carrying out the restoration the
Mikado's party held that the Shogun's assumption of the
right of making treaties with foreign Powers was just as
much a usurpation on his part as was his exercise of
authority in purely internal affairs. In order to emphasise
this view of the matter the foreign Ministers were invited to
an audience with the Mikado in Kyoto. The British and
Dutch Ministers accepted the invitation, the others declined.

The train of the British Minister, Sir Harry S. Parkes, was attacked by fanatic assassins and his life was saved by Goto, who by a sweep of his sword cut off the head of the assailant. The conversion of the Court of Kyoto was Conversion of instantaneous, and they became good friends Mikado's Court. with the men whom they had looked upon as unworthy to be in Japan. The action of Sir Harry Parkes on this occasion did much to bring about this happy result. It was determined, not only that foreign intercourse should be encouraged, but that Chinese customs, which had hitherto been the sole foundation of Japanese civilisation, should give way to European, and that European science and arts should be studied so that Japan might become a member of the comity of nations on terms of perfect equality.

Hitherto the Emperor, while looked upon with the greatest veneration by the people, had lived apart from all his subjects except a few court nobles, but it was resolved that in future he should take an active part in the government of the country and be as accessible as European sovereigns ; and to emphasise the change, Yedo, the capital of the Tokugawa Shoguns, became the new capital of the Empire, instead of Kyoto, the old seat of government, and its name was changed to Tokyo, meaning " Eastern capital." The Emperor was supported by those statesmen of both parties whose intellectual superiority had caused them to be recognised as leaders, and they united in adopting the modern progressive policy which ever since has guided the Japanese Empire.

On March 14, 1868, the Emperor, soon after his accession to the throne, proclaimed on oath the five principles that were to guide the Government newly established.[1]

First.—Deliberative assemblies shall be established on a broad basis, in order that Governmental measures may be adopted in accordance with public opinion (taken in the broad sense).

[1] Viscount Hayashi's translation.

Secondly.—The concord of all classes of society shall in all emergencies of the State be the first aim of the Government.

Thirdly.—Means shall be found for the furtherance of the lawful desires of all individuals, without discrimination as to persons.

Fourthly.—All purposeless precedents and useless customs being discarded, justice and righteousness shall be the guide of all actions.

Fifthly.—Knowledge and learning shall be sought after throughout the whole world, in order that the status of the Empire of Japan may be raised ever higher and higher.

In the same year a deliberative assembly was called together as a first step in carrying out the policy which had been adopted. It was composed of persons representing each of the Daimiates, who were chosen for the position by the Daimyos, and was intended to give advice to the Imperial Government. The inexperience of the members, however, rendered it of little use, and it resolved itself into a peaceful debating society of a very conservative character, and after a short and uneventful career it was dissolved.

Meantime it had become evident to the moving spirits of the revolution that national development and peace could Fall of never be secured while feudalism existed, as the feudalism. clan system was fatal to national unity, and they recognised the necessity for a reconstruction of the machinery of government and administration. With few exceptions the hereditary princes of the provinces had come to be merely formal chiefs of their Daimiates, and the real power was in the hands of the energetic and capable samurai who were employed to manage their affairs. These latter were not slow to recognise that any scheme for the transference of the political authority of the Daimyos to the central Government would render more important their services, and no doubt these motives prompted them to support a plan which at the same time advanced their interests and could be commended on patriotic grounds.

Matters were brought to a point by the presentation to the Emperor of an elaborate memorial signed by the Daimyos of Choshu, Satsuma, Tosa, Hizen, Kaga and others offering him the lists of their possessions and men. This memorial appeared in the official Gazette, March 5, 1869. Its preparation is attributed to Kido Takayoshi and bears supreme evidence to his learning and statesmanship. The example thus set was followed rapidly by others, and in the end only a small number remained who had not so petitioned. The Emperor accepted the offer thus made, and on the 25th of July a decree was issued, which stated that His Majesty, from a desire to assimilate the civil and military classes, and to place them on a footing of equality, abolished the designation of Court nobles (*Kugé*) and territorial princes (*Shoku*, more commonly called *Daimyo*) and replaced them by that of noble families (*Kwazoku*). By another decree the Government reserved to themselves the approval of all appointments or offices held under the late Daimyos, another obvious step towards the subordination of all the local administrations to that of the central Government. Thus, at almost one stroke, the whole institution of feudalism which had flourished for many centuries was cut away, although the forces which brought it about had been at work for a considerable time. In the sequel we shall see that adherence to the principles enunciated by the Emperor has within the short space of one generation brought Japan from conditions of feudalism to a strong position of con- solidated military power, able and determined to make its influence felt among the nations of the world, especially in all matters affecting Far Eastern policy; while in industry and commerce she has already made sufficient progress to ensure that she will be a most important factor in the evolution which will take place in all the countries bounded by the Pacific area.

BIBLIOGRAPHICAL NOTE

The complete study of the subjects mentioned in this chapter involves the whole of Japanese history, and that can only be done by those who are able to read Japanese books. Some of the more recent of these are very good and follow scientific methods. Some very interesting and important papers appear in the *Transactions* of the Asiatic Society of Japan, but general readers are likely to be content with the works of Murray, Griffis, Rein, Black, Adams and others. The official report of Perry's Expedition, Griffis's books on Townsend Harris and Perry, and those by Laurence Oliphant and Sir Rutherford Alcock on the early days of foreign intercourse with Japan, are all interesting in their way. Captain Brinkley's monumental work should be in the possession of every real student of Japan and Japanese history.

CHAPTER III

THE JAPANESE MIND

THE facts mentioned in the preceding chapter indicate the forces which brought about the fall of feudalism in Japan, and their study should help to dispel some of the mistaken ideas which prevail on the subject. Mistaken ideas about Japan.
Before proceeding further, however, it is necessary that we should form, at least, an approximate estimate of the mental and moral qualities of the Japanese, or what may be roughly called " the Japanese mind "; for, after all, these qualities form the chief determining factors in the progress of the nation. Japan is still looked upon by many people as a very interesting country for the globe-trotter and the curio-hunter, but few as yet have admitted the serious purpose which has guided all the changes of the last half-century, and fewer still have realised the extent of the developments which have taken place or the importance of the position which Japan now holds among the nations, as a factor in all the problems which affect Far Eastern politics.

In endeavouring to form an estimate of the Japanese mind it is evidently of the highest importance that we should ascertain, as far as that is possible, what were the chief motives which urged them on Motives of the Japanese. when they determined to give up feudalism and to replace it by constitutional government and Western science, industries, and commerce. No doubt, at first these motives were somewhat indefinite and probably considerably mixed, but those who know the history of the past fifty years will admit that

Dr. Inazo Nitobe is near the truth when he says: "In a work of such magnitude various motives naturally entered; but if one were to name the principal, one would not hesitate to name 'Bushido.' When we opened the whole country to foreign trade, when we introduced the latest improvements in every department of life, when we began to study Western politics and sciences, our guiding motive was not the development of our physical resources and the increase of wealth; much less was it a blind imitation of Western customs. The sense of honour which cannot bear being looked down upon as an inferior Power—that was the strongest of motives. Pecuniary or industrial considerations were awakened later in the process of transformation." [1] The mental attitude of the Japanese with regard to material subjects is well illustrated in another passage by the same author: "It has been said that Japan won her late war with China by means of Murata guns and Krupp cannon; it has been said that the victory was the work of the modern school system; but these are less than half truths. Does ever a piano, be it of the choicest workmanship of Erhard or Stanley, burst forth into the Rhapsodies of Liszt or the Sonatas of Beethoven without a master's hand? Or if guns win battles, why did Louis Napoleon not beat the Prussians with his Mitrailleuse, or the Spaniards with their Mausers the Filipinos, whose arms were no better than the old-fashioned Remingtons? Needless to repeat what has grown a trite saying, that it is the spirit that quickeneth, without which the best of implements profiteth but little. The most improved guns and cannon do not shoot of their own accord; the most modern educational system does not make a coward a hero. No! What won the battles on the Yalu, in Korea and Manchuria was the ghosts of our fathers, guiding our hands and beating in our hearts. They are not dead, those ghosts, the spirits of our warlike ancestors. To those who have eyes to see, they are clearly visible. Scratch a Japanese of the most advanced ideas and he will show a

[1] *"Bushido," The Soul of Japan*, p. 117.

samurai. If you would plant a new seed in his heart, stir deep the sediment which has accumulated there for ages,—or else, new phraseology reaches no deeper than his arithmetical understanding."

The secret of the developments which have taken place in Japan is to be found in the fact that the Japanese have a high sense of personal and national honour, which their critics not unnaturally put down to conceit and vanity. From the time that the first treaties were made with foreigners, they felt that some of the conditions were such that they were placed in a position of inferiority which they could not endure. I can recall the bitterness with which some leading Japanese spoke to me of the presence of a British regiment in Yokohama for the purpose of protecting the foreign settlement. They felt it as a national disgrace which ought to be got rid of as soon as possible, although they recognised its need for some time after it came. The terms of the treaties by which foreigners were placed under the jurisdiction of their own national authorities were considered humiliating to Japan. The responsible statesmen, of course, recognised that such arrangements were necessary until Japan had brought herself somewhat into line with Western nations as regards the methods and the administration of the law, but all classes of the community felt that the arrangements should not continue for any length of time. Their educational system was reorganised in order that men might be trained who would be able to discharge the national duties; legislation and administration were brought into harmony with Western ideas so that their claims for recognition as equals might be admitted by the other Powers.

The Japanese, however, were not long in learning that foreign Powers were more amenable to the arguments to be drawn from a large army and a powerful navy Necessity for a than those to be drawn from improvements in strong Japan. education and administration, and they determined to make themselves a strong military nation. The sound of the cannons at the Yalu River really awakened Europe and

America to a knowledge of the fact that a nation had been born in the Far East which had not only brought itself up to a considerable degree of Western culture, but had developed its administration to such an extent as to give it a strong claim for entrance to the comity of nations on terms of perfect equality. The effective action of the Japanese army and navy during the war with China, moreover, proved that they were able to enforce their rights with something stronger than mere arguments. Fortunately nothing more was needed.

One almost requires to have lived in Japan to understand what Dr. Nitobe means by saying that it was the ghosts of their fathers guiding their hands and beating in their hearts which won the battles on the Yalu, in Korea and Manchuria. In the absence of that experience no better guide can be found than Dr. Nitobe himself, and in what follows I shall be greatly indebted to him, Mr. Lafcadio Hearn, and Captain Brinkley. Probably some of the opinions of these writers may seem to be overdrawn and to a large extent sentimental, but I shall, for the most part, confine myself to an outline of those which I can confirm by my personal experience.

The distinguishing idea which differentiates Oriental from Occidental thought is that of Pre-existence, to understand which aright one requires to have lived for some years in the real living atmosphere of Buddhism. It shapes every thought and emotion, and the term *ingwa* or *innen*, meaning Karma as inevitable retribution, comes naturally to every lip as an interpretation, as a consolation, or as a reproach. It is very curious to note that Western philosophers have scarcely as yet recognised that the modern intellectual movement of science and philosophy is strangely parallel with Oriental thought, and that Buddhism and Science are more nearly at one in their view of the universe than the conventional form of Western theology. To the Buddhist mind expressions and thoughts which seem to require long psychological

Oriental and Occidental thought.

explanations to our minds, are matters of common experience and axioms of everyday life.

A complete study of what we have somewhat roughly called "the Japanese mind" would take us into many departments of Confucian philosophy and of Buddhist and Shinto religions. From the two former the Japanese were furnished with a sense of calm trust in Fate, a quiet submission to the inevitable, a stoic composure in sight of danger or calamity, and even a disdain for life and a friendliness with death. A soldier inspired with this spirit does not know the meaning of fear. A nation inspired with the spirit of Buddhism is continually striving to bring itself into harmony with the Absolute. The tendency of such a spirit is to lose itself in contemplation, and to become very indistinct; hence the neglect of material conditions which are necessary for moral and physical welfare. In the case of the Japanese, however, Shintoism supplied a corrective, to a considerable extent, for it brought into prominence the national as distinguished from the moral consciousness of the individual. As Dr. Nitobe puts it: "Its nature-worship endeared the country to our inmost souls, while its ancestor-worship, tracing from lineage to lineage, made the Imperial family the fountainhead of the whole nation. To us the country is more than land and soil from which to mine gold or to reap grain—it is the sacred abode of the gods, the spirits of our forefathers; to us the Emperor is more than the Arch-Constable of a *Rechtsstaat*, or even the Patron of a *Culturstaat* —he is the bodily representative of Heaven on earth, blending in his person its power and its mercy."[1] The two predominating features in Japanese national life are therefore patriotism and loyalty, and these to a large extent explain the circumstances which led to the overthrow of the Shogun and the restoration of the Emperor as the centre of executive authority in Japan. They also explain the national character of all the movements which have taken place since the

Constituents of Japanese thought.

[1] *Bushido*, p. 9.

Restoration. When once their meanings were fully grasped by some of the leading spirits, they rapidly spread throughout the nation, and even the poorest in the land-felt that they had to take a part in them and that the ghosts of their fathers were guiding their hands and beating in their hearts. Another point to be noted is that the real nature of the religious and national life of Japan has been and still is predominantly communal, and that individualism has only had a minor part in forming the nation. The combination of Shintoism, Buddhism and Confucianism which constituted the Japanese religion and philosophy was therefore not a mere mechanical mixture ; it was of the nature of a chemical compound which was very different from any one of its elements ; and this accounts not only for the essential difference of the Japanese mind from that of other Eastern nations, but also for the social order and in great part for the changes which have taken place in recent years in Japan.

It would take us far beyond our present limits if we examined in detail the nature of the compound which was
Resultant produced by the amalgamation and evolution
thought. of the various factors in Japanese religion, but a few notes are necessary in order to understand some of the features in the national character. Buddhism, in the process, became very much modified and simplified. The immeasurably deferred hope of the Indian Buddhist was brought down to everyday life by the prospect of immediate admission, after death, to the ranks of the deities, and its practical morality was condensed into five negative precepts and ten positive virtues, which are to be found in all the moral codes of the world. The former were—not to kill, not to be guilty of dishonesty, not to be lewd, not to speak untruth, not to drink intoxicants ; the latter were—to be kind to all sentient beings, to be liberal, to be chaste, to speak the truth, to employ gentle and peace-making language, to use refined words, to express everything in a plain unexaggerated manner, to devote the mind to moral thoughts, to practise charity and patience, and to cultivate

pure intentions. The practical Japanese mind could not accept the negation of all interest in the affairs of this world as necessary to the way of salvation, and while not neglecting meditation, it found scope for its religious zeal in the exercise of a charity which, if it had been practised as prescribed, would have made the devotees very good Christians. "It included the digging of wells, the building of bridges, the making of roads, the maintenance of one's parents, the support of the Church, the nursing of the sick, the succouring of the poor, and the duty of recommending these same acts to others. There were further noble precepts, and there was also an elaborate system of daily worship and prayer. All idea of abstention from the affairs of everyday life disappeared, and the hereafter became, not a state of absolute non-existence (*nirvana*), but the 'infinite perception of a beatific vision'; a condition in which each of the saved formed one of a band of great intercessors, pleading continually for their ignorant and struggling brethren upon earth that they might attain to the same heights of perfect enlightenment and bliss." [1]

The latest developments of Buddhism in Japan made a still further approach to the Christian ideals. Nichiren is one of the noblest and most picturesque of the Japanese saints, and his teachings included the conception of a God in whom everything lives and moves and has its being; an omnipotent, omnipresent and omniscient deity. All phenomena, mental and material, in all time and space, were declared by him to have only subjective existence in the consciousness of the individual. To the enlightened Buddhist all worlds were equally beautiful. "Hence, to proclaim the identity of this evil or phenomenal world with the glorious underlying reality, or noumenon; to point out the way to Buddhahood; to open the path of salvation; above all, to convince the people that one and all of them might become Buddhas, here and now—that was the mission of the sect of Nichiren." Captain Brinkley sums up the results of all the

---

[1] Brinkley, *Japan*, vol. v. p. 146.

changes which took place in these words : " Thus the
colours that Buddhism took in its transmission through the
Japanese mind were all bright hues.   Death ceased to be a
passage to mere non-existence and became the entrance to
actual beatitude.   The ascetic selfishness of the contemplative
disciple was exchanged for a career of active charity.   The
endless chain of cause and effect was shortened to a single
link.   The conception of one supreme, all-merciful being
forced itself into prominence.   The gulf of social and
political distinctions that yawned so widely between the
patrician and the plebeian, and all the other unsightliness of
the world, became subjective *eidola* destined to disappear at
the first touch of moral light.   The Buddha and the people
were identified."[1]   Captain Brinkley adds : " Buddhism in
the comparatively bright and comfortable garments with
which Japanese genius clothed it, is the faith of the masses,
but the scholar proposes to himself a simpler creed, an
essentially workaday system of ethics.   To be moral,
honest, and upright ; to be guided by reason and not by
passion ; to be faithful to friends and benefactors ; to
abstain from meanness and selfishness in all its forms ; to
be prepared to sacrifice everything to country and king,—that
is the ideal of the cultured mind, and in the pursuit of it
no priestly guidance is considered necessary.   If a Japanese
be asked to define the much-talked of *Yamato damashii*—
the spirit of Yamato—he will do so in the words set down
here."[2]   There can be little doubt that they express the conditions of the Japanese minds which exercised the greatest
influence in the country since the adoption of Western
methods and the introduction of Western arts, sciences,
and religion.   Confucian ethics, in Japan as in China, was
the basis of the philosophy of life to the educated classes, in
so far as they had a philosophy of life, and the Confucian
teaching only strengthened, deepened, and gave form and
outline to the sentiments of the Shinto religion.   Farther
on we will consider some of the changes which have taken

[1] Brinkley, *Japan*, vol. v. p. 151.   [2] *Ibid.* p. 159.

place in recent years in consequence of the developments in education and in social, economic, and political conditions.

Nothing illustrates the spirit of Old Japan so much as the institutions of suicide (*hara-kiri*) and redress (*kataki-uchi*), and they show, in a very clear manner, some Hara-kiri. of the characteristics of what we have called the Japanese mind, even of the present day ; for although they are not carried out as in former days, they indicate the attitude which the great body of the people still assume when there is any question either of national or individual importance under discussion. When a question of honour was involved, death was accepted by a samurai as a key to the solution to many complex problems. Redress did not descend to mere personal revenge, for it was justified only when it was undertaken on behalf of superiors and bene-factors. " One's own wrongs, including injuries done to wife and children, were to be borne and forgiven. A samurai could therefore fully sympathise with Hannibal's oath to avenge his country's wrongs, but he scorns James Hamilton for wearing in his girdle a handful of earth from his wife's grave as an eternal incentive to avenge her wrongs on the Regent Murray." [1] The recognition of this spirit helps to explain many of the features connected with Japanese history, not only under the old regime, but also during the transition period since the country had intercourse with foreigners.

In some respects the Japanese samurai resembled the ancient Greeks in that they always placed loyalty and duty to the State before self-interest, and their most popular literature abounds in illustrations of Duty to State always first. this. Viscount Hayashi has given English readers an excellent example of the ancient spirit of the Japanese in his book *For His People*, and the perusal of this and similar books will do far more to make people acquainted with the manners and thought of the Japanese than formal disquisitions on ethics and psychology, and to

[1] Nitobe, *Bushido*, p. 86.

such books we must refer our readers, as our space will allow
us only to touch on those parts of the subject which have
an immediate bearing on the chief aspects of modern
Japanese life, with which we propose to deal. A very
competent writer has made the following remarks on the
feature in the Japanese character we have been considering,
and they explain a great deal which to the ordinary foreign
mind is not apparent: " Something more than a profound
conception of duty was needed to nerve the samurai for
sacrifices such as he seems to have been always ready to
make. It is true that Japanese parents of the military class
took pains to familiarise their children of both sexes from
very tender years with the idea of self-destruction at any
time. The little boy was taught how the sword should be
directed against his bosom ; the little girl, how the dagger
must be held to pierce the throat ; and both grew up in
constant fellowship with the conviction that suicide must be
reckoned among the natural incidents of everyday existence.
But superadded to the force of education and the incentive
of tradition there was a transcendental influence. Buddhism
supplied it. The tenets of that creed divided themselves,
broadly speaking, into two doctrines, salvation by faith and
salvation by works, and the chief exponent of the latter
principle is the sect which prescribes ' meditation ' as the
vehicle of enlightenment. Whatever be the mental processes induced by this rite, those who have practised it
insist that it leads finally to a state of ' absorption ' in which
the mind is flooded by an illumination revealing the universe
in a new aspect, absolutely free from all traces of passion,
interest, or affection, and showing, written across everything
in flaming letters, the truth that for him who has found
Buddha there is neither birth nor death, growth nor decay.
Lifted high above his surroundings, he is prepared to meet
every fate with indifference. The attainment of that state
seems to have been a fact in the case both of the samurai of
the military epoch, and of the Japanese soldier of to-day,
producing, in the former, readiness to look calmly in the face

of any form of death, and in the latter, a high type of patriotic courage." With a spirit of this kind even very imperfectly developed fear of death disappears, and deeds of daring are possible which astonish the outside world.

Amidst all the intellectual and material changes which have taken place in Japan there have naturally been great changes in the religious ideals of large numbers of the people. One thing, however, has not changed. Shinto remains the unique creed of the Imperial house, and as this fact is of great national importance it is necessary to dwell on it a little in detail. Appended to the Constitution, by which freedom of conscience was unequivocally granted to the people, were three documents—a preamble, an Imperial oath in the Sanctuary of the Palace, and an Imperial Speech— every one of which contained words that left no doubt of the Sovereign's rigid adherence to the patriarchal faith of Japan. In the preamble His Majesty said: " Having, by virtue of the glories of our ancestors, ascended to the throne of a lineal succession unbroken for ages eternal ; desiring to promote the welfare and to give development to the moral and intellectual faculties of our subjects who have been favoured with the benevolent care and affectionate vigilance of our ancestors ; and hoping to maintain the pro- sperity of the State in concert with our people and with their support, we hereby promulgate," etc.; in the Imperial oath he said: " We, the successor to the prosperous throne of our predecessors, do humbly and solemnly swear to the Imperial founder of our house and to our Imperial ancestors that, in consonance with a great policy co-extensive with the heavens and with the earth, we shall maintain and secure from decline the ancient form of government. . . . These laws (the Constitution) contain only an exposition of grand precepts for the conduct of the government, bequeathed by the Imperial founder of our house and by our Imperial ancestors. That we have been so fortunate in our reign . . . as to accomplish this work, we owe to the glorious spirits of the Imperial founder of our house and of our other

Imperial ancestors"; and in the Imperial speech he says:
"The Imperial founder of our house and our other Imperial
ancestors, by the help and support of the forefathers of our
subjects, laid the foundation of our empire upon a basis
which is to last for ever. That this brilliant achievement
embellishes the annals of our country, is due to the glorious
virtues of our sacred Imperial ancestors and to the loyalty
and bravery of our subjects, their love of country, and their
public spirit." The sentiments embodied in these words
represent a force in the national life of Japan which
those who have not lived in the country cannot realise,
and its existence may bring about a combination of
Imperial and democratic power which may probably throw
a new light on the political and social problems of the
future.

At the same time it must be admitted that there has
been a great development of purely materialistic ideas. A
large proportion of the younger men may be said to belong
to the school of scientific agnostics, and their religion resolves
itself into a system of practical ethics, and is in fact a return
to the "Bushido" of the samurai. It may be said that the
code of moral principles embodied in that system was to a
large extent ideal and had little effect on real life, but I
venture to affirm that its principles entered more deeply
into the national life of Japan than do those of the
religion we profess into Western civilisation, which in
many respects is directly opposed to the spirit of
Christianity. The true samurai insisted on justice in all his
dealings with his fellow-men, and courage was not esteemed
unless it was exercised in the cause of righteousness, while
benevolence, magnanimity, sympathy and pity were ever
recognised to be supreme virtues, the highest of all the
attributes of the human soul. The courtesy and politeness
of the Japanese were simply the outward symbols of the
inward spirit which was the mark of the cultured man; who,
however, never allowed mere outward form to interfere with
the standard of veracity and conduct which was demanded

by his social position. The word of a samurai was sufficient guaranty of the truthfulness of an assertion.

Foreigners who have had commercial dealings with Japanese may find it difficult to reconcile these high ideals with the practice which they found to prevail, but Commercial it must be remembered that the social position of morality. the samurai demanded a loftier standard of veracity than that of the tradesman or the peasant. It cannot be denied that Japanese merchants gained a bad name by their want of commercial integrity, especially in the early days of foreign intercourse, but under the feudal system none of the great occupations of life were further removed from the profession of arms than commerce. The merchant was placed lowest in the category of vocations—the knight, the tiller of the soil, the mechanic, and the merchant. Commercial development was not possible to any great extent in feudal Japan, and the obloquy attached to the calling brought within its pale many who did not care for social repute. The initial consequence was that, while those belonging to it had a code of morals which guided them in their transactions with each other, in their relations with people outside their vocation their actions were in accordance with the low reputation which their class had acquired.

Such being the case, it can easily be understood that when the country was opened to foreign trade, the most adventurous rushed to the open ports to take part in the scramble with foreigners for their share of the wealth which was the main object of life at these places. Some of the samurai, and even of the nobles, went into trade, but their inexperience and their sense of honour led the majority of them into bankruptcy ; the Japanese side of trade was thus, for the most part, left in the hands of sharp, unscrupulous persons, to whom the spirit and teaching of " Bushido " were either unknown, or if known, altogether ignored, and their actions brought the whole Japanese nation into disrepute ; for foreigners are apt to generalise regarding Eastern peoples from their experience of those with whom they come into contact, and who are seldom, if ever, the representatives of the highest types. Under the old regime money and the love of it were ignored, and a man was honoured on account, not of his possessions, but of his social position, his character, or his wisdom.

We have hitherto dealt chiefly with the ethical aspects of Japanese character, but it will be necessary to glance at
Japanese mental some of their mental characteristics in order
characteristics. that we may better understand the wonderful progress which has been made. The common impression is that the Japanese have wonderful powers of imitation but little or no originality. This impression, however, is as superficial as many others which have been formed of Eastern peoples. The Japanese samurai, and to a very considerable extent all the other classes in the country, were fairly well educated, but it was not for the purpose of enabling them to pass examinations or to make money but to build up character. Intellectual superiority was of course esteemed, but with them intellectuality meant wisdom in the first instance and only knowledge in a very subordinate sense. The framework of " Bushido " was composed of Wisdom, Benevolence, and Courage, but in erecting this framework the mind was trained in such a manner that it obtained the capacity to undertake any study to which it was directed. When, therefore, Western learning and science were introduced they found a field well cultivated for their reception, and characters prepared to take full advantage of them. As, however, a very thoughtful writer has said, " although the 'occidentalization' of Japan is a fact unique in human history, what does it really mean? Nothing more than rearrangement of a part of the pre-existing machinery of thought. Even that for thousands of brave young minds was death. The adoption of Western civilisation was not nearly such an easy matter as unthinking persons imagined. And it is quite evident that the mental readjustments, effected at a cost which remains to be told, have given good results only along directions in which the race had always

shown capacities of special kinds. Thus the appliances of Western industrial invention have worked admirably in Japanese hands—have produced excellent results in those crafts at which the nation had been skilful, in other and quainter ways, for ages. There has been no transformation —nothing more than the turning of old abilities into new and larger channels. The scientific professions tell the same story. For certain forms of science, such as medicine, surgery (there are no better surgeons in the world than the Japanese), chemistry, microscopy, the Japanese genius is naturally adapted ; and in all these it has done work already heard of round the world. In war and statecraft it has shown wonderful power ; but throughout their history the Japanese have been characterised by great military and political capacity. Nothing remarkable has been done, however, in directions foreign to the national genius. In the study, for example, of Western music, Western art, Western literature, time would seem to have been simply wasted. These things make appeal extraordinary to emotional life with us ; they make no such appeal to Japanese emotional life. Every serious thinker knows that emotional transformation of the individual through education is impossible. To imagine that the emotional character of an Oriental race could be transformed in the short space of thirty years by the contact of Occidental ideas is absurd. Emotional life, which is older than intellectual life, and deeper, can no more be altered suddenly by a change of *milieu* than the surface of a mirror can be changed by passing reflections. All that Japan has been able to do so miraculously well has been done without any self-transformation ; and those who imagine her emotionally closer to us to-day than she may have been thirty years ago ignore facts of science which admit of no argument." [1]

This line of thought might lead us into many interesting discussions on the relations of European and Asiatic thought and into a consideration of the belief which is often

[1] Hearn, *Kokoro*, pp. 9-11.

expressed, but as often forgotten in practical action, that the East is separated from the West by a chasm that nothing Eastern people and Western thought. can bridge and is altogether impervious to influences from without, but meantime these must be postponed.   The quotations which we have given indicate the lines on which an Eastern people may be influenced by Western thought and the limitations to that influence.   The forces acting on Japan from without have been co-operating with those which acted from within and have merely changed their direction ; they have created little that is new.   If we compare her case with that of China, we at once see the cause of the differences of results.   It is customary to speak of China as having stood still for centuries, but if we examine her history we find that she developed on her own individual lines from age to age up to the time of the coming of Europeans, and since then she has slowly but surely retrograded ; because, as an experienced Eastern official in the British service has put it, " the external influence brought to bear upon her has been one essentially Results of European action. antagonistic to her whole spirit and genius, and has served to make development of a kind which was natural to her, and which was something wholly unlike, and far more subtle than the *progress* of modern Europe, an impossibility."   The same writer points out that in the thirteenth and fourteenth centuries and later the Chinese were remarkable among all the nations for the extraordinary care which was taken by high and low to secure the safety of the persons and property of strangers, travellers, and foreign merchants, and religions of all kinds were tolerated.   What has wrought this complete change in China, the reputedly unchanging and unchangeable ?   The writer from whom I have quoted says : " The answer, let us blind ourselves to it if we can, does not admit of a doubt. It is due solely and entirely to the influence of Europe, to the aggressive spirit which animated, and to a certain extent still animates, the white men in Asia ; the spirit which, coming into rude contact with that of the East, threw the latter violently back upon itself, stayed the tide of its *natural* development, and since the civilisations of Asia were thus prevented from advancing in their own fashion, and the law of Nature forbade that they should stand still, compelled them to retrogression."[1] The present condition of China is a disgrace to the Western Powers and a complete justification of the independent position which the Japanese have always taken in matters affecting the internal development of their country.

My own experience with Japanese students has always been, in every way, most pleasant. Eager and persevering in their studies, and with abilities which compare favourably with those of students in any part of the world, they retained a great part of their native politeness and gave no trouble to teachers in the course of their work. *Personal experience of Japanese students.* If occasionally one of the more boisterous spirits forgot himself, a word reminding him of the behaviour which was expected of a Japanese gentleman was sufficient to recall him to a sense of his duty, and during all the time I was in Japan no question of College discipline ever arose. The only change made in the Calendar of the Engineering College as I drafted it was the addition, on the suggestion of the Japanese authorities, of certain regulations with regard to discipline, but these were found to be unnecessary, and they appeared only in the first edition of that publication. In recent years, however, it is evident that a turbulent spirit has shown itself among certain classes of students, but this no doubt arises from the disorganisation of Japanese ideals and methods and the want of anything better to take their place, and indicates the necessity for the cultivation of " Bushido " suitable to modern conditions.

The charge of want of originality on the part of the Japanese is, as I have said, superficial and unfair. *Charge of want of originality.* How could originality be expected under a feudal system which penalised it in every form? I

---

[1] Hugh Clifford, C.M.G., "The East and West," *The Monthly Review*, April 1903, p. 133.

remember my apprentice master, Alexander C. Kirk, LL.D., writing to me when in Japan warning me not to expect too much in the way of science and engineering from the present generation of Japanese, for, as he said, " such things had to be bred in the bone." In the course of little more than a generation the Japanese have shown that they are not only able to adapt Western science to Japanese conditions, but to advance its borders by original investigation. The memoirs and papers published by Japanese students, both on scientific and literary subjects, will bear very favourable comparison with those of any other country, and while no Japanese Newton, Darwin, or Kelvin has yet arisen, there are men connected with Japanese universities and colleges of whom any learned institution in the world would have no reason to be ashamed. In the course of our investigations we shall have an opportunity of noting the practical work which has been done in engineering, industry, and commerce, and a mere outline will be sufficient to show that the Japanese are not simply book students, but are able to apply their knowledge to the practical affairs of life. As conditions develop, the opportunities for originality will increase, but we must remember that what we call originality is only another name for the resultant of the experience and spirit of the age ; genius simply translates that into language which can be understood.

It is too late in the day to continue to repeat what was a very common saying thirty years ago ; namely, that the Japanese were very clever imitators but that they had neither originality nor perseverance to accomplish anything great. Their whole history in the interval has disproved the charge. Their ardent patriotism, their high sense of personal and national honour, their keen intelligence have enabled them to work what is admitted to be the political miracle of the latter part of the nineteenth century. Early in their new career they formed very clear ideas of what they wished to attain. They made their plans with deliberation, they carried them out with

Disproved by recent history.

skill, and by their adaptations of Western methods to their national institutions they have created a new Power which will influence conditions in all parts of the world and especially in those countries bounded by the Pacific area. To show how they accomplished this will be our task in the following chapters.

A complete study of the mental and moral qualities of the Japanese—which have influenced the Revolution that has taken place in their country—would take us into many psychological and metaphysical problems. The spirit of the Revolution. Enough has been said to show that the spirit which dominated that Revolution is of a very complex nature. What has been called "the Soul of Japan" has been a very important factor in it; but, unlike other Easterns, the Japanese have brought the soul under the control of the brain, and each successive step in their evolution has been guided by an appeal to reason, which has enabled them to combine many of the qualities of the East and the West. What these qualities really were will be best understood, not by abstract discussions, but by a study of the results which have followed from their efforts. The advent of Christianity in its various forms in Japan has had the result of imparting new life to Buddhism and in many respects causing it to approach still more nearly to some of the Christian ideals. On the other hand, Christian missionaries now understand much better than they did the conditions of the Japanese mind and are not so disdainfully aggressive as they were, and, consciously or unconsciously, they are imbibing Eastern ideas which are causing them to modify the forms of presenting some of their Western theological doctrines. How far this process will go on is one of the problems of the future.

If I were attempting to sum up briefly the qualities of the Japanese which have enabled them to make such wonderful developments in such a short time, I would mention as the most important factor the intense loyalty of the people, which compels them to make any sacrifice—even life itself—when they consider it necessary for the honour of their country. This, combined with their great intellectual ability, enables them to take full advantage of the modern science and organisation necessary for the attainment of the objects of their ambition. Their great power of foresight prepares them for all their enterprises, both of peace and war, with an exact and scientific prevision not excelled by any other nation. While they are permeated by Eastern ideas they have been able to appropriate much that is best in Western thought, and thus they unite many of the best qualities of the East and the West.

BIBLIOGRAPHICAL NOTE

The Japanese mind is not to be understood from books alone. A lengthened residence in Japan and a careful and sympathetic study of the subject are necessary even for its approximate understanding. Still some books which have been written will be found useful, such as Dr. Nitobe's *Bushido, The Soul of Japan*, Lafcadio Hearn's *Kokoro* and other works, some of the chapters in Captain Brinkley's large work, and Professor Chamberlain's *Things Japanese*. Gulick's *Evolution of the Japanese, Social and Psychic*, contains a great deal of interesting but some of it debatable matter. Probably such books as Mitford's *Tales of Old Japan* or Viscount Hayashi's story *For his People* are more useful to general readers than formal psychological treatises.

CHAPTER IV

TRANSITION

THE formal abolition of feudalism in Japan was only the beginning of a long period of transition during which the government and the institutions of the country were fitted to the new conditions, and before entering on a description of the chief developments in the various departments of national life, it will be convenient to give a sketch of the more important events that occurred during the period of rapid change which we may consider to have ended with the war with China in 1894-5—a war which was the means of causing the strength of Japan to be recognised by the other nations of the world. Changes have, of course, been going on since that date, the more important of which will be noted under their appropriate headings; but during the period mentioned the foundations of the institutions of modern Japan were laid and their superstructures sufficiently developed to allow us to give an outline which will be of use in co-relating them to each other and to the general course of events in Japan. The task before the country and the people was a difficult one; and it is Problems of the not surprising that mistakes were made, and Revolution. that troubles arose which sometimes threatened serious results to the nation; but, on the whole, it is admitted even by their most severe critics that the Japanese have performed their task in a manner which, in many respects, affords an object lesson to the world.

On the publication of the decree abolishing feudalism

the ex-Daimyos returned to their provinces and assumed the functions of governors of their clans, and each provincial government received a uniform constitution. It was soon found, however, that the hereditary princes were, as a class, utterly unfit for the chief executive offices of their old provinces, and as vacancies occurred they were replaced by other more competent persons. The actual leaders in the central Government, after the Revolution, did not number among them a single Daimyo, although two or three were Men of the *Kugé* or Court nobles. Among the men who Revolution. have made modern Japan, the names of Okubo, Kido, Iwakura, Sanjo, Goto, Katsu, Okuma, Ito, Inouye, Soyejima, Oki, Saigo, and Yamagata deserve to be specially recorded, although many others who will be mentioned later on did much in their own departments to consolidate the new regime. Captain Brinkley, a very competent authority, has said: " Of the fifty-five men whose united efforts had compassed the fall of the Shogunate, five stood conspicuous above their colleagues ; they were Iwakura and Sanjo, Court nobles ; Saigo and Okubo, samurai of Satsuma ; and Kido, a samurai of Choshu. In the second rank came many men of great gifts, whose youth alone disqualified them for prominence—Ito, the constructive statesman of the Meiji era, who inspired nearly all the important measures of the time, though he did not openly figure as their originator ; Inouye, who never lacked a resource or swerved from the dictates of loyalty ; Okuma, a politician of subtle, versatile, and vigorous intellect ; Itagaki, the Rousseau of his era ; and a score of others created by the extraordinary circumstances with which they had to deal. But the first five mentioned were the captains, the rest only lieutenants." If we were studying the history of the time we would of course enter into the examination of the share which individuals had in public affairs, but, as already explained, our object is rather to give a broad outline of the national evolution, and therefore we can touch on the careers of individuals only in so far as their work bears directly on the subjects under consideration.

The Emperor was the source of all authority, but the actual work of the Government was carried on by the Daijokwan or Privy Council, composed, for the Central most part, of the leaders of the Revolution. Government. Under the Daijokwan were the Ministers of the different departments, who were called to take part in the Cabinet Councils of the Government when any questions relating to their department were to be discussed. The composition of the Privy Council from time to time caused serious dis-content among the members of the more powerful clans, who were dissatisfied with the share which they had obtained in the Government. Satsuma especially was troublesome, as the members of that clan looked upon themselves as the principal agents in the Revolution which had been the means of restoring the governing power into the hands of the Emperor, and their discontent came to a head in a very serious rebellion a few years later.

The first deliberative assembly having proved a failure, another attempt was made in 1870 but with almost equal want of success. The House was opened with some ceremony on the 26th of June, but it was found Deliberative that the members were so deficient in the informa- Assembly. tion necessary for the transaction of business and so much given to irrelevant discussion that they were eventually sent home, with the object of qualifying themselves for the task they had set to perform.

From time to time attacks were made on foreigners by Japanese who thought that their country was going on a wrong course by the adoption of foreign Attitude towards customs, but in many cases these attacks were foreigners. provoked by the imprudence or misconduct of the persons who suffered. On the whole, however, the anti-foreign policy was being abandoned, especially by the high officials of the clans, and by 1871 it was evident that a very important change was coming over the spirit of Japan. The people recognised that any attempt to return to the old system of isolation was impracticable, and they agreed with the Government in its resolve to respect the treaties and to encourage friendly relations with foreign Powers.

Public opinion changed very rapidly. On the one hand there were those who wished to adopt all kinds of foreign arts and inventions at once and to plunge into Western civilisation, and on the other those who, while recognising the necessity for an approximation to the methods of European countries, were anxious to retain what was good in Japanese customs and methods and to preserve the old institutions of the country. When opportunity arose I always took the side of the latter, and impressed on those with whom I came in contact that a nation which forgot its past was not likely to have a great future. While anxious that the Japanese should be assisted in every way to become a strong nation, I felt that if too great haste were displayed disastrous results would follow. For some years it was difficult to prevent the beginning of schemes which were doomed to failure, but as experience was gained more caution was shown, and gradually there occurred what many foreigners called a reaction against things European, but which, in reality, was only a recognition of the claims of things Japanese, and a clearer recognition of the conditions of real national progress.

Many young men and a considerable number of young women were sent to foreign countries in order that they Lines of might obtain a knowledge of foreign methods and Progress. be instructed in Western arts and sciences, but as they were quite unprepared to take full advantage of what they saw and heard, the results were, in the majority of cases, very unsatisfactory. Those, however, who settled down to a systematic course of study, as a rule, did well, and on their return to Japan were able to do very efficient work. It was, however, felt that it was absolutely necessary that arrangements should be made for a sound preliminary training being given in Japan to those who were likely to go abroad, so that they might be fitted to take full advantage of the opportunities which they had for the study of Western arts and sciences.

Frequent changes and developments took place both in the central and local Government with the object of meeting the new conditions which were arising. The most important of these we will note in subsequent chapters. The administration of the- law was improved, the Department of Education was established and a beginning was made with the organisation of national education and of public works which have been the means of changing to a large extent the general conditions of Japan. The various public works were united in one department, the Kobusho, under which a few years later was placed the Imperial College of Engineering. A telegraph was soon in working order between Yokohama and Tokyo, and the construction of a railway between these two points was begun. In order that navigation might be rendered safer, lighthouses were constructed at different parts of the coast under the superintendence of Mr. Brunton, a British engineer, and in short a beginning was made in a great many departments of national activity, all of which have had very important developments, to be noticed later on.

Those in power, however, felt that more complete information was required before a systematic attempt was made to reorganise thoroughly the national institutions, and accordingly it was determined by the Cabinet that an embassy should be sent to the United States and Europe on a tour of observation, for the purpose of learning the nature of the institutions of other countries and for gaining a more precise knowledge of their laws, commerce, and education as well as their naval and military systems.

Embassy to United States and Europe.

In addition to these reasons, however, there was another which probably had more direct effect in causing the appointment of the embassy. The Japanese Government and the people generally had all along felt that in the treaties with the foreign Powers the clauses which placed those of their nationality who were resident in Japan under the direct jurisdiction of the representatives of these Powers, were derogatory to the dignity of Japan, and that they should be altered as soon as possible.   The date fixed for the revision of the treaties was 1st of July 1872, and it was recognised that an important epoch was approaching.   The members of the Cabinet felt that it was their duty to make the Governments of the Treaty Powers acquainted with the changes which had taken place in the country since the treaties were signed, and explain the existing conditions and the policy which it was intended to carry out.

The chief of the embassy was Iwakura, the Junior Prime Minister, and with him with the title of Associate Ambassadors were Kido, Sangi ; Okubo, Minister of Finance ; Ito, Vice-Minister of Public Works; and Yamaguchi, Assistant Minister for Foreign Affairs.   There were in addition a number of secretaries, commissioners, and other officials ; so that the embassy attained considerable dimensions, as was becoming, considering the importance and variety of the functions which it was expected to perform.

The embassy did not succeed in bringing about the revision of the treaties, but it collected a great deal of information on many points relating to government and national institutions which no doubt has been largely used in shaping the policy which has since been followed. Personally I am interested in the embassy and its work, because, as I have mentioned, when it visited Britain Mr. Ito, one of its members (now Marquis Ito) arranged for the institution of the Imperial College of Engineering, of which I became Principal.   On my arrival in Japan in June 1873 I collected, with difficulty, about fifty students from the small schools and classes which had been started in con-nection with various departments, and we made a beginning with the College, using as temporary premises the *yashiki* or residence of an ex-Daimyo.   In order to provide properly prepared candidates for entrance to the College I started a large preparatory school, which was carried on with success for some years until the work of the Education Department was more fully organised, when it was discontinued. What ultimately became the University of Tokyo was also being rapidly developed, and a national system of education was being organised, but these and other matters connected with education will be noticed more fully in the next chapter.

Beneath the surface of the apparent calm in the country there was still a large amount of latent discontent, especially among the members of the Satsuma clan. As Signs of trouble. has already been explained, that clan took a leading part in the Revolution which brought the Emperor back to power, but its members were, as a rule, animated by a great dislike to foreign customs and methods, and indeed they made the action of the Shogun in favouring foreigners and making treaties with them the main reason for working for his overthrow. The Satsuma leaders were therefore justified in thinking that under the new order of things their services would be remembered, and that they would have a large share in the Government. Probably they were disappointed that they did not get as much as they expected in this respect, but subsequent events seemed to prove that some of them aimed at acquiring for themselves the executive authority of the extinct Shogunate, without its name, rather than at making the Emperor the real and effective depositary of supreme power. It is very difficult, if not impossible, to estimate men's motives, but there can be little doubt that these reasons and the contempt which they had for foreigners and their methods explained the action of many members of the Satsuma clan during the years which immediately followed the Revolution.

The story is a long one, and we can notice only those points in it which bear on the national evolution. Among the Satsuma men who had rendered good service at the time of the restoration of the Emperor was Saigo Takamori, and on the formation of the new Government he was appointed to an important post in the Ministry of War. Other members of the Satsuma clan had also received influential appointments, and amongst those was Okubo Toshimitsu, whose name is associated with all the more important changes carried out by the Mikado's Government in its early years. In November 1870 the members of the Satsuma clan who were then in Tokyo began to show signs of discontent; Shimadzu Saburo, the acting head of the clan, and Saigo presented a petition to the Emperor asking to be relieved from their service in Tokyo as part of the guard for the central Government. Okubo and Terashima, the two other members of the clan in the Government, did not support the petition, and there can be little doubt that the real grounds of the request which it contained were the discontent and disappointment of the two former statesmen at finding that the part in the government of the country allotted to them was infinitely less than what they considered they had a right to expect. These feelings were shared by the troops and the majority of the clan. Various unsuccessful efforts were made to appease them. Shimadzu and Saigo returned to their province, and under the name of a " private school " they carried on an establishment which was essentially a military training institution; all their resources were employed in the maintenance of armed forces, and as many as 30,000 men were being constantly drilled and exercised. They had a large arsenal, and connected with it were a cannon foundry and powder mills which were able to turn out considerable amounts of the munitions of war. They also held the fortifications which commanded the harbour of Kagoshima. In short, Satsuma was practically as feudal as ever, and all Satsuma men obeyed the orders of Shimadzu and not of the central Government.

An open breach, however, did not occur for some time, and in April 1873 the Government, after much negotiation, prevailed on Shimadzu to visit Tokyo, and he was offered high official position if he would modify his opposition to the projected changes. Shimadzu arrived in the capital about the end of April, accompanied by several hundred armed retainers, all wearing the old costume of the country and carrying their two swords, and their appearance in Tokyo caused no little sensation, where the samurai had already availed themselves of the permission granted them to lay aside their weapons. I arrived in Japan in the beginning of June of that year, and I can recall the Satsuma men with their swaggering gait and sometimes scowling aspect, and one was thankful when one got safely past them in the streets ; for there was no saying what an angry samurai might do on the spur of the moment. In order to conciliate him, Saigo was named commander-in-chief of the Emperor's land forces, but neither he nor Shimadzu modified their opposition to the progressive measures of the Government, and the latter, finding his advice unheeded, asked leave to return home. The Emperor refused his request and ordered him to remain in the capital until the return from Europe of Iwakura and the members of his mission. This took place in September of the same year, and shortly after a split took place in the Cabinet ; the reason which was given being a question arising out of the state of Japanese relations with the Kingdom of Korea.

These relations go back to the almost prehistoric times of the Empress Jingo (A.D. 201-269), but it is not till 1592 that we have exact historical records. In that year a Japanese army under the Regent Hideyoshi, a man with great warlike ambitions, landed in Korea and conquered it, and although the Japanese army was withdrawn after the death of Hideyoshi, the Koreans for more than two centuries sent tribute to the Tokugawa Shoguns. After the Restoration, however, they had refused to acknowledge the Mikado as Emperor of Japan or to have any official relations with his Government, which had given so much encouragement to Western barbarians. This caused great irritation to some sections of the Japanese, who held that the conduct of the Koreans deserved severe chastisement. On the other hand, Iwakura, the head of the embassy which had just returned from Europe, became the chief of the peace party which declared that the country was unprepared for war and that financial ruin would be the result of attempting it, and the counsels of that party prevailed.

The relations between Japan and Russia are at the present time the most important political questions in the Japan and Far East, but a glance at history shows that Russia. they are of very long standing. The present policy of Russia is only a continuation of the policy she has carried on for generations. Towards the end of the eighteenth century, Russia made several attempts to open up communications with Japan, but in vain. In the early years of the nineteenth century several raids were made by Russians on the northern parts of Japan, and their actions in burning, pillaging, and taking prisoners raised Japanese feeling very strongly against them. One of the prisoners was entrusted with a letter ending with the sentence : " If you comply with our wishes [to make a treaty of commerce] we shall always be good friends with you ; if not, we will come again with more ships and chase you about"—a communication which was not calculated to increase the friendship between the parties.

Among the students who about this time tried to obtain a knowledge of Western countries through the Dutch who were settled at Deshima was one Ono Kinshihei, and he, like all others who infringed the laws on these matters, soon had to make a difficult choice. He had collected information regarding the manners and customs as well as the military and naval organisations of Western States, and he had to choose between concealing information which seemed essential to his country's safety and revealing it at the certain cost of his own safety. He chose the latter, and published a book in which he not only gave all the information he thought would be useful, but warned the authorities that the Russians would one day show themselves in the north of Japan, and urged the advisability of building a fleet and constructing coast defences. His patriotism was rewarded by imprisonment and the confiscation of his publication.

Before he was five months in prison, events vindicated his wisdom ; the Russians appeared and attempted to carry out their objects by force, and their depredations impressed themselves in bloody letters on the memory of the Japanese. The great struggle which was going on in Europe at the time diverted the attention of Russia from the Far East, except for an occasional visit. In 1811 the Russian ship *Diana* was sent to survey the Kurile Islands, and by a stratagem the captain and a number of his officers were seized and kept prisoners by the Japanese for two years and treated with considerable cruelty. An interesting account of the experiences of the Russians was written by Golovnin, the captain, which gives some insight into Japanese ways and thoughts.

Gradually as the colonisation of Saghalin by the Russians from the north and that of the Japanese from the south came into contact, friction arose, and in 1854 Count Pontiatine endeavoured to arrange a boundary line, but without success. Then, as now, however, Russia combined silent but aggressive action with her diplomacy, and in 1857 she attempted to include the island of Tsushima among her colonies— Tsushima, which lies within sight of Japan on one side, of Korea on the other, and commands the principal entrance to the Sea of Japan. In 1864 the Government of the Bakufu (Shogun) sent a special envoy to St. Petersburg to discuss the questions at issue, and a sort of joint occupation was agreed to, which, however, was found to be unsatisfactory, and in 1869 trouble again arose. In one of his letters[1] Sir Harry Parkes thus alludes to the subject: "What a day I have had! A very important question has occurred in Saghalin to the north of Yezo, which if not carefully treated by the Japanese Government may occasion a rupture between them and the Russians, in which case the former would go to the wall. The Russians are reported to be concentrating 1200 men at the extreme south of Saghalin, with the object, I think, of taking Yezo if the

[1] *Life*, vol. ii. p. 239.

Japanese give them the chance. Yezo would be a most serious loss to the Japanese and a great gain to the Russians. I have advised the Japanese to throw force into Yezo, and not to quarrel about Saghalin, to which they have only a questionable right. In a weak moment, some years ago, they agreed with the Russians to a joint occupancy, which means of course that the whole island will be appropriated by the Russians. This cannot be helped, I fear, but Yezo may be saved."

In a recent letter to the *Times*[1] Sir Robert K. Douglas says: "It is interesting to observe the identity of the methods by which Russian diplomatists work out their political ends. Some years ago Russia began to cast longing eyes on the island of Saghalin, the most northerly island of the Japanese group, and, taking advantage of its detached position, utilised it as a convict station. The Japanese very naturally raised objections to this appropriation of their territory, and in reply Russia brought forward a proposal that the two empires should enjoy a common possession of the island, just as she now proposes that they should enjoy a common possession of Korea, only, in this instance, she substitutes 'spheres of influence' for 'common possession.' They mean the same thing in the Russian sense. When Russia made this proposal Japan was in her callow days and yielded the point, only to find shortly after that 'common possession' meant 'full possession by Russia.' Again, in 1867, Japan had occasion to protest against the continued encroachments of her northern neighbour in the administration of the disputed island and Russia answered her protest by the suggestion that in exchange for the full possession of Saghalin—an island containing 47,500 square miles—she should accept four insignificant islets in the Kurile group. This suggestion Japan refused to entertain and the two Powers returned to the pre-existing arrangement. Matters, however, did not work smoothly, and in 1875 Russia came forward with a

[1] February 3, 1904.

more liberal offer. She proposed to yield to Japan, in exchange for Saghalin, the eighteen islands which form the Kurile group, stretching between Kamtchatka and the Japanese island of Yezo. To this transfer Japan deemed it wise, in the existing circumstances, to consent, and Russia thus became legally possessed of Saghalin, just as she would surely become the owner of Korea if Japan were weak enough to fall in with her present proposal. But Japan has learnt her lesson." In the interval, however, she has had to pay dearly for her experience.

The outcome of the negotiations was that Saghalin was surrendered to the Russians and the Japanese received, as compensation, the Kurile Islands. The shame of the cession, unavoidable though it was, was deeply felt by the samurai, and it has sunk Saghalin exchanged for the Kurile Islands. deeply into the hearts of the Japanese. One of the last instances of *harakiri*—exclusive of the wholesale *harakiri* that followed the suppression of the Satsuma rebellion— was that of Ohara, a Yezo militia lieutenant, who dis-embowelled himself in 1889 before the tombs of his ancestors in Tokyo, driven to suicide by brooding over Russian encroachments. The surrender of Saghalin added to the discontent of the samurai, who thought that the Government had already made too many concessions to the demands of foreigners.

All these events had very important results on the national evolution of Japan. The decision that Japan would not go to war with Korea did not simply involve a question of peace or war, but the much wider question whether the country should halt or Results on Japanese affairs. advance on its newly adopted path of progress. It was recognised that Japan must be made strong, not only that she might be able to resist foreign aggression, but also that she should be united. A conscription law was therefore passed making service in the army or navy obligatory on the adult males of all classes of the population. The object of this was not only the formation of a strong national army and navy ; it **was** also intended to destroy all clannish feeling, cohesion and power, and to result eventually in the disarmament of all the samurai. This was another cause of offence to Shimadzu and Saigo, who saw that it would be the means of decreasing the influence of the samurai in the affairs of the Government.

Saigo and other officers left Tokyo and returned to their respective provinces. About the same time disorders broke out in Hizen, and shortly afterwards, in January 1874, an attempt was made to assassinate Iwakura, but which was unsuccessful. As soon as peace was restored in Hizen the Government became anxious to have Shimadzu and Saigo back in the capital, as it was felt that their presence would be a guarantee for the good behaviour of their clan. Saigo refused the invitation, but Shimadzu, after parleying for three weeks with the Imperial envoy, obeyed the summons. He was given the title of Sai-daijin, the second in point of rank in the Government, although his opinions with regard to the policy which ought to be followed by the Government do not seem to have been much modified.

The Liu-Kiu (Loo-Choo) Islands had a shadowy connection with Japan, and received an annual visit of one junk Liu-Kiu and from Satsuma to obtain the marks of nominal Formosa. vassalage, while the island of Formosa was to the Japanese a far-off land of fairy tales and adventure, in which, centuries before, Japanese buccaneers had won fame and glory. Indeed, in earlier historical times Japanese pirates had made themselves unpleasantly known in the Chinese seas generally. It was therefore not to be wondered at that a proposal to send a warlike expedition to Formosa should not only raise the enthusiasm of the fiery samurai, but also that the Government should take the opportunity of using it as a safety-valve for the purpose of cooling their warlike ardour. On more than one occasion shipwrecked Japanese and Liu-Kiuns who had been cast on the shores of Formosa had been murdered by the wild aboriginal tribes, and in 1874 an expedition was sent to

Formosa for the purpose of chastising these tribes and acquiring guarantees for the future security of Japanese ships and seamen. No doubt it was also intended as a means of outlet for the discontent of the samurai, especially those of the Satsuma clan, and of directing their attention away from home politics. The central Government also saw in it an opportunity for increasing the regular army, and thus of strengthening their position and controlling the samurai class. The expedition was placed under the command of a younger brother of Saigo, who had distinguished himself during the war of the Restoration, and it was completely successful in its object. The Formosan tribes were defeated, the Japanese troops returned in triumph in December 1874, and an indemnity was obtained from the Chinese Government for the expense incurred by Japan.

As has been mentioned, the decree of September 1871 made the custom of wearing two swords optional, and its effect was soon observed by the numbers which gave up the custom. In March 1876 the Government thought that the time was ripe for prohibiting the practice of wearing swords and limiting to the regular forces the right of bearing arms. This caused further irritation among the samurai, especially those of the Satsuma clan, which went on steadily increasing its military preparations. Meantime, however, the central Government was also consolidating its position and augmenting its army and navy. The postal and telegraph services were extended, and as they were of great use in directing the operations of the military and naval forces, they added to the strength of the Government.

At last, in the beginning of 1877, matters came to a crisis, and civil war broke out between the forces of the Emperor and those of Satsuma, the first overt act Satsuma being by pupils of the " private schools " breaking Rebellion. into the arsenal at Kagoshima and carrying off as many rifles and as much powder as they could remove. On the 5th of February the Emperor had gone south for the official opening of the railway recently constructed between Osaka and Kyoto, the representatives of the foreign Powers had accepted invitations to be present and the former capital was in festive garb for the occasion, when the news of the outbreak at Kagoshima arrived. Although these were considered grave, the ceremony was carried out as originally arranged, but, immediately after, a Cabinet Council was held and Admiral Kawamura despatched to Kagoshima to endeavour to arrange matters. The leaders of the Satsuma men, however, had decided that the time for action had arrived, and civil war was carried on in real earnest. The struggle was long and severe, and for some time the issue was doubtful. Both parties exerted themselves to the utmost. Among other things which were done, the engineering workshops which we had organised in connection with the Imperial College of Engineering were utilised for the provision of the munitions of war. Ultimately the resources of the Government told, and the Satsuma men were totally defeated. The final act was very characteristic of the Japanese nature. Saigo wounded by a bullet in the thigh, one of his lieutenants performed what samurai consider a friendly act. By one blow of his heavy sword he severed his chief's head from his body in order to spare him the disgrace of falling alive into his enemy's hands, and after handing the head to one of Saigo's servants for concealment, he committed suicide. The rest of the rebels who took part in that fight were either very severely wounded or killed. Admiral Kawamura, in the spirit of a true samurai, reverently washed Saigo's head with his own hands as a mark of respect for his former friend and companion in arms.

An Imperial Notification was issued on 25th September that the rebels had been overcome and peace restored. The news was received without much demonstration, but with a feeling of relief mingled with admiration and regret. The rebellion had the effect of causing the strength of the Government to be greatly increased. Fully 65,000 troops were employed in its suppression, and the naval forces and ships of transport were considerably increased in number ; so that the troubles in Satsuma had the effect of consolidating the power of the Government, which immediately applied itself to various developments in administration and to the rearrangement of financial affairs, such as the land tax, pensions, etc. Satsuma was placed under the same system of government as the other provinces, and the "private school" system was replaced by a garrison of Imperial troops at Kagoshima. The civil administration was placed in the hands of Imperial officials, selected without regard to the place of their birth, and the taxation was put on the same footing as elsewhere in the country. A final act in the tragedy must not be forgotten. On the 14th of May 1878, Okubo Toshimitsu, the Minister of the Interior, was assassinated as he was driving to attend a Cabinet Council in the Emperor's palace, being cut down by two men who thought him a traitor to his country and who were determined to revenge the death of Saigo. I can well recall the place where the event occurred, as it was one of my favourite walks. It has been described as "a sylvan dell, bounded on each side by grassy slopes, crested with grotesque old pine-trees, and studded here and there with bamboo groves—a dell where the philosopher might think undisturbed, and the painter find worthy studies for his canvas." As if to complete the tragedy, the remains of the murdered man were found by General Saigo (a brother of the Satsuma leader), who happened to drive past shortly afterwards, and were by him conveyed to Okubo's house.

Now that the troubles with the samurai were largely got rid of, the attention of the people was directed to political affairs, and a demand arose for the establishment of representative institutions. The agitation was led by Itagaki Taisuki, the chief man of the Tosa clan, and to this day an active worker in the fields of philanthropy and social politics. In July 1877 a memorial was addressed to the Emperor giving reasons for the proposals, and reminding him that in 1868, before the assembled Court and Daimyos, he had promised that a

Agitation for representative institutions.

deliberative assembly should be formed and that all measures should be decided by public opinion. We will trace the history of representative government in Japan later on, but meantime note that on July 22, 1878, a notification was issued by the Prime Minister stating that the Emperor had decided on the establishment of elective assemblies in all the provinces of the Empire. This, however, was only the beginning of a movement which led in 1881 to the promulgation of an edict announcing that a national assembly would be convened in 1891, and that a Constitution would be framed which would give the people a direct voice in the government of the country.

In the interval, however, great developments took place in education, administration, public works, industry, and com-

Developments on Western lines. merce, and for some time there raged what has been called the great "foreign fever," when Japanese society was literally submerged in the flood of European influence. Speculative companies of all kinds were formed for the purpose of carrying on public works and industrial undertakings, many of which came to grief through the inexperience of the promoters and the insufficiency of financial resources. The rude lessons of experience brought a reaction, and greater care was exercised in attempting to carry out new proposals. The methods of administration of the Government were reformed, and the excessive number of officials reduced. The laws were codified, and the administration of justice brought into harmony with Western ideas, with the result that in 1894 the long attempt at treaty revision was successfully carried out by the conclusion of a new treaty with Great Britain and a few months later with the United States of America. These, and other developments we will consider more at length in the special chapters devoted to them.

Among all the developments which had taken place in Japan, the most important, from the point of view of national evolution, was the growth of an army drilled and equipped in foreign style and a navy of considerable size and of great efficiency. In the summer of 1894 these were employed in a manner which showed that the Japanese had profited by the instruction they had received, and, moreover, that they had realised the nature of the arguments which had the greatest weight with the foreign Powers.

The early relations of Japan and Korea have already been mentioned. The irritation caused by the conduct of the Koreans after the Restoration was never Difficulties with allayed in Japan, although for some years Korea. Korea was left in her hermit-like seclusion. The Japanese maintained a small settlement at Fusan, the most southern port, but they knew little of what was being done in the interior of the country. Rumours, however, were current that the Russians were attempting to establish themselves in Korea. In 1875 an incident occurred which was the immediate cause of the opening of Korea to the world. A gunboat belonging to the Japanese, while surveying the coasts, was fired on by a small fort. The fire was promptly returned, the fort destroyed, the arms, banners, and other trophies were brought to Tokyo and exhibited in the military museum. The punishment which had been meted out to the Koreans did not satisfy the national pride of the Japanese, who now felt that they were in a position to impress their will on such a Power as Korea. An expedition was sent out to Korea, but fortunately matters were arranged without having recourse to war, and a treaty was concluded by the terms of which two ports were opened to the trade and residence of Japanese subjects. The other foreign Powers were not slow in following the example of Japan, and Korea was at length open to the world.

In the negotiations which were carried out Korea was treated by Japan and the other Powers as an independent nation, with which diplomacy was to be conducted on terms of perfect international equality. But although Korea had broken off the slight bonds of her vassalage to Japan, she still clung to China's suzerainty, and China retained a controlling influence in her affairs, both foreign and domestic, and this was always exercised in the direction of obstruction to improvements and of conservatism generally. The Japanese, on the other hand, wished to see developments in commerce and industrial undertakings and in all that was necessary to make them successful. They were not always fortunate in their methods or in those who represented them. Unscrupulous men in search of fortunes, without regard to the means they employed, treated the natives in a very offensive manner, with the consequence that the traditional hatred of the Japanese was revived, and in 1882 the Japanese Legation at the capital was attacked and burned by a mob; the Minister and his staff escaped with diffi- culty to the coast, twenty miles distant, where they were rescued by a British man-of-war which happened to be surveying in the neighbourhood. The Legation was very soon rebuilt, but from that time Japan claimed and exer- cised the right of maintaining a force of troops in the capital. This right was recognised by China, and in 1885 a convention was arranged between the two countries by which it was agreed that both should have the privilege of stationing troops in Korea, but that due notice should be given by each to the other of any intention to exercise it whenever it became necessary.

For nine years there were constant difficulties between Japan and China, for which it is impossible to apportion the responsibility. Matters were brought to a crisis in 1894, when a serious insurrection broke out in Korea, and the Government was unable to cope with it. The Japanese Government saw that it was necessary to put an end to the misrule and corruption which rendered Korea a scene of constant disturbance, and offered invitations to foreign aggression, which, if carried out, would be a source of danger to Japan. Russia especially was to be feared, and the Japanese recognised that if that Power got possession of Korea, the narrow straits which divided their country from Korea would not be sufficient protection from the further aggression of the great northern Power, of which they had already reason to be afraid.

I do not propose to enter into all the political or other questions involved, or even to attempt to defend the Japanese on all points from an ethical point of view. War with European Powers are not in a position to criticise China. their action, as nearly all they do in the Far East is dictated by pure selfishness—national or personal—which is generally prompted by the ambition of their representatives, who recognise that an active policy, if successful, leads to official promotion. Even the autocracy of the Czar is powerless before the influence of the Russian bureaucracy. The Imperial Rescript issued by the Emperor of Japan on declaring war with China intimated that while Korea was an independent State she was first introduced into the family of nations by the advice and under the guidance of Japan, but that it had been China's habit to designate Korea as her dependency, and both openly and secretly to interfere with her domestic affairs. On account of disturbances in Korea, China despatched troops thither, alleging that her purpose was to afford succour to her dependent State, and in virtue of a treaty concluded with Korea in 1882 and looking to possible contingencies, the Japanese sent a military force to that country. The Japanese Government invited that of China to co-operate with them in the maintenance of peace, not only in Korea but in the East generally, but China, advancing various reasons, declined Japan's proposals.

We need not follow the details of the negotiations or even inquire into the sufficiency of the reasons given by Japan for her action, for, as Professor Chamberlain remarks, "though Japan evidently lacked moral justification for her proceeding, the science of statecraft, as understood in the present imperfect stage of human culture, must approve her action." No doubt the Japanese saw that it was necessary that they should show their strength, and their quarrel with China afforded the opportunity. On this subject Captain Brinkley says: "The approximate cause of the war is readily discernible. China's attitude towards Korea, her fitful interference in the little kingdom's affairs, her exercise of suzerain rights while uniformly disclaiming suzerain responsibilities, created a situation intolerable to Japan, who had concluded a treaty with Korea on the avowed basis of the latter's independence. A consenting party to that treaty, China nevertheless ignored it in practice, partly because she despised the Japanese and resented their apostasy from Oriental traditions, but chiefly because her ineffable faith in her own superiority to outside nations absolved her from any obligation to respect their conventions, and the struggle was therefore between Japanese progress and Chinese stagnation. At the same time, Japan's material and political interests in Korea outweighed those of all other States put together. In asserting her commercial rights she could not possibly avoid collision with a Power behaving as China behaved. But there was another force pushing the two States into the arena ; they had to do battle for the supremacy of the Far East. China, of course, did not regard the issue in that light. It was part of her immemorial faith in her own transcendence that the possibility of being challenged should never occur to her. But Japan's case was different. Her position might be compared to that of a lad who had to win a standing for himself in a new school by beating the head boy of his form. China was the head boy of the East-Asian form. Her huge dimensions, her vast resources, her apparently inexhaustible " staying power," entitled her to that position, and outside nations accorded it to her. To worst her meant to leap, at one bound, to the hegemony of the Far East. That was the quickest exit from the shadow of Orientalism and Japan took it. This is not a suggestion that she forced a fight upon her neighbour merely for the purpose of establishing her own superiority. What it means is that the causes which led to the fight had their remote origin in the different attitudes of the two countries towards Western civilisation. Having cordially embraced that civilisation, Japan could not consent to be included in the contempt with which China regarded it ; and, having set out to climb to the level of Occidental nations, she had to begin by emerging from the ranks of Oriental nations."

We cannot enter into details of the war which followed. Both the Japanese army and navy did splendid work. The skill of the generals, the bravery of the soldiers, and the perfection of all the arrangements for the supply of materials, combined, no doubt, with the unprepared state of the Chinese, led to easy victories by the Japanese, in which the navy took a prominent part. Within a year the Chinese saw that it was useless to continue the struggle, and on April 17, 1895, a treaty of peace was signed by Li Hung Chang and Li Ching Fong on behalf of China, and by Marquis Ito, the Premier, and Count Mutsu, the Minister of Foreign Affairs, representing Japan, at Shimonoseki. By this treaty, among other things, the complete Treaty of Shimonoseki. independence of Korea was declared, the province of Liao-tung and the islands of Formosa and the Pescadores were ceded to Japan, and it was arranged that a war indemnity of 200,000,000 Kuping taels should be paid by China. Further additional commercial privileges were provided for, as well as a commercial treaty similar to those concluded by China with European Powers. While it was the sound of the Japanese cannons at the mouth of the Yalu River which awoke the nations of the world to a sense of the military and naval power of Japan, it was the terms of this treaty which impressed them with the political significance of that Power. Russia was busy constructing her Trans-Continental railway and was intent on obtaining a free opening on the Pacific, and both France and Germany had their own plans of aggrandisement. These three Powers lost no time in presenting a joint Note to Japan, suggesting that she should forgo her claim to the territory ceded to her on the mainland, since its retention would not make for the lasting peace of the Far East. Although this Note was quite polite, there could be no mistaking its meaning, and the suggestion was meant to have the force of a command. It says a great deal for the self-restraint of the Japanese that they received the Note as they did, but it must have been a severe blow to their national pride. An Imperial Rescript was published, simultaneously with the ratified treaty, in which the Emperor, proclaiming his desire to do all that in him lay to serve the cause of peace, " yielded to the dictates of magnanimity, and accepted the advice of the three Powers." Subsequent events threw a lurid light on the disinterested- ness of these Powers, and are illustrations of the morality which guides them in their dealings with Eastern peoples. Their actions, however, reacted on themselves, and had a pro- found influence on Eastern opinion ; for while Japan was denied a large part of the results of her conquests, the action of the European Powers was the cause of raising in her the larger ambition to become the champion of the down-trodden countries of the East, and by her counsel and, if necessary, her assistance enable them to obtain the same measure of independence and power as herself.

Under a pretext of " leasing," Germany seized Kiao- chow and asserted her claim over the greater part of the Shantung province, and Russia practically annexed the Liao-tung peninsula ; so that within four years from the time of her expulsion

Aggression of Russia and Germany in China.

from the territories belonging to her by right of conquest, Japan saw those territories appropriated by the very Powers that expelled her. The immediate result of the arbitrary conduct of Russia, France, and Germany in China was an increase in the belligerent force of Japan and a determination to make the army and navy strong enough to assert the rights of the country. The

Results on Japanese policy.

indemnity received from China as well as the revenue from increased taxation was spent on what was called the *post-bellum* programme, which provided alike for warlike and peaceful developments. The principal features in that programme were—(*a*) the expansion of military and naval armaments ; (*b*) the establishment of an Imperial

University at Kioto ; (*c*) the improvement of rivers for purposes of internal navigation ; (*d*) the colonisation of Hokkaido ; (*e*) the improvement of railway lines and the extension of the telephone service ; (*f*) the establishment of experimental farms and institutes for training in all branches of the silk industry ; (*g*) the encouragement of foreign trade ; and (*h*) the establishment of a Government work for the production of iron and steel.   We shall note some of the chief results of this programme in the sequel.

The Japanese recognised that something more than peaceful progress in Western industries and methods of administration was necessary to win respect from the nations of Europe and America, and Results in China. a large part of their energy and their money was devoted to the development of their army and navy.   Even the spirit of the Chinese Court was roused when they saw their territories being filched from them, piece by piece, but the great body of the people were apathetic.   Steps, however, were taken to form volunteer associations for the purpose of resisting foreign aggression.   From the want of proper control, these rapidly assumed the form of an anti-foreign rebellion, which led, in 1900, to cruel excesses in the provinces of Shantung and Chili, and placed the foreign communities in Tientsin and Peking in positions of extreme peril.   During the troubles which ensued, the Japanese won increased respect among the nations of the world and proved that they were able to bear themselves under very trying circumstances in a manner which compared favourably with that of the representatives of other nations.   When the foreign Legations in Peking were defending themselves against overwhelming odds, the Japanese contingent of the foreign troops in China came to their rescue and won the admiration of the world by their bravery, skill, and good conduct.   It has been truly said that "when all alike were tried in the same fire, the peoples of Europe learned to their humiliation that the largest measure of restraint was exercised, not by white men, but by the soldiers of an Oriental Power."

All who have made themselves acquainted with the history of events in Japan during the past half-century will
Alliance with
Great Britain.
agree with Professor Chamberlain that "whatever troubles Japan may have in store for her, —troubles financial perhaps, complications with foreign Powers, troubles arising from the constant yearning of small but influential sections of her people for radical changes in government,—one thing is certain;—the whole trend of recent events has made for stability and for safety, for increased commerce, increased influence, and national self-respect. New Japan has come of age." Her coming of age has been fitly recognised, not only by her admission as a member of the comity of nations on terms of perfect equality, but also by a political alliance with the Britain of the West.

During what we have called the transition period territorial expansion has been a feature in the history of the
Extent
of Japanese
Empire.
Japanese Empire, and it now includes the long chain of islands extending from Kamtchatka on the north to and including Formosa in the south. In that chain there are five large islands and about six hundred small ones. The most northerly latitude is 50° 56′, and the most southerly 21° 48′, so that the variety of climate is considerable. Its position has enabled it to become a focus of navigation routes in the Pacific and a great market in the Far East, as well as a naval power which will have a dominating influence in the whole of the Pacific area. In 1872 the registered population of Japan consisted of 16,796,143 males and 16,314,650 females, or a total of 33,110,793 ; while in 1900 it was 22,608,150 males and 22,197,806 females, or a total of 44,805,937. In addition the population of Formosa, which was ceded by China to Japan in 1895, was, at the latter date, 2,621,158. During recent years the population of Japan proper has increased at the rate of nearly half-a-million a year ; a fact which must be kept in mind when the foreign policy of Japan is being considered.

BIBLIOGRAPHICAL NOTE

A standard history of Japan for the period covered by this chapter has still to be written. The students of the subject must consult Government Reports and Blue Books, the files of the daily newspapers, and other contemporary publications. General readers may obtain a fairly good idea of the history of what I have called the Transition Period from some of the books which have been written, although these are usually of a somewhat superficial and one-sided nature. The following will be found useful :—Black, *Young Japan*; Adams, *History of Japan*; Griffis, *The Mikado's Empire*; Murray, *The Story of Japan*; Mounsey, *The Satsuma Rebellion*; Yamawaki, *Japan in the Beginning of the Twentieth Century*; Norman, *The Real Japan*; Stead, *Japan, our New Ally*; Diósy, *The New Far East*; as well as others mentioned in the Appendix. The best condensed account of the history of modern Japan is that given by Captain Brinkley in his articles on Japan in the supplementary volumes of the *Encyclopædia Britannica*. His large work, especially volumes v. and vi., should be carefully studied.

CHAPTER V

EDUCATION

"KNOWLEDGE and learning shall be sought after throughout the whole world, in order that the status of the Empire of Japan may be raised ever higher and higher." In these words, the Emperor, soon after his accession to the throne, when announcing the principles of the progressive policy which would in future guide the Government, not only stated the object which would be kept in view, but also indicated the means which were to be adopted for its attainment. That object was the raising of the status of the Empire of Japan among the nations of the world, and the chief means by which that was to be attained was by taking advantage of Western knowledge and experience. At first, no doubt, the ideas of those in power were very limited, as regards the nature and extent of the knowledge required, but, as is the case in all national movements, these ideas developed as the work progressed, until it was recognised that Japan could rise to her true position only through a system of national education conducted on the most approved methods. The development of education in Japan during the last quarter of the nineteenth century is, without doubt, the most striking example in the history of the world of the influence of education in changing the economic, industrial and social conditions of a country. We can only note its most important features ; details of organisation and of the work of special institutions may be studied in the publications mentioned at the end of this chapter.

Under the old regime, education in Japan was carried on strictly on Chinese lines. As has already been indicated, the samurai, consisting of about one-fifteenth of Education in the population, were highly cultured according Old Japan. to the ideas of the country and were characterised both by uprightness and by devotion to duty. The most important part of knightly pedagogics was the building up of character, and the subtler faculties of prudence, intelligence, and dialectics were left in the shade. Intellectual superiority was, of course, esteemed ; but the word *Chi*, which was employed to denote intellectuality, meant wisdom in the first instance and placed knowledge only in a very subordinate position. The tripod that supported the framework of Bushido was said to be *Chi, Jin, Yu*, respectively Wisdom, Benevolence, and Courage. A samurai was essentially a man of action. Science was out of the pale of his activity. He took advantage of it in so far as it concerned his profession of arms. Religion and theology were relegated to the priests ; he concerned himself with them in so far as they helped to nourish courage. Philosophy and literature formed the chief part of his intellectual training ; but even in the pursuit of these, it was not objective truth that he strove after—literature was pursued mainly as a pastime, and philosophy as a practical aid in the formation of character, if not for the exposition of some military or political problem.

The curriculum of studies according to the pedagogics of Bushido consisted mainly of fencing, archery, a knowledge of anatomy required for purposes of offence or defence, horsemanship, the use of the spear, tactics, caligraphy, ethics, literature and history. Finance and commerce and everything connected with them were regarded as low pursuits compared with moral and intellectual vocations. Money and the love of it being thus diligently ignored, Bushido itself could long remain free from a thousand-and-one evils of which money is the root. People whose minds were simply stored with information found no great admirers.

Of the three great services of studies that Bacon gives,—for delight, ornament, and ability,—Bushido had decided preference for the last, where their use was " in judgment and the disposition of business." Whether it was for the disposition of public business or for the exercise of self-control, it was with a practical end in view that education was conducted. " Learning without thought," said Confucius, " is labour lost ; thought without learning is perilous."

In the matter of science and of the outside world the higher-class Japanese were in a state of almost absolute ignorance, while the education of the common people, for the most part, consisted of varying degrees of knowledge of the Chinese classics, got up by mere force of memory, and of Japanese history and Government edicts, together with the ability to write and to reckon on the abacus. It was curious to note how much the people were the slaves of mechanical methods in their mental training. The abacus, for instance, was used for the most simple calculations which any fairly well-educated person could perform mentally or with a pencil and a slip of paper. Still, intelligence was very widely diffused, and few were unable to read and write, at least in the ordinary Japanese characters, although their knowledge of Chinese might be very limited or altogether nil. Learning by heart and copying constituted the greater part of the education of the Japanese youth, and the teacher did nothing to stimulate original thought. The schools were small and the scholars in each class seldom exceeded six ; so that the personal character of the teacher was a very important factor. There were three grades of schools—*Sho, Chin,* and *Dai-Gakko* ; or small, middle, and great schools. The latter, however, were found only in a few localities. The chief centres of learning were at Kyoto and Yedo (now Tokyo), where the highest educational institutions had something like university rank. Kyoto was the seat of ecclesiastical and æsthetic learning, while Yedo was the highest seat of Chinese learning in the land. In nearly every daimyo's provincial capital there was a school for the instruction of the sons of the samurai. Etiquette and good manners, for which the Japanese in olden times were so marked, were taught with special care. Under the forms of politeness, however, there were concealed many of the results of Eastern philosophy. As a well-known exponent of the best-known school put it : " The end of all etiquette is to cultivate your mind that even when you are quietly seated, not the roughest ruffian can dare make an attack on your person." Or as Dr. Nitobe has said : " It means, in other words, that by constant exercise in correct manners, one brings all the parts and faculties of his body into perfect order and into such harmony with itself and its environment as to express the mastery of spirit over the flesh." Japanese politeness was therefore not the superficial matter foreigners usually took it to be.

During the long peace which prevailed under the Tokugawa Shoguns considerable encouragement was given to literature and arts. There was a good deal of speculation and several systems of philosophy were produced ; sciences and arts began to emerge from the narrow sphere of Chinese philosophy, and to be gradually permeated with the influences of Western civilisation. As I have already indicated, there slowly filtered throughout the country, from Nagasaki, where the Dutch had their settlement before foreigners were generally admitted to the country, a certain amount of European science and literature ; but nothing of a systematic nature was done until the representatives of the Foreign Powers were forcing themselves on Japan and demanding treaties of commerce, when the Government of the Shogun recognised the necessity of training men in European languages and methods ; and in order that they might more successfully carry on negotiations, they instituted a school in Yedo with an English and a French department, which ultimately developed into the University of Tokyo. The missionaries who had arrived in Beginning of Japan in considerable numbers did excellent foreign schools. pioneer work in education, and among them the name of the Rev. Guido Verbeck deserves to be specially mentioned. He began his work in Nagasaki early in the sixties, and there he influenced men who afterwards took a leading part in the government of the country. After the Restoration he was invited to Tokyo to take charge of the school which had been instituted by the Shogun, and for some years he acted as its Principal. Thereafter he became adviser in general matters to the central Government, and during his later years he returned to purely missionary work, at which he continued till his death, in 1898. His name deserves to be held in remembrance by the Japanese, as he rendered good service to their country at a very critical period of its history.

After the Restoration, in 1867, as we have already seen, great changes took place in the administration, and the Government soon turned its attention to the improvement of education. In 1869 regulations relating to universities, middle schools and elementary schools were promulgated by Imperial decree. In July 1871 the Department of Education was established, and all affairs relating to general education were brought under its control. In August 1872 the Code of Education was promulgated. An Imperial Rescript was then issued indicating the course to be pursued by the people in general. The purport of the said Imperial Rescript was briefly as follows :—

" The acquirement of knowledge is essential to a successful life. All knowledge, from that necessary for daily life to that higher knowledge required to prepare officials, farmers, merchants, artisans, physicians, etc., for their respective vocations, is acquired by learning. A long time has elapsed since schools were first established. But for farmers, artisans, and merchants, and also for women, learning was regarded as beyond their sphere, owing to some misapprehension in the way of school administration. Even among the higher classes much time was spent in the useless occupation of writing poetry and composing maxims, instead of learning what would be for their own benefit or that of the State. Now an educational system has been established and the schedules of study remodelled. It is designed, henceforth, that education shall be so diffused that there may not be a village with an ignorant family, nor a family with an ignorant member. Persons who have hitherto applied themselves to study have almost always looked to the Government for their support. This is an erroneous notion, proceeding from long abuse, and every person should henceforth acquire knowledge by his own exertion."

In the Code of Education above mentioned various regulations were prescribed in regard to the grand, middle, and elementary school districts, school district committees, bureaux of inspection, the appointment of special school officials in the local Government offices, the subjects of study to be pursued in universities, middle schools, and elementary schools, school teachers and normal schools, pupils and examinations, students in foreign countries, school funds, tuition fees, etc. Rapid progress was made in carrying out the objects of the Education Code. For some years Dr. David Murray, a Scotsman by birth, but an American by education and experience, was engaged as adviser to the Department of Education, and he introduced some features of the American system into the elementary and secondary schools of Japan. The colleges were to a large extent staffed by men of different nationalities, and they of course caused them to be moulded, to a certain extent, on lines to which they had been accustomed. The staff of what has now become the Literature and Science Colleges of the Universities had representatives of almost all Western countries ; that of the Engineering College was British, and largely Scottish ; the Naval College was British ; the Medical College, German ; the Military College, French ; the Agricultural College, British ; the School of Art, Italian. In education, as in other departments, however, the Japanese have not been content to copy any system ; they have observed what they believed to be the good points in all systems, and they have now evolved an organisation of their own, which is very complete and well suited to the requirements of the country. It begins with the common school course, comprising a primary department covering four years, to which children at the age of six are admitted, and a secondary or higher grade covering another four years. Above this there is the middle-school course of five years for boys, and the high-school course of four years for girls, to both of which those who have been two years in the higher department of the common school are admitted. Above the middle school stand the higher schools, of which there are six in the country, and which provide three years' preparatory course for the Imperial University, mostly in languages and mathematics, as well as, in the case of some of them, four years' special training in medicine, law, or engineering, instruction being given in the vernacular. Only the graduates of the middle school are admitted to the higher middle school, through competitive examination. Lastly, at the head of all stand the two Imperial Universities of Tokyo and Kyoto—the former consisting of the colleges of law, medicine, engineering, literature, science, and agriculture ; the latter of the colleges of science, and engineering, medicine, law, and literature. There is a provision made for the post-graduate studies, called *Daigaku*—to which only graduates of superior scholarship are eligible. The system as tabulated stands as follows :—

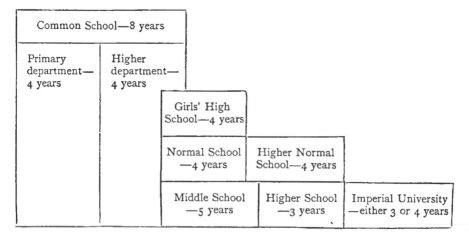

Common School—8 years

Primary department—4 years

Higher department—4 years

Girls' High School—4 years

Normal School—4 years

Higher Normal School—4 years

Middle School—5 years

Higher School—3 years

Imperial University—either 3 or 4 years

Supposing a scholar enters the elementary school at six years of age, and follows this complete course, he will be twenty-two when he enters the university.

The object of the elementary schools, as defined in the Imperial Ordinance, is as follows :—" Elementary schools are designed to give children the rudiments of moral Primary education. education, and of education specially adapted to make of them good members of the community, together with such general knowledge and skill as are necessary for practical life—due attention being paid to their bodily development." This object is explained more fully in the regulations relating to the elementary school course, in which the principles of teaching are defined and the chief points to be attended to in education are indicated. (1) In teaching any subject of study, special attention should be paid to those topics which are connected with moral education and with education specially adapted to make of the children good members of the community. (2) As regards the knowledge and skill to be imparted to children, those facts the knowledge of which is most necessary in daily life should be selected and taught, so as to enable them, by repeated exercises and study, to apply intelligently and practically what they have learned. (3) In order to ensure the sound and healthy development of the body, instruction in any subject shall be so regulated as to conform to the degree of growth, both mental and physical. (4) In teaching children, careful discrimination shall be made as to their sexes, so that education thus imparted might be best adapted to their respective characteristics as well as to their future life. (5) The instruction in different subjects of study shall be so conducted that they may be beneficially influenced by one another, the true object and the best methods of instruction being steadily kept in view at the same time. It is quite evident from these sentences that the Japanese do not make the mistake, which is so common in this country, of confounding instruction with education, and that the training in character is the chief object kept in view.

The number of ordinary elementary schools in Japan is 18,871, and of higher elementary schools, 8238, or a total of 27,109, showing a proportion of one elementary school for 1685 heads of population. Supplementary courses extending over two years are provided in 2136 ordinary elementary schools, and in 224 higher elementary schools for those who carry their education beyond the ordinary course. The local administration of the schools is almost entirely in the hands of the local authorities, a general supervision being exercised by the central Education Department. In city, town or village elementary schools tuition fees have hitherto been levied as a rule, but, according to the revised Imperial Ordinance relating to elementary schools, no tuition fees are to be levied in ordinary elementary schools. In special cases the local governor may allow fees to be charged, not to exceed 20 sen a month in cities, and 10 sen in towns or villages and in town and village unions. Almost the whole expenditure on elementary schools is borne by the city, town or village in which they are situated ; but as the expense of education is increasing from year to year, the difficulty of obtaining the requisite funds is becoming greater, and grants are given by the Central Department for the purpose of lessening the local burdens. All the indemnity received from China on the conclusion of the war of 1894-5 was not spent on the army and navy or other warlike purposes : a considerable part was devoted to industry and education. The sum of 10,000,000 yen was reserved as an educational fund, the interest of which is distributed among the schools in proportion to the attendance.

I must refer to special publications for details of the courses of study and of the organisation of elementary schools. These will be found to cover every part of elementary education, and to contain much information which is worthy of the attention of educationists in any country in the world.

The same remark applies to secondary education in all its aspects. It has been arranged that there shall be, at least, one secondary school in every town and province. Since the Japan-China war the desire for learning has become so great that the increase and extension of secondary schools has during the last ten years been remarkable. In 1893 there were 53 public and 15 private secondary schools, with 5 branches; while at the end of 1902-3 there were 207 public and 35 private secondary schools, with 22 branches; which shows an increase of four times in the aggregate. As to the size of the schools, the expenditure, the number of pupils, etc., the increase has been even more rapid. The subjects of study are—morals, Japanese, Chinese classics, foreign languages, history, geography, mathematics, natural history, physics, chemistry, law and economics, drawing, singing, and gymnastics. In some cases a few of these subjects are optional. The establishment and closing of schools of this class require the approval of the Minister of State for Education, but the expenses are borne by those who establish them. In public secondary schools tuition fees are charged, except in particular cases, but with private schools this matter is left to the will of the proprietor. The greater number of the private schools are supported by the tuition fees, which are usually higher than in public schools, and vary from one to three yen per month.

Special schools have been instituted for the purpose of affording the higher general education necessary for girls. In Japan, however, the women are in the minority, and the consequence is that almost all of them get married at about twenty years of age, and the demand for higher women's education has not arisen to any great degree. The objects kept in view in the girls' high schools is therefore the formation of character in women and the imparting of knowledge well calculated to make good wives and wise mothers, able to contribute to the peace and happiness of the family into which they wed.

Very complete arrangements have been made for the training of teachers for the various classes of schools, in the higher normal schools, the Higher Normal School for

Girls, the Teachers' Training Institute, the Tokyo Fine Art

Training of teachers.

School, and the Tokyo Academy of Music. These schools are all Government establishments, and the expenditure for their maintenance is kept distinct from the general items of expenditure of the National Treasury. By the accumulation of their yearly balances it is hoped that, in time, those schools may become independent and self-supporting.

In addition to the ordinary secondary schools there are others called Kotogakko, or higher schools, which prepare

Higher secondary schools.

students for entrance to the universities. There are now eight such schools, and they are situated in Tokyo, Sendai, Kyoto, Kanazawa, Kumamoto, Okayama, Kagoshima, and Yamaguchi. They are all Government institutions and are supported in the same way as the higher normal schools, with the exception of the one at Yamaguchi, which is supported by donations. The courses of study are divided into three sections, each extending over three years. In the first section are taught those who wish to enter the College of Law or the College of Literature ; in the second, those wishing to enter the College of Science, the College of Engineering, the course of pharmacy in the College of Medicine, or the College of Agriculture ; and in the third section, those intending to enter the course of medicine or the course of pharmacy in the College of Medicine,—and they each give a very complete preparation for the work of the universities.

The Imperial universities of Japan are stated to have for their object the teaching of such arts and sciences as are

University education.

required for the purpose of the State, and the prosecution of original researches in such arts and sciences. Each Imperial university consists of a university hall and colleges ; the university hall being established for the purpose of original research, and the colleges for that of instruction, theoretical and practical. At present there are two universities, namely, the Imperial University of Tokyo and the Imperial University of Kyoto.

The latter is of very recent origin, having been established in 1897, while the former dates almost from the Restoration.

After that important event the Imperial Government revived an institution known in the Tokugawa period as Kaiseijo, and in the following year it was designated Daigaku Nanko; and from this originated the present University of Tokyo. In 1873 the name was changed and the institution was called Kaisei Gakko. In 1877 it was combined with the Tokyo Igakko, or Medical School, to form the Tokyo Daigaku, or Tokyo University, with the four departments of law, medicine, literature, and science.

In so far as the Kobu-Daigakko, or Imperial College of Engineering, is concerned, I shall quote verbatim from the last edition of the Calendar of the Imperial University of Tokyo, which says: "As at present organised, the Tokyo Teikoku Daigaku, or Imperial University of Tokyo, is of no very great antiquity, for it came practically into existence in March 1, 1886, when an Imperial Ordinance fused the two independent institutions of the Tokyo Daigaku and the Kobu-Daigakko into one, under the title of Teikoku Daigaku, or Imperial University." After giving a somewhat detailed account of the various developments of the first named of these institutions, the account proceeds: "The history of the Kobu-Daigakko (Imperial College of Engineering), the second component factor in the Imperial University of Tokyo, is much shorter and much less complicated than that of the Tokyo Daigaku (Tokyo University). Originally known as the Kogakko, it was established at Toranomon-uchi, in connection with the Bureau of Engineering in the Public Works Department of the Imperial Government. In 1872 it was divided into the College proper and the Preparatory School (which latter opened in Yamato-Yashiki, Tameike, in 1874), and in 1876 an Art School was established in connection with the College. [This Art School was discontinued in 1877.] In 1877 the Bureau of Engineering was abolished, and the College, now established in its new buildings at Toranomon, was officially named the Kobu-Daigakko (Imperial College of Engineering). The abolition of the Department of Public Works in 1885 caused the Kobu-Daigakko to be transferred to the control of the Department of Education. And on March 1, 1886, Imperial Ordinance No. 3 was promulgated for the organisation of the Teikoku Daigaku or Imperial University, and the Kobu - Daigakko and the Tokyo Daigaku were merged in the new institution. Two years later (July 1888), the College of Engineering was removed from Toranomon to the new brick building then completed for it in the Kaga Yashiki grounds at Hongo." The professors and students of the Kobu-Daigakko were transferred to the new buildings, and the work of the Engineering College has been carried on with success, although there are not now the same opportunities for practical work as when it was in the Department of Public Works. The students have now, for the most part, to depend on private undertakings and on visits to Government establishments. In the interests of the students and indeed of Japan more complete arrangements are required for practical training.

In June 1890 another college, that of Agriculture, was added to the Imperial University as the result of two Imperial Ordinances. That college had been instituted in 1874 by the Agricultural Bureau of the Department of Agriculture and Commerce, and the buildings are still on the original site at Komaba, at a considerable distance from the other university buildings ; a fact which, of course, does not prevent it from being an integral part of the university, which now consists of the six Colleges of Law, Medicine, Engineering, Literature, Science, and Agriculture. The buildings of the first five of these institutions stand within the grounds of the old Kaga Yashiki, on the north-eastern slope of the Hongo plateau.

The following figures from the latest published Report of the Minister of Education give the numbers of professors, instructors, and students in the different colleges :—

	No. of Professors and Assistant Professors.					Students and Pupils.			Graduates.		
	Professors.	Assistant Professors.	*Shokutaku.*	Foreign Professors.	Total.	Students.	Pupils.	Total.	Students.	Pupils.	Total.
University Hall	...	...	...	...	...	467	...	467	*44	...	44
College of Law	17	3	9	4	33	969	26	995	106	2	108
College of Medicine	23	7	4	1	35	398	124	522	97	133	230
College of Engineering	20	14	23	2	59	421	6	427	98	5	103
College of Literature	12	4	22	7	45	285	17	302	71	3	74
College of Science	18	5	5	...	28	65	3	68	19	1	20
College of Agriculture	14	18	9	4	45	65	275	340	15	37	52
Total	104	51	72	18	245	2670	451	3121	406 *44	181	631

* Students whose term of study in University Hall had expired.

The Calendar of the University gives very complete information regarding the courses of study in the various colleges ; that publication must be referred to for details, and its perusal will show that the youth of Japan have now opportunities for higher education which will compare very favourably with those of almost any other country in Europe or America. Besides the colleges, there are several other organisations which add to the completeness of the arrangements, such as the Library, the Institute for Natural History, the Hospital, the Institute of Botany, the Astronomical Observatory, the Seismological Observatory, experimental farms, etc. Each of the colleges is well equipped with laboratories for experimental work, so that the teaching is made thoroughly practical and encourages original thought and not mere book-learning.

The courses of study extend over three years, with the exception of those of law and medicine, which extend over four years, and on satisfying the examiners, the graduates receive titles indicating the courses which they have followed. The total number of graduates of all classes up till September 1903 was 5459, and of these 391 had died.

The Imperial University of Kyoto, though of very recent

establishment, being scarcely seven years old and consequently far from complete in its equipment, seems to be satisfying the expectations of the students belonging to the various colleges. It is developing rapidly, and thus laying a foundation for larger usefulness in the future. At present it consists of the University Hall and the Colleges of Law, Medicine and Science and Engineering. The following table shows the number of professors, instructors, and students for the year 1901-2, and is taken from the last published Report of the Minister of Education :—

	No. of Professors and Instructors.					Students and Pupils.			Graduates.		
	Professors.	Assistant Professors.	*Shokutaku.*	Foreign Professors.	Total.	Students.	Pupils.	Total.	Students.	Pupils.	Total.
University Hall	...	...	...	...	...	30	...	30	...	...	...
College of Law	10	2	4	...	16	157	15	172	...	...	...
College of Medicine	12	4	2	...	18	71	9	80	...	...	...
College of Science and Engineering	21	14	12	1	48	202	7	209	39	1	40
Total . . .	43	20	18	1	82	460	31	491	39	1	40

Not only are the teaching arrangements becoming more complete, but the external organisations which are connected with the University of Kyoto are developing, and there can be little doubt that she will emulate the example of her elder sister in Tokyo. The Government proposes to establish another university in some other part of Japan as soon as circumstances permit, with a view of realising more fully the aspirations of those numerous students who are eager to pursue the highest course of study in Japan.

All the expenses of university students are defrayed by themselves. Each student is required to pay a fee of 2 yen for admission, and 25 yen annually for tuition fees. An incidental fee of 10 yen for each academic year, to cover the cost of materials used, is also required of each student in the Colleges of Engineering and Science. To help those who have not the means of meeting the necessary expenses, a system of Loan Scholarships has been established in the University of Tokyo, and these have been of considerable advantage to the class of students for whom they were intended.

The higher branches of technical education are of course important in the colleges of the Imperial universities, but in order to give a fairly good training in both Technical theory and practice to those who will be in charge education. of the more practical aspects of industry and who cannot proceed to the universities, numerous technical schools have been established. Since the Japan-China War the Japanese Government has put much weight upon technical education, and during the past ten years it has made very rapid progress. There are at present the three higher Technical Schools of Tokyo, Osaka, and Kyoto, and a large number of others of a more elementary and practical nature. The following table shows the increase in the number of technical schools, public and private, since 1892 :—

Kind of Schools.	Industrial Schools.	Agricultural Schools.	Commercial Schools.	Nautical Schools.	Apprentices' Schools.	Supplementary Schools.	Total.
(’92) 25th year { Number of schools	5	12	11	...	?	?	28
,, ,, scholars	714	191	1629	...	?	?	2934
(’00) 33rd year { Number of schools	18	56	38	4	22	150	288
,, ,, scholars	1605	5040	8269	319	1642	8850	25,725
(’01) 34th year { Number of schools	21	79	41	5	25	221	392
,, ,, scholars	1993	7778	9842	533	1528	12,992	34,666
(’02) 35th year { Number of schools	25	102	50	7	32	629	845
,, ,, scholars	2590	9847	11,370	715	2192	30,882	57,596

An adequate description of the different kinds of schools and of the work done in them would require a large volume, but the following statistics for last year give an approximate idea of the extent of the movement for technical education in Japan:—

Kind of Schools.	Number of Schools.			Number of Pupils.	Number of Graduates.	Expenditure.	Aid of the National Treasury.
	Public.	Private.	Total.				
						Yen.	Yen.
Industrial Schools	23	2	25	2590	417	508,700	62,330
Apprentices' Schools	31	1	32	2192	469	125,799	29,230
A-class Agricultural Schools	55	2	57	7146	1919	1,031,697	110,090
B-class Agricultural Schools	47	2	49	2701	572	154,435	
A-class Commercial Schools	34	7	41	9882	1021	611,300	53,210
B-class Commercial Schools	16	1	17	1488	573	48,395	
A-class Nautical Schools	7	0	7	715	93	83,407	13,820
Supplementary Industrial School — Industrial	42	1	43	3042	479	17,564	16,573
Supplementary Industrial School — Agricultural	482	21	503	22,933	1804		
Supplementary Industrial School — Commercial	69	13	82	4880	501		
Supplementary Industrial School — Nautical	1	0	1	26	6		
Sum	807	50	857	57,596	7854	2,739,297	285,253

The courses in these schools include the subjects which are indispensable to artisans and others engaged in industrial and commercial occupations. The programme includes morals, arithmetic, geometry, chemistry, and drawing, together with those subjects directly connected with handicrafts and practical work. When convenience requires it, any subject except morals may be left out or taught simply as an elective subject. The length of the course is from six months to four years; the season for teaching may be fixed according to the convenience of the locality, and lessons may be given on Sundays or at nights. Very complete arrangements have been made for the training of teachers for technical schools. Special institutes for this purpose are attached to some of the colleges of Tokyo University, and various independent training institutions have been established.

The events at the Restoration upset all the arrangements for the teaching and practice of art; for some years purely Japanese art suffered a check and many of those who practised it were reduced to very Art and music education. great straits. What was formerly done from love of art and in conformity with Japanese ideals had now, very often, to be done to obtain a bare living, and to conform to what were supposed to be the tastes of the foreign purchasers. Gradually, however, a revival took place, and facilities were given for the culture of art by various educational institutions and societies.

In a future chapter the subject of art industries will be considered; so that meantime a few notes on existing institutions are all that is necessary. After various attempts had been made to re-establish art training on a proper basis, none of which turned out very successful, a commission was sent in 1886 to Europe and America to study the methods and organisation of art education; on its return to Japan in 1888 a new institution was founded under the name of the Tokyo Fine Art School. Several changes and improvements have since been introduced into the constitution of the school, and it has now reached a remarkable stage of development and progress and is the chief centre of art education in the empire. The school gives instruction in painting, designing, sculpture, architecture (omitted for the present) and industrial arts, with the object of training youths as professional artists or teachers of drawing. Each course of study extends over four years, besides one year of preparatory work. For details of which, however, reference must be made to special publications.

There is a considerable number of private institutions connected with artistic education, the most important of which is the Bijitsuin, of which the leading spirit is Mr. Kakasu Okakura, to whom frequent reference will be made in subsequent chapters. The object of this institution is to endeavour to keep art more closely in touch with Japanese ideals than is done in the Government institution, while at the same time allowing it to develop to a considerable extent on Western lines. This is a very difficult task, and we need not be surprised to learn that it has not been altogether successful. There are now many private studios in which pupils are taken; and as regards painting, we find the original Japanese school, the European school, and a mixture of both, so that a most interesting development is now going on, and it is probably in art that we will first see a combination of the ideals of the East and the West. Instruction is now given in many institutions, both public and private, in the applications of fine arts to industry. Art in Japan enjoys the enlightened patronage and powerful support of the Court, and the official recognition of distinguished artists by the Imperial Household has greatly stimulated progress.

Music in Japan goes back to the remotest antiquity and has taken its development from various sources. In 1879 the Department of Education began to take an interest in musical education, and sent a Commission to Europe and America for the purpose of investigating the subject. A school was established in 1883, and the curriculum was constituted as follows :—Morals, Singing, Pianoforte, Organ, Koto, Kokyu, Special Instruments, Harmonics, Theory of Music, History of Music and the Methods of Teaching Music. After undergoing various modifications the Tokyo Academy of Music took its present form. The school provides five courses—the Preparatory, Principal, Post-Graduate, Normal, and Elective Courses. The principal course is not by any means confined to music in the narrow sense of that term, but gives a very complete education, through music and its allied subjects and the other courses allow a considerable choice for special study in any department. Outside the Tokyo Academy of Music there is no school, either public or private, for systematic musical education. There are, however, many musical societies and associations with different objects, with which the fellows of the Tokyo Academy of Music are mostly connected, so that there are opportunities for musical education apart from the formal training of the Academy. There are, besides, special institutes of musicians, such as the Board of Musicians which takes charge of affairs relating to music in the Imperial Court, and to that of the army and navy. In recent years much more attention has been paid to musical education in the higher circles of society, and in almost all the schools singing and music are taught as a part of general education.

There are many schools in various parts of Japan for special purposes, which cannot be strictly classified under any of the preceding headings ; such as Special schools. the Tokyo Foreign Language School, the Nautical College, the Higher Commercial School, and the institutions connected with the army and navy, some of which will be mentioned later on. Considerable attention has been paid to the education of the blind and of the deaf and dumb, and the Institution in Tokyo which was started so far back as 1874 has rendered very effective service to an afflicted part of the community. The subjects of study in the ordinary course for the blind are Japanese, Arithmetic, Conversation, and Gymnastics ; and those in the industrial course, Music, Acupuncture, and Massage. The ordinary course for the dumb includes Reading, Writing, Composition, Arithmetic, Written Conversation, and Gymnastics ; and the industrial course, Drawing, Carving, Joinery, and Sewing. A similar institution has been in existence in Kyoto since 1878, and the subsequent careers of those who have passed through these two schools show that they have been fitted to earn their living in an honourable manner.

(B 207)

H

	No. of Schools.				Instructors and Teachers.				Students and Pupils.				Graduat[es].			
	Gov.	Public.	Private.	Total.	Gov.	Public.	Private.	Total.	Gov.	Public.	Private.	Total.	Gov.	Public.	Private.	Total.
Elementary Schools .	2	26,485	369	26,856	31	91,767	1101	92,899	1,124	4,622,930	59,544	4,683,598	318	736,907	8,580	5,80
Blind and Dumb Schools	1	1	9	11	15	15	25	55	231	196	194	621	14	8	12	3
Normal Schools . .	...	52	...	52	...	958	...	958	...	15,639	...	15,639	...	7,323	...	7,32
Higher Normal Schools	2	...	...	2	110	...	...	110	803	...	...	803	180	...	...	18
Middle Schools . .	1	183	34	218	22	3,067	659	3,748	321	64,051	13,943	78,315	40	5,584	2,163	7 78
Higher Female Schools	1	44	7	52	19	525	114	658	306	9,746	1,932	11,984	91	1,832	637	2 56
Higher Schools . .	7	...	...	7	345	...	...	345	5,684	...	...	5,684	1019	...	...	1 01
Imperial Universities .	2	...	...	2	291	...	...	291	3,240	...	...	3,240	633	...	...	63
Special Schools .	3	4	41	48	128	81	734	943	968	1,447	10,985	13,400	138	210	1,687	2,03
Technical Schools .	9	265	23	297	238	1,382	137	1,757	1,730	23,599	2,126	27,455	349	4,406	249	5,00
Miscellaneous Schools	...	122	1195	1,317	...	90	4273	4,363	...	4,817	80,117	84,934	...	721	15,783	16,50
Total . . .	28	27,156	1678	28,862	1199	97,885	7043	106,127	14,407	4,742,425	168,841	4,925,673	2782	756,991	29,111	111

A very imperfect outline has been given of the educational organisation of Japan ; to do it justice much more space would be required than can be given to
it in this chapter. The preceding summary,
however, gives a good idea of the extent of
the work which is done. The figures refer to the year
1900-1901, the latest published.

Summary of educational statistics.

The Government schools are those directly under the control of the Education Department ; the public schools are those which are managed by the local authorities, subject to the general supervision of the Department ; while the private schools are those which are instituted and carried on by private persons with the authority of the Education Department.

Space will not allow a detailed account of all the financial arrangements in connection with the organisation of education, but the following figures showing the main items of expenditure for the year mentioned will be found interesting :—

	Regular Expenses.	Special Expenses.	Total.
	Yen.	Yen.	Yen.
The Department Proper . . .	392,813	1,377,612	1,770,425
Earthquake Investigation Committee .	28,094	...	28,094
International Geodetic Committee .	14,333	...	14,333
Central Meteorological Observatory .	36,910	...	36,910
Observatory for measuring Latitudes .	4,898	...	4,898
Dependent Institutions . . .	2,027,398	...	2,027,398
Salaries for the Directors of *Fu* and *Ken* Normal Schools	53,167	...	53,167
Local School Inspection . . .	161,469	...	161,469
Grant for Technical Education . .	249,984	...	249,984
Grant for Elementary Education .	1,487,637	...	1,487,637
Total	4,456,703	1,377,612	5,834,315

The following table shows the expenditure for the same year on the institutions named :—

	Regular Expenses.	Special Expenses.	Total.
	Yen.	Yen.	Yen.
Imperial University of Tokyo	882,167	67,062	949,229
Imperial University of Kyoto	326,342	101,253	427,595
Higher Normal School	157,287	...	157,287
Higher Normal School for Females . .	83,824	4,932	88,756
Supporo Agricultural School	58,737	2,500	61,237
Higher Commercial School	54,346	...	54,346
First Higher School	127,581	...	127,581
Second Higher School	83,721	2,659	86,380
Third Higher School	103,473	...	103,473
Fourth Higher School	78,673	...	78,673
Fifth Higher School	122,768	13,713	136,481
Sixth Higher School	20,041	10,000	30,041
Yamaguchi Higher School	37,830	3,083	40,913
Tokyo Technical School.	85,286	36,392	121,678
Tokyo Foreign Languages School . . .	55,574	...	55,574
Tokyo Fine Arts School.	57,704	...	57,704
Tokyo Academy of Music	29,010	...	29,010
Osaka Technical School	50,377	7,000	57,377
Tokyo Blind and Dumb School . . .	12,255	1,498	13,753
Imperial Library	23,577	...	23,577
Total	2,450,573	250,092	2,700,665

These figures prove that the Japanese believe that money spent on education is a good national investment.

There are many organisations in Japan which, although not directly educational, all help the progress of education. Miscellaneous organisations. Educational societies exist in almost every locality for the purpose of diffusing and developing education and interesting the people in it. They organise discussions and lectures on educational subjects ; their proceedings are published in journals and thus they are able to make their opinions known. They are also engaged in the compilation of school books, the establishment of teachers' institutes and the organisation of educational exhibitions. There are now numerous scientific and technical societies (the most important of which will be mentioned in a subsequent chapter) which are devoted to the interests of special departments of science and industry and the transactions of which testify to the ability of the members. The scientific memoirs issued by the members of the universities will bear favourable comparison with those issued by European and American universities. Libraries of considerable extent are now to be found in many parts of the country, and new books published in Europe and America are eagerly purchased. The Tokyo Academy, somewhat on the lines of the French Academy, was established, under the control of the Minister of State for Education, for the promotion of science and arts, with the view of exercising a beneficial influence on education in general, and is composed of members selected from among old and venerable men of learning; the number of members is limited to twenty-five. One was selected by His Majesty the Emperor, while the others were elected on the recommendation of the members. Addresses are delivered by the members of the departments of learning in which they are interested, and these are published in a magazine. Among the contributions made to the Academy during the last year for which a report has been issued were 10 volumes of books, 378 copies of magazines and 40 copies of catalogues or reports.

The figures which have been quoted show that there is, in Japan, a considerable number of private educational institutions of all grades. The demand for Private education in recent years has been so great that educational the capacity of the Government and public institutions. institutions is too limited to meet it, and consequently part of the educational work has been undertaken by private individuals. Some of the more important private institutions have been started by men who wished to have greater freedom in the choice of subjects and methods than was possible in the official institutions, and in my opinion such a line of development ought to be encouraged, not only to give variety in the educational arrangements and methods, but also to induce a healthy rivalry in the training of men and women of high character and ability. The most important of these private institutions are the Keio Gijiku, the Waseda University in Tokyo, and the Kyoto Doshisha, each having its characteristics derived from its founder, its origin or its methods of instruction ; and these institutions are entitled, side by side with the Government special schools of various descriptions, to the credit of having been pioneers in the advancement of civilisation of the country.

The Keio Gijiku, as its name shows, was established during the Keio Era (previous to the Restoration of Meiji), and is consequently the oldest establishment of all the special schools, public or private, now in existence. Its founder, Yukichi Fukuzawa, was one of the most prominent characters modern Japan has yet produced, and his name will be long remembered not only as an educationist, but also as a writer and philosopher, who did more than any other man to promote the introduction of Western ideas into Japan. His life and his writings should be carefully studied by all who wish to understand the current of events in modern Japan. The institution which he founded has trained a great many of the politicians and public men who now occupy very important positions, and it has thus been a most important factor in the national evolution. It is now provided with a university course, an ordinary course of the standing of a middle school and a primary school course. The university comprises four departments ; namely, those of Political Economy, Law, Politics, and Literature. At present the number of students and pupils is over 2000, and it has sent out 3318 graduates.

The Waseda University was established in 1882 by Count Okuma, one of the most distinguished statesmen in the country, and some of his followers. It consists of a university course, a special course, and a higher preparatory course. The university course embraces three departments ; namely, those of Political Economy, Law, and Literature ; while the special course consists of six departments, namely, those of Politics and Economics, Law, Administrative Law, Japanese Language and Chinese Classics, History and Geography, Law and Economics, and English. In addition, it is provided with a post-graduate course. The number of graduates of the special course has already exceeded 2000, and the number of students and pupils is at present over 3000.

The Doshisha, in Kyoto, was established in 1875 by Jo Niijima, who had received a Christian education in America. At first it was called the Doshisha English School. Later on, a theological seminary, a girls' school, and a preparatory school were added to it. In 1883 the courses were much enlarged and the institution was about to become the Doshisha University—a scheme, however, which was not realised owing to the lamented death of its founder. At present the Higher School Course of the Doshisha is treated as a Special School. It consists of the Harris Science School, the department of politics and law, and the department of literature. In addition, this institution is provided with a theological seminary, an ordinary school, and a girls' school of the standing of a middle school, together with a library, a school of nursing, and a hospital. The graduates of the departments number about 1000, some of whom have become exemplary Christians, having no doubt been inspired by the noble and self-sacrificing spirit of its founder, while others have made themselves conspicuous in other fields, such as politics and literature.

Besides the foregoing Special Schools, there are others which provide courses in Law, Political Economy, and Politics; such as the Meiji University, the Hogakuin University, the Hosei University, the Nihon University, the Senshu Gakko, etc., as well as special schools of medicine, science, and pharmacy. Among the institutions devoted to instruction in literature and pedagogics may be mentioned the Kokugakuin and the Tetsugakkwan. Two universities have been established by the Buddhists, the East Honganji and the West Honganji, and they are noteworthy, not only as regards their design and equipment, but also because they are indicative of the religious and intellectual revival which has taken place in Buddhism.

No notice of the educational developments which have

taken place in Japan would be even approximately complete unless due praise was given to the work of Christian missionaries. The Doshisha in Kyoto has already been mentioned, but in the early days of foreign intercourse many of the missionaries devoted a great part of their time to the work of teaching. Now that the educational work of the country has been organised, this is not necessary to the same extent, but still there are a good many who are engaged in teaching, and their influence over numbers of the students has been considerable. Some of these have become professing Christians, but many others have had their ideals of life and conduct moulded by Christian principles.

In educational institutions of every grade in Japan the teaching of "morals" has a place in the curriculum,
Moral education. but except in those which are conducted by religious organisations, nothing is taught in the shape of religious dogma. The subject, however, is very much discussed both in newspapers and in books, and a very great variety of opinions is expressed. The following paragraphs from an article on the subject by Mr. Tokiwo Yokoi, one of the most thoughtful men in Japan, indicate its present position and are sufficient for our purpose :—

"The ethical teaching in the schools remains still the most important unsolved problem with the educators of the country. The various methods that have been tried during the past fifteen or more years, such as the use of Confucian classics, or the worshipping of the letter of the Emperor's Rescript on morals, have all proved inadequate to solve the great problem with which the nation is confronted. The greatest difficulty in the way of its solution is probably caused by the presence of two factors which must be taken into consideration. These two factors are the relation of religion to education, and the bearing of the changed social conditions of the country on the kind of ethics to be taught in the schools."

"Secular education in its barest form is the system that has been in vogue ; but it is a question which, I believe, is now beginning to engage the serious attention of many of our leading educational thinkers whether education in order to be secular must necessarily be so completely detached from religion—or anti-religious—as has been the case hitherto. To Viscount Mori is attributed, whether rightly or wrongly I know not, the dictum which has ruled the educational world of Japan for past years, that the minds of the pupils must be kept completely blank as far as religious ideas are concerned, until they attain to years of discretion. It is questionable, however, whether young minds can be kept entirely blank and free from religious bias for many years. Weeds grow and fill up gardens if useful plants are not cultivated. The actual result of this policy seems to be that the gain in the form of freedom from bigotry or superstition is counterbalanced by a lack of ethical ideals and intellectual depth among the educated people. Secularism in education, as emphasised by the Japanese authorities, seems to go hand in hand with shallowness and worldliness. When there is no sense of the eternal that maketh for righteousness, when no great and ennobling ideal pervades the thought, when martial glory and national splendour are all that call forth the ambition of youth in a country, who can expect great results from the teaching given in the schools? I am far from thinking that education in Japan should be given over entirely to Buddhist priests or Christian missionaries, or that endless disputations should be brought into the lecture-room. I believe in secular education in the sense of its separation from sectarian religious systems or bodies. But secularism does not necessarily imply anti-religion, or hostility towards any one form of religion." These opinions and the discussions which take place in the newspapers and elsewhere prove that the exclusion of religious teaching from the schools has not by any means settled the question, and its future development will be watched by many educationists in all parts of the world. How far Eastern and Western religious thought will approximate to the same ideals is one of the most interesting and important problems of the future.

The outline which has been given of the educational organisation in Japan shows that the recent developments Results of which have taken place in that country have been education. laid on a solid basis of national education. The Government has taken the lead in encouraging and supporting educational institutions of all kinds, and the people have eagerly responded to the facilities which have been offered to them. All classes were quick in perceiving that from a personal and national point of view it was their duty to equip themselves in such a manner that they might be able efficiently to discharge the duties which the new conditions would place upon them. Moreover, higher education in Japan, as in Germany, is encouraged by the fact that the graduation certificate of a common middle school not only carries considerable weight as a general qualification, but it also entitles a young man to volunteer for one year's service with the colours, thus escaping two of the three years he would have to serve as an ordinary recruit.

The results of the educational arrangements which have been made in Japan will be evident from a perusal of the following chapters, dealing with the most important national developments. The Japanese have not been content merely to absorb Western learning, but they have also, by original researches, extended its boundaries and have engaged in scientific, historical, and philosophical investigations of great interest and value. During a stage of such rapid transition, however, as has taken place in Japan, it was only natural that at first the new learning should be sought for chiefly for its practical applications in national affairs, and especially in the development of the natural resources of the country. At the Southport meeting of the British Association last year, the President, taking as his subject "The Influence of Brain-Power on History," traced convincingly and conclusively the intimate relation that exists between the provision made by a nation for the higher education of its people and the position taken by that nation in the ceaseless competition between the great countries of the world. After a searching comparison between the facilities for university education in this country on one hand and in the United States and in Germany on the other, Sir Norman Lockyer said : "But even more wonderful than these examples is the 'intellectual effort' made by Japan, not after a war, but to prepare for one. The question is, Shall we wait for a disaster and then imitate Prussia and France ; or shall we follow Japan and thoroughly prepare by 'intellectual effort' for the industrial struggle which lies before us ? " I have given an outline of the earnest and thorough attempt which the Japanese have made to establish a complete system of education, and in succeeding chapters evidence will be given of the profound and comparatively immediate effect which a well-considered scheme of education can have on national prospects.

The study of law, economics, and politics has had great attractions to large numbers of Japanese, no doubt in order that they might fit themselves to take part in the government of the country. In a recent official report it is stated that "the prevalence of a desire for such abstract forms of learning as law and politics in this country is no doubt due to the fact that people have become aware of the importance and necessity of pursuing these studies, since they live under a Constitutional Government ; but for this state of things another reason is assignable at least, as powerful as the one just given. Great importance is attached by our countrymen to what is called governing a country and saving its people—an idea which has been implanted in the mind of the nation by the study of Chinese literature. So deeply rooted is this idea in their minds that it has come to be almost a hereditary trait of Japanese character. This sentiment it is which impels the most promising young men to give themselves to the study of law, politics, and the like." It is now, however, being recognised that any attempt to govern a country and save a people by too close attention to technical education and material ends only sharpens the tools which may possibly drive them to destruction, while the training of an official class which is content with the machinery of government altogether overlooks the higher elements necessary for real national welfare. As a distinguished Japanese author put it a short time ago: "No system of education which is not based on sociological conditions can ever be thoroughly successful, and therefore a study of ethnology, sociology, and of evolution generally is absolutely essential to a thorough understanding of the educational questions awaiting solution." The Japanese are now face to face with many of the problems which confront all industrial nations, and it is to be hoped that, having organised their education generally and in some respects given an example to Western nations, they will go a step farther and show that it is possible to combine industrial development with the welfare of all classes of the community.

BIBLIOGRAPHICAL NOTE

The subject of education in Japan is touched upon in almost all the recent books on Japan, but usually in a very imperfect and superficial manner. A very complete official account of it has recently been published by the Education Department for the St. Louis Exhibition. The annual Reports of the Minister of Education should be studied in order that the progress made from year to year may be known. Details of the various institutions must be got from the Calendars, Prospectuses, etc., which they publish. The Life and writings of Yukichi Fukuzawa, the speeches and writings of Count Okuma and others who take a special interest in education, and the discussions which appear in the newspapers and journals must be studied in order that the opinions of the Japanese on the national aspects of education may be understood.

CHAPTER VI

ARMY AND NAVY

FOR our present purpose it is sufficient to consider the Japanese army and navy as factors in the national evolution, and it is not necessary to enter into details of their organisation, although a few particulars will be given regarding them. As in other departments, the ideas of the Government on the subject of national defence developed with the changes of conditions, both internal and external. The existence of the samurai had accustomed the people to the idea of a class whose chief object in life was to do the fighting which was required, and after the Restoration the problem that presented itself was to consolidate, under the control of the central Government, all the fighting material in the country. At that time foreign politics did not to any great extent affect the action of the Government; therefore the army received the greatest attention; and it was not until the relations with other Powers became considerable that a powerful navy was considered essential. Even at the outbreak of the war with China the Japanese had no battleships, but the action of some of the European Powers after that war showed them very clearly that if they were to receive the respect which was their due they must be strong enough to command it. They soon recognised that a complete system of national education by itself would not do this, and that if their country was to obtain a position of equality with the foreign

Army and navy as factors in the national evolution.

Reorganisation of fighting material.

Powers, the most effective arguments were a strong army and navy, which could be depended upon to enforce their claims, if that were necessary.

This, in great part, accounts for the developments which have taken place, especially in recent years, in the military Causes of recent and naval resources of the Japanese. They developments. were not animated by any desire for territorial expansion, or even for warlike glory, but they were determined to claim their full independence and the position which was due to them among the nations of the world, while at the same time they took full advantage of Western arts, sciences, and industrial arrangements. It is a sad commentary on Western civilisation when we find that an Eastern Power could not qualify itself for entrance to the comity of nations without, in the first place, spending a large part of its revenue on the appliances of destruction, and which could have been used to far greater advantage in improving the general conditions of the people. Recent events in the Far East have clearly proved that if the developments in national strength which have taken place in Japan during the past quarter of a century had been neglected, the national existence of the country would have been in danger. Moreover, Japanese statesmen have recognised that not only is the centre of importance of the commerce of the world moving in the direction of the Pacific area, but also that that area is destined to be the scene of great political events in the not very distant future, and therefore that Japan must be prepared to take her due share in the working out of the great changes which will profoundly affect conditions in all the countries bounded by that area.

Under the feudal system each daimyo had his own fighting men—the samurai—and although peace reigned in The Army Japan for two and a half centuries before the under the Restoration of 1868, all the military forms of feudal system. an earlier period were kept up. The events accompanying the Restoration caused these to be shattered,

and made a new military system a national necessity. The Emperor's Government rested chiefly on the reverence inspired by his sacred name. This moral force had been assisted by the actual support of the three great clans of Satsuma, Choshu, and Tosa, whose chiefs had taken the lead in surrendering their possessions and men to His Majesty, but under the changed conditions it became absolutely necessary that an Imperial army should be formed, which would give stability to the new Govern-   New system
ment. It was therefore arranged that the   introduced.
three clans named, who were the most powerful from a fighting point of view, should furnish the central Government with a certain proportion of troops who were to be transferred to Tokyo and entirely handed over to the Sovereign for the purpose of forming the nucleus of an Imperial army. Contingents from the other clans were to be added subsequently. Foreign officers were engaged to teach the Western methods of drill and tactics, and before long the Imperial Government had a considerable number of troops who were armed and drilled in foreign style.

It was, however, soon perceived that something more complete was necessary to consolidate the Government and to do away with the feeling that it was to a large extent the creation of the three most powerful clans and mainly supported by them. In 1873 the conscription system was therefore introduced. This, indeed, was only a return to what existed in the early days of Japan, when every man was a soldier and when civil duty was not differentiated from military. This measure practically put an end to the dominance of the samurai class, and no doubt it was one of the causes of dissatisfaction which arose among the samurai, and which came to a point in the Satsuma rebellion, noticed in a previous chapter.

That rebellion, although it was the means of causing great hardships—financial and warlike—on the country, had the effect of strengthening the Imperial army and making it a truly national institution including all classes of the people.

It was thought that the farmers, artisans, and tradespeople, after centuries of exclusion from the military pale, would be found to be deficient in the military spirit, but subsequent events dispelled this fear.   At twenty years of age every male Japanese becomes liable for conscription, and the con- duct of the Japanese troops in the war with China and in the more recent disturbances in that country showed that they may be trusted to fight their country's battles both at home and abroad.

When the new system was introduced French officers were engaged to assist in organising the army and elaborat- ing its system of tactics and strategy, and they rendered most valuable aid to the Japanese.   A few British officers were employed in special departments and latterly some German officers, but ultimately all foreign services were dispensed with, and now Japan sends her picked men to Europe to complete their studies ; on their return they are appointed to positions in which they are able to intro- duce the latest improvements, and it cannot be doubted that in organisation and efficiency the Japanese army will compare favourably with any other army in the world, while the spirit which animates it makes it a weapon, both for offence and defence, which is far more formidable than its numbers would seem to indicate.

As I have already stated, for our present purpose it is not necessary to enter into details of the organisation of all departments of the Japanese army ; our object is not to look at it as an end in itself, but simply as one of the factors in the evolution which has taken place in Japan. Still, a few particulars may be given.   There are four principal kinds of service ; namely, service with the colours (*genyeki*) for three years ; service with the first reserves (*yobi*) for $4\frac{1}{3}$ years ; service with the second reserves (*gobi*) for five years ; and service with the territorial troops (*kokuminhei*) up to the age of forty.   There are also two bodies of supernumeraries (*hoju*).   The first consists of men who, though liable for conscription and medically qualified, have escaped the lot for service with the colours. The second consists of those similarly liable and qualified, who have escaped not only the lot for service with the colours but also the lot for service with the first supernumeraries. The period for the first supernumeraries is $7\frac{1}{3}$ years, and that for the second $1\frac{1}{3}$ years; after which both pass into the territorial army. Their purpose is to fill vacancies in the troops with the colours, but in time of peace that liability devolves upon the first supernumeraries alone, and during the first year after conscription only. After reaching the territorial army a man is relieved from all further training. The total number of youths eligible for conscription each year is over 430,000, and over 60,000 are taken for service with the colours, and fully 130,000 are drafted into the supernumeraries. When the scheme of army organisation adopted in 1896 after the war with China is completed in 1905, the strength of the army on a peace footing will be 150,000 of all ranks, with 30,000 horses, and the strength on a war footing, 500,000 men, with 100,000 horses.

The Emperor is the Commander-in-Chief of the army, and theoretically the sole source of military authority, which he exercises through a general staff and a war department, with the assistance of a board of field-marshals. The officers of all ranks are kept in a high state of efficiency, and there are several schools for their education. The most important of these institutions is the Rikugun Daigakko, or Army College, where officers are prepared for service in the upper ranks and for staff appointments, and there are other schools for special departments of training. Captain Brinkley, a very competent authority, says: " The Japanese officer is one of the strongest features of the army. His pay is small, according to European standards, but his mode of life is frugal. Quarters are not assigned to him in barracks. He lives outside, frequently with his own family, and when duty requires him to take his meals in barracks, food is brought to him in a luncheon-box. His uniform is plain and inexpensive, and he has no desire to change it for

I

'mufti,' as so many Occidental officers have. Being thus without mess expenses, contribution to a band, or luxuries of any kind, and nearly always without private means to supplement his pay, his habits are thoroughly economical, and a campaign involves comparatively few privations for him. He devotes himself absolutely to his profession, living for nothing else, and since he is strongly imbued with an effective conception of the honour of his cloth, instances of his incurring disgrace by debts or dissipation are exceptional."

At the beginning of 1902 the following were the figures for the strength of the commanding staff on peace footing:—

Kind of Service.	Active Service.	First Reserve.	Land-wehr.	Total.
Generals and non-combatants of equivalent rank	110	27	10	147
Gendarmes	91	54	27	172
Infantry	4427	1654	873	6954
Cavalry	421	95	28	544
Artillery	1519	239	98	1856
Engineering	474	98	42	614
Commissariat	252	73	34	359
Paymaster	712	307	168	1187
Surgeon	932	526	128	1586
Veterinary Surgeons . . .	148	45	27	220
Band	7	...	...	7
	9093	3118	1435	13,646

Large and very completely equipped arsenals, for the manufacture of small arms, cartridges, and the implements Factories. and tools pertaining to small arms, are situated in Tokyo and Osaka, and turn out highly efficient work. There are powder factories at Meguro, Itabashi, and Iwahana, and the powder manufactured has very special qualities. The Osaka arsenal undertakes the manufacture of guns, cannon-balls, and other munitions of a like nature, and it maintains the powder factory at Uji and the arms workshop at Moji. Attached to the War Department there is a large factory at Senju, near to Tokyo, which manufactures woollen goods for the clothing of the army.

The Japanese army under its new organisation had its baptism of fire in the suppression of the Satsuma rebellion (which we have mentioned in a previous chapter), and its behaviour showed that a conscript army could overcome the *élite* of the samurai. It however proved its efficiency still more strikingly in the three over-sea wars in which Japan has been engaged since the abolition of feudalism. In each of these the naval forces were also engaged, and therefore before noticing them briefly, it will be advisable to give a few particulars regarding the Japanese navy. First fighting of new army.

Although the modern navy of Japan only dates from the last days of the Shogunate, the Japanese are not without a long naval history which proves that in the early days they were bold and adventurous seamen. For more than 200 years the policy of national seclusion enforced by the Shoguns of the Tokugawa dynasty stifled all maritime enterprise. As far back as 1185 there are records of naval battles between the rival factions in Japan for national supremacy, and later on, in the Middle Ages, battles at sea more than once decided the final issue. The Japanese made many piratical descents on China and Korea, culminating, in 1594, in the great invasion of Korea under the Shogun Hideyoshi, by, according to the native annals, a military force of 500,000 men. Even when rigidly confined to their own shores by the most drastic penal sanctions, the fishermen and coasters were bold and adventurous sailors, and showed that they were capable of furnishing material which required opportunity only and training to develop into ocean seamen of the best type of efficiency. Foundation of modern Japanese navy.

The advent of foreigners was the immediate cause of the foundation of the modern Japanese navy. When the Shogun was carrying on the negotiations in connection with the first treaties, he soon recognised the necessity for the possession of a navy, if Japan was to hold her own with the foreign Powers, and, as a preliminary, he despatched a few young men to Holland for instruction, and among them was one who afterwards became well known as Admiral Enomoto. At the same time the foundations of the present great Naval Arsenal at Yokosuka were laid by French engineers, and the services of British naval officers were obtained for the organisation of a naval school. The chief of these officers was Commander, now Admiral Sir R. Tracey. The troubles at the time of the Restoration prevented this school from being organised, and after a short time the officers returned home.

The first steamship owned by Japan was a small yacht of 400 tons, named the *Emperor*, which was presented by Lord Elgin to the Shogun, on behalf of Queen Victoria, when he negotiated the first treaty in 1858. When the Japanese students were in Holland, a wooden frigate of 2000 tons and 26 guns, with engines of 400 horse-power, which was named the *Kayo Maru*, was ordered in Holland, and in it the students returned to Japan. On his return from Holland Enomoto was appointed to the command of the ships belonging to Japan; which besides the vessels I have named consisted only of one obsolete vessel of war (a wooden paddle-ship, which had been originally known as the *Eagle* in the British Navy and had fought in the Crimean War), and of some half-dozen equally obsolete merchant steamers. Enomoto being an adherent of the Shogun, made a stand for his master in the struggles of the Restoration, and in this he was ably assisted by two men who afterwards became my colleagues in the Imperial College of Engineering, and who since that time have rendered high service in many ways to the Government of the Emperor; namely Viscount Hayashi, now Japanese Minister in London, and Baron Otori, formerly Japanese Minister in Korea. My first lessons in Japanese history were from Viscount Hayashi when he was my fellow-passenger to Japan in 1873, and his accounts were most interesting. Into these, however, we cannot at present enter; it is sufficient to say that he and his friends fought for the Shogun, not because they were opposed to the Emperor becoming the head of the actual Government, but because they believed that those who were fighting against them were animated by selfish motives and wished to displace the Shogun in order that they themselves might assume the executive power. The issue is well known ; the Imperialists had purchased from the United States Government the *Stonewall Jackson*, an ironclad ram, which though only of 1200 tons burden, carrying one ten-inch and other guns, was in those days a powerful ship, and were thus able to overpower Enomoto and his colleagues and bring the struggles of the revolution to a close.

On the restoration of peace the Government directed its attention to the creation of a national navy, and the first step was the establishment, on a large scale, of a Naval College and barracks, in Tokyo. A few months after my arrival in Japan, Commander (now Admiral Sir Archibald) Douglas, assisted by a staff of British naval officers, took charge of the instruction in the College, and for some years did excellent work in the training of officers and men, and their students are the admirals and senior officers in the Japanese navy at the present time, many of whom have distinguished themselves in active service. A few years later Commander L. P. Willan and Lieut. T. H. James (now of the Nippon Yusen Kaisha, London) joined the staff of the college, and these officers first took charge of Japanese ships of war on distant cruises to Australia and India ; their work gave the Japanese confidence in their own powers, and now Japanese ships of war have no difficulty in finding their way to any port in the world. Another name which must be mentioned in this connection is that of Lieut. Hawes, who organised a corps of marines whose smart appearance won for them good opinions wherever they were seen, and who initiated that state of efficiency which has made the men in the Japanese Navy the acknowledged equals of those of the best navies of the world.

The Naval College in Tokyo.

For some years the development of the Japanese navy was slow, as those in authority recognised that their first Development of duty was the training of officers to take charge Japanese navy. of the ships and men to work them, and it was not till 1877 that the Government seriously entered on the acquisition of modern fighting ships. In that year the first ship specially built for them in England, a broadside central battery ship of 3700 tons, designed by Sir Edward Reed, was launched on the Thames, and she was soon followed by several small but powerfully armed ironclads. Still, when the war with China broke out, the navy of Japan was by no means strong, as it did not contain a single battleship. It had, however, a considerable number of fast and heavily armed cruisers, and it was with these that she won the great naval battle of the Yalu, though fighting against armoured battleships; thus proving the high efficiency of the officers and men and the skilful manner in which they conducted their operations.

The three over-sea wars in which Japan has been engaged since the abolition of feudalism have already been Over-sea wars. mentioned in Chapter IV., when we were considering the most important events in recent Japanese history. The first of these was the expedition in 1874 to Formosa, the second the war with China in 1894, and the third was on the occasion of the anti-foreign and anti-dynastic rebellion, which broke out in China in 1900. On each of these occasions the arms of Japan were distinguished for bravery, efficiency, and skill. We must refer to special histories for detailed accounts of these expeditions; all that we can do meantime is to note some of their results on the national evolution, and the effect they had in causing the other nations in the world to recognise the advance which had been made by Japan, not only in western methods of war, but also in all those departments of national life which were necessary to enable her to claim a position of equality in the comity of nations.

The expedition to Formosa was undertaken at a time

when, as we have seen, the affairs of the nation were in a very critical condition. The steps which were taken had the effect of consolidating the army, and of adding to the strength of the navy. Moreover, they gave a great impetus to the Japanese mercantile marine, which rapidly became important in itself, and a very necessary adjunct to the navy for purposes of transport. The success which attended the expedition to Formosa should have taught the Chinese authorities that Japan was not to be despised ; but that she was able and determined to take any measures which were necessary to maintain her national dignity. Fortunately, through the good offices of the British Minister in Peking, the war which was threatened between the two empires was avoided, and the matter was settled by Japan agreeing to withdraw from Formosa, and by China indemnifying her to the extent of half a million dollars (about £100,000) on account of the expenses of the expedition.

The war with China in 1894-5 marked a most important epoch in the history of Japan and gave a great impetus to every department of its national life. The War with China circumstances under which that war broke and its results. out have already been noted, and reference must be made to special books for its details. Even Japan's best friends had doubts as to the ultimate issue when they considered the immense numbers and resources of the Chinese ; but in modern warfare mere numbers are powerless before efficient equipment with the most improved appliances and methods. The Chinese cannot be accused of want of bravery, or rather of the fear of death. If they were properly armed and led, they could face any troops in the world ; a fact which has been certified by such an eminent authority as Lord Wolseley. On land the war was a succession of triumphs for Japan, and the great naval battle which took place on September 17th, 1894, near the mouth of the Yalu river, that forms the northern boundary of Korea, not only showed that the Japanese could make good use of their navy, but it also awoke the nations of the world to the fact that a new Power had arisen in the Far East, which in future would require to be taken into account when any political problems arose. The Yalu victory practically gave Japan the control of northern China, and before long the Chinese authorities recognised the hopelessness of the struggle and agreed to the terms of the treaty already mentioned.

Besides a large addition to the "ordinary" expenditure on the army and navy the *post-bellum* programme included the following items for "extraordinary" expenditure :—

A. *Military Expansion Scheme :—*

	Yen.
Construction of coast batteries . . .	14,071,893
Furnishing arms, repairs, etc. . . .	17,334,890
Manufacture of arms	8,486,766
Extension of arsenals	2,949,105
Buildings	479,577
	43,322,231

B. *Naval Expansion Scheme :—*

	Yen.
Construction of war-vessels . . .	47,154,576
Manufacture of arms	33,751,162
Buildings	13,870,506
	94,776,244

The spending of these sums was spread over five years, but before the first programme was completed, the "Second Period Expansion Programme" was initiated, and again the chief features were concerned with the expansion of the army and navy. The following were the military and naval parts of the second programme :—

A. *Military Expansion :—*

	Yen.
Coast batteries	6,460,520
Barracks, etc.	19,363,746
Manufacture of firearms	9,854,538
Making up deficits	2,679,790
	38,358,594

B. *Naval Expansion :*—

	Yen.
Construction of war-vessels . . .	78,893,399
Manufacture of arms	33,176,329
Various building purposes . . .	6,254,990
	118,324,718

Adding together the amounts for military and naval expansion included in the two programmes, and including the addition to the ordinary expenditure, we arrive at a total expenditure for naval expansion of 360,000,000 yen. In some cases, however, the estimates were exceeded, and the total amount of expenditure for army and navy expansion by Japan, consequent upon and subsequent to the war with China, has been estimated at 400,000,000 yen, or £40,000,000.

Both programmes have practically been carried out, and Japan has now a navy which is, in offensive and defensive armament, in steaming capacity, both in speed and distance, and in homogeneousness, equal to any in the world of the same size. The majority of the ships have been built in Britain—on the Thames, the Clyde, the Tyne, and at Barrow-on-Furness—and the construction of the most of them has been superintended by my former students of the Imperial College of Engineering, and whom I had often the pleasure of meeting when they were in this country.

Present conditions of Japanese navy.

The following figures give the personnel of the Navy at the beginning of the year 1902 :—

Kind of Service.	Active Service.	First Reserve.	Second Reserve.	Total.
Admirals and non-combatants of equivalent rank	47	22	14	83
Senior Officers	639	22	60	721
Junior Officers	1,060	23	70	1,153
Cadets	330	...	...	330
Special Warrant Officers . . .	631	10	54	695
Warrant Officers	5,802	163	...	5,965
Seamen	22,036	4036	1793	27,865
Students	834	...	...	834
	31,379	4276	1991	37,646

The latest published returns, those for 1902, give the total tonnage of ships in commission or reserve as 252,180 tons, with an indicated horse-power of 459,599, distributed as follows :—

		Tons.
6	First-class battleships . .	86,399
2	Second-class battleships . .	11,112
6	Armoured cruisers . . .	58,778
9	Second-class cruisers . .	38,518
5	Third-class cruisers . . .	14,078
10	Coast-defence vessels . .	18,215
2	First-class gunboats . .	3,557
14	Second-class gunboats . .	8,013
13	Destroyers	3,957

The remainder is made up of despatch vessels, tenders, etc. In addition there were over sixty torpedo-boats of various sizes, with a tonnage of 4675, and this number has been considerably increased since the returns were published.

The Japanese navy is well supplied with dockyards and arsenals, there being four first-class naval stations. The oldest is that at Yokosuka near Yokohama, which was started over forty years ago by French engineers and naval architects, but has since been greatly extended. The most important station is Kuré on the Inland Sea, which, in addition to a well-equipped dockyard and a magnificent harbour, possesses a fine arsenal for the manufacture of large modern breech-loading steel guns, and also of large-calibre steel shell. Sasebo (or Saseho), in Kyushu, is rapidly becoming of great importance, and its position, in the south of Japan and near to the coast of China, would make it of great use in case of hostilities. The fourth station at Maizuru, on the Sea of Japan, was opened only in 1901, but it is also being developed. There is also a very complete arsenal in Tokyo for the manufacture of appliances required in the Navy, and the Shimose powder factory supplies ammunition of very high explosive power.

A survey of the resources of the Japanese navy shows that, for its size, it is the most thoroughly equipped navy in the world ; while the bravery and efficiency of its officers and men will enable it to give a very good account of itself should it be required to defend the rights of Japan.

As an illustration of the thoroughness with which the Japanese make their plans, of the completeness with which they carry them out, and also of their Training of Japanese naval officers. power of adapting arrangements to their own conditions, a sketch may be given of the training of Japanese naval officers. That training was, as we have seen, founded on the British system, but in some respects they have improved on that system. It may be divided into the following sections :—(1) Entrance of cadets and their education in the Imperial Naval College at Yetajima; (2) education of midshipmen ; (3) education of sub-lieutenants and lieutenants in their respective duties afloat and ashore ; (4) education of officers in the Imperial and Higher Naval College at Tokyo ; and (5) education of officers in the torpedo and gunnery schools at Yokosuka. In each of these sections the course is very complete. The whole expense of training, food, and clothing is provided out of Government funds. The cadets are selected after a physical examination of the candidates, as well as one testing the state of their education in those preliminary subjects which are necessary for naval officers. The course extends over three years, and the instruction is given partly in college and partly in the tenders attached to the college. It includes the physical sciences and their applications to engineering, navigation, gunnery, and the other departments of the duties of naval officers. In addition, elementary courses of international and civil law and naval history are provided. When the cadets pass the final examination they are promoted to midshipmen.

The education of midshipmen is divided into training in the special training ships and training in the ships of the standing fleet, the object being to show them how to apply practically what they had been taught in the college and to give them the foundation of the experience necessary to perform their duties as junior officers. After the completion of the course the midshipmen are distributed among the ships in commission—almost invariably to the ships of the standing fleet, where there is no regular course. They perform junior officers' duty under the supervision of the superior officers, but it is, as a rule, the custom for the captain of the ship to choose a very competent officer to take charge of them, besides giving orders to the gunnery, torpedo, and navigating officers to instruct them in their own special branches. As sub-lieutenants and lieutenants their studies are continued, although not according to any fixed programme, but it is the practice of the captains to set each officer a subject for a "yearly essay" on either theoretical or practical questions of naval interest. The subject varies according to the officer's rank, special duty, and capacity. After being criticised by the superior officers, these essays are printed in book form and distributed throughout the fleet and naval barracks. Special lectures are from time to time given on recent developments of naval science and practice.

The courses in the Higher Naval College in Tokyo are provided for those who have shown special ability; their nature and extent depend on the object in view, and they are very similar to the special courses given at the Royal Naval College at Greenwich. Besides all this, there are special schools for instruction in gunnery and torpedo practice; moreover, when some new weapons had been introduced, or some new scientific discovery had been made, or drills had undergone changes, a number of officers were summoned from various parts to bring themselves up to date in such matters and to teach their comrades or those under their command what they had themselves just acquired. The success of the Japanese navy is evidently not of a haphazard nature, but is the result of a long, systematic training, combined, of course, with the fearless bravery of the officers and men.

The share which the Japanese forces took in the operations which were carried on in China in 1900 by the
Foreign Powers was the means of still further Japanese soldiers
directing attention to the efficiency of the in the
Japanese army. On account of the troubles Boxer troubles.
with the Boxers, the foreign communities of Tientsin and
Peking were placed in situations of extreme danger, and it
was impossible for any European Power or the United States
of America to organise efficient and prompt measures of
relief. On the other hand, Japan was near, with a well-
equipped army and a powerful navy; but, knowing the
suspicion of the Foreign Powers in such matters, she hesitated
to intervene, and it was not until Europe and America made
it quite plain that they needed and desired her help that she
sent a division (21,000 men) to Pechili, and it was admitted
by all competent observers that they practically saved the
situation. Their coolness and bravery under very trying
circumstances won the admiration of all who saw them, and,
fighting side by side with European and American soldiers
and under the eyes of competent critics, they acquitted themselves in such a manner as to establish a high military
reputation. Probably most important of all, the conduct of
the Japanese soldiers was in every respect worthy of com-
mendation and in some ways worthy of emulation by their
foreign comrades. The Government of Japan acted in harmony with all the other Governments, and sought no special
advantages, on account either of the part their troops had
taken in the operations in China, or of the special interests
which they had because of their proximity to that empire; thus
showing that there were no grounds of any kind for the suspicion with which they had been regarded in some quarters.

A mere statement of the facts connected with the
Japanese army and navy is sufficient to show their
importance as factors not only in the develop- Japanese power
ment of Japan, but also in that of the Far as factors in
East generally. In many respects Japan the Far East.
closely resembles Great Britain. Both countries consist of

a group of islands, with almost similar area and population, and the one has the same geographical position relatively to Asia that the other has to Europe. The Pacific area is destined to become the most important commercial area in the world, and Japan is nearer that centre than Britain. The Japanese were not slow to recognise that the circumstances which had led Great Britain to rely for trade on a great mercantile marine, and for defence mainly on her fleet, applied in her own case with almost equal urgency, and for some years they have been rapidly building up their commercial power by means of a great mercantile marine, which now trades with all the chief countries of the world ; at the same time they have been adding to their fighting strength by means of a navy which is now a very important factor in the political forces in the Far East. Their army is relatively large, well equipped, well organised, and capable of doing very effective work if required. The expenditure on the naval and military forces bears a considerable proportion to the total national income, and one of the problems before Japan is how best to provide for the defence of the country without crippling its financial and industrial resources.

It must be recognised that this expenditure is part of the price which Japan is paying for her membership of the comity of nations, and it is very sad that it should be so. Captain Brinkley has truly said that "no one who should tell the Japanese to-day that the consideration they have won from the West is due solely to their progress in peaceful arts would find serious listeners. They themselves held that belief as a working incentive twenty years ago, but experience has dissipated it, and they now know that the world took no respectful notice of them until they showed themselves capable of winning battles. At first, they imagined that they might efface the Oriental stigma by living up to civilised standards. But the success they attained was scarcely perceptible when suddenly their victorious war with China seemed to win for them more esteem in half a year than their peaceful industry had won for them in half a century. The perception of that fact upset their estimate of the qualifications necessary for a place in the 'foremost files of time,' and had much to do with the desire they henceforth developed for expanded armaments." While the expenditure may be regretted, it is not difficult to give sufficient reasons for the policy which was adopted, and looked at simply from an offensive or defensive point of view even their most severe critics admit that the Japanese army and navy are in a high state of efficiency. Professor Chamberlain gives the opinion of all who have had opportunities of observing the powers of the Japanese army and navy when he says : " We cannot help expressing our admiration of and belief in the Japanese navy, and of Japan altogether as a military power. Though it may not be for us to judge of the technical excellences of ships and docks, it is perhaps given to an old resident who has travelled widely, and read a great deal, and mixed much with all classes, to appreciate the existence of those qualities of intellect and *morale* which go to make a good fighting man, whether on land or sea. To our thinking, any foreign Power that should venture to attack Japan in her own waters would be strangely ill-advised." The high state of efficiency to which the Japanese army and navy have been brought has proved not only that the Japanese are able to take advantage of all the applications of Western science to military and naval matters, but also that all classes of the people are now animated by the true samurai spirit which knows no fear and which prefers death to either personal or national dishonour. Modern military and naval appliances are merely the tools which are used ; the " Soul of Japan " which animates those behind them is the source of the strength of the army and navy.

BIBLIOGRAPHICAL NOTE.

An excellent account of the Japanese army and navy is given by Captain Brinkley in his articles on Japan in the supplementary volumes of the *Encyclopædia Britannica*, and an interesting sketch of the *Growth of the Japanese Navy* by Mr. Longford, late of the British Consular Service in Japan, appeared in the *Nineteenth Century* for September 1903.   *The Imperial Japanese Navy*, by Fred T. Jane, gives plans, photographs, and full descriptions of all the ships in the navy, of the Japanese dockyards and arsenals, as well as official reports on the Japan-China war.   H. Yamawaki's *Japan in the Beginning of the Twentieth Century* contains statistics of the army and navy, with an outline of their history and organisation.   *Heroic Japan*, by Eastlake and Yamada, records the doings of the army and navy in the war with China.   Many books and reports on this war have been published, which must be consulted for details.

CHAPTER VII

MEANS OF COMMUNICATION

As soon as the Japanese had determined to introduce Western methods of national life into the country, they recognised that one of the first necessities, not only from an industrial but also from a political point of view, was improved means of communication, and that of these the most important was a national system of railways. When I went to Japan in 1873 the only railway in the country was the short one of eighteen miles between Tokyo and Yokohama, which had been opened with considerable *éclat* by the Emperor a few months previously, and the illustrations of that event published in the *Illustrated London News* were the first things which specially directed my attention to Japan. Little did I think that in a short time after reading the account of the opening of the first railway in the country I would be at the head of an institution which was to be the chief means of developing not only the railways and other means of communication, but also all the other industries of Japan. Students of the Imperial College of Engineering (Kobu Daigakko) are to be found in important positions in almost all the undertakings which have caused so great a change in the economic, industrial, and political conditions of Japan, and it would be interesting to enter into some details regarding their work, but these must be reserved for another occasion. Meantime I can only briefly sketch the developments which have taken place and which have enabled Japan to rank as an equal in the comity of nations. It may be thought that in some respects she has paid very dearly for this position, but there can be little doubt that if these developments had not taken place, she would have fallen under the domination of one or other of the foreign Powers which are so anxious to extend their influence in the Far East.

Under the feudal system the means of communication were very imperfect; indeed those in authority deliberately

Communications under the feudal system. kept them so. Each province was to a large extent self-contained, both economically and politically, and the central Government did not exercise much control over ordinary affairs. The Tokugawa Shoguns and the feudal nobles took care that the highways leading to the capital should cross deep defiles and bridgeless rivers, where all passage might be barred by a small force. Thus one of the main thoroughfares from Kyoto to Yedo was led over the Hakone pass and the other over the Usui; and any one taking a circuitous route so as to avoid the guardhouses at either of these precipitous places was liable to be put to death. At the same time the feudal chiefs were required to keep the roads and bridges within their territories in fairly good order and to provide post-horses and ferry boats within the limits of their provinces.

There were, indeed, a number of Imperial roads, somewhat like the old coach roads in Britain, and those were largely used by the Daimyos and their retainers when they made their visits to Yedo to pay their respects to the Shogun. Of these the two best known are those already mentioned; namely, the Tokaido, or Eastern Sea Road, running along the sea-shore between Kyoto and Tokyo, and the Nakasendo, or Central Mountain Road—so named in contradistinction to the Tokaido and the comparatively unimportant Hokurokudo, or Northern Land Road, in Kaga and Etchu, between which it occupies a middle position. There were several other main roads of less importance, all provided with *honjin* or specially fine hostelries, for their lordships and their retainers to sleep at. The changed conditions have caused the glories of these institutions to depart.

About the beginning of the seventeenth century a regular transport service was organised between Yedo and Kyoto, and a scale of charges for coolies and pack-horses was fixed by law; later on the merchants of Osaka organised a land transport service to Yedo, and gradually the system was extended to other parts of the country for the carriage of both goods and letters. A considerable maritime carrying trade was organised between the most important sea-ports, and this fell into the hands of guilds, which obtained a practical monopoly. At the Restoration, however, the means of communication were still in a comparatively primitive condition, and it was determined to improve them not only in order that the country might be welded into one organisation, but also that full advantage might be taken of its economic possibilities. Not only improved roads but also railways, telegraphs, steamships, and other means of communication were therefore the natural results of the new conditions brought about by the Restoration, and the demand for them was the immediate cause of the institution of the Imperial College of Engineering. For some years a considerable number of foreign experts were engaged by the Public Works Department, but as the graduates of the College and other Japanese trained in other institutions and in foreign countries gained experience, the work to a large extent fell into their hands, and a very large part of the civil engineering undertakings have been carried out entirely by Japanese. No doubt many mistakes have been made, but no unbiassed critic will deny that the development which has taken place in Japan in the ways and means of communication has been wonderful.

In feudal times the only methods of travelling were on foot, on horseback, or in *kago*. The latter is a kind of basket made of bamboo, with a light roof atop, and swung on a pole which two men—one in Roads.
front and one behind—bear on their shoulders, and it is

still used in mountainous districts. The old *norimono* of the towns, which was largely used in the Daimyos' processions and by rich people, was simply a glorified *kago*. The jinrikisha, which is now so well known and so much used, rapidly displaced the *kago*. The origin of this useful little carriage is sometimes attributed to an American missionary, named Goble, although it is also traced to several Japanese sources. After the Restoration the necessity for better means of communication between the different parts of the country caused attention to be directed to the roads. The old thoroughfares were repaired and improved in many ways and bridges were built over rivers which formerly had to be forded; so that the more important roads were made available for carriage and bullock-cart traffic as well as for jinrikishas with passengers. The local authorities being responsible for the cost endeavoured to be as economical as possible. Although improvements and developments have been made during recent years, many of the roads in Japan are still in a very unsatisfactory condition. The developments which have taken place in the railways and shipping have probably been the cause of attention being directed from the ordinary roads, as they have now become of secondary importance in the carriage of goods. The advent of the cycle in its various forms and of the motor car for all sorts of purposes will no doubt lead to an improvement in the roads and to their extended use as feeders to the railways.

The initiative in the construction of railways in Japan was undertaken by Mr. Horatio Nelson Lay, who in 1869 arrived in Tokyo with proposals to offer a loan to the Government on behalf of certain British capitalists to be used for the formation of a railway between Tokyo and Osaka, with a branch to Yokohama. The amount of the loan was one million pounds sterling at twelve per cent interest, the capital being repayable in twelve years. The railway was to form part of the security to the lenders, who were further to have a lien on the

Railways.

customs duties arising from the foreign trade at the open ports. Mr. Lay had stipulated that he was not only to be the chief commissioner of railways, but that he was also to have the appointment of all the engineers and other foreigners whom it would be necessary to employ, and the ordering of everything that had to be imported. Mr. Morel, a gentleman of experience and ability, was engaged as engineer-in-chief, a considerable number of subordinates were appointed and they at once set to work to make the necessary surveys. It was determined to make a start with the line between Yokohama and Tokyo, and before the end of 1870 the work had fairly commenced.

It is not necessary to enter into the details of Mr. Lay's financial arrangements ; it is sufficient to say that they fell through, and that the business was taken in hand by the Oriental Bank, and for some years the financial arrangements of the railways were under the supervision of the Bank—Mr. W. W. Cargill, acting as director of railways on behalf of the Bank, and Mr. R. Vicars Boyle, C.S.I., becoming engineer-in-chief, with Dr. William Pole, F.R.S., as consulting engineer in London. For some time the work of railway construction proceeded at a comparatively slow rate, partly on account of financial reasons but also because the Japanese Government had determined to use the construction of railways as a practical training school for Japanese engineers. At first fully two hundred foreigners were employed in railway construction, but the services of these were gradually dispensed with as students of the Imperial College of Engineering and others, trained partly at home and partly abroad, were able to undertake the work, and now very few foreigners remain in the railway service.

As already mentioned, in 1872 the only line of railway in Japan was that between Tokyo and Yokohama, a distance of eighteen miles. The original intention of the Government was to construct a trunk line from Tokyo to Kobe and Osaka and Kyoto by way of the Nakasendo, or Middle Mountain Road,

Outline of history of railway construction.

but it was found that this would involve great labour and expense, on account of the mountainous district through which it passes; it was abandoned, and the Tokaido route adopted instead. The part between Kobe and Kyoto was proceeded with slowly, under the superintendence of foreign engineers. The construction was under the control of the Department of Public Works, the railways at first being entirely State undertakings. In 1885 the Department of Public Works was abolished, and the Railway Bureau was then placed under the direct management of the Cabinet. In 1890 the Railway Bureau changed its name to Railway Board, and it was at the same time affiliated to the Home Office. This connection with the Home Office came to an end in 1892, when the Department of Communications was created, and the Railway Board, which had restored to it its old designation of Railway Bureau, was brought under the control of the new Department.

The main line between Tokyo and Kyoto *via* the Tokaido proceeded slowly. The people of Japan were quickly appreciating the importance of railways in the development of the country, and as Japanese engineers were being found qualified to undertake the work, it became necessary to devise a more rapid means of extension, and permission was given to private companies to undertake the work. The pioneer of private enterprise in Japan was the Nippon Railway Company, which in November 1881 obtained a charter for laying the Tokyo-Aomori line. As it was impossible to form any exact estimates of cost or expenditure, far less to calculate the probable amount of traffic and the consequent return on the capital invested, the Government undertook to guarantee its profit within a certain limit, and moreover gave it every facility for carrying on the work. In a short time the work was begun and carried on with great zeal and activity, and the period of private railway work was ushered in. Since then it has developed at a rapid rate. Indeed, in 1896 and 1897, immediately after the war with China, there was something .approaching a railway mania, like that in England during the early days of railways ; numerous schemes were proposed, many of which came to nothing practical, as they issued from the brains of speculators, whose object was not to construct railways but to make money out of the unfortunate investors. Since that time the greater part of railway construction in Japan has been carried out by private enterprise, although the Government completed and has still retained the management of the first lines which were designed. It has also carried out extensive railway developments in the Hokkaido, in order to encourage the promotion of industry and agriculture in that rather inhospitable part of the Japanese Empire. No doubt political and military reasons have also had considerable weight. The question of the sale of the Government railways to private companies has often been discussed in Japan, but as yet no definite proposals have been made on the subject. So far as can be gathered from the opinions expressed in the newspapers, there is a strong feeling that the railways ought to be directly under Government control, not only for military reasons, but also that they may serve, to the greatest advantage, the general wants of the country.

It is not necessary to enter into details of the various railways in the country, but the following figures show their distribution throughout the Empire :—

	Area sq. miles.	Population.	Railway Mileage.	Mileage per 100 sq. miles.	Mileage per 10,000 Inhabitants.
Honshu . .	86,329	34,196,471	3165	3.67	0.74
Kyushu . .	13,771	6,586,682	425	3.07	0.52
Hokkaido .	30,123	1,003,751	360	1.16	3.48
Shikoku . .	6,858	2,961,714	75	1.08	0.20
Total . .	137,081	44,748,618	4026	2.75	0.72

The following table gives the rate of construction for State and private railways since 1872 :—

Year.	Mileage open to Traffic.					
	State Railways.		Private Railways.		Total.	
	Miles.	Chains.	Miles.	Chains.	Miles.	Chains.
1872 . .	18	0	.. .	...	18	0
1873 . .	18	0	...	...	18	0
1874 . .	38	27	...	...	38	27
1875 . .	38	27	...	...	38	27
1875–1876	38	27	...	...	38	27
1876–1877	65	11	...	...	65	11
1877–1878	65	11	...	...	65	11
1878–1879	65	11	...	...	65	11
1879–1880	73	22	...	...	73	22
1880–1881	76	37	...	...	76	37
1881–1882	100	38	...	...	100	38
1882–1883	114	63	...	...	114	63
1883–1884	125	51	63	00	188	51
1884–1885	125	51	80	63	206	34
1885–1886	167	62	129	76	297	58
1886–1887	208	64	165	77	374	61
1887–1888	244	40	293	24	537	64
1888–1889	445	19	406	38	851	57
1889–1890	550	49	525	22	1075	71
1890–1891	550	49	848	43	1399	12
1891–1892	550	49	1166	40	1717	9
1892–1893	550	49	1320	26	1870	75
1893–1894	557	49	1367	77	1925	46
1894–1895	580	69	1537	33	2118	22
1895–1896	593	22	1679	75	2273	17
1896–1897	631	62	1800	9	2431	71
1897–1898	661	65	2282	37	2944	22
1898–1899	768	37	2642	57	3411	14
1899–1900	833	72	2802	49	3636	41
1900–1901	949	69	2905	16	3855	5
1901–1902	1059	48	2966	48	4026	16
1902–1903	1226	64	3010	64	4237	48

We cannot enter into details either of the working of the railways or of their financial arrangements, but a few
Working and financial returns. of the main figures may be given. The regulation gauge of the railways is 3 feet 6 inches, but for light railways it is 2 feet 6 inches. The details of rolling stock vary considerably, the capacity naturally advancing with the progress of railway business. The ratio of vehicles to mileage under traffic is, according to the latest returns, 33.5 locomotives, 112.5 passenger cars, and 492.3 waggons per 100 miles.

The actual capital invested at the beginning of 1902 was as follows :—

					Yen.
Government Railways	.	.	.	.	127,167,852
Private Railways	.	.	.	.	219,709,432
					346,877,284

The dividends paid on the capital have, as a rule, been very good, those on the larger railways being from 10 to 12 per cent per annum, and very few being below 5 per cent. The net earnings of the Government Railways in 1901 were 8,418,128 yen, and of the private railways 16,547,242 yen, or a total of 24,965,370 yen. Both the passenger and the goods traffic have increased at a rapid rate, but there is still great room for development. The latest statistics show that the number of persons, per head of population, per annum who travelled was only 2.39, and that the distance travelled was only 40.5 miles, while the number of tons of goods carried per head of population was only 0.30 tons and that only for a distance of 16.4 miles. Mr. K. Inuzuka, Director of the Railway Bureau, after an examination of these figures, says : " These analyses impress on the mind of one that the benefit taken of the railway by our people is still in a state of infancy " ; and he adds : " To afford a more enlightened use of the facilities by railways at the minimum cost of performing the service, it is necessary on the one hand to accomplish a more direct communication, and on the other to adopt all the most important modern improvements in railway appliances and methods, so as to induce the public to enjoy the benefit of railway travelling." It is evident therefore that great as has been the development of railway construction in Japan in the past, we may expect a considerable development in the future.

Various legislative measures relating to railways have from time to time been passed, but it is not necessary to enter into details of these. A few of the main points, however, may be noted. In 1872 the Railway legislation. first measures were published, and they provided general

rules about railway work; these were amended and extended from time to time. In 1879 and 1883 the general
and punitive rules which had been issued for Government
railways were made applicable also to private railways.
From time to time special regulations relating to loans and
the construction of special lines were issued, and in 1900
the laws relating to private railways were codified. The
following are the points in these which deserve special
notice :—

1. Shares of the capital must not be acquired except
by the payment of money.

2. Unless in virtue of a decision arrived at by a general
meeting of shareholders and with the sanction of the minister
concerned, no railway can be chartered or hired or its
management entrusted to others.

3. Unless with the sanction of the minister concerned, and
after not less than one-fourth of the share capital has been
paid up, a railway company must not issue debenture bonds.

4. With the approval of the minister, a company may
contract a loan by mortgaging its railway with accessories,
but they must not be used as objects of right of mortgage.

5. The debenture bonds and loans together must not
exceed the total sum of the paid-up capital.

6. No company must declare dividends unless after the
principal and interest of the bonds and loans payable every
year have been subtracted from the proceeds.

7. Except in cases specially approved of, the gauge must
measure 3 feet 6 inches.

8. The minister concerned may order an alteration of
tariff rate, when such alteration is judged necessary in the
public interest.

9. The tariff rate of third-class passengers must not
exceed 2 sen per mile.

10. A company shall be held responsible to offer its
lines in accordance with the provisions determined by law or
ordinance for the use of the army or the navy either in time
of war or in time of peace.

11. The Government reserve the right of purchasing the line with all its appurtenances after full twenty-five years from the time of granting a permanent charter.

The Japanese Government has paid considerable attention to the improvement of the rivers of the country and have spent large sums of money on the work. For instance, in the last Budget, there appeared the River improvements. sum of 3,220,000 yen for river engineering works. The rivers of Japan are peculiarly difficult to keep in order, and their beds are subject to sudden changes which often cause floods of a very serious nature. The engineering works are chiefly for the purpose of preventing such floods, but the improvements which have taken place have made many of them much more useful as a means of communication for the transportation of goods and passengers, and the traffic on some of the larger of them is of considerable and increasing importance.

The early records of Japan show that a considerable maritime trade was carried on not only between the ports of Japan but also with foreign countries ; but in Shipping. 1614, on account of the political intrigues of the foreigners who had settled in Japan and the fanaticism excited by the ill-judged measures of the propagandists of Christianity, Iyeyasu, the then Shogun, issued a proclamation ordering the banishment of the propagandists and leaders of Christianity and the destruction of their churches and the compulsory recantation of their doctrines. A period of persecution followed, which culminated in the imprisonment of the Dutch at Deshima in 1641 by the grandson of Iyeyasu, the third Tokugawa Shogun. In order to make his edict more effective he ordered that all vessels of sea-going capacity should be destroyed and that no craft should thenceforth be built of sufficient size to venture beyond home waters. Some vessels were built for coast defence, but their design was very crude and they were utterly useless for the purpose for which they were intended, while the trading junk, as modified by official instructions, was as little capable of navigating the

high seas as of fighting, and the Japanese remained without anything that could be called a mercantile marine until after the advent of foreigners and the signing of treaties of trade and commerce with the representatives of the foreign Powers.

After the restoration of the Emperor to power, in 1869 and 1870, the Government made repeated announcement to

Beginning and development of modern Japanese mercantile marine. the effect not only that any person might keep any number of ships of foreign type, but also that liberal protection would be afforded to him in his undertaking. For some years a considerable number of antiquated and in some cases worn-out ships were sold to the Japanese, who, however, soon found that what seemed cheap bargains were, in the end, very expensive, and they determined to build up a mercantile marine on sound business methods. In 1872 the Nihonkoku Yubin Jokisen Kaisha (Japan Mail Steamship Company) was organised, which was superseded five years later by the Yubin Kisen Mitsubishi Kaisha (Mitsubishi Mail Steamship Company). Afterwards the Kyodo Unyu Kaisha (United Shipping Company) and the Osaka Shosen Kaisha (Osaka Merchant Steamship Company) were created in 1882 and 1884 respectively, both of them being supported by the subsidies of the Government. In 1885 the Mitsubishi Kisen Kaisha and the Kyodo Unyu Kaisha, after a desperate competition, were united into one company under the title of Nippon Yusen Kaisha (Japan Mail Steamship Company), the greatest navigation company in Japan ever since. After the war with China, and in consequence of the encouragement and assistance given by the Government, shipping and shipbuilding made very rapid progress. In 1896 the Toyo Kisen Kaisha (Oriental Steamship Company) was established. The success which has attended the efforts of the Japanese to build up a mercantile marine is one of the factors which establishes the claim of Japan to the name of the Britain of the East. The following table shows the development of Japanese shipping since 1870 :—

At the end of—	Steamers.		Sailing Vessels.		Total.		Japanese Junks.	
	No. of Ships.	Gross Tonnage.	No. of Ships.	Gross Tonnage.	No. of Ships.	Gross Tonnage.	No. of Ships.	Gross Tonnage.
								Koku.
1870	35	?	11	?	46	?	?	?
1871	71	?	31	?	102	?	?	?
1872	96	?	35	?	131	?	18,640	3,312,281
1873	110	?	36	?	146	?	22,693	3,835,402
1874	118	?	41	?	159	?	22,673	3,766,221
1875	149	?	44	?	193	?	21,260	3,577,853
1876	159	?	51	?	210	?	19,919	3,397,183
1877	183	?	75	?	258	?	18,964	3,251,425
1878	195	?	123	?	318	?	19,135	3,333,406
1879	199	?	174	?	373	?	19,285	3,254,759
1880	210	?	329	?	539	?	19,092	3,273,709
1881	298	?	379	?	677	?	17,638	3,032,345
1882	344	?	428	?	772	?	17,331	2,930,842
1883	390	?	419	?	809	?	16,149	2,655,763
1884	412	?	402	?	814	?	16,427	2,798,780
1885	461	95,975	509	57,292	970	153,267	17,006	2,854,632
1886	460	100,112	688	60,328	1148	160,440	16,757	2,786,818
1887	486	115,395	798	64,416	1284	179,781	17,194	2,851,247
1888	524	129,836	896	67,529	1420	197,365	17,878	2,969,695
1889	563	141,805	843	57,624	1406	199,429	18,796	3,216,158
1890	585	150,058	865	54,989	1450	205,047	19,375	3,302,385
1891	607	154,749	832	53,387	1439	208,136	18,589	3,153,210
1892	642	165,764	780	49,085	1422	214,849	18,205	3,069,816
1893	680	176,915	746	48,303	1426	225,218	17,209	2,878,462
1894	745	273,419	722	46,959	1467	320,378	17,300	2,876,131
1895	827	341,369	702	44,794	1529	386,163	17,360	2,960,887
1896	899	373,588	644	44,055	1543	417,643	17,612	3,066,128
1897	1032	438,779	715	48,130	1747	486,909	19,097	3,320,284
1898	1130	477,430	1914	170,894	3044	648,324	19,099	3,049,035
1899	1221	510,007	3322	286,923	4543	796,930	18,479	2,713,646
1900	1329	543,365	3850	320,571	5179	863,936	18,796	2,785,114
1901	1395	583,532	4020	336,436	5415	919,968	19,758	2,921,565

Statistics relating to the gross tonnage for the years prior to 1884 inclusive are inaccessible. Only Japanese junks, the capacity of which are over 50 koku, are taken into account in this table.

A few particulars may be given of the three great steamship companies which now carry on the ocean-carrying services of Japan. At the time of the amalgamation which resulted in the formation of the Nippon Yusen Kaisha the foreign trade carried on in Japanese-owned vessels was of a very limited nature, the only foreign services opened being between Yokohama and Shanghai, Nagasaki and Vladivostock, and Kobe and Inch-'yen. The new company

opened regular services to Niuchwang and Tientsin, and in
1892, in order chiefly to bring a supply of Indian cotton
for the rapidly developing cotton industry, the line to
Bombay was opened.   When the war with China broke
out in 1894 the company furnished fifty-seven transports
with over 130,000 gross tonnage for the use of the Government for military purposes, and thus helped materially in
the victory over China.   After the war, a great extension
took place in the foreign services of the company, and as a
first step its capital was increased to 22,000,000 yen and
a considerable number of new ships were constructed in
Britain for its trade.   In March 1895 one of its ships
made its first voyage to Europe, as an experiment, and the
result was so satisfactory that a regular service was instituted
between Kobe and Europe.   In August and October 1896
a similar service was started to America and Australia
respectively.   The four lines, namely the European, the
American, the Australian, and the Bombay lines are the
prescribed routes specially ordered by the Government.
In the two former the vessels are despatched fortnightly
and in the latter monthly.   In addition the company has a
regular service to all the chief ports of Japan, China, and
Korea, the total length of lines on which the company is
now running regular steamship services is 44,418 miles.

The necessity of connecting the city of Osaka, the
centre of trade of the western part of the Empire, with the
most important trading ports such as Kobe and Nagasaki
and Shikoku, Kyushiu, and many other islands lying to the
west of Osaka, induced a number of large shipowners, in May
1884, to combine and establish the Osaka Shisen Kaisha.
At the time of the combination their trade was confined to
coast service, but in 1891 and 1892 the Osaka-Fusan and
the Osaka-Inch-'yen services were respectively opened.   In
1896 the company began a regular service to Taiwan
(Formosa), one to the Yangtze in 1898, another to south
China in 1899, and others to various ports in Korea in
subsequent years ; thus facilitating the means of communica-

tion between Japan, China, and Korea, and between Japan
proper and Formosa, and at the same time improving the
coast services; so that the company is now considered one
of the most important shipping companies in the Far East.
During the war with China in 1894-5 it furnished the
Government with thirty or more transports with a gross
tonnage of 12,500 tons. The total length of lines on
which the company is now running regular services is
19,727 miles.

The Toyo Kisen Kaisha, which came into existence as
one of the *post-bellum* undertakings, was established in 1896
but did not begin actual operations until the end of 1898.
The original plan of the company was to open a regular
service to New York and Batoum, but changing it subsequently, the company selected the route to San Francisco
via Shanghai and Hongkong, the steamers being now
despatched once or twice a month.

The following shows the development of the Japanese
mercantile marine in the larger size of ships during the
years 1892-1902 :—

	From 1000 to 2000 tons.	From 2000 to 3000 tons.	From 3000 to 4000 tons.	From 4000 to 5000 tons.	From 5000 to 6000 tons.	No. of Ships.	Total Tonnage.
1892	39	10	2	...	...	51	8,645,912
1893	43	11	2	...	...	56	9,574,843
1894	46	29	9	2	1	87	18,367,228
1895	58	40	13	2	1	114	24,291,045
1896	64	45	14	2	1	126	26,569,602
1897	69	47	14	2	1	140	32,197,885
1898	68	44	16	2	1	144	35,708,600
1899	65	47	17	3	1	148	38,239,974
1900	70	52	17	3	1	156	41,053,741
1901	74	56	17	3	2	170	44,372,346
1902	81	60	17	4	2	182	46,995,000

A survey of the growth of the Japanese mercantile marine
shows that it has been one of the most striking features in the
national evolution, and its past history makes it quite clear
that Japan means to follow the example of the Britain of the
West and become a great maritime nation.

At present there are thirty ports open to foreign trade ; namely, Yokohama, Kobe, Nagasaki, Hakodate, Niigata, Ebisu,

Open Ports and Harbours. Osaka, Shimizu, Taketoyo, Yokkaichi, Itozaki, Shimonoseki, Moji, Hakata, Karatsu, Kuchinotsu, Misumi, Izuhara, Sasuna, Shikami, Naba, Hamada, Sakaye, Miyazu, Tsuruga, Nanao (southern basin), Fushiki, Otaru, Kushiro, and Muroran. With the object of maintaining order in these ports having much shipping traffic, in 1898 an Imperial Ordinance was issued containing Harbour Regulations, and the ports of Yokohama, Kobe, and Nagasaki were at once placed under this legislation, which was extended two years later to Moji.

In May 1864, while the Shogun's Government was still in existence, Japan agreed, in accordance with Article XI. of the Tariff Convention concluded with Great

Lighthouses. Britain, France, United States of America, and Holland, to construct lighthouses and other nautical signals in foreign style and in the vicinity of the open ports. Sir Harry Parkes, the British Minister, took much interest in this matter, and having referred it to his Government, the Board of Trade undertook to procure the lighthouse apparatus required by the Japanese Government ; to appoint and send to Japan suitable persons to erect the lighthouses and to organise an efficient lighthouse system. The Board of Trade engaged the services of Messrs. D. and T. Stevenson, engineers to the Commissioners of Northern Lights, Edinburgh, and these gentlemen designed and superintended the construction of all the apparatus which was sent to Japan. They also selected the chief engineer, Mr. R. H. Brunton, and the artisans and lightkeepers who were sent out, the Board of Trade in each case approving the selection and making the appointment.

Mr. Brunton arrived in Japan in August 1868, and a Lighthouse Engineering Department was established at Benten, Yokohama. Mr. Brunton remained in the service of the Japanese Government for eight years, and during that time he superintended the construction of a large number of lighthouses and other signals at the most important parts of the Japanese coast, and thus made navigation comparatively safe. Since that time the number has been considerably increased and the Japanese coasts are now well lighted. The nautical signals of Japan are divided according to construction and method of maintenance into three classes ; namely Government, communal, and private. At the end of 1901 there were 162 Government signals of various kinds, 51 communal, and 16 private, or a total of 239.

Among the Western apparatus presented by Commodore Perry to the Shogun in 1853 were two sets of telegraph instruments, but they were never used for any practical purposes. The Shogunate was, as we Telegraphs. have seen, in the midst of very serious troubles, which ended in its disappearance, the officials or people had no time to study telegraphy and the instruments were left to mould and decay in a storehouse.

It was not until after the Restoration that Japan had its first line of telegraphs, when in 1869 under the super-intendence of Mr. Brunton, the engineer of the Light-house Department, Tokyo and Yokohama were connected by telegraph wires. For some time the pioneer line suffered from the ignorant masses, who looked upon the telegraph as a species of witchcraft and frequently broke down the line ; so that the guarding of it was no easy matter. The Govern-ment, however, was firm in its determination to maintain the service, and spared no trouble to extend and improve it ; the people were soon convinced of its utility and gave up their attempts to destroy it.

The system was slowly extended to other parts of the country, but without any definite plan and with very imperfect construction and appliances, and breakdowns were frequent. Soon after my arrival in Japan I impressed on the Vice-Minister of Public Works the desirability of a more complete organisation, and on my suggestion Mr. Edward Gilbert of the North British Railway Company's service was engaged, along with a competent staff of assistants, to organise and develop the system. In a comparatively short time considerable extensions took place and the service was placed on a proper basis. Its importance and utility were fully demonstrated during the civil war in Kyushu, and its use gave the Government troops a great advantage over the rebels. In the following year the Emperor made a tour round Japan and many telegraph offices were opened ; shortly afterwards the country joined the Telegraph Union, and thus both internally and externally the telegraph service was placed on a fair road to satisfactory development. That development was hastened by the work of the graduates of the Imperial College of Engineering and by the operators and workmen who were trained under their superintendence. In a recent report it is stated that " in short, the technical knowledge possessed by Japan in the work of constructing lines and apparatus has been advanced to a state of efficiency, and both in respect of applying the latest developments of science and art and of training the staff of operators and experts, our telegraphic service can well stand comparison with that of Western countries " ; and there can be no doubt that this claim is well founded. Besides the offices maintained in the interior, the Government also possesses telegraph offices at Fusan, Seoul, and Jinsen, all in Korea. There are now about 2200 telegraph offices throughout Japan, and they are being increased as the demand arises for them as quickly as means will allow, and it is expected that before long all the post offices in Japan will be connected by telegraph lines. In the more thickly populated districts of Japan proper, that is in Kyushu and Shikoku, the offices are at the rate of one per nine square *ri* approximately. The latest developments of electrical science and the most improved appliances have been fully utilised in the telegraph system of Japan.

The following table shows the development of telegraphs in Japan since 1869 :—

	Telegraphs.			
	Number of Offices open to the Public.	Length of Lines.	Length of Wires.	Number of Messages.
		Ri.	*Ri.*	
1869 . .	2	8	8	?
1870 . .	4	19	19	?
1871 . .	4	19	19	19,448
1872 . .	18	160	185	80,639
1873 . .	28	354	536	186,448
1874 . .	34	433	1,325	356,539
1875 . .	47	637	1,590	525,930
1876 . .	51	672	1,626	690,162
1877 . .	68	947	1,946	868,970
1878 . .	97	1310	2,828	1,037,884
1879 . .	112	1518	3,211	1,659,702
1880 . .	155	1722	4,037	2,041,372
1881 . .	169	1871	4,666	2,585,663
1882 . .	185	1990	5,116	2,978,763
1883 . .	195	2056	5,496	2,678,860
1884 . .	213	2216	5,803	2,723,613
1885 . .	216	2243	5,921	2,670,311
1886 . .	219	2265	5,948	2,540,928
1887 . .	231	2346	6,209	2,647,536
1888 . .	251	2452	6,723	2,842,331
1889–1890	311	2574	7,275	3,675,802
1890–1891	408	2900	8,218	4,316,366
1891–1892	524	3244	9,245	4,728,728
1892–1893	633	3557	10,052	5,466,095
1893–1894	716	3836	10,388	6,556,109
1894–1895	762	3983	11,670	8,359,774
1895–1896	787	4044	12,408	9,410,985
1896–1897	1125	4903	15,659	11,099,150
1897–1898	1259	5872	19,158	14,296,378
1898–1899	1272	6127	21,500	15,188,008
1899–1900	1450	6534	25,302	14,496,130
1900–1901	1651	6999	28,606	16,789,543
1901–1902	1856	7361	31,170	16,596,806
1902–1903	2198	7628	33,584	17,635,461

Some time in 1877 I had a set of telephone instruments sent out from London, which were the first in Japan, and having connected my office in the Engineering College with that of the Public Works Department, they were shown in operation to a large number of visitors. Other instruments were gradually introduced and used for short distances, but it was not till some years later that telephones became largely used as public means of

Telephones.

communication. The first long line was constructed in 1888 between Tokyo and Atami. The scope of operations was next extended as far as Shizuoka, and then to Osaka, and with success in both cases. During the past ten years especially great progress has been made in telephonic communication in Japan, and it is now being used freely, not only for business purposes, but also for social intercourse. Reference must, however, be made to special reports for details.

Among the methods of communication which have been the means of causing great changes in Japan, a prominent Postal place must be given to the postal services, that services. have now attained a high standard of efficiency. From an early period a very rudimentary form of postal service existed in Japan. As I have already mentioned, early in the seventeenth century a service was established by the Tokugawa Shoguns. At first this was limited to official uses, but later on it was imitated by business men. The intervals, however, between the despatches were considerable, and the methods of delivery crude and uncertain, but for more than two centuries this primitive system of postal service was in vogue.

The great changes which took place in the country after the Restoration convinced the Government that the postal services could not be carried on with efficiency and benefit as private enterprises, and it was decided to run them as official undertakings. In January 1871 the new Postal Service System was promulgated, and it was put in force by way of trial between Tokyo, Osaka, and Kyoto in March of the same year, and very soon developments took place all over the country.

In June 1877 Japan joined the International Postal Union, and from that date every effort was made to keep the arrangements of the Post Office Department up to the standard of Western countries. On June 20, 1902, on the occasion of the twenty-fifth anniversary of the admission of Japan into the Union, a great celebration was held to mark the occasion and to recount the work done. For some time Japanese letter postage was the cheapest in the world, being based on a silver standard which naturally shared in the universal depreciation of that metal. Inland letters went for 2 sen, that is about a halfpenny; post-cards for half that sum. In 1899 these rates were raised fifty per cent; so that domestic letters now cost 3 sen (for $\frac{1}{2}$ oz.), post-cards $1\frac{1}{2}$ sen. Foreign postage to all countries included in the Postal Union is 10 sen ($2\frac{1}{2}$d., though originally intended to be equivalent to 5d.). There is an excellent system of postal savings-banks which at the end of the year 1902 had 27,196,802 yen in deposit in the names of 2,363,335 individuals. The money orders and parcel post are largely made use of. The following figures show the increase in ordinary mail matter in ten years :—

Year.	Letters.	Post-cards.	Newspapers and Magazines.
1892	74,991,639	133,260,804	50,829,871
1897	148,254,148	287,069,246	88,266,273
1901	190,951,188	436,673,345	139,116,263

The dead-letter office in Japan has very light work, as it is the universal custom for correspondents to put their own name and address on the back of the envelope; a custom which is now becoming somewhat common in other parts of the world. A detailed study of the work of the Post Office Department of Japan affords a very good index of the national progress in many of its aspects.

The sketch which has been given of the development of the means of communication shows most distinctly that they must have been very important factors not only in the formation of Japan into an organic unity instead of a group of isolated feudal clans, but also in the promotion of national and international industry and commerce in all their departments. Some of the most important of these we will now proceed to consider.

BIBLIOGRAPHICAL NOTE

The Reports of the Public Works Department and of the Departments of Communications give statistics of the development of the means of communication in Japan. A very complete résumé is to be found in the *Financial and Economical Annual* issued by the Department of Finance, and in another annual issued by the Imperial Cabinet, namely the *Résumé Statistique de l'Empire du Japan.* Chapter vii. of H. Yamawaki's *Japan in the beginning of the Twentieth Century* gives the most connected account which has been published. The British and American Consular Reports have noted the progress which has been made from year to year, and several special reports have been issued on the railways and shipping. Almost all the recent foreign books on Japan contain an outline of the arrangements and extent of railways, shipping, telegraphs, etc.

CHAPTER VIII

INDUSTRIAL DEVELOPMENTS

FOR some time after the fall of feudalism the progress of Western industries in Japan was comparatively slow. The attention of the new Government was too fully occupied with problems of administration and finance to allow them time to consider the reorganisation of industry, and few among the people had either the capital or the knowledge to enable them to make industrial developments on Western lines. As affairs settled down in the country, however, considerable numbers of foreign experts were engaged to superintend the working of special industries, but the success which attended their operations was not great. Some of these industries were started under the superintendence of the Public Works or some other department of the Government, while others were undertaken by private individuals. In many cases the Japanese had to pay somewhat dearly for their experience. Not infrequently they were unfortunate in the selection which they made of their foreign employees, and occasionally the unsuitable economic conditions of the localities selected for the works brought about failure. Sometimes the want of success was due to an attempt to carry on the works entirely by Japanese before they had gained the requisite experience. Withal, progress *was* made, and especially when men who had been educated in the colleges in Japan, and who had supplemented their training by experience in Europe and America, returned to their native

Introduction of foreign industries.

country. From about 1880 onwards, the progress has been wonderful, and for some years there was quite a boom in industrial undertakings, some of which, however, were of too speculative a nature to be successful financially. The war with China in 1894-5 marked an epoch not only in the political history of Japan, but also in its economic and industrial history, and its successful termination gave an impetus to every department of national activity; which had a great effect on industrial development.

While that development has been very great, especially in the neighbourhood of large towns, it must not be imagined
Conditions of native industries. that all the industries of old Japan have disappeared or changed their methods to any great extent. Mr. Stafford Ransome has truly said: "Any one whose business it might be to visit the modern factories in the Japan of to-day, and who afterwards might pick up Rein's *Industries of Japan*, thoughtful and excellent in every way as is that work, might well imagine that what he had seen and what he reads in that book had to do with two absolutely different countries. This does not mean that the industrial Japan described so ably by Rein has ceased to exist, but that during the last few years, side by side with the picturesque, effective, and time-honoured native handicrafts, there have sprung up into being the essentially progressive but inartistic factory chimney, and its accompanying and still more hideous workshops, built on the most approved-of European and American designs. My advice to the visitor to Japan, who wishes to enjoy himself and improve his mind, is to study the industrial Japan depicted by Rein; for though less obtrusive, it still remains, and is far more interesting than its modern congener. Let him see the making of cloisonné ware, embroidery, rice-mats, and carving, and admire the curios, toys, hand-weaving, and painting, while those are arts still to be seen as now carried on; for my conviction is that, if the old Japan is destined to die, as we are so often told is to be the case, mortification will first attack its native industries."

I shall discuss the probable future of the artistic industries of Japan in a future chapter, but as native industries are still carried on to a considerable extent and as their products still form a large part of the industrial output of the country, a few notes regarding them will meantime be convenient. .

Methods of native industries.

During the Tokugawa period, extending over two hundred and sixty years, Japan was in a state of perfect tranquillity, and the feudal chiefs did a great deal to encourage and protect manufacturing industry, especially that of an artistic nature. The energy which was formerly spent on internecine war was expended in friendly rivalry in the industrial arts, and the consequence was that a very high standard of excellence was attained. The best work was not made for sale, but for use or presentation ; time was not money, and the artificers and artists threw their personalities and all their skill into their work. Both artists and workmen were free to work when they felt in the mood to do justice to their objects, and equally free to seek repose the instant fatigue notified them of their failing powers. They therefore had real pleasure in their work, and each of the products was a distinct specimen of skill, perfect, novel, and idiosyncratic. Nothing short of what they considered perfection was allowed to pass ; for their honour as craftsmen and artists was at stake. Usually they worked by themselves in their own cottages, or else with a few sympathetic associates, on such branches of art as had been perfected by many generations of their ancestors through the fostering care of their feudal lords. Skill passed from fathers to sons or adopted sons, and surrounded by their own domestic circle they carried on their work under conditions which were almost perfect from an artistic point of view. Qualified critics and fellow-workers kept up a spirit of healthy emulation, and the worker unconsciously imbibed in a more or less degree some of the purity, poetry, and refinements of the motives which actuated his art.

It cannot be wondered that the specimens of Japanese

industry which found their way to Nagasaki, and from there
to Europe, when the Dutch were the only people who had intercourse with the Japanese, are still looked upon as the best
specimens of Japanese art work, and that the Tokugawa
period is considered the golden age of Japanese art.   Some
of the best products of the period are now better represented
in European museums than in Japan.   The industries were
fairly well diffused over the country, although naturally
certain districts became specially noted for their products.
Textile fabrics in silk, hemp, and cotton were produced in many
parts of the country, and porcelain wares in those districts in
which clay of good quality was to be found.

The economic and social changes which took place on
the fall of the feudal system played havoc with all the
Japanese art industries, even with those of a
purely mechanical nature, and great hardships
were inflicted on the workers.   Many were reduced to
poverty, and others were compelled to undertake work of a
menial kind.   As affairs settled down production for sale
and profit took the place of production for use and enjoyment, with a consequent debasement of taste and workmanship, and the art products were made to suit what were
believed to be foreign tastes.   In recent years, however,
great improvements have taken place, and it is now possible
to obtain specimens of Japanese art workmanship, which
are of a high standard of excellence but with modified
ideals of art and under conditions approximating to the
factory as distinguished from the domestic system.   The
modern factory system as applied in all the chief industries
is crushing out many of the smaller trades of a domestic
nature, although the combination of industries of various
kinds with agriculture still prevails to a large extent.   The
spare time of the farmers and of their wives and families is
utilised in those domestic industries, and in this way they do
not compete directly with the large factories.   They are
thus likely to exist for a considerable time, although as
industry and commerce are more organised and specialised

they are certain to become of less importance and probably ultimately to disappear.

The factory system has made remarkable progress in Japan; modern industries are now dotting themselves about all over the country, and many of the larger towns have become industrial centres of considerable importance. Even Tokyo is becoming distinguished for its high chimney-stalks and manufacturing establishments, but being spread over a great area they are not so self-evident as in other parts of the country. Osaka is rapidly developing into an industrial city pure and simple, and Englishmen sometimes call it the Manchester, Scotsmen the Glasgow, Frenchmen the Lille, Germans the Hamburg, and Americans the Chicago of Japan; but, as Mr. Stafford Ransome has truly remarked, while one " of course sees the idea which gave birth to these respective similes, yet Osaka is not in the least like any one of the cities mentioned, and never will be; for the individuality of the Japanese will always be strong enough to prevent the possibility of their adopting any of our Western methods in their entirety, even in the carrying out of their modern industries."

The changes which have taken place in the life and industry of Japan have caused a very largely increased demand for wood for manufacturing, engineer- Supply of ing, and other purposes. Moreover, large timber. quantities have been exported to China and Korea. This has caused greater attention to be paid to the forestry industry. Not only has the Government taken steps to prevent the destruction of existing forests, but also to introduce the most improved methods, so that the natural capabilities of the forests may be developed and the demands of the new conditions of the nation more fully met. The Forestry Department has issued very complete reports on the subject, but meantime we can do little more than mention it. According to the Government statistics for 1901 (which are the latest published) the area of the forests of Japan is 23,087,365 *cho*, that is over 59 per cent of the area of the whole country, and of these 13,125,320 *cho* are State forests, 2,091,755 *cho* imperial forests, and 7,870,260 *cho* people's forests, and the variety of woods is very considerable, depending on the nature of the soil and the climate. The different classes of forests are in the following proportions in the forest areas of Japan .—

Conifer forests	21	per cent
Broad-leaved forests	25	,, ,,
Conifer and broad-leaved forests . .	45	,, ,,
Thinly-stocked or blank areas, etc. . .	9	,, ,,
	100	,, .,

The great demand for wood which has arisen for purposes of construction and industry caused a large amount of thoughtless deforestation ; in recent years the Government has taken steps to prevent this, definite regulations have been drawn out which are now rigidly enforced, and when they have been in operation for some years they will revolutionise the conditions of the forests, and greatly develop their production. According to the existing system, the Minister of Agriculture and Commerce has the supreme supervision of all matters relating to State forests and to forests at large, and, subject to his control, the Forestry Bureau takes charge of all matters relating to the administration and scientific treatment of forests. Under this supervision many marked improvements have been made in recent years.

Modern improvements in Japanese forestry.

These improvements are, to a very considerable extent, the result of the developments which have taken place in arboricultural education. Not only is very complete instruction given in the College of Agriculture of the Imperial University of Tokyo, but higher courses are given in the Sapporo Agricultural College and the High Agricultural and Dendrological School at Iwate. In each of these institutions attention is paid to the training of specialists who are to combine adequate scientific and practical knowledge of forestry, and who on leaving are qualified to attend with efficiency to the duty of managing and improving the forests. The Government is giving special encouragement to the study of this useful science, by offering to the graduates comparatively good posts. For the subordinate posts there are secondary schools where special courses are given in the practical sides of the work.

A considerable number of Laws and Ordinances have been issued with regard to the regulation of forestry conditions, and altogether the work which has been done in this Department is not the least noteworthy of the national developments which have taken place in Japan. The Japanese have always been distinguished for their love of forests, and many are inclined to think that they owe much of their patriotism and æsthetic sense to the influence the forests have exercised upon them.

The people of Japan were not slow to recognise the fact that the Britain of the West in great part owed its predominant position among the nations of the world to its abundant mineral resources, and especially those of coal and iron, which enabled it to carry on all kinds of manufacturing industries, and they determined to develop the mineral resources of their country as rapidly as possible. In some respects the mineral resources of Japan are limited, but some of the most important harbours are very conveniently situated for trade with China, from which abundance of raw materials can be obtained at a cheap rate.

Mining and metallurgy.

Nothing accurate is known about the origin of the mining industry in Japan, but history records that, as early as the seventh or eighth century, gold, silver, copper, iron, coal, and petroleum were produced in various parts of the country, but the operations were carried on on a small scale. Since the Restoration, however, great progress has been made in almost every department of mining. The following table shows the production in the more important departments since 1886 :—

Year.	Gold. Momme.	Silver. Momme.	Copper. Kin.	Iron. Kwan.	Antimony. Kin.	Manganese. Kin.	Coal. Ton.	Petroleum. Koku.	Sulphur. Kin.
1886	123,888	8,982,577	16,290,325	3,669,054	3,994,209	669,775	1,374,209	40,113	10,745,414
1887	138,838	9,498,097	18,439,613	4,071,546	2,589,971	517,113	1,746,296	39,303	17,968,462
1888	167,788	11,396,894	22,290,711	4,851,851	2,039,985	1,348,294	2,022,968	39,605	31,659,766
1889	204,939	11,458,127	27,090,181	5,347,931	2,911,988	1,566,731	2,388,614	55,871	27,460,321
1890	193,762	14,091,754	30,192,447	5,603,481	2,164,885	4,319,131	2,608,284	54,399	34,499,523
1891	192,560	15,645,273	31,721,799	4,616,785	3,780,810	5,372,025	3,175,844	55,983	36,548,417
1892	186,805	16,063,426	34,544,539	5,031,466	2,305,433	8,363,750	3,175,670	72,893	34,142,610
1893	196,372	18,469,285	30,025,201	4,535,305	2,748,895	26,737,715	3,319,601	94,145	39,814,386
1894	209,509	19,209,527	53,186,229	5,182,463	2,618,551	22,240,739	4,268,135	151,986	31,257,166
1895	239,041	19,272,544	31,856,887	6,879,306	2,805,729	28,520,061	4,772,654	149,497	25,884,250
1896	256,519	17,156,666	33,464,615	7,299,579	2,237,615	29,893,267	5,019,690	208,400	20,863,373
1897	276,427	14,478,485	33,982,217	7,464,364	1,951,068	25,701,496	5,188,157	231,220	22,636,870
1898	309,145	16,118,242	35,039,592	6,296,225	2,061,829	19,162,323	6,696,033	280,742	17,202,173
1899	446,716	14,978,060	40,459,709	6,151,033	1,568,462	18,893,440	6,721,798	474,406	17,062,186
1900	566,535	15,681,595	42,182,353	6,624,447	716,477	26,384,526	7,429,457	767,092	24,064,196
1901	660,653	14,598,749	45,652,927	18,680,043	911,462	27,115,884	8,945,939	983,799	27,580,478

Taking the last of these years, the following table gives an approximate estimate of the value of the more important of the mineral products :—

Kinds.	Units.	Quantity.	Value.
			Yen.
Gold	Momme	652,356	3,261,780
Silver	,,	14,174,489	2,055,301
Copper . . .	Kin	45,652,927	16,252,442
Lead	,,	3,004,983	246,409
Pewter	,,	23,422	13,749
Iron . . .	Kwan	18,680,043	2,947,684
Pig Iron . .	,,	14,686,801	2,041,465
Matte . .	,,	335,551	32,884
Wrought Iron .	,,	412,246	172,319
Steel . . .	,,	3,245,445	701,016
Sulphate of Iron .	,,	4,690,270	27,782
Silica . . .	Kin	17,187	1,633
Quicksilver . .	,,	1,250	1,688
Antimony . .	,,	911,462	13,814
Refined . .	,,	714,276	117,856
Sulphate . .	,,	197,186	16,958
Manganese . .	,,	27,115,884	108,464
Coal . . .	Ton	8,945,939	30,592,971
Bituminous . .	,,	8,811,903	30,207,203
Anthracite . .	,,	86,554	230,407
Natural Coke .	,,	47,482	155,361
Lignite	,,	9,740	16,343
Petroleum . .	Koku	983,799	2,278,418
Sulphur . . .	Kin	27,580,478	386,127
Black-lead . .	,,	146,495	17,433
		Total Value	58,343,038

In feudal times the operations of mining and metallurgy were carried on in very primitive methods, but now full advantage is taken of all the latest appliances. In the latter days of the Shogunate, that is in the year 1867, an Englishman, Erasmus Gower, introduced into the country the use of explosives, which he employed in the silver-gold mine in Sado, and about the same time an American, Raphael Pumpelly, also used an explosive in the Yurap lead mine in Hokkaido. In 1868 the feudal lord of Saga, in conjunction with a Scotsman, Thomas Glover, sank a shaft in European style at Takashima, and this was the beginning of the development of the now celebrated coal mines of that district, which supply with coal many of the ships that visit Japan.

At the Restoration the new Government undertook the mining business itself, and placed the Sado, Ikuno, Muoi, Ani, Kosaka, Kamaishi, and Okuzu metal mines, as well as the Takashima and Miike collieries, under its direct control. Foreign engineers were employed and Western methods adopted in carrying on the work. As the graduates of the Imperial College of Engineering and others who had studied in foreign countries were able to take charge, very rapid developments took place, an example was set to private mining companies and many of these were started. They were not always successful, but on the whole good progress was made. Gradually the Government handed over their model mines to private companies, and mining in Japan is now almost entirely carried on by private enterprise. For details, however, we must refer to special reports.

Japanese copper is of high quality and free from impurities, and thus of great value for electrical purposes; already it has been the cause of a wide application of electrical power for manufactures and to the development of industries connected with electricity. Gold and silver mining, as will be seen from the figures quoted above, is attaining considerable importance. The production of sulphur is large and finds many applications in the chemical industries. The petroleum industry is developing. At first the sinking of wells was done by manual labour, but in 1890 the Japan Petroleum Joint-Stock Company introduced American oil-well boring machines with success, and this, with other improved appliances, is rapidly causing an important industry to be built up.

As will be seen from the figures which have been given, the production of coal has increased at a rapid rate, and it is capable of great development—a fact which is of great importance from an industrial point of view.

Still more important is the production of iron and steel, as it forms the basis of engineering in all its forms.

Although the deposits of iron ore in Japan are considerable, they are not in themselves sufficient to allow a great development of the iron and steel industries, and the recognition of this fact has already led to arrangements being made for the supply of iron ore from China, where the supplies are very large. In this as in other departments of industry a close connection between Japan and China is necessary, not only for the supply of raw materials, but also for the disposal of the manufactured products.

The Government has established large steel works near Wakamatsu, an excellent harbour in the north-western corner of the island of Kyushu, ten miles distant from the important port of Moji. They are connected by a branch of the main line of the Kyushu railway, are in the immediate vicinity of the most abundant and cheapest coal-producing districts of Japan, and have an abundant supply of excellent water conveyed from the river Itabitsu, and amounting at the ordinary water-level to nearly 2,000,000 gallons per diem. They are divided into three principal departments— (1) pig-iron, (2) steel, and (3) rolling mills. The first is fitted with coke ovens and blast-furnace plants, the second has mixed Bessemer and open-hearth plants, and a steel foundry, and the third, blooming rail mill, large, middle, and small bar-mill, sheet-mill, middle and large plate-mill plant. In addition there are a central pumping station, an electric central station, repair shops, iron foundry, pattern and boiler shops, smithy, and chemical and mechanical laboratory. Every one of these is provided with a complete outfit of all the necessary machinery and appliances, all of the most modern and efficient types of German manufacture.

The works have evidently been designed on an extremely comprehensive and ambitious scale, but unfortunately due regard has not been paid to the financial conditions necessary for success. Their cost has far exceeded the estimates, and although a beginning has been made in the production of iron and steel, the cost is much greater than that of imported material. The Government would have been well advised to have started the works on a much smaller scale and developed them as experience was gained. Although a mistake has been made in this respect, there can be no doubt that these works will ultimately have a very important influence on the industrial development of Japan. Their excessive cost is part of the price which Japan has had to pay for her experience.

The record given in the preceding chapter proves that in all the ordinary branches of what are usually called civil

Civil and mechanical engineering.

engineering construction the Japanese are now able to carry on the work entirely on their own responsibility. They can construct their roads, railways, bridges, docks and harbours all in very good style and at moderate cost. In all these departments they are continually sending their most promising young men to foreign countries to learn the most improved methods, and to make themselves acquainted with the latest design, so that there is little danger of the various works falling behind the times. The Japanese keep a very sharp look-out on all that is done in Europe and America.

Considerable progress has been made in the various departments of mechanical engineering. When I went to Japan in 1873 comparatively small mechanical engineering establishments were found in Tokyo, Yokohama, Kobe, and Nagasaki, but they were inadequate for the proper training of students, and large works were started under my management in connection with the Public Works Department at Akabane, Tokyo, in which the majority of the students of the Imperial College of Engineering spent considerable time, and they were of great use in the practical training of the students. I insisted on all the students of the various departments of engineering spending some time in the workshops before they took up their special work, and they found this preliminary training of the greatest value. I wish to record my high opinion of the efficient service rendered by George S. Brindley, the superintending foreman at the Akabane works.

There are now in connection with the railways, the shipbuilding and shipping companies, the navy and the army, as well as other departments of the Government, a considerable number of well-equipped workshops, all turning out on the whole fairly good work, while private establishments of all grades of size and efficiency are to be found in many parts of the country. These are now able to turn out all the ordinary machines and mechanical appliances, as well as the land engines and boilers for factories, electric lighting and pumping. Almost all the marine engines and boilers for the home-built boats are made in Japan; in some cases the designs have been got from abroad, and the work done in the Japanese workshops; they also make their own dynamos and electric motors and electric fittings of all kinds. The number of electric tram-roads is increasing steadily throughout the country. Some of the tramcars are imported, some have parts imported and the rest made in Japan. A considerable number of machines and appliances of all kinds are still bought abroad, especially if they are wanted in a hurry, but if not pressed for time, they are usually made in the workshops in Japan.

The railway workshops are mostly confined to repairs, but at Kobe several new locomotives have been constructed, and there is a private locomotive building establishment in Osaka which has built a number of locomotives and a considerable quantity of general rolling stock. An Anglo-Japanese Locomotive and Engineering Company has been formed, and plans have been made for the erection of a large establishment in Yokohama which will undertake the manufacture of locomotives and all other kinds of railway rolling stock. The value of the machinery made in Japan in the year 1899 (the latest for which returns have been published) is given as 4,175,144 yen.

One of the earliest Western industries to be introduced into Japan was the coinage of money, and it has been one of the most successful. Article VI. of the Convention

signed at Yedo on June 25, 1866, between a Minister of Foreign Affairs in Japan and the representatives of Great
The Imperial Mint. Britain, France, the United States of America, and Holland stipulated for the establishment of a free mint on certain conditions. The Japanese Government purchased from the British Government a mint which had been established at Hong-Kong, but which the latter had resolved to discontinue. Major Kinder and a staff of officials were engaged to superintend the operations which were begun in Osaka in 1869, and the establishment was completed and opened with great ceremony on April 4, 1871, the foreign representatives having been invited to be present. Among the members of the staff the best known were Mr. E. Dillon, B.A., F.C.S., technical adviser and assayer, Mr. W. Gowland, F.C.S., Assoc. R.S.M. (now Professor of Metallurgy at the Royal College of Science, London), technical adviser, chemist, and metallurgist, and Mr. R. MacLagan, engineer ; all these gentlemen rendered very efficient service to the establishment. The latest report of the director, that for the year ending March 31, 1903, shows that the work is being carried on in a very satisfactory manner. The coinage during that year consisted of 10 yen gold and 50 sen silver coins, amounting to 5,351,126 pieces of the value of 38,300,563 yen, against 21,354,919 pieces of the preceding year valued at 15,903,726 yen, in six denominations of gold, silver, nickel, and bronze coins. In addition to these, 668,782 pieces of silver yen were struck during the year for the reserve fund of the Taiwan Ginko (Bank of Formosa). On the whole the Imperial Mint has been one of the most useful establishments in Japan. In this connection it may be mentioned that there is a large Government establishment in Tokyo for the printing of bank and other notes, so that Japan is thoroughly well equipped for the provision of all that is necessary for the currency.

In Chapter VII. the rise and progress of the modern Japanese mercantile marine has been sketched, so that meantime it will be sufficient to give a few details regarding the shipbuilding industries and those otherwise directly connected with shipping. The following returns Shipbuilding of the shipbuilding output for last year, as and shipping. supplied by the special correspondent of the *Glasgow Herald*, gives a good idea of the present condition of the industry :—

	Steam.		1902.
	Ves.	Tons.	Tons.
Yokosuka Dockyard	5	3,940	4,413
Kure Dockyard	8	1,710	3,420
Sasebo Dockyard	3	270	270
The Mitsu Bishi Works	6	14,940	14,561
Kawasaki Dockyard Company	8	5,218	3,280
Osaka Ironworks	5	3,518	1,582
Owaki's Shipyard	1	1,628	1,526
Fuginagata Shipyard	3	1,382	523
Other firms	*20	2,805	5,457
	59	35,411	35,032

* Includes 11 sailers of 640 tons.

THE IMPERIAL DOCKYARD, YOKOSUKA.

Vessel.	Type.	Displt.	I.H.P.	Registry.
Otowa	3rd cl. cruiser	3000	10,000	Jap. Govt.
Hayatori	T.b.d.	380	6,000	Jap. Govt.
Asagiri	T.b.d.	380	6,000	Jap. Govt.
Two vessels	T.b.'s	180	2,400	Jap. Govt.
		3940	24,400	

THE IMPERIAL DOCKYARD, KURE.

Vessel.	Type.	Displt.	I.H.P.	Registry.
Kari	1st class t.b.	152	4,200	Jap. Govt.
Uji	Gunboat	646	1,000	Jap. Govt.
Aotaka	1st class t.b.	152	4,200	Jap. Govt.
Hato	1st class t.b.	152	4,200	Jap. Govt.
Tsubame	1st class t.b.	152	4,200	Jap. Govt.
Hibari	1st class t.b.	152	4,200	Jap. Govt.
Kiji	1st class t.b.	152	4,200	Jap. Govt.
Sagi	1st class t.b.	152	4,200	Jap. Govt.
		1710	30,400	

THE IMPERIAL DOCKYARD, SASEBO.

Vessel.	Type.	Displt.	I.H.P.	Registry.
Three vessels	T.b.'s	270	3600	Jap. Govt.

Also a caisson for new dry dock to take 1st class battleships.

THE MITSU BISHI WORKS, NAGASAKI.

Vessel.	Type.	Tons.	I.H.P.	Registry.
Kojima Maru	Ferry t.s.s.	220	320	Shimonoseki.
Tamamo Maru . . .	Ferry t.s.s.	220	320	Shimonoseki.
Niigata Maru	Cargo s.s.	2100	1200	Tokio.
Yeiko Maru	Passenger s.s.	1900	1500	Tokio.
Nikko Maru	Passenger s.s.	5500	6500	Tokio.
Ceylon Maru	Cargo s.s.	5000	3200	Tokio.
		14,940	13,040	

KAWASAKI DOCKYARD COMPANY (LTD.), KOBE.

Vessel.	Type.	Tons.	I.H.P.	Registry.
Heijo Maru	Spardeck s.s.	1208	1185	Osaka.
Kagawa Maru . . .	Spardeck s.s.	614	949	Osaka.
Yehima Maru . . .	Spardeck s.s.	614	955	Osaka.
Two vessels	T.b. (2d class).	178	2400	Jap. Govt.
Otori	T.b. (1st class).	152	3500	Jap. Govt.
Hashitaka	T.b. (1st class).	152	3500	Jap. Govt.
Taisei Maru	Aux. t.s. barque.	2300	900	Tokio.
T.b.'s are displacement.		5218	13,389	

OSAKA IRONWORKS AND DOCKYARD.

Vessel.	Type.	Tons.	I.H.P.	Registry.
Tensho Maru	S.s.	528	350	Osaka.
Korin Maru	S.s.	750	500	Osaka.
Siang Kiang Maru	T.s.s.	935	750	Tokio.
Yuen Kiang Maru	T.s.s.	935	750	Tokio.
Reibun Maru	S.s.	370	300	Otaru.
		3518	2650	

OWAKI'S SHIPYARD, SHINAGAWA.

Vessel.	Type.	Tons.	I.H.P.	Registry.
Kwannon Maru, No. 26 . . .	Wd. s.s.	1628	1500	Shinagawa.

FUJINAGATA SHIPBUILDING YARD, OSAKA.

Vessel.	Type.	Tons.	I.H.P.	Registry.
Nagata Maru, No. 13 . . .	W.d. s.s.	580	450	Not stated.
Kaishun Maru	W.d. s.s.	112	85	Not stated.
Ikuta Maru	S.s.	690	500	Not stated.
		1382	1035	

ONO'S SHIPYARD, OSAKA.

Vessel.	Type.	Tons.	I.H.P.	Registry.
Kyodo Maru, No. 7	Wd. s.s.	548	440	Tokushima.

SORA SHIPBUILDING YARD, OSAKA.

Vessel.	Type.	Tons.	I.H.P.	Registry.
Uwajima Maru	Wd. s.s.	464	482	Not stated

KISHIMOTO SHIPBUILDING YARD.

Vessel.	Type.	Tons.	I.H.P.	Registry.
Shin-Yu-Maru	Wd. s.s.	415	330	Kishiwada.

CHUJIO'S SHIPBUILDING YARD, TOSA.

Vessel.	Type.	Tons.	Registry.
Juho Maru	Wood sailer	147	Kochi.
Kaitsu Maru	Wood sailer	159	Kochi.
		306	

THE URAGA DOCK COMPANY (LIMITED).

Vessel.	Type.	Tons.	I.H.P.	Registry.
Uraga Maru, No. 2 . . .	Tug s.s.	173	200	Uraga.
One vessel	Dredger	14	50	Uraga.
Two vessels	Hopper barges	52	—	Uraga.
		239	250	

MIYAGAWA SHIPBUILDING YARD, OSAKA.

Vessel.	Type.	Tons.	I.H.P.	Registry.
Teshiogawa Maru	W.d. s.s.	180	150	Osaka.

THE ISHIKAWAJIMA S. & E. CO. (LTD.), TOKIO.

Vessel.	Type.	Tons.	Registry.
One vessel	P.s.	52 }	Not stated.
Six vessels	Barges.	122 }	
		174	

NAKAMURA'S SHIPYARD, OSAKA.

Vessel.	Type.	Tons.	I.H.P.	Registry.
Taisei Maru	Wd. s.s.	164	130	Not stated.

OKUBO SHIPBUILDING YARD, OSAKA.

Vessel.	Type.	Tons.	Registry.
Shoun Maru	Wood sailer	160	Osaka.

FUKUI SHIPBUILDING YARD, OSAKA.

Vessel.	Type.	Tons.	I.H.P.	Registry.
Kanei Maru	Wd. s.s.	155	200	Kobe.

YOKOHAMA DOCK CO. (LTD.),

have docked and repaired about 100 vessels, and repaired a large number out of dock.

MARINE ENGINEERING.

The following table summarises the Japanese marine engineering of the year, details of which appear in the shipbuilding returns :—

	Total I.H.P.	1902. I.H.P.
Kure Dockyard	30,400	10,000
Yokosuka Dockyard	24,400	25,075
Sasebo Dockyard	3,600	3,600
Kawasaki Dockyard Company	13,389	4,450
The Mitsu Bishi Works	13,040	12,265
The Osaka Ironworks	2,650	2,688
Owaki's Shipyard	1,500	1,100
Fuginagata Shipyard	1,035	280
Other firms	1,982	4,662
	91,996	64,120

The most important shipbuilding establishment in Japan is that of the Mitsu Bishi Company at Nagasaki ; it is now able to turn out vessels of 6000 tons, which as regards design and workmanship will bear favourable comparison with those built in Europe. The works are thoroughly well equipped in every respect, and the docks capable of taking in the largest steamers which go to the Far East. The other important private shipyards are the Kawasaki works at Kobe, the yard connected with the Osaka Ironworks, and the establishments belonging to the Ishikawajima Company at Tokyo, and the Uraga Dock Company near the entrance of the Bay of Tokyo, all of which are now turning out good work.

The three most important Government dockyards are (1) Yokosuka, in the Bay of Tokyo ; (2) Kure, in the Inland Sea ; and (3) Sasebo, on the west side of the island of Kyushu. They are all equipped for repairs rather than for new work, and in this respect form a contrast with the private yards. Third-class cruisers have been built at Yokosuka and Kure, but all the larger vessels in the Japanese Navy have been built abroad, chiefly in Britain.

All these three Government establishments, on the other hand, have magnificent graving docks and all the appliances necessary for repairs in time of war, and in that contingency they would be able to render very effective service.

All these establishments, both private and Government, naturally involve a large number of subsidiary industries of all kinds, but into details of these we cannot enter.

After the war with China the Government of Japan resolved to encourage both the shipping and the shipbuilding of the country, and in March 1896 the Navigation Encouragement Law was promulgated, which provides that any subject of Japan *Subsidies for shipping and shipbuilding.* or any commercial company, the partners or shareholders of which are Japanese subjects, engaging themselves in the conveyance of passengers or goods between the empire and foreign countries or between foreign ports, with their own vessels of 1000 tons or more, registered in the shipping list of the empire, shall be granted subsidies in proportion to the distances traversed and the tonnage of the vessels used for the lines concerned, as is prescribed in the law. At the same time the Shipbuilding Encouragement Law was enacted, by which bounties were granted for the construction of vessels above 700 tons to any subject of the empire or any trade company engaged in shipbuilding, the partners and shareholders of which are Japanese subjects. Since these laws were passed the shipping and shipbuilding industries have made rapid progress. In a paper read by Mr. K. Uchida (Director of the Marine Bureau), before the Institution of Naval Architects in Japan, it was stated that under the shipbuilding law there had been built, up till the end of 1902, a total tonnage of 86,000 (gross) and 71,000 indicated horse power. The following are the amounts paid to the steamship companies mentioned in Chapter VII. for their most important lines.

The routes run by the Nippon Yusen Kaisha, and the respective subsidies, are as follow :—

Yokohama to Melbourne, employing three steamers of 3500 tons and above : speed, 16 knots and above. A monthly service. Subsidy £53,600. Contract runs from April 1901 to March 1906.

Yokohama to Bombay, employing three steamers of 3000 tons and above; 10 knots and above. A monthly service. Subsidy, £18,200. Contract runs from April 1901 to March 1906.

European line, employing twelve steamers of 6000 tons and above ; 14 knots and above. A fortnightly service. Subsidy £272,800. Contract runs from January 1900 to December 1909.

Hong-Kong to Seattle, employing three steamers of 6000 tons and above; 15 knots and above. A four weeks' service. Subsidy, £66,700. Contract runs from November 1901 to December 1909.

Also mail routes :—

1. Yokohama to Shanghai, employing three steamers of 2500 tons and above ; 14 knots and above. A weekly service.

2. Kobe to North China, employing three steamers of 1400 tons and above ; 12 knots and above. A weekly service, except in winter.

3. Kobe, Korea, and North China, employing one steamer of over 1400 tons : speed, over 12 knots. A four weeks' service.

4. Kobe to Vladivostock, employing one steamer of over 1400 tons and 12 knots. A four weeks' service.

5. Kobe to Otaru, employing twelve steamers of 1400 tons and above ; 14 knots and above. Two routes : eastern, ten times a month ; western, weekly.

6. Aomori to Mororan, employing three steamers of 700 tons and above, 10 knots and above. A daily service.

The joint subsidy for the foregoing six mail routes is £56,100. Contract runs from October 1900 to September 1905.

The Toyo Kisen Kaisha have the following route and subsidy :—

Hong-Kong to San Francisco, employing three vessels of 6000 tons and above, and 17 knots and above. A four weeks' service. Subsidy, £103,400. Contract runs from January 1900 to December 1909.

The Osaka Shosen Kaisha have the following :—

Shanghai to Hankow, employing three steamers of 2000 tons and above ; 11 knots and above. A bi-weekly service ; in winter, three times a fortnight. Subsidy, £25,000. Contract runs from January 1898 to December 1907. Hankow to Ichang, employing two vessels of 1500 tons and above ; 10 knots and above. Service, six times a month ; in winter four times. Subsidy, £11,200. Contract runs from January 1899 to December 1907. Kobe to Korea, employing two steamers of 700 tons and above ; 10 knots and above. A three weeks' service. Subsidy, £3100. Contract runs from October 1900 to September 1905.

The first two of the other companies mentioned run services on

Chinese rivers and on the Japanese sea respectively, and receive subsidies, the one of £5900, the other of £14,000.

The total annual payments on account of the special services above detailed amount to £630,000.

The cotton-spinning industry is the one which has made the most rapid development, and which appeals most directly to British manufacturers, as its pro- Cotton-spinning. ducts compete with them. The following table shows its growth and extent :—

Year.	Number of Cotton Mills.	Gross Amount of Capital invested.	Average Number of Spindles used daily.	Quantity of Raw and Ginned Cotton demanded.	Total Production of Cotton Yarn.	Waste Cotton.	Waste Cotton Yarn.
		Yen.		Kwan.	Kwan.	Kwan.	Kwan.
1888	24	?	113,856	1,807,066	1,593,103	140,986	16,025
1889	28	?	215,190	3,859,464	3,358,042	311,971	51,971
1890	30	?	277,895	5,962,484	5,132,588	598,651	88,565
1891	36	8,715,510	353,980	8,995,293	7,689,938	823,003	232,371
1892	39	9,103,237	403,314	12,240,788	9,997,208	906,116	304,851
1893	40	11,271,005	381,781	11,531,307	10,666,744	1,178,059	298,466
1894	45	13,308,030	476,123	17,179,774	14,620,008	1,816,333	191,017
1895	47	16,392,058	518,736	21,771,346	18,437,011	2,423,361	251,879
1896	61	22,860,709	692,384	24,803,618	20,585,485	2,915,950	328,159
1897	74	36,414,728	768,328	32,068,243	26,134,120	3,706,510	1,177,099
1898	77	42,342,080	1,027,817	42,544,656	32,163,239	4,980,687	558,409
1899	83	33,023,317	1,170,327	42,962,406	43,052,402	4,923,207	587,343
1900	80	35,908,512	1,144,027	38,323,770	32,419,641	3,889,848	786,457
1901	81	36,690,567	1,181,762	38,681,886	33,115,829	4,092,460	477,364

The distribution of the cotton-spinning industry in different parts of the country is shown by the following figures, which give the latest published returns of the value for the year of the yarn produced in the various districts :—

	Yen.			Yen.
Tokyo	2,278,953		Okayama	3,743,899
Kyoto	821,880		Hiroshima	912,591
Osaka	12,264,578		Wakayama	791,763
Hyogo	4,954,766		Kagawa	363,557
Nara	1,114,763		Ehime	704,740
Miye	2,380,858		Fukuoka	1,681,073
Aichi	2,242,658			

Cotton-spinning in Japan was started by the Daimyo of Satsuma at Kagoshima in 1865. The machinery came from England and consisted of 6000 spindles. A few years later another factory was opened in Sakai, Idzumi province. In 1870 Mr. Kajuna Manbei started a similar factory, near Oji in the vicinity of Tokyo, and these were the only establishments of the kind in the country when I went to Japan. After some of the graduates of the Imperial College of Engineering, who had been to Britain and studied the construction and working of cotton-spinning machinery, had returned to Japan there was quite a boom in the erection of cotton mills; the progress made was most remarkable, and many of the cotton mills in Japan will now bear favourable comparison with the best of those of England in organisation, equipment, and extent. They have as a rule been successful financially, many of them paying from 10 to 20 per cent per annum. On the other hand, some have not been so successful, partly on account of extravagant financial arrangements and partly because of excessive production before the markets were prepared. The latest published returns give the average rate of dividend of each company at 6.2 per cent for the first half of the year, and 3.5 for the second half; but averages in such cases do not give much information, as so much depends on management and on local and other conditions.

The question of the supply of raw cotton for Japan is one of great importance and is receiving considerable attention from those who are interested in the industry. It is a somewhat remarkable fact that the cultivation of cotton in Japan has gradually but steadily declined. The principal cause seems to be found in the fact that the native cotton is of much shorter fibre than the imported, and consequently not nearly so well adapted for spinning purposes. The chief supply of raw and ginned cotton comes from British India, China, Dutch India, Egypt, and the United States, with small quantities from other Eastern countries. The variations in the price brought about by the action of speculators and other causes are very troublesome, and have directed attention to the necessity of improving the cultivation of cotton in

Japan. In recent years Japanese farmers have been devoting their attention to the introduction and cultivation of American upland cotton, with considerable success. The area available for this purpose is not great, and it is not improbable that the Japanese may turn their eyes to various parts of the world in order that they may have a more secure supply of the raw material for what has proved to be their most important manufacturing industry.

A full discussion of the economic conditions and the future prospects of that industry would require much more space that can at present be spared, but sufficient has been said to show the rapid progress which has been made and the important place which it has taken in the national economy.

Sericulture, or the art of rearing silk-worms, in Japan is said to date from the " Age of the Gods "; since then it has always been of importance, and has shared *The silk* in the modern developments consequent on the *industries.* introduction of Western science and appliances, and a great deal might be written about it, if space allowed. The following is a résumé of the industry in 1901 :—

Silk-worm raisers (families engaged)	.	. 2,475,819
Egg-cards (number manufactured) .	.	. 3,856,683
Cocoons (in *koku*)	.	. 2,526,181
Egg-card manufacturers (families) .	.	. 18,138
Raw Silk manufacturers (number of)	.	. 421,941
Raw Silk output (in *kin*) . .	.	. 10,972,981
Raw Silk exported (in *kin*) . .	.	. 8,697,706

Thus it will be seen that silk-producing forms one of the most important industries of Japan. Indeed, silk comes close after rice in importance as an article of domestic production, while as an article of export it has no compeer. It may even be said that silk holds the balance of Japan's foreign trade.

Under feudalism the reeling of raw silk was carried on in the domestic system as subsidiary to agriculture, and the appliances were of a somewhat elementary nature, but in 1870 the Government erected a model filature at Tomioka, Joshu, and engaged a French expert as superintendent.

Japane farmers have be:
the intrduction and cultiva:. n
, with cosiderable success. The
rpose is ot great, and it is nut
ese may irn their eyes to vari us
that theymay have a more secu::
l for wha has proved to be the:r
ring indury.
economiconditions and the future
would rjuire much more space
pared, bu sufficient has been said
ss which as been made and the
has taken the national economy
of rearin silk-worms, in Japan is
Age of tl Gods"; since then it
tance, andhas shared
ts consecent on the   industries
cience an appliances, and a great
about it, f space allowed. The
he industr in 1901 :—

s engaged	2,475,819
factured)	3,856,683
	2,526,181
families)	18,138
number of	421,941
	10,972,981
)	8,697,706

t silk-proucing forms one of the
of Japan. Indeed, silk comes close
s an articl of domestic production,
rt it has o compeer. It may even
e balance f Japan's foreign trade.
reeling of raw silk was carried
m as subdiary to agriculure, and
somewh elementar but
erected a model filature a,
French epert as sup

Since that time numerous other establishments of a similar kind have been started which have brought about a large increase in the production. The industry is not, however, by any means confined to large factories, as even those who were formerly contented with hand-reeling now took up frame-reeling, and adopted the practice of selling their product jointly by unifying its quality. According to the official returns for 1900, the output by machine-reeling was 6,193,869 *kin*, as against 4,779,575 *kin* by frame-reeling. The number of machine-reeling factories was 2072, employing 122,116 pans, and of frame-reeling establishments 597, employing 55,022 pans, the figures being in each case for factories which employ ten workers or more.

The following table gives the value of the out-Value of output of put in the principal textile industries for the textile industries. year 1900, and it is sufficient to give an idea of their relative importance :—

	Yen.
Silk, raw	86,233,957
Silk Yarn	4,296,883
Cotton Yarn	73,619,589
Silk Fabrics, etc.	166,936,604
Silk Handkerchiefs	4,318,553
Cotton Fabrics, etc.	122,652,764
Silk-cotton Fabrics	20,275,823
Hempen Fabrics	2,851,981
Woollen Fabrics	5,034,720
Various (about)	20,000,000
Allied Industries—	
Straw Plaits	2,926,127
Hats and Caps	424,321
Umbrellas (European)	2,918,085
Matting for Floor	3,039,795

The printing press has been one of the most powerful factors in the evolution of modern Japan ; for it has been the The printing means not only of spreading useful knowledge industry. but also of educating public opinion on all matters affecting the national welfare and uniting the country for purposes of education, industry, and commerce, as well as of defence. Printing is now one of the most important modern industries in Japan, the latest returns showing that there were 108 companies engaged in it, with a capital of 2,121,956 yen, and the number of newspapers, journals, and books which are printed is now very large.

The rapid growth of journalism is one of the facts that forces itself on the attention of every one observing Japan's modern career. When it is remembered that little over thirty years ago it was practically non-existent, and that now there are probably more than 1000 newspapers, magazines, etc., published in the empire, we can form an idea, not only of the extent of the printing industry but also of the influence of the press. The daily papers cost from 25 to 50 sen per month. Many of the journals are of a high standard, both as regards the quality of their matter and their tone, but others pander to tastes that are demoralising, and indulge in language which is far from creditable. In Japan, as in other countries, newspapers are made to sell, rather than to instruct and elevate. Captain Brinkley says : "Already the press occupies a very low place in the estimation of educated Japanese. They recognise its political capabilities, but regard journalism, on the whole, as a low calling. Public opinion does not help ; its restraints are practically inoperative in Japan. People uncomplainingly endure many things besides journalism." Still, after everything has been discounted, there can be little doubt that modern Japan would not have been in its present condition if it had not been for the press.

In the early days of the open ports the foreign journals which were there published were often marked by a narrow, selfish spirit, and were very unfriendly to the Japanese, although there were some honourable exceptions. Examples might be given of writing which appeared in them at very critical times in the history of Japan which in any other country would have caused the suppression of the paper and the expulsion of those responsible for it. Now, a more reasonable spirit prevails, much of the captious criticism no longer appears, and while not hesitating to criticise when that is necessary, they are sympathetic to the Japanese and appreciative of the progress which they have made.

Not only are many journals and books written and published in Japan, but many of the best books of Europe and America are translated into Japanese, and the booksellers freely import books of all kinds ; so that the Japanese have now every opportunity of making themselves acquainted with the latest developments in every department of thought and action.   Japanese engineers and scientific men are often found better informed regarding the contents of British journals than are many in this country.

The number of chemical and miscellaneous industries now carried on in Japan is very large, and the majority of them have, on the whole, been very successful. Chemical and miscellaneous industries. Among those of a chemical nature may be mentioned the manufacture of sulphuric acid, sulphate of potash, phosphate of soda, soap, matches, brewing and distilling, tanning, sugar-refining, tobacco-manufacture, glass, cement, and brick-making.   Those of a mechanical nature, in addition to what is usually included under mechanical engineering, are very numerous, including clock-making, the appliances connected with electric-lighting and motor work, telephony and telegraphy, and the numerous appliances connected with the larger industries which have been mentioned.   The manufacture of foreign clothing, boots and shoes and furniture, has now assumed considerable importance.   In short, it would be difficult to name any department of foreign manufacture in which something has not been done with more or less success, the ambition of the Japanese evidently being not only to supply their own wants but also to become a manufacturing nation like the Britain of the West, and thus not only provide for its rapidly increasing population but also claim its share in the markets of the world, especially in those of the Far East.   Meantime space will allow only the following figures from the

latest returns showing the value of the annual output of
some of the more important industries :—

	Yen.		Yen.
Sulphuric acid	559,492	Glass ware	1,493,044
Soap	794,823	Cement (Portland)	2,372,266
Matches	5,886,388	Bronze and Copper	1,106,907
Sulphate of potash	260,968	ware	
Phosphate of soda	867,910	Porcelain and	6,873,693
Paper (European)	7,001,111	Earthenware	
Paper (Japanese)	13,985,437	*Shippoki*	315,676
Leather or Hide	2,592,412	Glass ware	1,493,044

Manufactured articles used for food will be mentioned in
Chapter XI.

The changes which have taken place in every department of national life have naturally caused great developments in the building industry, as applied not The building only to engineering and industrial purposes but industry. also to public institutions, commercial houses, and domestic residences ; and as is always the case in transition periods there has been a great mixture of styles. In fact, it has been remarked that what is termed the " foreign style " of building is so named because it is foreign to all the known styles of architecture. Some of the public buildings are handsome and do credit to their designers ; some of the industrial establishments are substantial and well adapted to the purposes for which they are intended, and a few of the main streets of the larger towns have been Europeanised, with, however, a considerable number of Japanese modifications. A comparatively small number of rich men have houses in foreign style (although always with Japanese annexes), but the greater number of the buildings are still of an unsubstantial nature ; a fact which is explained partly by the frequency of earthquakes and partly by the want of means to erect them in a more substantial manner.

The following list of Government factories gives a convenient résumé of the most important Government manufacturing establishments directly under factories. the Government :—

Names of Factories.	Locality.	Kinds of Enterprises.	No. of Engines used.
Woollen-cloth Manufactory at Senju	Senju, Tokyo	Manufacture of Woollen Clothes and Hats used for Military Purposes	Steam 8
Yokosuka Naval Arsenal	Yokosuka, Kanagawa Prefecture	Construction and Repairs of War Vessels	,, 27
Sasebo Naval Dockyard	Sasebo, Nagasaki Prefecture	Manufacture of Hulls and of Steam Engines and Boilers for Ships' Use	,, 7
Kuré ,,	Kuré, Hiroshima Prefecture	Torpedo-tubes, Steam Engines and Boilers, Puddled Steel and Iron, Iron Wares hammered and cast, and Drawings	,, 17
Factory for the Manufacture of Articles needed for Telegraph and Lighthouse Services, at Tokyo	In the Enclosure of the Department of Communications	Telegraphs and Telephones	,, 2
Do. at Yokohama	Yokohama	Articles needed for Lighthouse Services	{ Steam 2 / Water ? / Electric ? }
Tokyo Military Arsenal	Tokyo	Cannon Accessories, Muskets and Bullets	Steam 17
Osaka ,,	Osaka	Cannons and other Ammunitions	,, 16
Mint Bureau	,,	Coins and Medals	,, 2
Yokosuka Naval Arms Factory	Urazato, Miura District, Kanagawa Ken	Arms	,, 4
Sasebo ,, ,,	Sasebo, Higashi Sonoki District, Nagasaki Prefecture	Do.	,, 2
Moji Military Arms Factory	Moji	Do.	,, 31
Kuré Naval Arsenal	Kuré, Hiroshima Prefecture	Arms and Ammunitions	,, 4
Shimbashi Factory, belonging to the Government Railway Works Bureau	Tokyo	Manufacture and Repair of Carriages, Machines and Tools needed for Railway Services	

			Motive Power	Number
Kobe Factory, belonging to the Government Railway Works Bureau	Kobe	Do.	Steam	6
Nagano Factory, belonging to the Government Railway Works Bureau	Serida, Kami Mizuuchi District, Nagano Prefecture	Do.	"	1
Itabashi Gunpowder Factory, belonging to the Tokyo Military Arsenal	Itabashi, Tokyo		Steam / Water / Electric	? ? ?
Meguro Gunpowder Factory, belonging to the Tokyo Military Arsenal	Meguro, Yebara District, Tokyo	Do.		?
Iwahana Gunpowder Factory, belonging to the Tokyo Military Arsenal	Iwahana, Gumma District, Gumma Prefecture	Do.	?	
Uji Gunpowder Factory, belonging to the Osaka Military Arsenal	Uji, Uji District, Kyoto	Do.	Steam	3
Osaka Animal Lymph Manufactory	Tokyo, Osaka	Animal Lymph, Do.		
Paper Factory, belonging to the Government Printing Office	Oji, Kita Toshima District, Tokyo	Public Loan Bonds, Convertible Bank Notes, Paying Orders, Postage Stamps, Various Stamps and Bills	Steam	10
Central Military Food Manufactory	Tokyo	C and Beef	"	1
Printing Office, belonging to Drawing Section in Military Survey	In the Enclosure of the General Staff, Tokyo	Maps	Lithographic	1
Printing Department of the Government Printing Office	Tokyo	Postage Stamps and Cards, Revenue Stamps, etc.	Steam	3
Typographical Printing Department of the Government Printing	"	Official Gazette, Statutes and Red-books	"	2
Total			Steam	165

Instead of going into further details of special departments of industry, it will be sufficient for our present purpose Manufacturing if we take a general view of the manufacturing establishments. establishments in Japan. Appended is a table showing the number of workshops (employing not less than ten workpeople) and of manufacturing companies :—

Year.	No. of Workshops.		Total.	No. of Companies.
	With Motor.	Without Motor.		
1899	2763	3788	6551	2253
1898	2003	4067	6070	2164
1897	1971	4346	6317	1181
1896	1967	4403	6370	1367

The falling off in the number of establishments without motors in 1899 as compared with the preceding year was because the workshops engaged in mining were withdrawn from the total, and no doubt also that many which were without motors supplied themselves with them. The following table shows the number of manufacturing companies, their aggregate amount of capital, the amount paid up, and the reserves :—

Year.	No.	Aggregate Capital.	Paid-up Capital.	Reserves.
		Yen.	Yen.	Yen.
1900	2554	216,766,903	158,851,730	17,697,540
1899	2253	222,673,634	147,783,280	13,467,802
1898	2164	183,657,046	122,066,653	11,642,993
1897	1881	165,232,633	105,381,106	7,581,535
1890	1367	143,617,530	89,900,900	7,404,980

Those figures show a very rapid rate of increase.

The workshops may be broadly analysed into the following kinds :—

    I. Fibre workshops (raw silk, spinning, weaving, cord-making).

2. Machine shops (machine - making, shipbuilding, furniture-making, casting).
3. Chemical workshops (ceramics, gas, paper mills, lacquering, leather - making, explosives, drugs, manures, etc.).
4. Miscellaneous workshops (brewing, sugar - refining, tobacco manufacture, tea - curing, cleaning of grains, flour mills, lemonade, mineral water, confectionery, preserved fruits and vegetables, printing and lithography, paper-work, wood and bamboo ware, feather ware, reeds and straw plait ware, lacquer ware, etc.).
5. Special workshops (electricity and metallurgy).

The following are the figures relating to each of these classes :—

A. Run by Motors :—

	Workshops.	Horse Power.	Workpeople.
Fibre	1921	32,094	196,723
Machine	208	4,274	18,412
Chemical	190	8,349	12,966
Miscellaneous	348	5,220	18,425
Special	36	12,194	33,766
Total	2763	62,131	288,292

B. Not run by Motors :—

	Workshops.	Workpeople.
Fibre	1803	50,394
Machine	157	4,205
Chemical	650	25,625
Miscellaneous	1065	27,391
Special	113	5,002
Total	3788	112,617

The ordinary working-hours of operatives are 12 hours

per day, but sometimes they extend as long as 16 or 17 hours. In cotton mills 12 hours are the standard, for Working-hours, both day and night workers, in filatures the wages, etc. regular hours are 13 to 14, and in power-loom factories 12. In hand-weaving workshops a great diversity prevails, the general rule being 12 to 15, according to the season, though in some rare cases the hours are as long as from 16 to 17. In the larger establishments, such as ship-building yards, vehicle and machine shops, the working hours are far more regular, being in general 10 hours, occasionally with one or two hours of overtime.

Wages are usually paid by the day, although payment by the month also prevails to some extent. Usually the amounts are settled once or twice a month, though in some cases they are settled every six months or once a year. In filatures, payment is made according to the amount of work done and by the month, though in some cases a yearly account system prevails. In cotton mills those who receive daily wages constitute about 40 per cent of the whole, and those who are paid by piece-work about 60 per cent. In such establishments as shipbuilding yards and machine and other similar shops day's-wages are usual, although at times a piece of work is given out on contract to one or more artisans. In match workshops the payment is by piecework, and in general this method of payment is becoming common where the amount of work done can be definitely computed.

The rate of wages for adult males employed in cotton mills and weaving-shops is about 30 sen per day, while that of females is about 20 sen. In shipbuilding yards and machine shops the rate is usually about 50 or 60 sen per day, but skilled artisans are paid more than one yen. In match factories the rate is only from 12 to 20 sen for ordinary female operatives, and from 5 to 13 sen for little girls. In tobacco factories and printing shops, ordinary females get about 20 sen, and males from 40 to 50 sen. The following table gives the average wages of workers in the years 1887, 1897, and 1901 :—

Kind of Labourers.	1887.	1897.	1901.
	Yen.	Yen.	Yen.
Carpenter	0.224	0.434	0.593
Plasterer	0.225	0.436	0.590
Stone Mason	0.250	0.474	0.670
Sawyer	0.205	0.430	0.580
Shingle Roof Thatcher . .	0.205	0.420	0.540
Tile Roof Thatcher . . .	0.243	0.469	0.640
Brick Maker	?	0.483	0.440
Mat Maker . , . .	0.218	0.387	0.513
Maker of Doors, Screens, etc. .	0.211	0.396	0.560
Paper-hanger	0.215	0.380	0.535
Joiner	0.209	0.388	0.553
Wooden Clog Maker . . .	?	0.318	0.420
Shoemaker	?	0.384	0.505
Carriage-builder . . .	?	0.352	0.498
Tailor (Japanese Clothes) .	0.189	0.305	0.453
Do. (Foreign Clothes) . .	0.399	0.461	0.620
Dyer	0.173	0.287	0.305
Blacksmith	0.217	0.394	0.488
Lacquerer	0.205	0.362	0.503
Tobacco-cutter	0.171	0.353	0.473
Compositor	0.223	0.287	0.395
Gardener	?	0.404	0.568
Male Weaver	0.127	0.225	0.293
Female Weaver . . .	0.074	0.150	0.193
Day Labourer	0.160	0.290	0.399

These figures show a rapid rate of increase and indicate the tendency for wages of the same class to approximate to the same amounts in all industrial countries, and as industrialism in all its aspects becomes more and more international this tendency will become more pronounced. Moreover, it must be remembered that the rate of wages is not by any means an accurate index of the cost of production. High wages are, as a rule, economical, as they indicate a high state of intelligence and therefore of efficiency on the part of the workers ; a fact which ought to be kept in mind when the fear is expressed of undue competition of Eastern countries in the markets of the world.

The general arrangements for education have been described in Chapter V. Every part of it has had a more or less direct effect on the industrial development which has taken place in the country. In recent years especially, great attention has been paid to those

Industrial training.

subjects bearing directly on industrial occupations, and the colleges in the Imperial Universities and the higher technical schools have trained many of the men who are now in charge of the most important undertakings.

As, however, already stated, with the object of still further diffusing technical knowledge and imparting a general idea of science to apprentices and young mechanics, the Government has made liberal grants to special technical schools in different parts of the country, and these efforts have been supplemented by local authorities and private individuals. Attached to a considerable number of the primary schools, for the benefit of those who cannot attend school in the daytime, are commercial and supplementary schools somewhat similar to the continuation classes in this country, and they are beginning to occupy an important place in the educational system in Japan.

All these arrangements have caused the apprentice system which formerly prevailed almost to disappear. It retains any semblance to its former status only in such departments as hand-loom weaving, pottery, and dyeing. In some of the larger factories and in the engineering establishments and shipbuilding yards the foremen take a number of the boys under their special supervision for the purpose of instructing them in the methods and details of their trades. In Japan, as in other parts of the world, however, the system of division of labour, especially in the mechanical industries, is rapidly causing the old, all-round system of training formerly given to apprentices to be superseded by a course of training in a technical school, supplemented by such practical experience as can be picked up in the factory or workshops. The want of more thorough training in the practical side of the work, however, places the young men, for a considerable time, at a disadvantage. A due combination of theoretical and practical training is one of the problems which have still to be solved for those who are intended for industrial occupations.

In addition to what are usually considered educational

institutions, there has grown up in Japan a considerable number of scientific associations which have had great effect on the progress of industry. The first of them was the Institution or Society of Engineers, which I inaugurated when the first set of graduates left the Imperial College of Engineering. I drafted the regulations somewhat on the lines of the British Institution of Civil Engineers, and the Institution of Engineers and Shipbuilders of Scotland, making, however, modifications and improvements where I considered them necessary. My friend Viscount Yamao became the first President,—I am glad to say that he still occupies that position,—and in the interval he has rendered great service not only to engineering but also to industry generally. Although Viscount Yamao's name will not figure to any great extent in political history, he deserves to be remembered as one of the men who did good service to Japan in a quiet, unobtrusive manner, and also as a good friend of all who were working for the progress of the country.

Technical associations.

I arranged for the Engineering Society to have sections representing the various departments of the Imperial College of Engineering, and it still includes engineers of all types; but in Japan, as in Britain, the tendency has been to start societies for special departments, and there are now Mechanical Engineering, Electrical Engineering, Chemical Engineering, and Shipbuilding Societies, all in a flourishing condition and each publishing valuable transactions. There are, in addition, a considerable number of societies, each devoted to a special department of industry, and all performing very useful functions, not only in collecting and distributing information with respect to their special interests, but also in cementing the bonds of friendship between those engaged in them.

After the Restoration the Japanese were not slow in recognising the necessity for encouraging invention and originality in design. In 1871 a measure was passed for protecting inventions,

Patents, trade marks, etc., inventions.

but the difficulty of carrying it out was so great that it was rescinded in the following year, and for about fourteen years from that time Japanese inventors were left unprotected, although encouragement in various ways was given to them. In 1884 the regulations protecting trade marks were enacted, and in the following year those relating to the protection of patents.

According to the existing system all matters relating to patents, designs, and trade marks are controlled by the Patent Bureau of the Department of Agriculture and Commerce, which adopts the regular system of examination before granting a licence, and patent agents are subject to the control of the Patent Bureau. The number of agents duly registered at the end of the year 1902 was 193. Up till that date 24,412 applications for licences had been made, and of these 5500 had been granted for patents, while for designs there had been 4694 applications and 1277 granted, and trade marks 28,925 and 18,200 granted.

Reference must be made to special publications for details of the regulations, which on the whole follow more closely those of America than those of Britain. When a foreigner, not residing in Japan, wishes to secure a letter patent or to have his design or trade mark registered, he must file an application through his attorney appointed from among those in Japan, and must further appoint, when his application has been accepted by the Patent Bureau, an attorney to represent him in all dealings with the Bureau and in all possible civil or criminal actions. The neglect to appoint such an attorney without justifiable reason within six months will invalidate the efficacy of his patents or registration. A patent must be worked within three years from the time the licence is granted, and if this is not done or if the patentee refuses without justifiable reason to assign or permit the use of the patent under reasonable conditions by a third party who has applied to him for such assignment or permission, the patent is liable to be revoked.

The figures which have been given are sufficient to

disprove the statement that the Japanese have no original ability. In mechanical engineering all over the world the designs of almost all the principal machines are essentially the same, the variations being in details to suit special conditions, and in this respect Japanese engineers have not shown themselves deficient. Not only have they modified Western designs to suit the conditions in Japan, but they have in many respects shown decided originality.

It would take up too much space to enter into details of this subject in the various departments of engineering, but what the Japanese have done in connection with appliances for military and naval purposes is sufficient to prove their ingenuity. The ships of their navy are probably the best illustration of the Japanese method of procedure. In naval matters they accepted all the guidance the Western world could give them, but at the same time they struck out a line of their own, and the fleet which they have created is unique in the character of its units. British designs have, in many respects, been improved upon, with the result that they have obtained in their latest ships many features which have won the admiration of the world. Among the inventions which have added materially and conspicuously to the fighting efficiency of the navy may be instanced the gun-rack of Rear-Admiral Yamanouchi, the water-tube boiler of Engineer-Admiral Miyabara, the smokeless powder of Dr. Shimose, the percussion cap of Vice-Admiral Ijuin, the floating mine of Commander Oda and Captain Taneda, and several others which might be mentioned ; all of great practical utility in real warfare, and the use of which may revolutionise the methods of war in the future. In the army the Japanese have shown themselves masters of tactics, not merely copying Western methods but introducing many of their own. The Murata rifle was an improvement on those of Europe, but that has been displaced by a still better weapon of Japanese invention, the Arisaka rifle. Not only in the arts of peace but also in those of war have the Japanese shown that they are

able to think and act for themselves.   The discoveries of
Dr. Jokichi Takamine in the department of chemistry, and
of Dr. Kitazato in that of bacteriology, and of many others
who might be named in other fields of investigations,
prove that the Japanese are able not only to apply existing
knowledge but also to extend its boundaries.   I am proud
to add that Dr. Takamine and Dr. Shimose are graduates
of the Kobu Daigakko.   Dr. Kitazato is a graduate of the
Medical College.

In a recent letter which I had from Professor C. D.
West, of the Engineering College of Tokyo University, he
says : " I suppose it is necessary to say something with
regard to the inventive power of the Japanese ; this is a
much vexed subject.   Some people assert that they have no
inventive power at all, but I don't think this is so.   It must
be remembered that the power of making absolutely new and
original designs is confined to very few people indeed ;
' Inventor nascitur, non fit,' like the poet.   Almost any one
with good abilities can be trained to design, and this the
Japanese certainly can do ; but between inventing, pure and
simple, and designing, there is no hard-and-fast line ; there
is room for all intermediate grades of inventive capacity.

" It is to this intermediate capacity of designers that
almost all our machines are due, even the most complicated,
by a process of gradual improvement and development.   I
see no point in this designing process at which the Japanese
must necessarily stop short, and I know of several things
they have produced that must come under the head of
inventive designing."   If we remember the conditions which
existed in old Japan, when originality of all kinds was
severely repressed, and consider what the Japanese have
already done, we must admit that they have all the qualities
which are necessary for the success of a great industrial
nation.

As a means of encouraging the progress of industry and
manufactures, the Japanese Government has, at various
times, caused exhibitions to be organised at home, and

has also taken part in those opened abroad. The first Domestic Exhibition was held in Tokyo in 1878, and I arranged a machinery department in which were shown some of the machines and appliances Industrial exhibitions. made at Akabane (the works which were connected with the Engineering College), as well as a few from private establishments; but at that time comparatively small progress had been made in mechanical engineering. Two similar exhibitions were held in Tokyo later on, which showed considerable developments in Western arts. The fourth exhibition was held in Kyoto in 1895, and the fifth in Osaka in 1903. This last was the most complete illustration of the progress which had been made in Japan in Western arts and manufactures, and attracted a considerable number of visitors from all parts of the world. It was international to a certain extent. Of course very large exhibits were not to be expected from Europe and America, but many of the foreign manufacturers who are in the habit of sending goods to Japan exhibited specimens. The following, from a report which was published at the time of the exhibition, not only gives a good idea of its contents, but also serves as a résumé of the developments which have been made :—

" Considering that only thirty years ago Japan had no such institution as a factory, and knew nothing whatever of iron foundries or machine shops, the Japanese-made machinery display at the exhibition at Osaka is astonishing. There we find silk-weaving and mat-making machines, electrical motors and generators, gas and oil engines, locomotives, electrical fittings, tools, beltings, match-making machine, fire-brigade appliances, rice-cleaning machines, huge steam navvy, oil tanks, soap-making machines, printing machines, massive hoisting engine, tea - refining machinery, heavy mining machinery, and many other smaller machines ; all of Japanese manufacture, admirably made and well adapted to the purposes designed.

" In general manufactures the empire makes a good

showing in certain lines. Straw braid in all conceivable styles and uses ; *shibori*, a beautiful dyed stuff, making pretty dress material ; woollen serges and woven silks, cheap and good cotton blankets, Japanese towels, artistic designs in tiles and roofing materials, drain-pipes, fire-proof bricks. In drinkables, also of home manufacture, there is beer by the cart-load, *saké*, the famous native drink, enough to quench the thirst of an army.

" One of the best exhibits is in clocks, some of them very handsome and very cheap, made by one or other of the twelve Japanese clock companies. The porcelain exhibition is good, consisting of beautiful vases, artistic porcelain trays, basins, tea-cups, etc. The exhibit of Japanese-made shoes is quite creditable. Other native manufactures exhibited are bamboo furniture, whatnots, overmantels, fire-screens, shell buttons, paper lanterns, fine silken rugs, shawls, paper, camphor, oils, soap, all kinds of sauces and relishes, silks of every hue and description, silk lace, gold and silver thread, linen, duck, tent cloths, ivory work, hinges, lacquer and silver work, surgical instruments, pianos, organs, and other musical instruments, bicycles, gymnastic and athletic goods, microscopes, cameras, barometers and almost every kind of educational apparatus.

" The natural products of the country are exhibited to good advantage. Rice, tobacco (manufactured and raw), silk-worms, various varieties of silk cocoons, tea, huge oranges, sugar, furs, woods, pearls, coral, fish (dried and salted). Mushrooms are a special exhibit of one prefecture, tea of another, and so on. The whole section of the agricultural experiment station is complete and admirable in every way."[1] Besides the national exhibitions, Japan has also participated in the World's Fairs held in Vienna, Philadelphia, Chicago, Paris, St. Louis, not to speak of various other exhibitions of limited scope.

All matters relating to manufactures are under the control of the Bureau of Commerce and Manufactures,

[1] From *Japan and America*, by Walter J. Ballard.

and are in direct charge of the Section of Manufactures, which forms part of the Bureau. The Section in question deals with matters relating to experiments made with the view of improving manufactures and manufactured goods, the position and construction of workshops, the control of boilers, the employment and engagement of operatives and apprentices, together with their relief, education, etc. In consequence of the rapid development of the factory system and of the problems arising therefrom, a temporary Factory Committee was created in the Section of Manufactures for the purpose of inquiring into matters concerning factories and operatives. Various draft measures have been put forward for factory regulations, but as yet none of any importance has been passed into law. The first legislative measure enacted bearing directly on manufactures was that issued by the Department of Agriculture and Commerce in 1884, relating to the formation of guilds, the object of which was to encourage different interests to form themselves into guilds and to provide against the provision of shoddy goods. The regulations relating to these guilds have been improved and extended from time to time. The provisions regarding trade marks and patents for inventions have already been noticed. In February 1901 rules were issued relating to the establishment of local and commercial industrial experimental laboratories, or manufacturing training schools; the object of the enactment being to encourage the improvement and progress of manufacture. It was arranged about the same time that matters relating to the control of boilers, factories, and operatives be left in charge of the respective local offices.

Not only has the formation of limited liability companies for commercial and industrial purposes been largely developed in Japan, but the practice which is now so common in other industrial countries for the combination of groups of companies and individuals having common interests in any given branch of manufacture or industry is now a feature in the organisation

Industrial legislation.

Combinations of employers and workers.

of the country.   The first step in this direction in connection
with Western industries was the formation in 1882 of the
spinners' union, which exists to-day in a somewhat modified
form.   It undertakes all matters which are supposed to
further the common interests of the members ; it despatches,
for instance, merchants or experts to Bombay to inspect the
condition of the cotton market or of the cotton crop, and
enters into contracts with the Nippon Yusen Kaisha (the
Japan Shipping Company) for the import of raw cotton from
Bombay.   Agreements are also made as to the rates of
wages and the general conditions of work in connection with
the industry, so that there may be no unfair competition
between the members.   Almost every industry of any
importance has some form of combination or guild for the
protection of its interests, and the latest returns show that
there were nearly 200 such guilds in existence, which seem
to have in them the germ of what may lead to an organised
system of industry, the evolution of which will be watched
with interest.

Meantime the workers are also beginning to organise for
the protection of their interests ; for they have not been long
in finding that when all the organisation is on the one side,
the other is certain to be subjected to unfair conditions.
Under the feudal system, as already mentioned, guilds
existed in the various trades, and these have now been
transformed into something like Western trade unions.
Strikes are by no means uncommon, and many of the labour
problems of Europe and America are now to be found in
Japan.   The labour unions on Western lines include the iron-
workers, the ship carpenters, the railway engineers, the railway
workmen, the printers, and the European-style cooks, and
some of these organisations have become so strong that they
have in some disputes been able to dictate their own terms.
The supply of workmen trained in foreign style being still
rather limited, it can easily be seen that the labour
organisations have a great advantage in Japan.   Their
members, however, are beginning to look beyond mere trade-

union efforts and to think of the possibilities of a system of co-operation which would make strikes impossible. Co-operative stores are to be found in various parts of Japan, while whose who study the problems involved recognise the possibilities of co-operation, both in production and distribution. The progress of the labour movement in Japan is largely due to the efforts of a young man, Mr. Katayama Sen, who has spent ten years in America and made a special study of social problems. He is the head of Kingsley Hall, a social settlement in Tokyo, similar to the settlements now somewhat common in this country, and which are the centres of varied social activities and investigations. He is also the editor of the *Labour World*, which is looked upon as the special organ of the working classes, and which should be studied by those who are interested in social problems in the Far East. These problems are part of the price Japan has paid for her use of Western methods, and it will be interesting to watch the attempts which are made at their solution.

While it is admitted that the progress made by the Japanese in many departments of industry has been remarkable, and that their aptitude for Western manu- Foreign factures is very great, even their greatest admirers advisers. think that in many cases they have paid too dearly for their experience by dispensing with their foreign advisers and assistants before they were able to replace them by fully qualified natives. While a love of independence is to be admired, it should be remembered that it involves neither personal nor national loss of honour to employ foreigners who have had special experience in any new development of industry, and if the right men be selected, they will be worth their salaries many times over. Captain Brinkley, who cannot be suspected of being unfriendly to the Japanese, says : "A visit to Japanese factories often shows machinery treated carelessly, employés so numerous that they impede rather than expedite business, and a general lack of the precision, regularity and earnestness that characterise successful industrial enterprises in Europe and America. Achievement in one direction and comparative failure in another, although the factors making for success are similar in each, indicate, not incapacity in the latter case, but defects of standard and experience. The vast majority of the Japanese have no adequate conception of what is meant by a highly-organised industrial or commercial enterprise. They have never made the practical acquaintance of anything of the kind, nor even breathed a pure business atmosphere." He emphasises his criticism by referring to the railways and the posts. He says: "The Japanese have long been able to survey, plan and build their own lines of railways, to run the trains and to manage the traffic. For these achievements they deserve much credit. But their arrangements for handling, forwarding and delivering goods are very defective, when judged by good Occidental standards, and their provision for the comfort of passengers leaves a great deal to be desired. So, too, their postal service invites criticism in some very important respects, if it merits praise in others. All such defects would soon be corrected if free recourse were had to the assistance of foreign experts, who have the advantage of familiarity with higher standards. It is unfortunate that a people so liberal in their adoption of the best products of Western civilisation should hesitate to avail themselves of the best means of learning to utilise them."

Surprise may be expressed at this state of affairs after we have seen the high state of efficiency and organisation in the army and navy, but, as Captain Brinkley points out, for elaborating their military and naval systems they have had access to foreign models, every detail of which could be carefully scrutinised, and they availed themselves freely of the assistance of foreign experts—French, German, and British ; but in the field of manufacture and trade their inspection of foreign models is necessarily superficial, and they are without the co-operation of foreign experts. He thinks that the Japanese attitude in these matters is to be explained by two considerations—one legal, the other sentimental.

The treaties forbade foreigners to hold real estate or engage
in business outside the limits of the settlements ; thus rendering it impossible for them either to start factories on their
own account or to enter into partnership with native
manufacturers ; and an almost morbid anxiety to prove their
independent competence impelled the Japanese to dispense
prematurely with the services of foreign employés. The
unsympathetic treatment which Japan received from Western
Powers in the matter of treaty revision prejudiced her against
foreigners in all capacities, and the opportunity was lost of
co-operating with Japanese in matters of industry. Captain
Brinkley believes that there is clear evidence that this sus-
picious mood on the part of Japan, which is so injurious to
her own interests, is being replaced by more liberal sentiments,
but in the meantime she has been induced to stand aloof
from alien aids at a time when they might have profited her
immensely, and to struggle without guidance towards
standards of which she has as yet only a dim perception.

As the status of foreigners under Japanese law, especially
in matters affecting industry, is a subject of growing practical
importance, the following extracts from Status of foreigners
an address delivered by Dr. Masujima under Japanese
before the New York State Bar Association industrial laws.
in January 1903 will be read with interest, as they touch
on the most important points :—" The cases in which
foreigners are restricted in the enjoyment of private rights
are the ownership of land and Japanese ships, the right to
work mines, to own shares in the Bank of Japan or the
Yokohama Specie Bank, to be members or brokers of
exchanges, to engage in emigration business, or to receive
bounties for navigation or shipbuilding. Any company
must, in order to own Japanese ships, have its principal office
in Japan, and all its members in case of a *Gomei Kaisha*,
all unlimited liability members in case of either a *Goshi
Kaisha* or *Kabushiki Goshi Kaisha*, and all directors in case
of a limited company, must be Japanese subjects. Otherwise
foreigners are as free as Japanese to own shares in any

Japanese commercial companies organised by themselves alone, or in combination with the Japanese, or to engage in any manufacture or other commercial operations.

"Foreigners may hold a long lease of land to plant trees or erect permanent structures, which may be arranged for an indefinite term almost perpetual, such as one thousand years, or as long as may be agreed upon. Such a holding is called 'superficies,' and it is very much like a long English lease, the only difference being that trees or buildings do not at the end of the term revert to the landlord, his right being only that of pre-emption at current valuation. The most advisable way for the enjoyment of the actual and permanent holding of land is for a foreigner to buy land himself through a Japanese, as bare trustee, and to secure its superficies for the period of as long a term as may be desirable for his purposes."

"Although no foreigners may work mines individually, they may be taken on mortgage, and a company registered as a Japanese organisation is entitled to engage in mining; the theory is that foreigners as members may merge themselves in the entity of a Japanese corporation, although it may be composed of foreigners exclusively."

"No railway or tramway business is allowed to be carried on unless by a limited company, and a concession for such purpose has to be secured from the proper authorities. No such railway can be pledged, but it may be hypothecated. Japanese pledge corresponds to English mortgage, differing therefrom, in that immediate transfer of possession and holding the pledged property absolutely is essential. Hypothecation does not carry possession or the right of entry. This condition of Japanese railway law has not satisfied capitalists as not affording sufficient security to induce investment by them. There has been some attempt to have this law altered, but it has not yet been accomplished."

"Banking, insurance, shipping and all other kinds of commercial business may be carried on in Japan by foreign companies by observing the treaties and certain regulations, such as the registration of their branch offices, their representatives, or other matters prescribed by law."

" There are two kinds of civil corporations, the one consisting of persons associated together and the other an estate of aggregate property somewhat like a trust in English law, formed or established for the purpose of religious worship, teaching, art, charity, education, or any other object of public benefit, not aiming at the making of a profit. Such a corporation can come into existence only with the permission of the competent authorities, while Japanese commercial corporations may be formed without it. No foreign association of persons or trust property is accorded the same rights and privileges as are enjoyed by similar Japanese corporations ; such a foreign corporation has no standing whatsoever in the Japanese courts, and the only way in which it could obtain protection would be to appear in the individual names of its members, just as used once to be the case in partnership actions."

" If foreigners wish to do business in combination with the Japanese, the best way would be to form a *Goshi Kaisha*, or limited partnership, they themselves carrying unlimited liability. To control a *Kabushiki Kaisha*, or limited company, they should own more than half the amount of capital, either by holding themselves or through their nominees, and shares should be tied up so as not to allow their transfer without the consent of the board of directors. The advantage of any business being organised as a Japanese corporation consists, as the law now stands, in owning land and having the full rights of Japanese subjects."

The question of the employment of foreign capital in Japanese industrial enterprises is one which is at present receiving considerable attention. The Japanese have sunk a great part of their floating capital in engineering and industrial enterprises, and as a natural consequence they find themselves in want, not only of working capital, but also of what is required for further natural developments, and various proposals have been made for the purpose of inducing foreign capitalists to invest in Japanese undertakings. Some have done so, but as yet the number is limited.

The introduction of foreign capital into Japan is a matter which requires very careful consideration. Capitalist domination is becoming one of the features in every industrial community in the world, and in many respects it leads to conditions which are worse than those of the feudal system from which Japan has freed herself Herbert Spencer in a letter to a Japanese correspondent, written some years before his death, was very emphatic on this subject, and said : " There should be not only a prohibition of foreign persons to hold property in land, but also a refusal to give them leases, and a permission only to reside as annual tenants. I should say decidedly prohibit to foreigners the working of the mines owned or worked by Government. Here there would be obviously liable to arise grounds of difference between the Europeans or Americans who worked them and the Government, and these grounds of quarrel would be followed by invocations to the English or American Governments or other Powers to send forces to insist on whatever the European workers claimed, 'for always the habit here and elsewhere among the civilised peoples is to believe what their agents or sellers abroad represent to them.' In the third place, in pursuance of the policy I have indicated, you ought also to keep the coasting trade in your own hands, and forbid foreigners to engage in it. The distribution of commodities brought to Japan from other places may be properly left to the Japanese themselves, and should be denied to foreigners, for the reason that again the various transactions involved would become so many doors open to quarrels and resulting aggressions." The policy indicated in these lines is, in my opinion, too drastic, as I believe that it is quite possible to find many opportunities for the investment of foreign capital which would not only be advantageous to Japan but also offer safe and sufficient returns to the capitalists. Whatever opinions we may hold as to the future relations of capital and labour, the present time is one of transition, and no sudden change can be made in the methods adopted. The welfare of the people, not the returns to the capitalists, should be the chief object kept in view, and as the social spirit develops we may expect many radical changes in the methods of owning property of all kinds. Municipal and State ownership and control are rapidly extending, and it will be very interesting to note how the Japanese face the problems which are now engaging the attention of thoughtful men in all countries of the world. Before any criticism is offered of their action, we ought to put ourselves in their place and consider how we would act under the same conditions. They are likely to take to heart not only the lessons to be learnt from social and economic conditions in Western countries, but also those from their own past history. A return recently published by the *Nichi Nichi Shimbun* gives the following figures as the amounts invested by foreigners in undertakings established and conducted by themselves in Japan :—

	Capital.	Amount paid up.
	Yen.	Yen.
Breweries	600,000	450,000
Machine Companies . .	2,290,000	229,000
Kerosene	24,000,000	16,500,000
Raw Silk	1,850,000	1,850,000
Carrying Companies (land and sea) . . .	132,340,000	130,400,000
Miscellaneous . . .	2,401,000	2,401,000
Agencies (commission). .	50,000	50,000
Purveyors	1,500,000	1,300,000
Banks	23,750,000	23,750,000
Commercial companies .	17,245,000	17,245,000
Insurance	5,000,000	3,750,000
Newspaper and printing .	227,000	227,000
Wholesale dealers . .	780,000	780,000

In addition to these sums foreign capitalists and even small investors have considerable amounts in Japanese undertakings and stocks of various kinds.

The facts and figures given in the preceding pages show the great progress which has been made in Japan in industry during a comparatively short time, but it is evident that past developments are far from satisfying the ambition of the Japanese. A short time ago one of the leading journals, the *Jiji Shimpo*, which takes a great interest in industrial and economic subjects, had an article of which the following is a translation of the more important parts :—"The talk about Japan having become a commercial and industrial country has in recent years been on everybody's lips. In reference to the question of what is the best economic policy for us to follow in future, with the exception of that small section of the community engaged in agriculture, everybody recognises the necessity of our making commerce and industry the foundation of the country's wealth. It would seem at first sight as though as a country we were very favourably situated for pursuing this policy. But the question is, how far have we actually followed it ? Though various differences appear in countries owing to their adoption of diverse economic systems, there are three unmistakable signs of commercial and industrial countries ; which are (1) that the raw produce imported from foreign countries should be utilised for manufacturing purposes ; (2) that imported food should go to support the people of the home country ; and (3) that the interest of the money sent abroad and the profits derived from general business should be received in the form of imports, which should always be in excess of exports. We observe by the British Trade Report for 1901 that the value of food, liquor, raw produce, and manufactured articles imported and exported by England was as below :—

Marginal note: Japanese ambition regarding the future of commerce and industry.

IMPORTS.

(1) Articles of food and liquors	£224,763,000
(2) Raw produce	137,355,000
(3) Manufactured articles	93,609,000
(4) Other miscellaneous articles . . .	66,511,000
	£522,238,000

EXPORTS.

(1) Articles of food and liquors	£15,626,000
(2) Raw produce	33,777,000
(3) Manufactured articles	207,966,000
(4) Other miscellaneous articles. . . .	20,976,000
	£348,345,000

PERCENTAGE OF THE EXPORTS AS COMPARED TO THE IMPORTS.

(1) Articles of food and liquors	6.9
(2) Raw produce	25.0
(3) Manufactured articles	222·0

We see then that the proportion of food-stuffs, liquors, and raw produce imported by England corresponds to over three-fifths of the total value of her imports ; and that, on the other hand, the proportion of manufactured articles exported has reached two-thirds of the total value of her exports. It appears that in the case of food-stuffs and liquors the total value of the imports is about fifteen times that of the exports. It is quite natural that when a country is manifesting signs of making commerce and industry, instead of agriculture, its economic foundation, its imports and exports should take this course.

"When we come to inquire how our country stands to-day in reference to the above-named points, though our tables, being very incomplete and failing to distinguish between raw material and manufactured articles, do not allow of accurate comparison with the English tables, they suffice to give a general idea of our economic situation. According to last year's (1901) returns the total value of exports was 252,349,000 yen ; and the total value of imports, 214,929,000 yen. Out of this the value of food exported was 28,125,000 yen, and that imported 7,502,000 yen ; that is, food bore the proportion of 11.1 of the total exports and 3.5 of the total imports. This one thing of itself is enough to make it clear that Japan has not yet given up the economic principle of supporting herself on agricultural products. But, moreover, when we come to consider a variety of other articles of commerce this becomes still plainer. The total value of the exports of our four principal commodities, namely, refined copper, raw silk, woven silk, and coal, is put down at 100,270,000 yen ; that is, they constitute about one-half of the total exports of the country. On the other hand, as to the import trade, with the exception of ginned cotton, valued at 50,000,000 yen, it would seem that the imported articles consist mostly of railway locomotives, iron, steel, things made of iron, and kerosene ; which means that we still are in the condition of a country which exports raw produce and imports manufactured articles ; that is, that our position is the exact opposite of that of England, which may be regarded as a model type of a commercial and industrial country. Though our circumstances bring us into connection with those products which form the basis of commerce and industry, despite the fact that the necessity of our becoming a commercial and industrial country is pressed home upon us by so many writers and speakers, we cannot but acknowledge that the real truth is that we are still a very long way from attaining to that position." It is to be hoped that in the best interests of Japan she will not attempt to follow the analogy of the Britain of the West too closely, and that above all she will ponder "whether, among national manufactures, that of Souls of good quality may not at last turn out a quite leadingly lucrative one." Modern conditions in Western countries do not seem favourable either for the production of souls of good quality or for the attainment of physical and intellectual excellence. The economic conditions at the beginning of the twentieth century are very different from those which existed at the beginning of the nineteenth, when Britain began her industrial career, and the social and economic problems with which Western countries are confronted should cause Japan to recognise that the inordinate pursuit of merely material ends will not lead to the highest national welfare.

BIBLIOGRAPHICAL NOTE

The literature on the subject of purely Japanese industries is very extensive, but Professor Rein's book on the *Industries of Japan* will be found sufficient for ordinary readers. No systematic account has yet been published on the development of Western industries in Japan, and information must be sought in the Reports issued by the various Departments of Government, in the British and American Consular Reports, and in the files of the newspapers printed in English in Japan. H. Yamawaki's *Japan in the Beginning of the Twentieth Century* is most valuable for the statistics of the subject, as are also the Annuals issued by the Department of Finance and the Imperial Cabinet. J. Stafford Ransome's *Japan in Transition* contains an interesting and readable account of modern developments. Those interested in technical details should consult the articles by the same writer which appeared in *The Engineer* (1897-8). Clement's *Handbook of Modern Japan* contains a great deal of useful information on the subject. Practical details are not to be found in ordinary books. These can best be got by personal inspection, or from men connected with the various undertakings, supplemented by a perusal of the scientific journals and the transactions of engineering and other societies.

CHAPTER IX

ART INDUSTRIES

ALL real lovers of Japan, while admiring the energy and ability which have been displayed in the application of Western knowledge and experience to industry and commerce, and to the arts of war, would regret if, in the changes which are taking place, it lost those artistic qualities which have given it a unique position among the nations of the world. That world would be a very dreary place if everything in it were reduced to the level which is the inevitable result of the competitive struggle for existence. Europe paid too dearly for its industrial development by the decay of art, and it is only in recent years that attempts have been made to retrace the backward steps. Whether a complete revival is possible under present social and economic conditions is one of the problems which must be faced before real individual or national life can be attained.

Importance of Art in Japan.

Under the old regime in Japan all the workers were artists to a greater or less degree ; that is to say, each one impressed on his work his own individuality. This was true even of mechanical trades, but it was strikingly true of all artistic crafts, and was to a large extent the direct result of the social and economic conditions existing under the feudal system. In the early days of the Shogunate each daimyo based the reputation of his clan on its martial prowess ; but during the long peace of the Tokugawa period, art and industry were the. distinguishing

Art in Old Japan.

features of the different parts of the country, between which there was always a certain amount of friendly rivalry for excellence in their productions. Not only did the daimyos exchange with their friends objects of art as compliments, but some of the best specimens were periodically sent to the Shogun's court in Yedo and to the Emperor's court in Kyoto. The daimyos therefore became liberal patrons of art, and the artists and workers were usually attached to their households as pensioners. These latter could never become rich men, but the wish for wealth never entered their minds. They found their happiness in their work, and they had a sufficient allowance to meet their small personal wants. In those days time was not money, the artists were able to work in a leisurely manner and give full play to their genius, and all their products had the marks of their own individualities ; and these again were fashioned to a large extent by the spirit and conditions of the country.

One requires to have lived in Japan, and to have breathed its atmosphere, before he can appreciate its art. A Japanese painting is not a picture in the Western sense of the term ; it is rather a poem which portrays an emotion called up by a scene, and not the scene itself in all its elaborate complexity, and Japanese connoisseurs value simple works far more highly than those which are full of details. The artist therefore omits all that is irrelevant to the particular emotion which he himself feels, and which he wishes to draw out from those who look at his art. A very capable writer on the subject has truly said that a Japanese painting is "the expression caught from a glimpse of the soul of nature by the soul of man ; the mirror of a mood, passing, perhaps, in fact, but perpetuated thus to fancy. Being an emotion, its intensity is directly proportional to the singleness with which it possesses the thoughts. The Far Oriental fully realises the power of simplicity. This principle is his fundamental canon of pictorial art. To understand his paintings, it is from this standpoint they must be regarded ; not as soulless

Characteristics of Japanese Art.

photographs of scenery, but as poetic presentations of the spirit of the scenes. The very charter of painting depends upon its not giving us charts. And if with us a long poem be a contradiction in terms, a full picture is, with them, as self-condemnatory a production. From the contemplation of such works of art as we call finished one is apt, after he has once appreciated Far Eastern taste, to rise with an unpleasant feeling of satiety, as if he has eaten too much at the feast."

We cannot, of course, enter into a lengthened disquisition on the characteristics of Japanese art, but what has been said should be remembered as applying in a greater or less degree to art work of all kinds, whether painting, porcelain, lacquer, bronze, or silk. Many of the most elaborate specimens in each of those departments which have in recent years been sold to foreigners, while good in their way, have really been produced for the foreign market, and the designs are not truly Japanese, but have been made to suit what are supposed to be Western ideas. The influence of Japanese art has been much felt in Europe and America, especially in the department of ornament, and on the whole that influence has been in the direction of improvement, but the same cannot be said of the foreign influence on Japanese art. The ideals are essentially different, and, while Western ornament with a tinge of Japanese may be passable, any attempt to Westernise Japanese art simply takes all the soul out of it.

On the downfall of the Shogunate the halcyon days of the art workers disappeared, and many of them were thrown on their own resources, and as the native market was entirely disorganised during the troublous times following the Restoration, they were compelled to adapt themselves to the supposed requirements of the foreign markets. It has been truly said that this was the Brummagem period of Japanese art, and it is responsible for the gaudy, vulgar specimens which form the chief points of some foreign collections.

Western influences.

For a year or two after I went to Japan my time was so fully taken up with the Imperial College of Engineering and the industrial establishments connected with it, that the art side of Japanese life to a large extent escaped my attention.   Foreign School of Art.   I was led to take an interest in it by a proposal on the part of the Government to start a School of Art, in European style, in connection with the College.   All the more important foreign Powers were anxious to have a hand in what they were pleased to call the "civilising" of Japan.   The Americans were influential in general education, the British in the navy and public works, the French in the military service, and the Germans in medicine.   The Engineering College represented the United Kingdom, as we had on our staff graduates of English, Scottish, and Irish universities.   The Italians thought that their special sphere was that of art, and they were anxious that there should be a School of Art in which they could impart the methods and ideals of European art.   To please them the Government established such a school, which was, for convenience, connected with the Engineering College.   I remarked that while I could not object to the arrangement and to the introduction of European art into Japan, I sincerely hoped that something would be done to prevent all that was good in Japanese art from disappearing.   My old friend Mr. (afterwards Count) Sano took up the matter very   Japanese Art Society.   keenly, and he formed a society for the purpose of cultivating the different departments of Japanese art ; to him and his friends the country owes a debt of gratitude, as through their efforts, and those of others who have followed in their steps, there are now many artists in the different departments who produce work which will compare very favourably with the best of former days, and all that is wanted is suitable economic and social conditions for their encouragement.   There has been a certain amount of westernisation of style, but in recent years the great aim of all the artists worthy of the name has been to return, as far as possible, to the canons of Japan, and to the methods and designs of the days of feudalism.

A Japanese artist and scholar, Mr. Kakasu Okakura, who has done a great deal to revive the old spirit in
Criticism of Foreign Art. Japanese art, and who has written a very interesting book[1] on the subject, speaking of the attempts to introduce European art into Japan has said : " The art which reached us was European at its lowest ebb—before the *fin-de-siècle* æstheticism had redeemed its atrocities, before Delacroix had uplifted the veil of hardened academic *chiaro-oscuro*, before Millet and the Barbizons brought their message of light and colour, before Ruskin had interpreted the purity of pre-Raphaelite nobleness. Thus the Japanese attempt at Western imitation which was inaugurated in the Government School of Art— where Italian teachers were appointed to teach—grovelled in darkness from its infancy, and yet succeeded, even at its inception, in imposing that hard crust of mannerism which impedes its progress to the present day. But the active individualism of Meiji, teeming with life in other cycles of thought, could not be content to move in these fixed grooves which orthodox conservatism or radical Europeanisation imposed on art. When the first decade of the era was passed, and recovery from the effects of civil war was more or less complete, a band of earnest workers strove to found a third belt of art-expression, which by a higher realisation of the possibilities of ancient Japanese art, and aiming at a love and knowledge of the most sympathetic movements in Western art-creations, tried to reconstruct the national art on a new basis, whose keynote should be ' Life true to Self.' "

I feel that Mr. Okakura's condemnation of the methods adopted for the teaching of European art is fully deserved,
Renewed ideals. and it is satisfactory to find that the danger of the native art being entirely swamped is now past. The problem now is to evolve economic conditions

[1] *The Ideals of the East.* London : John Murray, 1903.

which will make true Japanese art possible. In a preceding chapter I have mentioned the arrangements of the Government School of Art at Uyeno, Tokyo, and of the Nippon Bijitsuin at Yanaka, in the suburbs of the city ; but, after all, Japanese artists are not so much trained in schools as under the eyes and direction of the masters, who do all they can to develop the powers of their most promising pupils. The biennial exhibitions of the Nippon Bijitsuin reveal clearly the vital element in the contemporary art activity of the country. Mr. Okakura, who takes an active part in the work of the institution, says : "According to this school, freedom is the greatest privilege of an artist, but freedom always in the sense of evolutional self-development. Art is neither the ideal nor the real. Imitation, whether of nature, of the old masters, or above all of self, is suicidal to the realisation of individuality, which rejoices always to play an original part, be it of tragedy or comedy, in the grand drama of life, of man, and of nature." Those who wish to make themselves acquainted with the spirit which now animates the best work in Japanese art cannot do better than read Mr. Okakura's book from which I have quoted.

Our present object is to enter into details neither of the ideals of Japanese art nor of the manufacture of the different kinds of art products, but rather to look at the social bearings of the subject, and to consider the possibility and probability of real art, and all that it means in the national life, surviving amid all the changes which are going on in Japan. Mr. Okakura truly says that "The simple life of Asia need fear no shaming from that sharp contrast with Europe in which steam and electricity have placed it to-day. The old world of trade, the world of the craftsman and the pedlar, of the village market and the saint's-day fair, where boats row up and down great rivers laden with the produce of the country, where every palace has some court in which the travelling merchant may display his stuffs and jewels for beautiful screened women to see and buy, is not yet dead. And however its form may change, only at a great loss can Asia permit its spirit to die, since the whole of that industrial and decorative art which is the heirloom of ages has been in its keeping, and she must lose with it, not only the beauty of things, but the joy of the worker, his individuality of vision, and the whole age-long humanising of her labour.　For to clothe oneself in the web of one's own weaving is to house oneself in one's own house, to create for the spirit its own sphere." [1]

He insists that it was some small degree of self-recogni-tion that re-made Japan and enabled her to weather the

Eastern ideals. storm under which so much of the Oriental world went down, and he generalises, that it must be a renewal of the same self-consciousness that shall build up Asia again into her ancient steadfastness and strength.　The opening paragraph of Mr. Okakura's book gives the key to the whole position.　He says : " Asia is one.　The Himalayas divide, only to accentuate, two mighty civilisations, the Chinese with its communism of Confucius, and the Indian with its individualism of the Vedas.　But not even the snowy barriers can interrupt for one moment that broad expanse of love for the Ultimate and Universal which is the common thought-inheritance of every Asiatic race, enabling them to produce all the great religions of the world, and distinguishing them from those maritime peoples of the Mediterranean and the Baltic who love to dwell on the Particular, and to search out the means, not the end of life."　These somewhat mystic words reveal the fundamental differences between the Eastern and the Western minds, differences which must be remembered when we are trying to explain the past, to understand the present, or prognosticate the future.　As a rule, Eastern peoples have a religious spirit (in the broad sense of that term) and try to live up to their beliefs.　Western minds are essentially materialistic (although there are some exceptions) and the majority of people spend their energies in searching for the means of life and forgetting the end.　The answer to

[1] *Ideals of the East*, p. 236.

the first question in the Shorter Catechism, What is the chief end of man? has become largely a form of words which has no bearing on practical life. Six days of the week spent in the worship of mammon, an hour or two on Sundays in church, and a few subscriptions to philanthropic institutions designed for the benefit of our social failures constitute the religion of the majority of well-to-do people in Europe and America. Some of them have picture galleries, but these are looked upon either as safe financial speculations, or are used chiefly to gratify their vulgar vanity and love of display. Under such influences true art is almost an impossibility. No doubt some artists of strong personality are able to develop their powers under the demoralising system of modern competition, but it requires a very strong man to resist the temptation to prostitute his talents in reproducing the figures of rich nobodies at £1000 apiece.

Art and economic conditions.

It may be asked, What has all this to do with Japanese art? Simply to show that national art depends largely on social and economic conditions and on the ideals which animate the lives of the people. Artists and art workers of all kinds should therefore have a special interest in social reform, so that they may be free to develop their own individualities, without which there can be no true art. Japanese art must degenerate unless conditions are evolved which allow the artists the same freedom which existed under the feudal system, and unless the ideals of national life are kept clearly in view. These indeed are the two great problems which lie before Japan. We will consider them a little further on, but meantime, looking at the subject from an economic and artistic point of view, I would insist on the necessity for the Japanese maintaining their individuality in art and art products. Their artistic ability has won for them a unique position, and while I would repel the suggestion that they should confine themselves to the rôle of curio-makers to the other nations of the world, I believe that they have a wide sphere of usefulness in supplying the artistic elements in their own national life and in supplementing those of foreign countries.

Notwithstanding the high ideals of Mr. Okakura and the practical efforts of the Bijitsuin, it cannot be said that Present condi- modern Japanese artists have yet been able to tions in Japan. translate their ideals into their works. They seem to be struggling between the ideals and methods of the East and those of the West. Writing of a recent exhibition held in Tokyo, a competent critic in the *Japan Daily Mail* says : " There are many pictures of considerable merit, but one carries away from the display a strong impression that no progress has been made since last year, and that there are even signs of retrogression. It should be premised, perhaps, that these are not pictures in the pure Japanese style. They represent an effort to wed the arts of the West and of the Far East ; an effort which has been watched with much interest for several years. Hence, when progress is spoken of in this context, the reference is to evidences that the marriage can be effected successfully and that its offspring will be attractive. We begin to entertain doubts. It appears that the Japanese artist has not yet ' found ' himself in such work. He is still groping after an undiscovered something. Fine ideas visit him : delicate ideas, romantic ideas, and even poetical ideas. But he can neither express them nor fix them so as to make them speak clearly from the canvas. He is living in a land of haze. His aspirations end in mist, and his struggle to be large finds no resource except the expanse of his canvas. Sometimes where his drawing is admirable, his composition well balanced, and his subject impressive, he fails in monotony of tone, in dreary absence of centralisation. Sometimes when he carries the spectator into an ethereal region where the impression of breadth and atmosphere is almost overpowering, he spoils everything by outlines that recall the studio of an immature observer. Yet there is in these pictures an indefinable something that suggests a noble idea in embryo. Several steps of development are necessary, however. Their nature, of course, cannot be accurately described. If it could, achievement would not be still distant. But hope remains though in the presence of considerable disappointment. The exhibition ought to be visited by every one that has any concern for the future of this school of Japanese artists, or, indeed, for the future of Japanese pictorial art. We do not allege that there are many striking pictures, or even many that rise above the level of mediocrity, but certainly there are many that offer much food for thought."

The standard of modern art metal work in Japan has been well maintained and many interesting developments have taken place, but it is still in a transition stage. Cloisonné enamel is a branch of applied art which may be considered of essentially modern development in Japan ; indeed it was only during the last quarter of the nineteenth century that it emerged from a condition of crudeness to one of unparalleled excellence. Captain Brinkley, a high authority on the subject, says : " There was no reason to anticipate that the Japanese would take the lead of the world in this branch of applied art. They had no presumptive title to do so. Yet they certainly have done so." In the department of pottery, although modern productions cannot yet equal the best porcelains of Hizen and Kutani and the faiences of Satsuma and Kyoto in the feudal times, still very good work has been done in recent years. For some time after the revolution a great deal of what was made was supposed to be designed to suit the tastes of foreigners, and much of it was utterly opposed to the canons of Japanese art, but in recent years there has been a return to Chinese ideals and a consequent improvement in the standard both of execution and of taste. Lacquer work of good quality can still be obtained, although the demand in Europe and America for cheap imitations of the old methods and designs has made it difficult to keep the standard of excellence up to the level of bygone days. In no department of applied art have the Japanese shown so much progress in recent years as in that of textile fabrics, and many examples are produced which are remarkable both for workmanship and for combination of colours. Although not much attention is now paid to the carving of *netsukes*, which attained a high standard of excellence in feudal days, the glyptic artists of Japan now devote their time to the production of works of greater importance, which are in many respects on a higher plane of excellence than the old work. Engraving in its several departments, work in gold and silver and many other applications of art to the articles of everyday life, all prove that it is possible for Japanese art productions to maintain something like their old standard of excellence, notwithstanding the great developments of Western industry and trade. While it is both desirable and necessary that these developments should continue in order that the standard of life in the country should be raised in all departments, all who really know and love Japan will agree with Captain Brinkley that " it would be an everlasting pity if the chief endowment of her people, their wonderful artistic instincts and their not less wonderful facility in expressing them, were left unutilised, because a party of fanatical radicals deemed it necessary to commit national suicide in order to be re-born into the comity of Occidental Powers." Japan has now been admitted a full member of the comity of nations because of the wondrous progress which she has made in every department of national life, and it is to be hoped that she will always retain those characteristics which have given her a special place among the nations of the world.

Sir George Birdwood in his book on *The Industrial Arts of India* says a good deal which applies with considerable Comparison force to the conditions of Japan, and his with India. remarks should be carefully studied by all who are able to exercise any influence on the future of Japan. Space will allow only of the following extracts :—" What is chiefly to be dreaded is the general introduction of machinery into India. We are just beginning in Europe to understand what things may be done by machinery, and what must be done by hand-work, if art is of the slightest ·consideration in the matter. But if, owing to the operation of certain economic causes, machinery were to be gradually introduced into India for the manufacture of its great traditional handicrafts, there would ensue an industrial revolution which, if not directed by an intelligent and instructed public opinion, and the general prevalence of refined taste, would inevitably throw the traditional arts of the country into the same confusion of principles, and of their practical application to the objects of daily necessity, which has for three generations been the destruction of decorative art and of middle-class taste in England and North-Western Europe, and the United States of America.

"The social and moral evils of the introduction of machinery into India are likely to be still greater. At present the industries of India are carried on all over the country, although hand-weaving is everywhere languishing in the unequal competition with Manchester and the Presidency mills. But in every Indian village all the traditional handicrafts are still to be found at work." After describing some of the general methods of some of these handicrafts, he concludes as follows :—" I do not mean to deprecate the proper functions of machines in modern civilisation, but machinery should be the servant and never the master of men. It cannot minister to the beauty and pleasure of life, it can only be the slave of life's drudgery; and it should be kept rigorously in its place, in India as well as England. When in England machinery is, by the force of cultivated taste and opinion, no longer allowed to intrude into the domain of art manufactures, which belongs exclusively to the trained mind and hand of individual workmen, wealth will become more equally diffused throughout society, and the working classes, through the elevating influence of their daily work, and the growing respect for their talent and skill and culture, will rise at once in social, civil, and political position, raising the whole country to the highest classes with them ; and Europe will learn to taste of some of that content and

happiness in life which is still to be found in the
Pagan East, as it was once found in Pagan Greece and
Rome."

The determination of the proper functions of machinery
in modern life is one of the problems which faces every
industrial country. Many of the social evils of the Western
world arise from the dull dead monotony of the work of the
people, and from the low, material, sensual ideals which large
numbers of all classes have of the meaning and object of
life. In Old Japan there was not only variety in the work,
but interest and pleasure in a great deal of it, and certainly
in all that which was of an artistic nature. Time was not
money and the feudal patrons encouraged the highest
excellence in every department of artistic work.
Under present conditions the foreign market
has to a large extent taken the place of feudal
patronage, but its demands are fitful and its tendency is to
reduce even the best artists to the production of pot-boilers
of little artistic value. The true spirit of Japanese art is
prostituted to the promptings of gain, and foreign tastes
have more influence than Japanese canons. A most essential
step is the organisation of the art workers in such a manner
as to ensure not only good payment for first-class work, but
also the maintenance of that standard of excellence and
purity without which all their efforts are for the most part
wasted. They must, however, be assisted by the men of
means who are becoming somewhat numerous in Japan.
They, like true patriots, should see it to be their duty to
take the place of the ancient daimyos in the encouragement
of art, in a truly national spirit, and under such conditions
of freedom as to allow the artists to develop their own
individualities. In addition the municipalities and other
local bodies as well as the central Government should give
every encouragement to artistic genius in the decoration of
public buildings; for, after all, the highest forms of art have
always been developed under some form of communism.
The temples and tombs of Japan and the churches of the

Future of Japanese art industries.

Middle Ages in Europe are illustrations of the results of such conditions.

In this way there would grow up a body of men who were free from the anxiety of earning a mere living, who would exercise a great influence not only on the national art, but also on the art products which are exported to Europe and America. Paintings and picture books are likely to be appreciated only by those who have been to Japan and who are really artistic in their nature and understand the motives and ideals of the artists, but there is a great field for the production of artistic articles which are intended partly for ornament and partly for use. The production of works in lacquer, pottery, bronze, silk and other materials is capable of immense development, and for these Japan might find a ready market in almost every country in the world. My past associations with Japan naturally make me anxious to see her take full advantage of the applications of Western science and machinery for the production of the requirements and conveniences of modern life, but it would be a disaster to the country if in the competitive struggle it lost its art and individuality. Other countries will be able to compete successfully with it in the manufacture of textile fabrics, engineering appliances, and chemical products, but I know of none which can take its place in art productions. If Japanese art be guided on right lines, it may interest every country in the world, not only from an artistic point of view, but also lead to that blending of Eastern and Western thought which, in my opinion, is necessary for the true progress of the world.

BIBLIOGRAPHICAL NOTE

A considerable number of books have been written in English and other foreign languages on the art industries of Japan. In Professor Chamberlain's *Things Japanese* will be found useful short articles on the different departments of Japanese art industries, with references to the most important books on the subject. Captain

Brinkley's article in the supplementary volumes of the *Encyclopædia Britannica* is the best condensed account which has been written. Clement's *Handbook of Modern Japan* (chap. xvi.) gives a very good outline, with a useful list of books on the subject.   Of these the following may be noted : Rein, *The Industries of Japan* ; Anderson, *The Pictorial Arts of Japan* ; Brinkley, *Japan, Its History, Art, and Literature*, and *Japan and China* (12 vols.) ; Audsley and Bowes, *Keramic Art of Japan* ; Huish, *Japan and its Art* ; and Conder, *Landscape-Gardening in Japan.*   *The Ideals of the East*, with special reference to the art of Japan, by Kakasu Okakura, should be carefully read, as it contains a great deal of useful and interesting information about Japanese art, and also indicates its relations to Japanese life and thought.

CHAPTER X

COMMERCE

THE history of commerce in Old Japan has many features of an interesting nature, but for details of these I must refer to special books on the subject. It will, however, be useful to note a few points which have considerable bearing on present-day conditions.

The earliest existing records of Japanese commerce take us back to the third century of the Christian era, at which early date things were in a very primitive condition. Under feudalism there was always a tendency to the multiplication of regulations and the increase of officialism, which prevented the free development of commerce. Some of the regulations were as quaint as they were absurd. They were for the most part based on the doctrine that the people's reward for the products of their labour must be regulated primarily with regard to the convenience of the ruling classes.

The commercial intercourse with China and Korea dates from a very early time, and a study of the relations which existed at different periods is very interesting in the present state of affairs. Such a study is necessary in order to understand the Japanese point of view. All the arrangements were controlled by officials who valued the merchandise as it arrived, and sales were afterwards made at greatly increased rates to the people, the difference going to the Treasury; so that in a sense the Government was the only wholesale foreign merchant.

Brinkley's article in the supplemental
Britannica is the best condensed ac
Clement's *Handbook of Modern Japa*
outline, with a useful list of books
following may be noted : Re, *The*
The Pictorial Arts of Japan Brinkle
Literature, and *Japan and China* (
Keramic Art of Japan ; Hah, *Jap*
Landscape-Gardening in Japa. Th
reference to the art of Japa. by K.
fully read, as it contains a great deal o
tion about Japanese art, and also in
life and thought.

Marine
˙ articles of
he had to
a profit of
silk crop in
n, gave the
ɛa appealed
ınd at once
tant export

ịn trade of
ments took
as develop-
ɔn, and the
ːhe increase
ɔreign trade
it consisted
se had to be
ıue unless a
t kind was
v materials
ports, and
ow goods
˙n foreign
n of im-

ɛ country,
in 1885,
some of
ıntime it
ɛ import
ıot only
ʉt also
ion to
ˑrcial
not
he

A very important feature in the internal commerce of Japan was the system of guilds or trusts, which practically controlled all departments of trade. The merchants, especially those of Yedo and Osaka, working under these trusts, gradually acquired great wealth and fell into luxurious habits, and they often resorted to arbitrary measures which caused great hardships and consequent discontent. In 1841, by the authority of the Shogun, the licences of the guilds were withdrawn and they were dissolved, and liberty given to all who wished to engage in commerce without let or hindrance. This sudden change, however, led to great inconvenience, as no other adequate arrangements had been made to take the place of the guilds, and after about ten years it was seen that a modified form of the old system would conduce to the public interest. Modified regulations were therefore made; the guilds were re-established and they remained until the beginning of the Meiji period (1867), when they shared the cataclysm that overtook all the country's old institutions. It will be interesting to note how far modern conditions will lead to a renewal of an organisation something like the guilds of former days. In Japan, as in every other industrial country in the world, the tendency is towards combination and monopoly.

The early days of foreign trade in Japan, under the conditions brought about by the events connected Results of new with the Restoration, were marked by great conditions. embarrassments, resulting from the difference between the silver price of gold in Japan and its silver price in Europe, at the time when the trade was opened. The difficulties were increased by the extraordinary appreciation of the prices of all the ordinary articles of commerce, in some cases amounting to as much as four hundred per cent, and seldom less than three hundred per cent. Such an increase inflicted great hardships on the consumers, who naturally attributed it to the advent of foreigners and the opening of new markets. On the other hand, the producers made large profits, as they obtained from foreign buyers such prices as they had never before realised. Marine products, raw silk, and tea were at first the chief articles of export, and notwithstanding the difficulties which he had to overcome, the foreign merchant frequently made a profit of from forty to fifty per cent. The failure of the silk crop in France, owing to a novel disease of the silk-worm, gave the silk trade in Japan a good start, while Japanese tea appealed so strongly to American tastes that a large demand at once arose for it, and it still continues the most important export to America.

For some years the increase in the foreign trade of Japan was comparatively slow, but as improvements took place in the administration of the country, and as developments were made in the means of communication, and the applications of Western methods to industry, the increase became very rapid. No great increase in the foreign trade of the country could be expected so long as it consisted chiefly in the importation of foreign goods. These had to be paid for, and the trade could not possibly continue unless a corresponding quantity of goods of a different kind was exported. Agricultural products and other raw materials were, as already stated, at first, the only exports, and they still form a very considerable part, but now goods manufactured not only in Japanese but also in foreign style are, as we have seen, assuming a position of importance.

The rapidly improving financial position of the country, and especially the resumption of specie payments in 1885, had very marked effects on trade. We will notice some of the financial measures in a subsequent chapter ; meantime it is sufficient to note here the inconvenience to the import merchant who purchased his goods with gold which not only appreciated constantly in value relatively to silver, but also the silver itself appreciated rapidly and sharply in relation to the notes paid by the Japanese consumers. Commercial operations became in great part a gamble, and it was not until the cause of the uncertainty was removed that the foreign trade was placed on a healthy basis, and developed with increasing rapidity. The natural resources of Japan have ample room for growth, while the growing intelligence of her people with regard to foreign countries will, no doubt, inspire the rising generation with a stronger desire to open up closer trading relations with the outside world. Some commercial men in Japan even think that in a comparatively short time their country will become the centre for the carrying trade of the Far East, and the geographical position of the country, as well as recent economic developments, justify their hope.

The development of the foreign trade of Japan since the Development of Restoration has been most remarkable, as is foreign trade. shown by the following table, which gives the amount of imports and exports during that period :—

Year.	Exports.	Imports.	Total.
	Yen.	Yen.	Yen.
1868	15,553,437	10,693,072	26,246,545
1878	26,988,140	32,874,834	58,862,974
1888	65,705,510	65,455,234	131,160,744
1892	91,102,754	71,326,080	162,428,833
1897	163,135,077	219,300,772	382,435,849
1901	252,349,543	255,816,645	508,166,188
1903	289,502,442	317,135,517	606,637,959

The principal exports are raw silk, *habutaye*, cotton yarns, matches, fancy matting, tea, camphor, marine products, Exports and copper, coal, etc. Of these, raw silk and imports. *habutaye* stand out conspicuous in volume and value, and have in the United States of America and France their best customers. Cotton yarns go mostly to China, Hong-Kong, and Korea ; matches and coal to China, Hong-Kong, and British India ; fancy matting to the United States of America, etc. ; marine products to China and Hong-Kong ; copper to Hong-Kong, England, Germany, etc. The following table gives the total value of classified commodities exported from Japan for the three years 1901-3 :—

	1903.	1902.	
Beverages and Comestibles :—	Yen.	Yen.	Yen.
Part 1. (Tea) . . .	13,935,252.710	10,484,017.060	8,854,326.70
Part 2. (Grains) . . .	5,170,066.600	6,822,574.610	7,037,432.00
Part 3. (Marine products) .	7,073,322.690	6,200,083.770	6,983,959.17
Part 4. (Others) . . .	6,254,803.110	5,222,161.150	5,250,132.88
Total . . .	32,433,445.110	28,728,836.590	
Clothing and accessories . .	3,473,566.740	2,860,393.640	2,442,764.28
Drugs, medicines, chemicals, dyes and paints	7,323,165.520	6,150,748.920	6,576,367.39
Metals and metal manufactures	18,329,564.350	12,796,450.650	15,821,272.72
Oils and waxes . . .	2,387,970.170	2,486,913.710	1,709,550.98
Paper and paper manufactures .	2,053,337.120	1,785,588.030	1,659,300.54
Skins, hair, shells, horns, etc. .	1,645,231.420	1,106,701.480	1,035,811.05
Tissues, yarns, threads, and raw materials thereof :—			
Part 1. (Silk) . . .	113,701,393.800	113,954,108.230	109,137,139.33
Part 2. (Cotton) . . .	39,928,259.470	27,110,732.590	28,029,194.55
Part 3. (Others) . . .	1,475,576.260	1,333,975.250	1,186,072.56
Total . . .	155,105,229.530	142,398,816.070	
Tobacco	2,127,580.380	2,365,792.830	
Miscellaneous . . .	61,092,533.010	54,994,774.570	
Grand total . .	285,971,623.350	255,675,016.490	
Re-exports	3,530,819.160	2,628,048.380	
Total exports .	289,502,442.510	258,303,064.870	

The imports into Japan are of a very miscellaneous nature, the most important items being machinery, iron ware, petroleum, sugar, raw cotton, cotton fabrics and woollen goods. Iron ware comes from the United States and Russian Asia ; sugar from China, Hong-Kong, and Germany ; ginned cotton from the United States, Hong-Kong, and British India ; cotton goods from England and Germany ; woollen goods from England, Germany, Belgium, and France. Under machinery the most important items are locomotives and cotton-spinning machinery, the former coming from Britain and the United States and the latter from Britain. In the requirements of the dockyards, both Government and private, British manufacturers still have most of the trade. The United States supplies a large part

f the electrical machinery. The following table shows the
ɔtal value of classified commodities imported into Japan
uring the three years 1901-3 :—

	1903.	1902.	1901.
	Yen.	Yen.	Yen.
s, clocks, watches, instruents, tools, and machinery	13,219,740.010	12,114,322.790	16,738,946.870
ɛrages and comestibles .	15,157,962.480	8,713,970.720	7,505,181.240
hing and accessories . .	1,374,489.710	1,327,499.860	1,351,432.230
gs, chemicals, and medicines	6,712,050.930	7,183,082.870	5,527,045.170
s, colours, and paints .	7,728,656.240	6,682,354.930	5,358,605.680
s and glass manufactures .	1,424,995.190	1,836,906.610	1,395,458.080
ns and seeds . . .	67,113,444.910	26,223,165.350	18,797,209.960
ns, ivory, skins, hair, shells, c.	3,271,610.660	3,076,050.940	2,977,177.620
als and metal manufacres :—			
art 1. (Iron, steel) .	21,918,767.650	18,768,763.120	19,998,203.560
art 2. (Others) . .	5,822,309.940	5,067,933.760	5,416,198.190
Total . . .	27,741,077.590	23,836,696.880	25,414,401.750
and waxes . . .	13,929,044.240	16,699,976.120	16,361,561.670
ɛr and stationery . .	4,855,425.630	4,947,869.610	3,216,852.810
ɪr	21,005,629.870	14,486,234.750	33,527,463.440
ues, yarns, threads, and raw aterials thereof :—			
art 1. (Cotton) . .	81,371,230.990	96,949,588.480	74,798,478.790
art 2. (Wool) . .	16,316,073.550	14,304,534.090	11,848,457.500
art 3. (Silk) . .	1,940,493.590	2,456,977.790	1,542,489.040
art 4. (Hemp) . .	2,072,927.240	2,102,936.890	1,665,692.750
art 5. (Others) . .	1,203,269.520	1,055,722.610	844,803.440
Total . . .	102,903,994.890	116,869,759.860	90,699,921.520
acco	1,117,858.340	995,976.250	121,090.750
es, liquors, and spirits .	769,236.900	695,790.140	698,243.180
ɔellaneous . . .	28,302,362.380	25,629,785.280	25,784,684.120
Grand Total .	316,627,579.970	271,319,442.960	255,475,276.090
mports	507,937.950	411,815.590	341,368.610
Total imports	317,135,517.920	271,731,258.550	255,816,644.700

The following table gives the total value of commodities
Distribution of exported to and imported from the various
apan's foreign trade. foreign countries for the year 1903 :—

	Exports.	Imports.	Total.
ASIA—	Yen.	Yen.	Yen.
China	64,994,179.640	45,458,057.420	110,452,237.060
British India . . .	8,086,798.150	69,894,197.280	77,980,995.430
Hong-Kong . . .	29,724,694.190	1,739,726.910	31,464,421.100
Korea	11,761,494.010	8,912,151.230	20,673,645.240
Annam and other French India	197,776.140	15,579,626.870	15,777,403.010
Dutch India . . .	912,419.440	10,842,779.850	11,755,199.290
Russian Asia . . .	2,239,986.850	8,267,652.090	10,507,638.940
British Straits Settlement	7,108,700.780	1,323,441.260	8,432,142.040
Philippine Islands . .	1,675,519.180	3,421,553.530	5,097,072.710
Siam	73,625.930	3,726,279.770	3,799,905.700
Total . .	126,775,194.310	169,165,466.210	295,940,660.520
EUROPE—			
Great Britain . . .	16,544,523.980	48,736,758.130	65,281,282.110
France	34,279,115.900	5,107,913.280	39,387,029.180
Germany . . .	5,185,658.490	26,958,976.670	32,144,635.160
Italy	11,003,607.190	311,020.990	11,314,628.180
Belgium . . .	487,173.130	7,578,590.990	8,065,764.120
Austria-Hungary . .	981,290.360	3,676,995.080	4,658,285.440
Switzerland . . .	264,738.220	2,187,954.190	2,452,692.410
Russia . . .	1,125,250.840	291,558.700	1,416,809.540
Holland . . .	224,043.000	814,705.930	1,038,748.930
Sweden	518.000	290,697.190	291,215.190
Spain	67,593.580	101,191.430	168,785.010
Turkey	105,959.370	2,044.520	108,003.890
Denmark . . .	29,447.710	18,002.120	47,449.830
Norway	1,727.560	19,804.990	21,532.550
Portugal . . .	998.800	17,999.260	18,998.060
Total . .	70,301,646.130	96,114,213.470	166,415,859.600
AMERICA—			
United States of America	82,723,985.610	46,273,870.930	128,997,856.540
Canada and other British America	2,923,539.730	499,039.860	3,422,579.590
Mexico	72,222.270	1,638.950	73,861.220
Peru	12,012,180	18,088.840	30,101.020
Total . .	85,731,759.790	46,792,638.580	132,524,398.370
ALL OTHER—			
Australia . . .	3,352,465.570	1,199,935.250	4,552,400.820
Egypt	322,664.420	2,401,598.460	2,724,262.880
Hawaii	2,253,782.630	6,218.480	2,260,001.110
Total . .	5,928,912.620	3,607,752.190	9,536,664.810
Other Countries . .	486,791.180	782,185.320	1,268,976.500
Unknown . . .	278,138.480	673,262.150	951,400.630
Grand Total .	289,502,442.510	317,135,517.920	606,637,960.430

If we examine the shares of the principal Western countries which supply Japan's requirements, we find that in 1883 more than one-half of the total imports came from the United Kingdom ; in 1890, about one-third ; in 1898, considerably less than one-fourth ; in 1899, little more than one-fifth ; and in 1900, one-fourth. Taking the three last mentioned years, the aggregate import trade of the whole British Empire bears a less favourable ratio to the whole import trade of Japan than did that of the United Kingdom alone in 1883. The trade of Germany has in the same period advanced from about one-twentieth to one-tenth of the whole, and of the United States (including Canada in 1883) from about one-ninth to over one-fifth. German trade is and has always been exclusively in articles which compete directly with British productions. It is only in very recent years, on the other hand, that the United States has become a competitor with the United Kingdom, the trade of that country having, until 1896, been almost entirely in such products as kerosene oil, flour, leather, and tobacco ; whereas it now includes machinery of all kinds, scientific and other instruments, metal manufactures, rails, railway and bridge materials, boots, clothing, cotton tissues, and even coal, etc., the supply of all of which was formerly considered under the exclusive control of the United Kingdom. The principal item in French trade, representing perhaps five-eighths of the whole, is the woollen staple *mousseline-de-laine*, the production of which is not seriously attempted by British manufacturers, and trade rivalry with France can therefore be said to exist only to a small extent.

While the trade of the United Kingdom has in the period referred to increased less than one-and-a-half fold, that of Germany and of the United States has, in each case, grown more than ten-fold. Not only is this the case at the present, but the most strenuous efforts are being made in both the latter countries to prepare the way for very considerable extensions in the future. I cannot enter into a detailed discussion of this aspect of the subject, but the following opinion by Mr. Consul Longford should be noted :—" While much of the success of Germany and the United States must be ascribed to the willingness of the manufacturers of both countries to cater specially for the requirements of the Japanese, to advertising, and to the energy and vigilance of agents, some of it, and not the least part, is undoubtedly due to facilities of through transport from the seat of production in both countries to the destination of the goods in Japan."

The most marked feature, however, in the foreign trade of Japan is the growth of that trade with the Asiatic Continent. In 1881 Europe stood at the head of the list in the volume and value of its exports, followed by America and Asia. Twenty years later, in 1901, the relative positions of these great divisions of the globe were reversed, and in the exports Asia came first, followed by America and Europe. In imports also Asia occupied the same position, after which came Europe and America. In the interval between the years mentioned Asia advanced by over seventeen-fold in the value of her exports, Europe by 460 per cent, America 680 per cent, Australia and others by over 325 per cent. In imports the rate of advance for the same interval was over fourteen-fold for Asia, over 450 per cent for Europe, over 2360 per cent for America, and over 5680 per cent for Australia and others. The importance to Japan of freedom to develop its trade on the Continent of Asia, and especially in China and Korea, is therefore evident, and this has a very important bearing on its foreign policy.

Since the opening of foreign trade the imports have exceeded the exports in value by a very considerable amount, and there can be no doubt that Japan's foreign trade is, at present, causing an outflow of her specie. Much of her floating capital has been invested in works which as yet are only partially productive, and is thus not meantime available for further developments. Still the balance of trade against Japan is not so great as it is sometimes made to appear. After the war of 1894-95 *Balance of trade against Japan.*

Japan received from China an indemnity of thirty-two millions of pounds, out of which she brought eighteen and two-third millions into the country. Further, in 1898 she sold bonds to the value of four and one-third millions in the London market and caused the money to be sent to Tokyo. Moreover, there are other sources of income which are not apparent in the ordinary returns. Her merchant marine brings in a large sum. She is selling coal and other ships' stores in her ports to foreign vessels, the value of which is not entered in the trade returns, and her 70,000 emigrants are bringing or sending their savings home. In addition to all this there is what may be called the foreign tourist industry. It is estimated that each foreign visitor spends on an average about £200 ; so that taking all these items into account the apparent debit balance is very considerably reduced. In the future the gross amount of that balance is not likely to be nearly so large as in the past, as much of the imports were designed to increase the exports and thus cause the balance to decrease.

The developments of all kinds which have taken place in Japan have caused a great increase in the prices of

Current prices of the chief articles of merchandise.

commodities in ordinary use, and this fact must be taken into account when the effects on wages and social conditions are being considered. It should also be remembered when the future of competition with Eastern countries is being discussed. The work of the engineer has caused economic conditions in all industrial countries to approximate to the same standard. The actual cost of production, not the rate of wages, is the proper basis of comparison. Skill, organisation, and the utilisation of the latest developments of science and machinery are the most important factors in modern industry. The following table gives the average prices of commodities throughout the country for the years named, from which it will be seen that rice, *saké*, coal and fuel have more than doubled in price in the interval considered, and other commodities have also greatly advanced in price :—

Kind of Commodities.	Unit.	1887.	1892.	1897.	1901.
		Yen.	Yen.	Yen.	Yen.
Rice	Per 1 koku	4.710	7.000	11.810	11.470
Barley	,,	2.360	3.310	4.880	4.070
Soja-beans . . .	,,	4.070	5.060	7.920	7.430
Table-salt . . .	,,	1.190	1.460	3.170	2.010
Soy	,,	8.290	9.380	13.330	18.120
Saké	,,	13.930	14.240	24.200	31.480
Tea	Per 100 kin	26.090	28.660	35.520	38.650
Leaf-tobacco . . .	,,	8.480	10.910	17.880	35.080
Japanese white sugar . .	,,	8.770	9.260	12.550	12.470
Foreign ,, ,, . .	,,	7.750	8.070	10.000	10.760
Japanese brown sugar . .	,,	6.180	6.470	9.110	9.370
Foreign ,, ,, . .	,,	5.020	5.570	6.670	8.120
Japanese ginned cotton . .	,,	18.520	18.890	23.870	27.550
Foreign ,, ,, . .	,,	16.640	17.750	21.460	25.740
Japanese cotton yarn . .	,,	31.040	26.950	31.080	57.000
Foreign ,, ,, . .	,,	30.830	28.580	37.510	54.480
White cotton cloth . .	Per 1 tan *	.310	.310	.370	.380
Foreign grey shirtings .	Per 1 kama†	?	2.480	3.100	4.030
Raw silk { Superior quality .	Per 100 kin	?	?	?	?
Average . . .	,,	?	?	682.000	706.000
Inferior . . .	,,	?	?	?	?
Kaiki (silk tissues) . .	Per 1 tan	2.580	2.800	4.460	4.500
Hemp	Per 100 kin	20.450	19.660	27.990	30.270
Japanese pig-iron . .	Per 1 kwan	.230	.260	.420	.500
Foreign ,, ,, . .	,,	?	?	.330	.320
Kerosene or petroleum oil {	Per box containing 2 cans	2.020	1.810	2.310	2.860
Coal	Per 1 ton	3.360	3.860	6.910	6.810
Fuel	Per 10 kwan	.110	.130	.240	.250
Charcoal . . .	,,	.290	.380	.730	.840
Manure { Dried sardine . .	,,	1.580	1.740	3.080	3.260
Residue of herring oil	,,	?	2.240	3.220	3.550
Rape-seed oil-cake .	,,	?	?	1.850	1.820

* 1 *Tan* varies from about 9 to 10 yards.   † 1 *Kama* contains 40 yards.

The Japanese have taken full advantage of the organisations for facilitating and encouraging business to be found in Europe and America. Though the custom of using commercial bills in trade existed long ago, it was only in recent years that clearing houses modelled on the Western system were established in Japan. The Osaka Clearing House, opened in December 1879, was the pioneer institution of this kind in Japan. Then followed the Clearing Houses of Tokyo, Kobe, Yokohama, and Kyoto. All these establishments partly partake of the Houses of London and New York in their

Provisions for encouraging commerce.

organisation and working, and they have been of great service in facilitating commercial and financial business.

Commercial and industrial bodies discharging the functions of regular Chambers of Commerce existed in Japan in feudal times, but it was only in 1890 that they were organised on modern lines. Since that time fifty-eight Chambers have been established throughout the country, and they undertake all the usual functions of such institutions for the encouragement of commerce and industry. Besides the Chambers existing in Japan, the Japanese subjects residing in the various parts of Korea, as Seoul, Fusan, Mukpho, Gensan, and Jinsen have Chambers of their own.

In 1896 the Government established the Higher Council of Agriculture, Commerce, and Industry for the purpose of devising measures for encouraging foreign trade, and in 1897 its organisation was amended so as to allow it to deliberate as well on matters relating to domestic trade, and a large number of measures have been passed on its initiative. For a number of years the Government has been despatching officials and commissioners to foreign countries for the purpose of investigating the conditions of trade, and especially with the object of promoting direct export trade by Japanese merchants. Besides Government officials, student commercial agents, student manufacturers and private individuals experienced in respective lines of trade have been despatched on similar missions, the Chambers supplying them with either the whole or part of their travelling expenses. There are thirty-eight Commercial Samples Museums in various parts of Japan, and these institutions have been of great service in promoting commerce and industry. Similar establishments have been attached to some of the Japanese Consulates in foreign countries. The Department of Agriculture, Commerce, and Industry issues valuable Reports on industrial subjects, especially in their bearing on foreign markets and the conditions of production in Japan. In addition the Reports forwarded by Japanese Consuls, student commercial agents and manufacturers, and also reports embodying the result of investigations made either at home or abroad on industrial and commercial matters have been published.

Mention has been made of the guilds which existed in feudal times. Some of these have been revived and extended to meet the requirements of modern trade and industry, and they now exercise great influence on existing conditions. The latest returns give the number of agricultural guilds as 112. In 1897 a law was passed for the regulation of such guilds, and it marked a new and important departure in legislation of this kind. It was rendered necessary owing to the production and export of an inferior class of goods and to the consequent injury done to the prosperity of the various branches of trade. Three years later the scope of the law was expanded to the shape in which it now exists. A very large number of guilds have been formed in connection with the modern developments of commerce and industry, and their chief object is to protect the interests of their members and advance the special trade or industry with which they are connected. Like other similar organisations in other parts of the world, while in many respects rendering useful service, they not infrequently are led to acts of an individualistic or selfish nature and contrary to the interests of the general community. These guilds, however, are destined to take a very important part in the future evolution of Japan, and their development should be carefully watched by all who are studying the subject.

In another chapter will be given an account of the negotiations connected with tariffs. The tariff on imports was originally fixed on a ten per cent basis; but in 1865 Japan consented, under heavy pressure and even armed menace, to reduce the rate to five per cent. This, too, was only nominal, for the conversion of *ad valorem* duties into specific was managed in such a manner that the sum actually levied on imports did not average as much as two and a half per cent of their value at the port of ship-

Commercial and industrial guilds.

Tariffs.

ment. Under the revised treaties it was arranged that Japan should recover tariff autonomy after a period of twelve years, and that in the interval a greatly increased scale of import duties should be applied.

The system promulgated in 1897 divided imports into three main classes, namely—dutiable goods, non-dutiable goods, and prohibited goods. The tariff for dutiable goods ranged from five to forty per cent, *ad valorem*, divided into sixteen grades. The schedule has as a standard rate, so to say, twenty per cent for ordinary refined goods, to decrease in one direction but to rise in another. Natural products, scientific instruments and apparatus, and raw materials, machinery, half-manufactured materials, and articles of ordinary consumption occupy the decreasing side of the schedule, while articles of luxury and liquors and tobacco occupy the other extreme. The new tariff was put in force in January 1899.

Since that time it has received several amendments, either in the interests of the inland revenue or with the object of encouraging home industries. Tobacco and liquors of all kinds are now made to pay very heavily, and the raw materials required by the State monopolies and match-making were relieved from all duties, as were also artificial and natural fertilisers. The regulations connected with the tariff were embodied in a law which was passed by the Imperial Diet in 1899. The passing of this law may be said to have ushered in a new era in the history of the Japanese tariff system, as it marked the introduction of Japanese tariff autonomy, and many matters which formerly led to diplomatic interference were henceforth transferred to the domain of ordinary administrative affairs.

When we recall the position merchants occupied in feudal Japan—the lowest in the social scale —we have little difficulty in understanding the opinions which were held by foreigners in the early days of foreign trade with Japan regarding the commercial morality of the Japanese

Social position and commercial morality of Japanese merchants.

trading class. These opinions were the results of experience with the sharpest and most unprincipled among the Japanese merchants who rushed to the foreign settlements in the hope of enriching themselves, and some of whom did succeed in amassing a considerable amount of wealth. Great improvements have taken place in recent years, and commerce and industry are now engaged in by men of high rank and honourable character, who are exercising all the influence in their power to raise the standard of commercial morality of their fellow-men. The bad reputation of former days, however, has left its mark, and many foreigners still hold the opinion that all Japanese merchants are untrustworthy, and in many cases they are able to support their opinions by examples from their own experience. Exceptions to honourable dealing are still to be found, but I doubt if they are more common in Japan than in other commercial countries, and I have no hesitation in saying that, if the caution and prudence which should mark all commercial dealings is exercised, there should be no more difficulty in carrying on trade with Japan than with any other part of the world. A well-informed writer in the *Quarterly Review*[1] recently said : " The Japanese nation, as a whole, is not dishonest. The Government has always scrupulously observed every engagement made by it, and even when, as not infrequently happened in its early days of inexperience, shamelessly tricked, it invariably fulfilled the obligations it had inadvertently assumed. There are old-established mercantile firms of which the same may be said—firms to which credit may be and is constantly given with the same confidence as to British firms of the best standing. The writer, throughout a long experience, has found the Japanese tradesman compare favourably with the English, and has met with many striking incidents of honesty in its best form on the part of domestics, artisans, and labourers. A Japanese policeman is absolutely incorruptible, and a railway guard or a postman would look upon a ' tip ' as an insult." Com-

[1] October 1902, p. 557.

mercial morality, even at its best in any country, is not much to boast of, and the worst sinners are not always those whose shortcomings are made public, but the prudent, respectable people who keep themselves within the four corners of the law, and are still able to enrich themselves at the expense of their more scrupulous competitors.

The position of foreign merchants in Japan is one of great interest. It must be admitted that it was chiefly through their exertions that the foreign trade of the country was built up. They acted as agents both for the Japanese producers and for the foreign purchasers. Both as importers and as exporters their knowledge, experience, and capital were of great service in developing the trade of the country. For some years fortunes were rapidly made (and very often as rapidly lost), but as things developed the competition of the foreign middlemen with each other enabled the Japanese to obtain the very best terms, and profits were cut down to a very small margin. The foreign merchants were, however, always in a position of unstable equilibrium, and as education developed in Japan and experience was gained in foreign methods of business, naturally the Japanese got more and more of the trade into their own hands. All reasonable people will agree with Captain Brinkley in saying that " In a measure the ambition (to manage their own trade) is quite natural. If a community of aliens settled down in the United States or in England, and obtained a dominant place in the management of the country's foreign trade, Americans and Englishmen would certainly endeavour to wrest the business from their hands. Every nation must desire to carry on its own commerce independently of foreign assistance, and since a community of strangers is not to be found discharging similar functions in any Occidental land, the Japanese would prefer that their land should not be exceptional in that respect." Statistics show that the efforts made by Japanese merchants to get the foreign trade into their own hands have been tolerably successful; for whereas,

Position of foreign merchants in Japan.

in 1888, their share was only twelve per cent of the total, it rose to twenty-five per cent in 1899. Yet Captain Brinkley thinks that there are strong reasons to doubt whether such a rate of change will be maintained in the future. He believes that the day is still distant when the Japanese tradesman can hope to establish with the Occident relations of such mutual intimacy and confidence as will enable him to take the place now occupied by the foreign middle-man.

Formerly the attitude of the Japanese in their employ-ment of foreigners for any part of their work was very severely criticised and especially by the foreign press in Japan, but now a more reasonable view is taken of the subject, and the legitimate ambitions of the Japanese are recognised as the natural results of the developments which have taken place. One of the oldest foreign journals[1] in Yokohama writing on the subject, after noting the changes which had been going on for years, expressed the following opinions, which on the whole may be taken as representing a reasonable view of the position :—" The underlying germ of truth is only misleading if the rest of the facts are not duly taken into account. In the first place, the growth of Japanese manufactures is accompanied by an immense increase in Japan's own requirements ; and they will continue to increase, because the law of supply and demand is always directly influenced by the law of progressive civilisation, which develops ever-increasing wants and is never satisfied. Where a Japanese fifty years ago would regard half-a-dozen kimonos as sufficient for a lifetime, he now has that number in a year. Where he used to go from Yokohama to Tokyo on foot, once a year, wearing out a few cents' worth of *waraji*, on bare human hoof, he goes now every month, and helps to wear out an infinity of things ; he does it because it pays him, for the outlay returns now vastly quicker than it did. So, consumption of everything is increasing and always will ; and Japan can no more live without imports than the

[1] *Japan Gazette*, May 20th, 1903.

United States can. True, the character of the trade changes, and that is where, in a certain sense, some foreigners are being and will be crowded out by the Japanese and gradually deprived of their livelihood ; or deprived of one line after another, but only to develop new lines all the time, and it hurts only those foreigners who are unadaptable, unprogressive, unforeseeing, and unenterprising. It is true that one old-established firm after another has had to close its doors and wind up its business ; but this proves only that those firms lacked enterprise and business activity. Such things happen all the world over, but they do not prove that it is becoming impossible to live.

"It is by no means impossible for European firms to flourish in India, though India also is building up her own industries even more than Japan. India has entirely ceased taking certain lines of cotton from Lancashire, but instead takes machinery, and develops a demand for finer grades of textiles which only Lancashire can make ; and the country is as far as ever from being closed against the white trader. There are British firms which flourish and prosper in France, Belgium, Germany, in every country ; and there are firms of every nationality doing a fine business in England. There is of course little or no scope in any country for alien competition in the commoner and simpler lines of trade, and it is not creditable on the part of foreigners in Japan to moan and groan about the bread being taken out of their mouths. The elementary branches of trade of course belong in the natural order of things to the people of the country, and if they have for a time been in the hands of aliens, this could not be expected to continue. The only excuse for business people to be in a country not their own, is that they conduct some business which the natives cannot do so well. If there is anything in the claim of superior abilities on the part of the white man, he should never have any uneasiness on the score of any other race cutting into his business. If it is a business which the Japanese are able to do, and do so well as to compete with the foreigner, then it is time for the foreigner to give effect to his business superiority, by developing a line in which they may follow at a distance but cannot catch up with him. It is unworthy of the foreigner to cling desperately to any line which can be quite satisfactorily handled by Japanese."

BIBLIOGRAPHICAL NOTE

Much interesting information is given regarding the conditions of commerce in Old Japan in Brinkley's *Japan and China*, and in Dr. Yetaro Kinosita's *The Past and Present of Japanese Commerce.* H. Yamawaki's *Japan in the beginning of the Twentieth Century* (Chap. v.) gives very complete statistics of the development of the foreign trade of Japan, as does also the Annuals issued by the Department of Finance and the Imperial Cabinet. British and American Consular Reports should be carefully studied by all who are interested in the commerce of Japan. Some of the special Reports are very valuable and give a useful résumé of the departments which are taken up. The volume in Harper's International Commerce Series by J. Morris on *Japan and its Trade* will be found useful. All books and reports on this subject, however, soon get out of date, and only the latest editions should be depended on for information regarding present conditions. The daily newspapers should also be read, as they notice all the most important developments which take place and discuss the conditions affecting trade.

CHAPTER XI

FOOD SUPPLY

AMID all the industrial and commercial developments which are taking place in Japan, it is satisfactory to find that due Population and attention is being paid to what is the oldest food supply. and after all the most important industry; namely, agriculture. Through the improvement of agricultural education, and consequently of the methods of farming, the increase per annum in the agricultural produce has kept up very closely with the increase of population. When from any cause there is a failure of the crops in any part of the country, or even when there is speculation on the part of the merchants and farmers, considerable quantities of food products require to be imported, but in ordinary circumstances the amount of the staple articles of food of the common people which is imported is nearly balanced by that exported. Moreover, as it is found that the allowance of rice per head of population of those above five years of age has also increased, as well as that of the other agricultural products, we infer that the average standard of living has improved.

It is very interesting to note the various influences which have been at work in causing attention to be paid to Agriculture in agriculture in Japan. When, at the beginning Old Japan. of the seventeenth century, the policy of seclusion was decided upon, the Government was confronted with the problem of supplying a large and rapidly increasing population from a comparatively small cultivated area. Not only were emigration and the exchange of the products of other countries forbidden, but the profound peace which lasted for two and a half centuries completely did away with the check to over-population furnished by the wars that had been so common. The result was, that great attention was paid to the art of cultivation, and the farmer class rose in the social scale, being placed next to the samurai, and above the tradesmen and merchants, the latter being the lowest in the scale. Individuality, independence, and skill were assiduously developed. The rural districts had a large amount of local self-government, and the consequence was that not only did they enjoy a fair amount of economic welfare and simple enjoyment of life, but they also displayed a loyal affection towards the central Government on account of the consideration which was shown to them by the authorities. It is said that the farmers took a positive pride and delight in the payment of the taxes. "Taxation, as understood or felt by the people of most countries, is a burden imposed, a kind of robbery of the hard-earned means of the people. But it was, as a rule, quite differently regarded by the people of Japan. The payment of taxes did not seem to be considered by the peasantry as a burden, but as a loyal duty in which they took more or less pride. The time of the annual payment of the rice at the collectors' storehouses, where each farmer's rice was submitted to inspection, instead of being an occasion of sorrow and irritation, was more like a fair where each vied with the other in presenting for official inspection the best return of rice. It was always a source of mortification for any one when his rice was rejected or declared improperly cleaned for market. Prizes were awarded for the best quality and yield, which stimulated the farmers in its production. The tax-rice was regarded as a precious thing not to be defiled." [1] This quotation is an illustration of the manner in which the spirit of "Bushido" permeated even the common affairs of Japanese life; everything was done in a spirit of loyalty to

[1] Knapp, *Feudal and Modern Japan*, vol. i. p. 84.

the country, and not simply with a view to personal considerations.

The rapid increase of population since the Restoration and the introduction of Western industries intensified the
New conditions. difficulty of the food problem, and it has even been stated by some foreign writers that Japan was being rapidly transformed from an agricultural to an industrial country and to a large extent (like Britain) becoming dependent on other countries for its food supplies. There is a considerable element of truth in this statement, but the statistics of the Agricultural Department to which I have referred prove that the pressure is not yet very great. The authorities have wisely recognised the necessity of making the most of the land, and they have done this not only for social and economic reasons, but also no doubt from that spirit of patriotism (foreigners are very apt to call it exclusiveness and selfishness) which we have already recognised as the chief motive in all the national movements in Japan; namely, a love of independence and a determination to stand in a position of equality with the other nations of the world. At the same time, not only the increase of population but the growth in general prosperity and the distribution of wealth among the poorer classes of the people have led to an increased demand for food products. Many who were formerly content with barley and millet now regard rice as an essential article of food, and the time is not far distant when large supplies of this cereal will have to be drawn from abroad. The same is true of timber, which the development of engineering and other works of construction has already made inconveniently scarce. The cotton and woollen industries have, as we have seen, in recent years attained considerable importance in Japan, but all the raw materials require to be imported. The growth of these and other industries has led to a great increase in that part of the population which is not engaged in the production of food, and therefore to the need for supplementing, by importation from other countries, what is supplied in Japan.

The area of Japan proper (exclusive of Formosa) is 24,794 square *ri*, or 38,555,229 *cho*, but of this only 6,120,519 *cho* is arable land, the remainder being hills or mountains not available for pur- Improvements in agriculture. poses of agriculture, so that the arable land is only about 15.7 per cent of the whole area of the empire. Rice being the most important article of food in Japan, the greater part of the arable land consists of rice-fields, which are usually in low and wet localities not suitable for other crops. The religious beliefs of the Japanese led them to avoid animal food, while the configuration of the country made it necessary to conduct farming operations on a small scale. In Japan agriculture is essentially tillage and has little to do with stock-farming.

During recent years full advantage has been taken of the applications of Western science and methods to agriculture, and as already indicated there has been a considerable increase in the amount of the products. That increase, however, is partly accounted for by the additional land which has been placed under cultivation, and also by the more efficient use of that already cultivated, through a re-arrangement of the fields and of the irrigation canals. In recent years there has been a tendency to an increase in the size of the holdings, and a consequent greater amount of co-operation in the irrigation and other arrangements. The great variety of climate in the Japanese Empire, extending as it does from the nearly Arctic regions of Yezo to the tropical climate of Formosa, makes a great diversity of agricultural operations necessary ; conditions which are advantageous from a national point of view. While rice and other articles of ordinary food are the most common agricultural products, some districts are most suitable for sericulture, others for tea and others for sugar. Stockfarming is never likely to become very important in Japan, as the development of railways, tramways, shipping and other means of communication has, to a large extent, rendered unnecessary the raising of animals for draught purposes, and the great majority of the people are likely to be content with vegetable products and fish as their chief articles of food. Agriculture and fishery will therefore in the future, as in the past, always be very important in Japan. The following table giving the amounts of the chief agricultural products for the years named shows the increases which have taken place :—

Year.	Rice.	Barley.	Soja-beans.	Potatoes.	Sweet Potatoes.
	Koku.	Koku.	Koku.	Kwan.	Kwan.
1886	37,191,424	16,033,960	?	?	?
1887	39,999,199	15,852,044	3,253,790	28,382,572	561,407,587
1888	38,645,470	15,311,658	?	?	?
1889	33,007,566	15,316,897	?	?	?
1890	43,037,809	10,723,107	?	?	?
1891	38,181,405	18,098,471	?	?	?
1892	41,429,676	15,951,146	3,110,665	40,491,431	568,371,606
1893	37,267,418	16,636,588	?	?	?
1894	41,859,047	19,822,000	2,943,478	49,752,903	495,948,701
1895	39,960,798	19,537,840	3,163,683	44,273,903	711,813,132
1896	36,240,351	17,340,466	2,999,490	44,220,605	725,942,023
1897	33,039,293	18,005,490	3,100,973	58,528,287	663,391,590
1898	47,387,666	20,462,053	3,108,708	34,088,550	716,956,146
1899	39,698,258	19,335,952	3,410,693	64,594,705	661,444,862
1900	41,466,734	20,391,673	3,562,176	71,775,433	756,935,532
1901	46,914,943	20,640,207	4,069,619	73,682,653	711,639,519

The cultivation of tea has always received great attention. For a long time, however, the use of tea was confined to the Cultivation wealthier classes and to the priests. In course of of tea. time the custom of tea-drinking began to wear an aspect of something like a ceremony, with nice and strict canons of etiquette surrounding it, and the ceremony finally came to play an important part in society as a regulator of social etiquette and as a means of promoting friendship.

Almost as soon as Japan was opened to foreign trade a great demand for Japanese tea came from America, and at the present time the United States and Canada take most of the teas which are shipped abroad, while Russian Siberia takes a small quantity of black tea and brick tea. The following figures give the amount (in catties) exported and consumed at home in the years 1891 and 1900 :—

	Total Output.	Import.	Total.	Export.	Home Consumption
1891	44,352,488	65,618	44,418,106	39,923,999	4,494,107
1900	47,576,175	113,985	47,576,175	32,240,147	15,449,963

For some years past there has been a tendency to a decrease not only in the total output but also in the amount exported. This arises from the increase of rivals in the foreign markets. On the other hand, there has been a marked increase in the amount of home consumption, which indicates an improved economic condition on the part of the population generally. The Government has been doing its best to promote the tea industry, and besides granting a subsidy has adopted measures for the improvement of the quality, and for keeping those interested well posted with regard to the state of the markets in foreign countries. The local authorities follow the example set by the central Government and are supplementing the efforts of the tea-growers and manufacturers in endeavouring to advance the prosperity of the industry.

The increased consumption of tea and of rice is not the only sign of an improvement in the dietary of the Japanese, there is now an increasing use of what may be considered food luxuries, such as sugar, *saké*, beer, tobacco, etc. Meantime we can give the figures for the value of the output of these only for the year 1900.

Sugar, saké, beer, tobacco, etc.

	Yen.
Sugar	6,216,206
Saké (liquor)	108,328,650
Soy (sauce)	23,782,840
Beer	2,809,874
Tobacco (cut) . . .	135,122,893
,, (cigars) . . .	5,528,600

The cultivated land covers about 5 million *cho*, yielding
Capital and labour about 1000 million yen worth of crops every
employed on   year.   Of that sum rice constitutes about
the land.   400 million yen in value.   The value of
the cultivated land is estimated at 7000 million yen.

The capital required in agriculture is invested in farm
buildings (which are not expensive), in the tools and implements required for the work, in live stock, and in manure and
fodder.   The Japanese have always been very economical in
the use of their manure, and apply it with great skill to their
lands.   Night soil and stable manure play a most important
part as fertilisers, but in recent years considerable attention
has been paid to other kinds of fertilisers, which are either
made at home or imported from abroad.   No department of
chemical industry has been so active as that for the production of chemical fertilisers, and especially the manufacture of
superphosphate of lime and other phosphate and nitrogenous
manures.

In Japan, as elsewhere, there is a tendency for the
wealthier classes to increase in all spheres of activity at the
expense of the poorer classes, and the consequence is that
farmers of limited means are in danger of having even these
absorbed by manufacturers or merchants of larger resources.
Special banks have therefore been instituted for supplying
capital, under proper conditions, to farmers who wish to
develop the resources of their land or otherwise improve their
conditions.   The Japan Hypothec Bank was started in 1896
for the express purpose of supplying the funds required for
the development of agriculture and industry; and in the
same year local Hypothec Banks were started in each of the
administrative localities for the purpose of supplying funds to
farmers of the middle and lower classes, and even of making
loans to organised bodies.   For smaller loans there are
Credit Guilds, somewhat after the style of the People's Banks
in Germany, and all these institutions have been very useful
in assisting the development of agriculture.

Exact returns are not obtainable for the farming population of Japan, but in 1900 it was estimated approximately at 28,000,000, with 4,800,000 households ; in other words, the farming population constitutes a little over 60 per cent of the whole population, and the number of farmers' households is a little less than 60 per cent of the total number of households.

In addition to the Agricultural College of the University of Tokyo and the other institutions for agricultural education mentioned in Chapter V., there is a considerable number of special organisations designed to en- courage agriculture, such as experimental farms, local training schools for the purpose of imparting to farmers' sons and to farming people generally some elementary knowledge of the principles of agriculture, surveying, meteorology, physics, chemistry, natural history, veterinary science, horse-shoeing, etc., local lectures in agriculture, sericultural training schools, experimental tea farms and laboratories for a variety of special investigations. Special attention has been paid to the breeding of horses, not so much for agricultural as for military purposes. Stock-breeding generally has also made some progress, but for the reasons already given it is not likely to become of much importance. Attention has been paid to the training of veterinary surgeons and farriers, to dairy-farming and meat-preserving, to the rearing of poultry and the keeping of bees ; in short, it is difficult to name a department of agricultural industry which has not in recent years been greatly developed by the Japanese. Arrangements have even been made for utilising the spare time of the farmers in subsidiary work of different kinds, so that in some cases they divide their time and labour almost equally between those " odd jobs " and their regular farming work ; being, therefore, partly farmers and partly manufacturers of goods, which, however, do not compete with those made in factories.

The Government has done a great deal by means of legislation to encourage agriculture. For instance, in 1899 the Law of Agricultural Societies was promulgated with the

Means for encouraging agriculture.

consent of the Diet, and the Rules of Operation of the same in the following year, the legislature providing, among Agricultural legislation. other things, a grant of not more than 150,000 yen every year to the societies established in conformity with the law. A large number of such societies have been established in the various prefectures, and in addition numerous sub-societies in rural districts or cities and in towns and villages, and these are certain before long to have a very great result on the agriculture of the country.

In 1900 a law was promulgated relating to Credit Guilds, but as it has been in operation only for a short time, it is still too early to speak of its results ; but there can be no doubt that the provision will be extremely useful. Even before the passing of this law there were considerable numbers of such guilds in existence, some of which were established as far back as 230 years ago on the rules laid down by the celebrated economist and moralist Ninomiya. Sufficient has been said to show the great interest which, under the new conditions existing in their country, the Japanese have taken in every department of agriculture.

Fish and marine products have always been very important parts of the food supply of the Japanese. Owing Fish and other marine products. to its geographical position, to the direction of the marine currents in its vicinity, and also to the abundance of suitable indentures along the well-wooded coast which can be used as harbours of refuge in the case of storms, Japan is an ideal country for fishermen. It is not surprising, therefore, that there are 900,000 families of fishermen or of persons engaged in the marine industry, or over 3,000,000 individuals, and that the number of fishing boats is over 400,000. With the steady increase of population and the development of the means of communication in the interior, the demand for fishing products has begun to show a striking advance—an advance which has been accelerated by an increasing demand from abroad. The following Tables give the values of raw and manufactured products during recent years :—

RAW PRODUCTS.

Year.	Sardine.	Katsuwo. (Bonito.)	Cuttlefish.	Mackerel.	Maguro. (Kind of Tunny.)	Buri. (Seriola quinqueradiata.)	Tai. (Species of Sea-bream.)	Shrimps.
	Yen.	Yen.	Yen.	Yen.	Yen.	Yen.	Yen.	Yen.
1894	3,501,795	1,719,765	994,573	652,802	747,382	836,725	1,369,032	494,973
1895	4,848,263	1,966,019	1,038,471	957,974	935,307	1,006,373	1,617,655	597,071
1896	4,595,022	2,407,828	1,605,910	1,069,663	1,312,700	1,048,636	2,214,377	648,982
1897	4,888,262	2,754,442	1,795,343	1,299,612	1,482,383	1,112,112	2,609,187	806,855
1898	5,195,855	3,404,265	1,787,827	1,475,716	1,386,834	1,098,463	2,695,830	876,128
1899	6,526,385	3,931,974	1,355,615	1,934,091	1,278,391	1,678,633	3,316,733	1,095,485
1900	7,275,614	4,347,887	1,562,951	2,158,976	1,755,392	2,219,435	4,109,802	1,345,340
1901	7,005,466	3,112,745	1,787,886	1,845,456	1,754,362	2,006,971	3,258,490	1,381,108

MANUFACTURED PRODUCTS.

Year.	Dried Cuttlefish.	Dried Sardine.	Sardine, boiled and dried.	Katsuobushi. (Dried Flesh of Bonito.)	Kanten (Colle Vegetable.)	Dried Herring.	Residue of Fish-oil. (Herring and Sardine.)	Dried Sardine. (Used as a Manure.)	Table Salt.
	Yen.	Yen.	Yen.	Yen.	Yen.	Yen.	Yen.	Yen.	Yen.
1894	1,540,533	505,081	585,039	1,552,582	317,265	858,284	5,812,765	543,058	3,483,078
1895	1,267,519	692,558	605,653	1,920,701	337,236	993,970	5,572,516	837,033	3,866,674
1896	1,776,339	686,747	900,402	1,796,137	581,061	191,625	6,722,253	948,064	7,620,616
1897	1,780,028	619,838	1,211,687	2,974,448	658,705	1,793,227	7,786,060	935,909	10,104,771
1898	2,050,234	683,900	1,172,284	2,951,907	675,711	1,332,322	5,428,040	790,972	8,218,514
1899	2,043,540	963,933	1,449,832	3,376,668	866,530	1,355,054	7,358,146	832,854	7,542,942
1900	2,465,004	941,603	2,138,777	4,881,303	1,153,003	1,204,332	7,058,117	1,400,319	9,388,694
1901	2,789,474	750,783	1,608,324	3,642,408	1,068,463	2,342,534	7,218,455	767,832	8,707,340

The average value of the seaweeds which are used for food or for industrial purposes has in recent years been about 850,000 yen, and of the whales caught in Japanese waters about 220,000 yen. Sea-otters are caught in the Kuriles, and fur-seals in the Northern Pacific and the Sea of Japan. Formerly these fell mostly into the hands of foreign sealers, but of late, owing to the encouragement given by the Government, the capture of these valuable fur animals of the sea by Japanese fishermen has become quite satisfactory.

Modern scientific methods have been applied by the Japanese to their fishing industry; fish culture is now ex-

Government encouragement to fisheries.

tensively carried out in both fresh and salt water, and the Government has given encourage-ment and assistance in various ways. Under the feudal system certain fees were charged the fishermen for the privilege of the exclusive use of shores, while fisher-men eligible for the maritime service of the Government were given similar privileges.

After the Restoration the practice of exacting fees was abolished and the seas were declared to belong to the State. In all other respects the Government left the matter to be regulated according to existing usages and customs. In 1886 fishery guild regulations were enacted, but soon these simple regulations proved inadequate to deal with troubles constantly arising among fishermen, until in 1902 the Government put in force a law regulating fisheries. In 1897 a law was passed for the purpose of giving encourage-ment to deep-sea fisheries, and State aid is now granted according to the tonnage of the ships employed in the work and to the number of the crew, provided such ships, whether steamers or sailing ships, engage in specified kinds of fishery approved by the Government. The latest returns show that the number of ships engaged in deep-sea fisheries was 22, with a total tonnage of 2042, and that the sum given during the year as State aid was 28,035 yen. Japanese fishermen were employed in fishery in Korean waters even before the Restoration, and since that event their numbers have largely increased. In 1883 and 1890 the Japanese Government made special arrangements with the Korean Government for their protection. In 1897 these fishermen established their own association at Fusan, and from 1900 the Government has given an annual grant in aid of its funds.

The progress of fishery education has been very slow compared with that of agriculture and commerce. In 1889 a course of instruction in fishery was arranged in the Agricultural College at Komaba, but it was shortly after discontinued. The Fishery Training School of the Japan Fishery Association did much to diffuse knowledge with regard to this important subject, and its work is being continued now as a Government institution. There are various associations and public bodies interested in fishing, some of a national and others of a local character ; all of which are useful in promoting the fishing industry and regulating its financial and commercial interests.

Notwithstanding the efforts of the Agricultural Department to improve farming operations and to increase the amount of the agricultural products, the supply *Importation* of food will evidently soon become a pressing *of food.* problem, as is seen from an examination of the trade returns for last year. The rice crops for that year were excellent, as were also the most of the other crops, and it was anticipated that there would have been sufficient food for the nation without purchasing much from abroad. The farmers, however, were anxious to recoup themselves for bad preceding years, and refused to sell until the price of rice had risen, and thus large amounts had to be imported from British and French India, Burmah, Siam, and Korea ; but rice cannot be kept stored in bulk in Japan for any length of time as it spoils very rapidly in the damp weather. With the free importation of rice the Japanese farmers find themselves face to face with a competition similar to that which has placed the landowners and the farmers of Britain in a difficult position. Still a certain amount of speculation on the part of the farmers and the merchants is possible, and it must be taken into account when studying the food supply of Japan in the future. Moreover, the Japanese are now using a considerable amount of foreign food materials which are not likely to be produced in Japan for some time, and they all, more or less, affect the question of food supply.

The following table shows the values of the grains and seeds imported last year :—

	Yen.
Beans, peas, and pulse—	
Beans, soja	6,369,081
Others.	1,624,331
Rice	51,960,272
Seeds, cotton	829,017
Seeds, sesame	373,113
Wheat	4,767,838
All other grains and seeds . .	1,189,789
Total . . .	67,113,441

Sugar was imported to the value of 21,005,629 yen, and in addition there was a long list of beverages and comestibles of foreign manufacture to the value of 15,157,962 yen, besides a considerable number of miscellaneous products used for food or drink. Evidently the problem of food supply must be taken into account when we are considering the forces which are likely to influence the foreign policy of Japan in the future.

BIBLIOGRAPHICAL NOTE

The Reports of the Agricultural Department showing the developments which have taken place in agriculture in Japan should be studied. A very good synopsis of the subject is given in Part II. of H. Yamawaki's *Japan in the beginning of the Twentieth Century*, as well as of the fishing industries. A large number of special articles and reports have been published in Japan on these subjects and will be found of great interest by specialists. The volumes prepared for the Paris Exhibition of 1900 may be specially mentioned. The *Annual Returns of the Foreign Trade of the Empire of Japan* issued by the Department of Finance should be studied for details of food imported and exported.

CHAPTER XII

COLONISATION AND EMIGRATION

NOTWITHSTANDING the improvements in agriculture and fishery, as we have seen, the population is beginning to press on the supply of food produced in Japan. The Pressure of population. Britain of the East is now passing through the same stage as did the Britain of the West in the earlier part of last century. Modern sanitary, social, and economic conditions have been the chief causes of the rapid increase of population in recent years. For some time past that increase has been between four and five hundred thousand per annum, and the Japanese Government has in consequence been compelled to consider the problems which have arisen. As an influential Japanese writer recently put it : " Of her habitable dominions Japan has made the best ; not a jot of land has been left uninhabited. Still she finds herself obliged to make some further arrangements. What by necessity and what by policy she is prompted to take, not as heretofore a stay-at-home policy, but to push forward and neglect no opportunity in planting settlements in any places of the earth not yet occupied by others, and favoured, even in a moderate degree by nature in productions and climate." He supported his arguments by pointing to the examples of other nations, but of course it is evident that such proposals are only of limited application. After all, there is not a very large part of the surface of the globe unoccupied or at least unappropriated, and if all nations followed the same policy, every inch would soon be taken up.

As yet, however, the population problem has not pressed very hard on Japan, and indeed the development of industries has to a large extent provided for the increase of population, and has even, in some districts, caused a dearth in agricultural and other labour. No doubt these industries will increase in number and size, and Japan, like Britain, may be made to sustain a very large population, which may be to a considerable extent supported by the food imported from other countries. This policy also has its limits, and it is doubtful if it is wise, from a national point of view, to follow it too far. We have seen that the Japanese authorities recognise the problems involved, and have been improving their methods of agriculture, and bringing more land under cultivation. The belief, however, prevails that Japan, like Britain, must become a great manufacturing country, which would send her products to the markets of the world, and especially to those in the Far East. Hence the attention which has been given in recent years to colonisation, to the outlying parts of the Empire, and to emigration to foreign countries, especially to Korea and China, and the influence which this has had on the foreign policy of the country.

In the strict sense of the term Japan has no colonies, for all the so-called colonial settlements are within the empire and under its central Government. What has been attempted is not colonisation, but immigration from one part of the empire which had a surplus population to another part which was comparatively unoccupied. There are Japanese settlements in China, Korea, Hawaii, and to a smaller extent in Siam and other parts of the world, which are sometimes called colonies, but which are simply concessions from the respective Governments on terms similar to those of other nations. The administration of those parts of the Japanese Empire in which immigration has taken place is in some respects special, and we will therefore note some of the measures which have been taken to advance the objects in view and to develop their natural resources.

While the annual increase in the population in Japan was still small, and chiefly for political reasons, one of the first undertakings of the new Government was the institution of a special department, called Kaitakushi, for the encouragement of emigration to the island of Yezo, and for the development of its resources. Department of Kaitakushi. The Ainos (or Ainu), the aboriginal inhabitants of Yezo, are supposed to be the remnants of the people which formerly spread over the whole of the Japanese archipelago, and on the arrival of the Japanese proper from the north-west, they were gradually pressed towards the east and north. Early in the eighteenth century they were completely subjugated and confined to the northern island of Yezo. Japanese colonists had, however, proceeded in considerable numbers to that island, and up till the time of the Restoration its affairs were administered by officers of the Shogunate. During the troubles of 1868 Admiral Enomoto took the Shogun's fleet to Yezo, captured Hakodate, and proclaimed a republic, but in the following year he was compelled to capitulate. Soon after Yezo was placed under the special department of the Government already mentioned and called the Kaitakushi (Colonisation Commission), and the island became part of Japan proper, receiving the designation of Hokkaido, or North Sea Circuit. It was divided into ten provinces, and arrangements were made for the development of its resources.

Up till that time Yezo was chiefly important for its fisheries, but of course its position gave it great political importance. Its possession gave a command of the Eastern seas, a fact which even then had been recognised by the Russians, who endeavoured to obtain a footing in the island, but the opening of Japan to foreign intercourse nipped this encroachment in the bud. These and similar actions by the Russians were, however, not forgotten by the Japanese. Their earlier attempts at colonisation in Yezo had therefore a significance of a political nature, and cannot be judged entirely from their financial results.

A considerable number of Americans, with General Capron at their head, were engaged by the executive for the purpose of developing the agriculture of the island. Large sums were expended on model farms and public works, but it was soon recognised that a strong navy would be far more useful, from a political point of view, especially as it was found that many of the agricultural and colonisation experiments had a very limited success, and in 1881 the Kaitakushi was dissolved. Since that time the Government of the island has undergone repeated reorganisation, into the details of which, however, we need not enter. One Military Colonies. attempt at increasing the population may, however, be noted. In the year mentioned the Government resolved to found military colonies, in which it was intended that the soldiers should at the same time engage in agricultural cultivation ; but the combination was found to be inefficient, both from the point of view of soldiering and of agriculture, and after some time the experiment was abandoned. In order to guard against Russian aggression, an army corps is now always stationed in the island, and emigration, agriculture, fisheries, and other industries are allowed to develop in a natural manner.

An Agricultural College was instituted in Sapporo in the early days of the Kaitakushi, and it has been of considerable service in training men who have Agriculture and marine products. improved the methods of agriculture. Moreover, many of the chief agricultural officials have been educated in the Agricultural College of Tokyo University, and in addition have visited foreign countries for the purpose of observing operations which are likely to be of use in Yezo. Although the climate is somewhat against the agricultural development of the island, great improvements have taken place both in the cultivation of the land and in the fisheries. The tinned-fish industry has assumed considerable importance. Other marine products have also been largely increased, and their annual value now amounts to a considerable sum.

The Government has laid out a very complete system of railways which will open up the resources of the Hokkaido, and a considerable part of it has been con-   Railways, structed under the superintendence of my friend   mining, and former student Dr. Tanabe Sakuro, now   and other industries. Professor of Civil Engineering in the University of Kyoto. The Tanko Tetsudo Kaisha (the Coal Mining Railway Company) has done a great deal to develop the mineral resources of the island and it now does a very large and prosperous business. The island has not only very large deposits of coal but has also a considerable number of other mineral resources, including silver, manganese, sulphur, petroleum, some of which are capable of offering employment to large numbers of people. Industries of various kinds have been started and carried on with considerable success. Sapporo beer has been favourably known for nearly thirty years, the paper industry is being developed, and many smaller industries have been started, especially those connected with fisheries and marine and agricultural products, and in order to meet the requirements of the shipping a dry dock has been constructed at Hakodate and other facilities for the encouragement of trade have been given. In short, Hokkaido will in future be treated like the other parts of Japan ; that is to say, its resources will be developed without artificial support or assisted emigration, and its success will depend on its economic conditions and the manner in which these are taken advantage of.

Notwithstanding the encouragement which has been given by the Government, the attempts to settle a consider- able population in Hokkaido have not been Immigration and very successful. This is accounted for, no doubt, Population. to a great extent, by the inhospitable climate in the winter time and the comparative isolation of the island from the rest of Japan. As, however, the means of communication are improved and the industrial resources are developed, there is certain to be a large increase in the number of settlers. The following figures show the population since 1868 :—

Year.	Population.	Year.	Population.
1868	58,467	1895	678,215
1872	111,196	1896	715,172
1877	191,172	1897	786,211
1882	239,632	1898	853,239
1887	321,208	1899	803,413
1892	509,609	1900	810,111
1893	559,959	1901	800,102
1894	616,650		

The island of Formosa (called Taiwan by the Japanese) came under the control of the Japanese Government on the termination of the war between Japan and China in 1895, being ceded as one of the conditions of peace between the two nations, and in consequence the Japanese found themselves face to face with some very difficult problems. Although they cannot as yet be said to have solved all these problems, they have by their tact, good sense, and, I may add, unselfishness, gone a long way towards making Formosa an integral part of the Japanese Empire, not only politically but also in every other respect.

Formosa.

The past history of Formosa is very interesting, but for it I must refer to other books, and notably to that by Mr. James W. Davidson, formerly the Consul of the United States of America in Formosa, now of Antung, Manchuria; all meantime that I can attempt is a short outline of the work which has been done by the Japanese since they obtained possession of the island.

It is very rich in tea, camphor, sugar, fruits, and vegetables of every kind, while its mineral resources are considerable, although these have, as yet, not been fully investigated. The Japanese did not enter into peaceful possession. A large part of the island is inhabited by aborigines of a savage nature, who have to be brought under control; while many of the Chinese in the island, animated in some cases by patriotism, and in others by real or fancied grievances, have given great trouble. The difficulty of finding men who were capable of undertaking work of such an intricate and novel kind would have been found great by any country in the world, and the Japanese Government has had trouble from the inefficiency and misconduct of some of its officials; but this is now being overcome, and under the administration of Lieut.-General Baron Kodama, Governor-General, and of Dr. Shimpei Goto, Civil Governor, efficiency is rapidly being attained and misconduct is disappearing; so that now even the most severe critics have nothing but praise for the work of the administration.

Previous to the occupation of the island by Japan in 1895 there was not a single Japanese resident in Formosa. The first civilian arrivals were not a very desirable class, being, for the most part, adventurers, and they led to considerable trouble. Many died from the effects of the climate, combined with insanitary conditions and their own bad habits, and many more were glad to return to Japan on the first opportunity. After the restoration of order a better element arrived. Merchants in Japan sent representatives to report on the prospects of trade; scientific and professional men visited the island for the purposes of research and the investigation of its resources, while shopkeepers and tradesmen of various kinds established themselves in the cities with the object of carrying on business. At first the mortality among the Japanese residents was very great, on account of the bad sanitary conditions, but with better houses and attention to sanitation, matters have greatly improved. Mr. Davidson says: "Given a sanitary neighbourhood, upper-storeyed quarters, plenty of fresh air and light, good food and protection for the head when exposed to the sun's rays, and life can be made quite as healthy as can be expected in a warm climate. The author's experience of six years in the island without a single day of sickness entitles him to speak with some authority on this point."

In 1900 the Japanese population of the island was about 40,000, being an increase of nearly 8000 during the year; the total population being 2,690,387. The following table shows the occupations of the Japanese population :—

	Males.	Females.	Total.
Officials	5214	697	5911
Educationists . . .	116	30	146
Agriculturists . . .	54	11	65
Manufacturers . . .	2255	230	2485
Merchants . . .	4458	3597	8055
Labourers . . .	1260	146	1470
Possessing no regular trade	165	84	249
Miscellaneous . . .	3912	2832	6743

With the exception of some wealthy firms, who are interesting themselves in plantations, the Japanese do not take to agricultural employment, and they are not likely ever seriously to compete with the Chinese in this department, who are not only accustomed to the work, but have also great powers of endurance under a hot sun. Formosa is not therefore likely to offer much scope for the influx of a large number of Japanese agricultural workers, not only for the reasons mentioned, but also because the greater part of the cultivated land is already in the hands of Chinese. For artisans, overseers, and shop assistants, and for general, professional, and skilled labour there is, however, an opening. The present Japanese population is therefore found scattered throughout the cities and villages. During the early days of the Japanese occupation wives and children were rarely brought to the island; now family life is more in favour, and the number of Japanese females is consequently on the increase, although even yet the males outnumber them by 3 to 1. Taking into account the increase of Japanese population and its general welfare, Mr. Davidson says : " All things considered, it would appear that the Japanese are finding life in Formosa worth living."

The administration of Formosa and of the neighbouring islands is wholly under the central Government of Japan, there being no local representation. The laws of Japan do not apply to Formosa unless special provision to that effect has been entered in the law itself. The supreme executive authority is vested in the Governor-General, Administration. who has as his immediate advisers the Chief of Civil Administration, Chief of Military Staff, and the Chief Councillor, who have power to issue ordinances for the government of the island, which come into force after they receive the sanction of the Emperor. Under the Department of Civil Administration are the Section of Police Affairs and the following Bureaux :—General Affairs, Finance, Communications, Agriculture, and Industry and Public Works, each with an adequate staff of officials. Local administrative offices or *cho* (as in Japan) have been established at a sufficient number of points, and the work of administration generally is approximating to that of Japan proper.

Under the Chinese Government education in Formosa was almost entirely neglected, there being only two missionary schools, confined almost exclusively to the Education, children of well-to-do parents who could afford justice, and sanitation. to pay for it. The Japanese Government have been doing a good deal to encourage education, and there are now 120 Government public schools scattered throughout the island, many of them in buildings specially built for the purpose. Progress must of course be slow, but it is intended to have the same system as in Japan. In addition to the primary schools which have been established the Government supports a number of special schools. First in importance comes the Medical School attached to the splendidly equipped Central Hospital at Taihoku, the chief city in the island. An agricultural school has been established in connection with the Taihoku Prefecture agriculture station and a number of other special schools of an industrial nature. In addition nearly every village possesses a school on the old Chinese style, with which the Government does not interfere.

For many years much good educational work has been

carried on by the missionaries of the Canadian and English Presbyterian Churches, for details of which, however, reference must be made to special publications. Among the latter my old fellow-student the Rev. Thomas Barclay, M.A., has since 1874 been taking a very prominent part. Courts of justice have been established over the island and law and order now prevail where formerly there were crime and disorder. Considerable attention has been paid to sanitation, with the consequence, as already indicated, that public health has much improved.

The Japanese have greatly developed the means of communication in Formosa. New roads have been made

Means of communication.

and the old ones repaired, and at the present time over a thousand miles are in process of construction at a very considerable cost. The first railway in Formosa was built by the Chinese Government and was completed in 1893. On the arrival of the Japanese, some 62 miles in length came into their possession, but it was found to be in such a wretched condition that a satisfactory train service could not be maintained, and the rolling stock was very limited and entirely unsuited to the requirements. The greater part of the line was reconstructed. At first the railway was under the control of the Military Department, but in 1897 it came under the control of the Civil Department. A private limited liability company was organised for the purpose of completing the Formosa railway system, but it failed to obtain the financial support of the public, and in 1898 the Formosan Government announced its intention of carrying on the work itself Under the able direction of Chief Engineer Hasegawa, and of the Assistant Engineer Mr. S. Niimoto, the plans were soon arranged; in 1899 work was commenced on the southern line from Takow north to Tainan, a distance of 28 miles, and it was completed in November 1900. The Kelung and Shinchiku (Teckcham) lines were repaired, much rolling stock was added, and in the autumn of 1900 work was commenced on the short branch line from Taihoku (Taipeh) to Tamsui

(Hobe), which was completed in June 1901. Over 200 miles of narrow-gauge tramway have been constructed in the island, primarily for the transport of military supplies, but it is also used for general freight and passengers. The main line runs from Shinchiku (Teckcham) in the north to Tainan in the south, a distance of 140 miles, and there are two branch lines. In order to meet the cost of improving the existing railway and extending it to form a complete trunk line, as well as to construct a harbour at Kelung, erect Government offices, and make a cadastral survey, the Diet authorised the Colonial Government of Formosa to raise loans to the amount of three and a half millions sterling, the principal and interest to be paid out of the revenue of the islands. Formosa now possesses twelve open ports, though only four—Kelung, Tamsui, Takow, and Anping—are utilised by merchant steamers engaged in foreign trade. The remaining ports are visited by coasting vessels and by Chinese and native-owned junks engaged in the China and Formosa trade.

There are now considerable facilities for steamship communications between Formosa and Japan and China, encouragement being given by the Japanese Government in the shape of subsidies. The chief line of steamers trading to Formosa is the Osaka Shosen Kaisha, although the Nippon Yusen Kaisha, the most important steamship company in Japan, has also some traffic with the island. Unfortunately, Formosa possesses no good natural harbours, and plans have been made out for considerable engineering works for harbour improvement. The large mail steamers running between the island and Japan have Kelung as their Formosa terminal, which is in fact the only harbour for big ships in the island. The steamers destined for Hong-Kong and other China ports sail from Tamsui and Anping.

The Japanese have instituted a very efficient post-office and telegraph service in Formosa. Every village has now a post office, and mail matter is delivered to any city in the island at the regular rate existing in Japan proper. The telegraph is under Government control and is run in connection with the posts. Over 2000 miles of telegraph and 600 miles of telephone wire, with cables between Formosa, the Japanese mainland and the Pescadores, have been laid.

The chief agricultural products of Formosa are rice, tea, sugar, cane, sweet potatoes, ramie, jute, turmeric. The value

Products and foreign trade. of the marine products, although it is increasing, is not yet very great. The mineral resources are being developed, gold to a considerable extent, while the output of sulphur is now of importance, and the output of coal is rapidly increasing. Camphor is a Government monopoly and yields a revenue of about £400,000 a year.

There has been but little increase in the value of the exports from Formosa since it was ceded to Japan in 1895. But the Japanese occupation has had a stimulating effect on imports, which now include many of the products of Western civilisation. Formosa, however, being an integral part of Japan, there is a rapidly growing trade with and *via* Japan, and therefore the outline of the foreign trade of the empire which we have given in a previous chapter will be sufficient for our present purpose.

Mr. Davidson says that " the Japanese occupation will improve the position of the masses throughout the island ;

General effects of Japanese occupation of Formosa. of this there can be little doubt. It will bring thousands within the reach of modern con- veniences, the railway, improved shipping facilities, good roads, etc. It will afford them modern medical treatment, the advantages of modern education, and will offer encouragement to the development of the island's resources and the utilising of machinery and other improved methods of manufacture." It is yet too early to attempt to tabulate definite social and economic results, but already a considerable part of the population finds its wages doubled, and the farmers obtain higher prices for their products ; a fact which reduces somewhat the actual value of the wages. Still the purchasing power of the masses has been considerably increased, with a consequent increase of comfort and welfare.

Dr. Shimpei Goto, the Civil Governor, thus summarises the reforms which have been introduced :—(*a*) The administrative system, for which General Baron Kodama is at present responsible, has since 1898 answered all requirements, and has given contentment to a population which is composed of many elements inclined by nature to be more or less antagonistic to one another. (*b*) As to sanitation, whereas the Chinese had paid no heed whatever to such matters, and the death-rate was extraordinarily high at the time when the island became the property of Japan, steps were at once taken by the new owners to remedy the defective drainage of the towns, to supply pure drinking-water by boring artesian wells and establishing water-works, and to reduce the number of mosquitoes and other noxious insects, which previously were veritable plagues. Hospitals were indispensable to the fulfilment of the scheme, and no fewer than eleven of these institutions are now rendering excellent service. (*c*) The cadastre, upon which the land tax is collected, is being pushed forward, and its effects, as exhibited in a largely enhanced revenue from this source, are already plainly visible, though the work is necessarily one which demands time for its complete accomplishment. (*d*) The educational measures adopted are far-reaching and are certain to be effective. (*e*) Public works, in the direction of lighthouses, railways, and telegraphs, and the improvement for the accommodation for shipping at various ports, are all receiving their due share of attention. (*f*) The banking affairs and monetary system of the colony have been placed upon a satisfactory footing. With all this Dr. Goto claims that already Formosa is no longer a financial burden to the central Government, and he justly claims this as proof of a vitality and of capabilities in general that are indubitably above the average. He believes that its future is eminently hopeful, as it is based upon rich agricultural and mineral resources which will form valuable adjuncts to those of

Japan proper, and the development of which will not only give a considerable outlet for the surplus population but also add greatly to the wealth of the empire.

One very interesting item in the action of the Japanese in Formosa is their treatment of the opium problem. When they took possession of the island they found there a population more or less addicted to the drug, and it was decided to abolish the practice by degrees. Only those who have already suffered from its effects to the extent that it occasions them intense pain to deprive them of the pipe are now permitted by a special warrant which they are obliged to procure to continue the use thereof. It is strictly forbidden to begin the practice, under severe penalties, and in order that the Government might have full control, and also to facilitate the final extinction of the habit, it has retained the sale of opium in its own hands. The revenue derived from the monopoly amounts to about £400,000 a year.

The rapidly increasing population of Japan has compelled the Japanese to look beyond the boundaries of their own territories for outlets for their surplus people, and naturally Korea and China have been looked upon as the most eligible countries, not only on account of their proximity, but also because of their historical associations. Mr. T. Nakahashi, a well-known Japanese politician, has said: "It admits of no doubt that nothing is more urgent for Japan at the present time than to find and develop the resources of new districts beyond the sea, with a view to the increase and prosperity of her own race in the world. In fifty years or so the number of the people will be nearly thrice as large as it is now. The number has been increasing yearly by four or five hundred thousand. As the increase is made invariably in regular advance it may be safely inferred that in a few score years the Japanese people will number a hundred millions.

"Granted that the Japanese should in every possible way be encouraged to emigrate to some convenient countries with a view to their future greatness, then Korea and Manchuria are the very places, and their next step should be to open and develop the means of communication with the proposed colonies.

" By an expenditure of sixty million yen spread over twenty years, two or three millions of Japanese settlers could be sustained in Korea and Manchuria. However great may be the number of emigrants from Russia, that Power will find herself always outdone by Japan.

" Japan must work out her own greatness, if necessary, in spite of her allies. Friendship is one thing, self-aggrandisement another. Even at the risk of peace, her colonisation policy must be carried out according to the plan she thinks best. Not a few collisions with the interests of the various nations may arise as a consequence of this struggle for existence. But each must carry out her respective international policy in spite of all obstacles."

These sentences prove that the modern Imperial spirit which has shown itself in almost all other parts of the world is not unknown in Japan, although they cannot be looked upon as in any way representing the policy of the Government. Still their existence cannot be overlooked, as their influence is certain to be felt in a greater or less degree. All that the Japanese ask, at the present time, is freedom of trade and of reasonable settlement ; in short, that their countrymen in Manchuria and Korea shall have fair-play, and that there shall be " the open door" for commerce. The official returns show that at the end of 1901 the numbers of Japanese in China were 5686, in Korea 4843, in Siam 16, in Hong-Kong 371, in Manilla 150, in Singapore 173, and India 42.

The emigration of Japanese to other countries, especially to North and South America and Australasia, is certain to cause a certain amount of discussion, if not Emigration to more serious trouble, in the not very distant other foreign future. The dislike of these countries to countries. crowds of Chinese is well known, and drastic legislation has been passed to prevent their arrival. Such legislation equally affects the Japanese, but in many respects their case is different from the Chinese. In the first place, their numbers are never likely to be very great, as the majority of those who wish to emigrate will naturally give a preference to countries nearer home ; and in the second, those who do leave Japan will, as a rule, not be of the labouring classes, but rather have special qualifications as merchants, engineers, or craftsmen. The latest published returns show that there were over 9000 in the United States or their colonies. A good many of these were in Hawaii, which at the time they settled there was an independent kingdom, and the climate and industrial conditions of which are very suitable for Japanese. Of the number mentioned 554 were students, and 2851 were engaged in trade. In Britain and British colonies the same returns show that there were 8215 Japanese, while Russia and Russian colonies had 3953. The other countries, apart from Korea and China, had only insignificant numbers ; so that the question of Japanese emigration with them is not as yet of practical importance.

In Britain proper it is never likely to become a burning question, as its geographical position makes it unlikely that large numbers of Japanese will ever settle there. Moreover, the economic conditions are against such a probability. In Australasia and Canada, however, the cases are different, and the same laws apply to Japanese as to Chinese, and it will not be surprising if the subject becomes one of general and diplomatic discussion. It is to be hoped that it will be settled in a common-sense manner, and that in British territories at least Japanese will be welcomed as likely to advance the welfare of the communities in which they settle.

In this chapter I have confined myself to a description of what has been attempted by the Japanese in the way of colonisation and emigration, but, after all, such methods of solving the population question can have only a very limited result. The solution of the real problem lies much deeper, and it is to be hoped that the Japanese will recognise that their influence in the world will depend much more on the quality of the people in their own country than in the numbers scattered over the other countries. It is further to be hoped that their national pride will not allow them to become hewers of wood and drawers of water to the other peoples of the world. Japan, like other industrial countries, is now face to face with many economic and social problems, and a resort to emigration on a large scale only results in the postponement of the solution of these problems. When free immigration is allowed in any country it has two bad effects. In the country to which immigrants are admitted it blinds people to the real causes of unemployment and starvation in the midst of superfluous wealth, while in the country from which the emigration takes place it, to some extent, relieves the pressure of competition and enables both the Government and the people to shut their eyes to the real causes of the evil.

While anything in the shape of what may be called artificial or forced emigration should be discouraged, natural emigration, depending entirely on economic considerations, should not be interfered with. Each nation should be expected to solve its own social problems, and economic conditions determine to a large extent how this is to be done. The Japanese are never likely to send great numbers to any parts of the world, except probably to neighbouring countries in the Far East; and Europe, America, and Australia must recognise that unless they receive on favourable terms those who go to them on legitimate business or work, their conduct may lead to measures of retaliation which would not only be unpleasant but also probably result in great financial loss. Already some questions have been raised, and it is to be hoped that they will be considered fairly and in all their aspects by the nations concerned, and that arrangements will be made which will conduce to the peace and welfare of the world.

BIBLIOGRAPHICAL NOTE

There is not much literature dealing directly with the subjects of this chapter. Many of the books on Japan, however, touch on it incidentally. Government Reports and the files of the daily newspapers are the chief sources of information. Mr. Davidson's large book on Formosa deals fully with the history, resources, government, etc., of that island. Chapter xiv. of Stafford Ransome's *Japan in Transition*, and Chapter vi. of M. Dumolard's *Le Japon, politique, economique et social,* contain some useful information on the subject. On the more general question of colonisation and emigration there are no special books, although there has been a great deal of discussion on it in the newspapers.

CHAPTER XIII

CONSTITUTIONAL GOVERNMENT

THE first of the principles enunciated by the Emperor soon after his accession to the throne, and which were to guide the actions of the Government, was to the following effect :— " Deliberative assemblies shall be established on a broad basis in order that governmental measures may be adopted in accordance with public opinion." For some years before these words were spoken there were in Japan a considerable number of students of constitutional government as it existed in Europe and America, but probably those in authority had little idea of the actual shape which the measures proposed in Japan would take. In this, as in other matters, their ideals developed as they gained information and experience.

First principle enunciated by the Emperor.

The Government of Japan under the Shoguns, while nominally an autocracy, was tempered to a considerable extent by various influences. The local autonomy enjoyed by each fief was not exercised by the daimyo himself but by his leading vassals, and even the nominal powers of the Shogun were wielded by a large body of ministers and councillors. Although there was no direct representation from the other clans, still the more powerful among them exercised a considerable amount of influence in a more or less indirect manner, as they were jealous of the practical absolutism which had been developed by a family which legally was in precisely the same position as themselves. On the arrival

Tempered autocracy.

of the American fleet under Commodore Perry, the Shogun thought it politic not only to inform the Emperor of the demands of the Americans but also to summon a council of the feudal chiefs in order that they might consult as to the steps to be taken under the circumstances. No doubt he saw that it was impossible to refuse the demands which were being made, but at the same time he felt that to grant them was a dangerous step to take on his own responsibility. The opinions of the daimyos were by no means unanimous on the subject. Some were inclined to open the country to foreign commerce on account of the profit which would result, others were prepared to resist the demands of the foreigners, even at the risk of war. The position of the latter was strengthened by the attitude of the Emperor Komei (the father of the present Emperor), who, being absolutely ignorant of political affairs in the exterior world, looked upon the arrival of the American squadron as a foreign invasion, sent letters to the dignitaries of the Buddhist and Shintoist priesthoods asking their prayers for the expulsion of the foreigners, and in this position was supported by the whole of the Imperial Court.

The first attempt at representative government in Japan therefore came to naught, and it was evidently made more for the purpose of appeasing the jealousy of the larger clans than of obtaining the opinions of the body of the people. That jealousy brought about years of agitation and many assassinations until the death of the Emperor Komei in 1867, and shortly afterwards the Shogun, Keiki Tokugawa, resigned his powers into the hands of the present Emperor.

During the next year a *Kogisho* or Parliament was called together, and great hopes were entertained of its usefulness. First attempts at representative government. It was composed (1) of representatives of the daimyos, (2) of functionaries of the departments of the central Government, and (3) representatives of the higher schools in Tokyo. It turned out a peaceful debating society, whose function was to give advice to the Imperial Government. Moreover, it was decidedly conservative and adhered to all the old customs of the country, as was shown by the practically unanimous votes against the proposals to abolish the privilege of *hara-kiri* and the wearing of swords. After a short and uneventful career the meeting was dissolved in the autumn of the same year, never to reassemble, as it was very evident that the country was not yet ripe for anything which was really worthy of the name of Parliamentary government.

Although the first attempt at a representative assembly in Japan was a comparative failure, still the evolution proceeded in various ways. The modifications that took place in the machinery of the central Government (and which will be noticed in the next chapter) were all in the direction of widening the influences which were brought to bear on the executive, and, although these influences were indirect, still they were by no means to be neglected. Public opinion, in many ways, was able to make itself felt, and these rapidly developed a demand for a representative assembly composed of members directly elected by the people. In April 1875 an Imperial Decree was issued which, in addition to certain administrative developments, ordered that an annual meeting of provincial governors should be held, so that they might discuss the affairs of their own districts and of the country generally. The Satsuma rebellion and other troubles, both internal and external, occupied public attention for a considerable time, and the agitation for constitutional government subsided. Meantime the Government slowly developed representative institutions in the various prefectures and cities (as will be explained more fully in the next chapter), but these steps did not satisfy the leaders of the agitation, as their purpose was to overthrow the clique of clansmen who, holding the reins of administrative power, monopolised the prizes of officialdom, and the development of local government did nothing to attain this end.

Evolution in direction of representative government.

In 1879 the agitation was renewed, chiefly on the initiative of Itagaki Taisuke (now Count Itagaki), a Tosa

Agitation led by
Itagaki. samurai who had taken a prominent part in the movement for the Restoration, and meetings were held in many parts of the country for the purpose of discussing the question. In March 1880 a general meeting of the leaders of the movement was held in Osaka and a new organisation was formed for the purposes of active propaganda. Under the leadership of Itagaki there was formed an association called *Jiyuto* (Liberals), which was the first political party in Japan, and was composed not only of men who held advanced opinions, but of many others who had or thought they had personal grievances against the Government, through their loss of office. The words and even the actions of some of these men were sometimes very violent, and in order to restrain them the police were entrusted with certain powers of control over the press and the platform. The somewhat drastic use of these powers enabled the Liberals to pose as victims of official tyranny, and prosecution (or persecution as some might call it) had its usual result; the movement grew in popularity and political agitation spread rapidly. In 1881 Okuma Shigenobu (now Count Okuma), who had held high position in the Government and was an authority on financial matters, seceded from the administration, and with his adherents organised an independent party calling themselves *Shimpoto* (Progressists), who not only stood aloof from Liberals but even assumed an attitude hostile to them; a fact which proves that the first political parties in Japan were grouped not about principles but about persons. However, it is not necessary meantime to enter into details of party politics or of constitutional and legislative enactments. For our present purpose it is sufficient to note the chief points which seem to have a direct bearing on the national evolution.

As already mentioned—the outcome of the agitation which was carried on—in 1881 an edict was published announcing that a national assembly would be convened in 1891. It was naturally supposed that this would have stilled the agitation, and that the Japanese spirit of patriotism would have caused merely Edict announcing national assembly. personal considerations to be put aside and united all parties in their efforts to make constitutional government a success. Unfortunately this was not the case; for having seemingly attained what was stated to be their object, the leaders of the movement directed their energies to the dissemination of anti-official prejudices among the future electors, somewhat after the manner of party politicians in every country in the world, and for ten years a very active anti-Government propaganda was carried on, both on the platform and in the press, and not infrequently scenes of violence occurred, proceedings which did not augur well for the smooth working of the future Parliament.

Meantime the statesmen in power resolutely pursued their path of progressive reform. Captain Brinkley has summarised their work during this period in Legislative and administrative reforms. the following paragraph, which is a model of condensed information:—"They codified the civil and penal laws, remodelling them on Western bases; they brought a vast number of affairs within the scope of minute regulations; they rescued the finances from confusion and restored them to a sound condition; they recast the whole framework of local government; they organised a great national bank, and established a network of subordinate institutions throughout the country; they pushed the work of railway construction, and successfully enlisted private enterprise in its cause; they steadily extended the postal and telegraphic services; they economised public expenditures so that the State's income always exceeded its outlays; they laid the foundations of a strong mercantile marine; they instituted a system of postal savings banks; they undertook large schemes of harbour improvement and road-making; they planned and put into operation an extensive programme of riparian improvement; they made civil service appointments depend on competitive examination ; they sent numbers of students to Europe and America to complete their studies ; and by tactful, persevering diplomacy they gradually introduced a new tone into the Empire's relations with foreign powers. Japan's affairs were never better administered."

As a step towards providing some of the machinery required by the new constitution, the Emperor, on the advice New orders of of Mr. Ito (afterwards Marquis), instituted five nobility. orders of nobility (apart from the princes of the blood), the English equivalents of which were princes, marquises, counts, viscounts, and barons. The greatest of the territorial nobles received the title of prince, the smallest that of baron, and titles of various degrees were bestowed on men who had rendered service to the country as statesmen, soldiers, sailors, or scholars, without regard to their original social status. In 1900 the princes numbered 11, the marquises 33, the counts 89, the viscounts 363, and the barons 280. The Japanese have been sneered at for this imitation of foreign customs, but they only followed the national evolution from feudalism to a constitutional monarchy and gave modern names to those who either by birth or service were entitled to recognition in framing a Constitution.

That Constitution was promulgated in 1890 with imposing ceremonies. Marquis Ito had been entrusted with Marquis Ito and the duty of framing it, and his name will live the Constitution. in history not only for his great services to his country as a statesman and administrator, but also as the chief author of a measure which gave Japan a constitutional Government ; and the Japanese people point proudly to his work as the only charter of the kind voluntarily given by a sovereign to his subjects. Although, as we have indicated, there was a certain amount of agitation, there were none of those long struggles between ruler and ruled which marked the rise of constitutional government in Europe. Marquis Ito studied parliamentary institutions in Europe and America, noted their methods, and his proposals were of a very cautious or even conservative nature, and the actual Constitution was fashioned more after that of Germany than of Britain. The minimum age of the electors and of the candidates was fixed at twenty-five, and the property qualification at a payment of direct taxes to the amount of 15 yen (30 shillings) annually. The result was that only 460,000 persons were enfranchised out of a population of 42 millions. As is usually the case in constitutional governments the two-chamber system was adopted for the Diet, the Upper House being in part elective, in part hereditary, and in part nominated by the Sovereign ; the Lower consisting of 300 elected members. By a subsequent development the qualification of electors was reduced to 10 yen annually, the number of franchise-holders being thus raised to about 800,000, and various modifications were at the same time introduced into the machinery and methods of election. The Constitution guaranteed freedom of conscience, of speech, and of public meeting, inviolability of domicile and correspondence, security from arrest or punishment except by due process of law, permanence of judicial appointments ; in short, all the essential elements of civil liberty as found in free countries. The Diet was given full legislative authority and control of taxation and financial matters except the payment of the salaries of officials, which the Sovereign reserved the right to fix at will. In the Emperor were vested the usual prerogatives of a constitutional sovereign, such as the power of declaring war and making peace, of concluding treaties, and of appointing and dismissing officials, of approving and promulgating laws, of issuing urgency ordinances to take the temporary place of laws, and of conferring titles of nobility.

The provision, however, round which has centred the chief difficulties in the working of the Constitu- Difficulties tion is that which made the Cabinet's tenure of in working office to depend solely on the Emperor's will, Constitution. and causes it to take its mandate from the Throne and not from Parliament. The Diet was not long in existence till these difficulties appeared. Loyalty to the Emperor compelled all parties to accept as a tenet which was not to be disputed that the sanctity and inviolability of the Imperial prerogative was to be observed; but the most radical among the Members of Parliament soon showed that they were of opinion that a Cabinet not acknowledging responsibility to the Legislature was virtually impotent for law-making purposes. The authors of the Constitution, no doubt, thought that the transition from an oligarchy to full Parliamentary government was too sudden a transition and was likely to be attended with danger. Probably they were right. Constitutions must develop with the conditions of the country, and already, although the printed words remain as at first, Parliamentary decisions have frequently had great effect on the actions of the Government, and have, in fact, more than once decided its fate. The future development of this part of the Constitution is probably the most important internal problem which faces Japan, for on it depends the solution of many other problems.

In addition to this constitutional question personal elements have to a large extent influenced the action of Personal the Japanese Parliament. The provision alluded elements. to evidently gave the opportunity for the continuance in power of practically the same men as those who wielded it before the promulgation of the Constitution and of what were called the "clan" administrators. The Government, for the most part, continued to be formed of those who belonged to the powerful clans who had taken an active part in the struggles of the Restoration, and while every unbiassed critic admitted that they did their work well, still the jealousy of the men of the other clans brought about constant struggles in the Diet, and in fact the opposition was directed against men, not measures, and obstruction of a very determined kind became the weapon of political parties. Legislation and finance were rendered very difficult, and for some time it looked as if constitutional government in Japan was not only a failure, but that it would be the cause of serious disaster to the country. Domestic and personal squabbles were, however, forgotten during the war with China (1894-95), and all parties united to give all the support which was required to make the war successful.

It is not necessary to follow the rise and fall of ministries or the changes in political parties ; the broad fact is evident that the government of Japan combines the features of an autocracy, an oligarchy, and a constitutional government. That the two former are still all-powerful has been made plain by recent events, when Parliament has been repeatedly dissolved while the same Ministry has continued to hold office. At the same time it cannot be said that the representatives of the people have been without influence in many important ways. In matters of finance they have been able to influence the Government proposals to a very great extent, in general legislation they have broadened the foundations of many public institutions, and in both domestic and foreign politics they have made their opinions felt in a very marked manner.

Making a survey of all that has happened since the promulgation of the Constitution, we must agree with Marquis Ito, its chief author, not only that there has been the experimental period, but also that excellent results have thus far been obtained, when it is remembered how sudden has been the transition from feudalism to representative institutions. However able the framers, no Constitution can be turned out which is perfect, and it must be modified to suit the changing conditions. As the *Japan Mail* put it, " it would be altogether extravagant to expect that Japan's new constitutional garments should fit her perfectly from the first. She has to grow into them, and of course the process is destined to be more or less awkward."

The first attempt at the compilation of a criminal code was made in 1870 and was amended three years later.

This code was far from perfect, being based mainly on ancient Japanese customs modified more or less by Chinese

Legislation.   laws.   One of the first serious pieces of work undertaken after the Restoration was the codification of the laws of Japan on the basis of the laws of Europe.   Foreign experts were engaged to assist in the work, and no efforts were spared to adopt the best principles of Occidental jurisprudence without doing violence to the customs and traditions of the country.   The Civil Code, the Code of Civil Procedure, and the Commercial Code are modelled chiefly on the laws of Germany; the Criminal Code and the Code of Criminal Procedure on the laws of France.

In 1882 the Criminal Code and the Code of Criminal Procedure were enforced.   The latter was subjected to a thorough amendment in 1899, while the amended draft of the former was introduced into the Diet in the eighteenth session, but the dissolution which occurred did not allow time for the consideration of the measure.   The principal statute laws thus far enforced are as follows :—

Imperial Constitution	1889
Law for the Operation of Laws . . .	1898
Law of Nationality	1899
Criminal Code	1898
Criminal Procedure	1890
Civil Code	1896–8
Civil Procedure	1890
Commercial Code	1890–8
Insurance Law	1900
Law relating to Registration of Real Estate .	1899
Law relating to Organisation of Courts of Law .	1890
Law regarding Ships	1899
Law regarding Crews of Ships . . .	1899

Reference must be made to special publications for details of these laws.   Other measures relating to finance, public works, and administration have been mentioned in the chapters dealing with these subjects.   It was very significant that one of the first Bills introduced in the Diet in 1891 was one for the removal of all restrictions on freedom of speech, but on account of the opposition of the Peers, who shared the opinion of the Government that to grant a large measure of liberty would certainly encourage licence, it was not until 1897 that the Bill was passed ; and the results have falsified all sinister forebodings. No doubt, in some of the journals, the language used is sometimes extreme, but in the majority of cases it is marked by a moderation of tone which has made the press of Japan a most influential instrument in the education of public opinion, and in moulding the empire into a harmonious unity.

BIBLIOGRAPHICAL NOTE

The subject of this chapter is chiefly of interest to specialists, and for general readers there is little need to enter into details. Marquis Ito's Commentaries on the *Constitution of the Empire of Japan* and Lay's *History of Japanese Political Parties* (*Trans. Asiatic Society of Japan*, vol. xxx. part 3) should be studied. More systematic history of the subject will be found in Iyenaga's *Constitutional Development of Japan* and H. Furuya's *Système Représentatif au Japon*. Knapp's *Feudal and Modern Japan* is well written and interesting. Chapter ix. of Clement's *Handbook of Modern Japan* gives a very good outline of the subject. A large number of articles dealing with its different aspects have appeared in British and American reviews. W. Petrie Watson, in his book *Japan, Aspects and Destinies*, has several chapters on the subject which are very clever, but he sometimes sacrifices exactness for effect. On legal subjects many books and papers have been published, but it is sufficient to mention Gubbins' translation of the *New Civil Code*, Longford's *Summary of the Japanese Penal Codes*, and other papers which appear in the *Transactions of the Asiatic Society of Japan*. Captain Brinkley's article on Japan in the supplementary volumes of the *Encyclopædia Britannica* contains an excellent digest of the history of Constitutional Government in Japan and its more important results.

CHAPTER XIV

ADMINISTRATION

ALTHOUGH the formal abrogation of the feudal system in Japan seemed very rapid and simple, it was, as we have
Problems of administration after the Restoration. seen, the result of forces which had been acting for a considerable time, and it left the new Government face to face with many problems of a complex and difficult nature in adapting the institutions of the country to the new conditions. If foreigners had not forced themselves on Japan, a revolution would still have taken place, but in all probability it would have stopped with the establishment of an autocratic administration, with the Emperor not only as the source of all honour and power, but also as the head of the actual government. The introduction of democratic ideas from the West, however, led to great developments of which even the most advanced thinkers in Japan had no conception.

As I have already pointed out, those in authority were not long in recognising that if Japan were to attain what they believed to be her proper status among the nations, a system of education which fitted for all the activities of national life was an absolute necessity, so that commerce and industry might be developed in such a manner as to supply the means of raising the standard of life, and that a strong army and navy were necessary to command respect. The development of constitutional government and the reconstruction of the laws of the country in harmony with the ideas of Western countries broadened the basis of administration and made the solutions of the problems which lay before the Government more difficult. A detailed account of all that was done to improve the national organisation is far beyond our present scope ; all that I can do is to give an outline of the most important steps in the development.

After the Restoration a Constitution was drawn up detailing the various Departments of Government and the duties of the officers in each. These Depart- New central ments were :—1. Supreme Administration ; Government. 2. Shinto Religion ; 3. Home Affairs ; 4. Foreign Affairs ; 5. War ; 6. Finance ; 7. Judicial Affairs ; 8. Legislative Affairs. The work of the central Government was carried on chiefly by the Daijokwan, or Cabinet or Council of State, and it is interesting to note the names of those who composed it in 1869 and their former positions and clans. They were :—

Sanjo Udaijin	(former Kuge)	
Iwakura Dainagon	,,	
Tokudaiji	,,	,,
Nabeshima	,,	(ex-Prince of Hizen)
Okubo Sangi	(Satsuma)	
Soyejima	,,	(Hizen)
Okuma	,,	,,
Hirozawa	,,	(Chishiu)
Kido	,,	,,
Sasaki	,,	(Tosa)

It is impossible to give exact equivalents of the ranks of the various members. Sanjo was First or Prime Minister. Iwakura, Tokudaiji, and Nabeshima were Chief Councillors or Junior Prime Ministers, and the Sangi were Councillors. Under the Daijokwan were the Ministers of the different Departments, who were called to take part in the Cabinet Councils of the Government when any questions relating to their Departments were to be discussed. Sometimes they were all called in to deliberate on matters of great importance.

In 1871 the Daijokwan, or Council of State, was turned

into Sei-In, or Chief College. It was composed of the Daijo, Sai, and Udaijin and of the Sangi, and formed the Council

Changes in Government. or Cabinet of the Emperor. Sanjo was raised to the rank of Daijodaijin ; that of Saidaijin remained vacant. Iwakura became Udaijin, and Saigo, Kido, Itagaki, and Okuma—representing Satsuma, Choshiu, Tosa, and Hizen—were the Sangi. The chiefs of Departments were constituted the U-In, or Right College or House ; while the Left College or House, which was intended to be of a somewhat representative nature, was composed of members nominated by the Emperor, and consisted of a President, Vice-President, and a number of subordinates of different ranks. The executive part of the Government consisted of the Ministers and Vice-Ministers of the eight Departments—Religion, Treasury, Foreign Affairs, War, Education, Justice, Public Works, and Imperial Household.

From time to time various changes took place in the arrangements of the central Government. For instance, in 1885 the Department of Public Works was abolished. That Department had been started for the purpose of initiating public works and various branches of industry, and by the date mentioned it was evidently thought by the Government that sufficient progress had been made to render direct assistance and supervision unnecessary, and that private enterprise should be encouraged. A large number of limited liability companies were started and undertakings of all kinds were initiated. The functions of the Public Works Department were distributed among the other Departments, that of Communications taking over the Government Railways, Posts, Telegraphs, etc., while the Imperial College of Engineering was, as already mentioned, transferred to the Department of Education, and became part of the Imperial University of Tokyo.

It is not necessary that we should enter into the minor changes which have taken place from time to time; it is sufficient for our purpose to give an outline of the existing arrangements. The Privy Council is the supreme advisory organ of the Emperor, while the Cabinet is the central administrative body. It has under it nine Departments of State; namely, those of Foreign Affairs, Home Affairs, Finance, War, Navy, Justice, Education, Agriculture and Commerce, and Communications. The heads of these Departments are the Ministers of State and they form the Cabinet, under the direction of a Minister President of State who is Premier; and in obedience to the Em- Functions of peror they deal with all matters relating to the Cabinet. administration. The principal matters to be determined by the Cabinet are as follows :—

- (*a*) Drawing up of projects of laws and compilation of Budgets and settled accounts.
- (*b*) Matters relating to treaties with foreign countries and to international questions.
- (*c*) Imperial Ordinances relating to official organisations or the operation of laws.
- (*d*) Disputes between the Departments of State as to jurisdiction.
- (*e*) Petitions of people sent in, either to the Emperor or to the Diet.
- (*f*) Disbursements not covered by the Budget.
- (*g*) Appointments and promotion of officials of *chokunin* rank and of local governors.

Matters of importance coming under the direct supervision of the Ministers of State may also be laid before a Cabinet Council. Attached to the Cabinet is the Legislative Bureau, which deals with matters relating to the drafting of projects of law or of ordinances or their amendment or revocation, whether such drafting is done at the instance of the Cabinet or of a Department of State or at its own initiative. It is also entitled to express its own opinion about those matters. The Cabinet, as I have already stated, is by the Constitution responsible only to the Emperor, by whom each Minister is appointed and dismissed at will, although as we have seen Parliamentary votes and public opinion have had considerable influence in the unmaking of Ministries and on the resignation of individual Ministers.

The Minister who has charge of a Department of State is empowered to issue Departmental Ordinances. The portfolios of War and the Navy are subject to ministerial changes, but there is a growing tendency to regard them as technical and administrative, and therefore to make their tenure independent of the Cabinet's life. The affairs and estates of the Imperial Household are managed by the Household Department, under a Minister who has not a seat in the Cabinet and is independent of changes of Ministry. Under the control of the central administration, but not forming part of it, are the Bureau of the Tokyo police, the Hokkaido Bureau, the governors of prefectures, and the staff of the Government of Formosa.

The Privy Council is the supreme advisory body of the Emperor, and attends to (*a*) matters relating to the Imperial

Privy Council House Law ; (*b*) matters relating to projects of
and other laws and ordinances pertaining to the Constitu-
advisory and
administrative tion ; (*c*) matters relating to a state of siege,
bodies. to the issue of urgency ordinances to take the place of laws when the Diet is not sitting, and to primitive provisions of the Constitution ; (*d*) matters relating to treaties and international agreements, matters relating to the organisation and rules of the Privy Council ; (*e*) other matters on which it is ordered by the Emperor to deliberate. At the present time Marquis Ito is the President of the Council ; so that although he is not a member of the Government in the ordinary way, it has the advantage of his experience and advice.

There are also a number of special Councils or Commissions intended to assist with advice the higher executive bodies,—such as the Codes Investigation Commission, the Central Sanitary Association, the Public Works Commission, the Higher Educational Commission, the Higher Council of Agriculture, Industry, and Commerce, and the Railway Council ; and attached to the various Departments there is a considerable number of special administrative offices, but into details of these it is not necessary to enter.

Although Shintoism remains the religion of the Imperial House, neither it nor Buddhism can lay claim to State protection in modern times, except that a grant of 216,000 yen annually is given for the support of Shinto shrines. No aid whatever is given to Buddhism. Under the Shogunate there was a class of officials whose duty it was to administer the secular laws in all matters relating to religion, and the Church was thus removed beyond the pale of the ordinary tribunals. The revival of pure Shintoism during the eighteenth century assisted so materially to re-establish the doctrine of the Throne's divinity, and thus prepare the way for the Restoration, that the new Government naturally identified itself with a creed of such practical utility. The old officials of religion were abolished, a new authority was created which ranked above all the State Departments, and there can be little doubt that the aim of the more radical reformers of the time was the ultimate suppression of Buddhism, and the elevation of Shinto to the rank of a State Church; but Buddhism had entwined its roots too strongly round the hearts of the people to be thus easily set aside. In 1872 a further change was made by the creation of a Department, with the name of Kyobu-sho, of a lower status than that which previously existed, but still very high in the administrative organisation, and from this office the priests of the two religions received equal recognition.

The spirit of the Revolution, however, was too rationalistic to maintain an intimate connection between Church and State, and the attempt to identify their interests gradually ceased to have practical force, until (in 1884) the ranks and titles of the priests were abolished, and the various sects were declared perfectly free to manage their own affairs. The only official connection of the State with religion is through the Bureau of Shrines and Temples, which administers the grant which is given for the preservation of the sacred buildings, but this is much more a matter of historical interest than of religious importance. The last tie that bound the Church to the State was severed when the new Constitution was promulgated in 1889, the twenty-seventh article of which declares that, "within limits not prejudicial to peace and order, and not antagonistic to their duties as subjects, Japanese subjects shall enjoy freedom of belief."

In no department of national life is the difference between Old and New Japan so distinctly shown as in the Administration of justice. methods of the administration of justice. Under the feudal system those in authority were too much inclined to visit summary and cruel punishment on slight pretext. It has, however, been clearly shown [1] that there was in Old Japan "a legal system, a body of clear and consistent rules, a collection of statutes and of binding precedents." The chief characteristics of Japanese justice under the old regime, were the following :—(1) Making justice "personal, not impersonal," by balancing "the benefits and disadvantages of a given course, not for all time in a fixed rule, but anew in each instance," and thus "to sacrifice legal principle to present expediency"; (2) the feudal spirit, especially in criminal law, as illustrated by the use of torture, humiliating forms of procedure, and awfully severe punishments ; and (3) the attainment of justice "not so much by the aid of the law as by mutual consent," by means of definite customs, applied, however, "through arbitration and concession"; so that there was "a universal resort to arbitration and compromise as a primary means of settling disputes," and only a *dernier ressort* to the process of law. In these as in other matters it is necessary to study their history in order that we may understand certain traits still prominent even in New Japan.

Having codified their laws on Western principles, the Japanese organised the machinery necessary to put them in operation. Their judicial system is divided into four grades ;

[1] Wigmore, *Transactions, Asiatic Society of Japan*, vol. xx. Supplement.

namely, the Supreme Court, the Appeal Courts, Local Courts, and District Courts. The last is the lowest tribunal and is conducted by a single judge, while in the Local Courts three collegiate judges sit on a case, in the Appeal Courts five collegiate judges and in the Supreme Court seven collegiate judges. Public Procurators are attached to each Court, on commission from the Minister of Justice. Security of tenure is guaranteed by the Constitution to the judges, and their appointments and those of the Public Procurators are obtained by passing a regular examination. The position of barristers is regulated by the Barristers' Law, and strict measures are in force with regard to their qualifications, rights, and privileges, and they are amenable to the same disciplinary law as that enforced in the case of judges.

The following table shows the number of Courts and the staffs at the end of 1901 :—

	No.	No. of Judges.	No. of Procurators.
Supreme Court .	1	25	7
Appeal Courts .	7	121	29
Local Courts . .	49	399	140
District Courts .	310	557	159

Great improvements have taken place in the Japanese prison system within recent years, and it will now bear favourable comparison with that of any Western country.

The dignity of the law in Japan is most commonly seen by "the man in the street" in the person of the policeman, and it must be admitted that he very worthily upholds it. The police of Japan are a very superior body of men, resembling the *gendarmerie* of France. They are in reality an excellent body of soldiers, who receive much higher pay and broader training than do the conscripts, and are almost without exception of high character and with a due sense of the dignity of their office.

Japanese officials are divided into four classes : the first comprising those that receive their commissions directly from Officials. the Emperor and are entitled to report personally to him ; the second, those that receive their commissions through the Minister of a Department and have the *entrée* to the palace on State occasions ; the third, those commissioned similarly to the second class but not having the *entrée* to the palace ; and the fourth, those temporarily engaged and having the status of mere employees. There is also another classification into nine ranks, each having two grades. The place occupied by an official in this list is granted by the Emperor as a recognition of merit, and the designation is prefixed to the name, like a title in official documents. Admission to officialdom is by examination, except in the case of candidates possessing certain duly attested educational qualifications.

The problems connected with local government which arose after the Restoration were even more difficult than Local those of the central Government, as they involved government. so many details directly affecting the daily lives of the people. At first the old machinery was utilised as far as possible, but it was found utterly inadequate to the changed conditions, and in August 1871 the daimiates were converted into prefectures or *ken*. The following is a translation of the message of the Emperor, and it is interesting as indicating the reasons for the change and the objects which it was desired to attain :—" We are of opinion that in a time of radical reform like the present, if We desire to give protection and tranquillity to the people at home and abroad to maintain equality with foreign nations, words must be made to mean in reality what they claim to signify, and the government of the country must centre in a single whole.

" Some time ago We gave Our sanction to the scheme by which all the clans restored to Us their registers ; We appointed Chiji for the first time, each to perform the duties of his office.

" But owing to lengthened endurance of the old system

during several hundred years, there have been cases where the word only was pronounced and the reality not performed. How is it possible for Us, under such circumstances, to give protection and tranquillity to the people and to maintain equality with foreign nations?

" Profoundly regretting this condition of affairs, We do now completely abolish the *han* and convert them into *ken*, with the object of diligently retrenching unnecessary expenditure and of arriving at convenience in working, of getting rid of the vice of the unreality of names, and of abolishing the disease of the government proceeding from multiform centres.

" Do ye, Our assembled servants, take well to heart this Our will."

The radical change thus announced appeared bold and hazardous to foreigners, but the Cabinet had confidence in the success of the new proposals, and that has been fully justified. At first the daimyos were appointed governors of the prefectures, but it was found that in many cases they were utterly unfit to perform the chief executive offices of their old provinces. Hence gradually other more competent persons were appointed to the vacancies as they occurred, until it was understood that fitness was to be the requisite qualification for such appointments. As the schools and colleges turned out graduates, they were appointed to the subordinate positions, and these as they gained experience proved very efficient officials. No doubt there are cases of inefficiency, and in recent years it is much to be regretted that cases of corruption have been painfully common, of which, however, the most is made by both the Japanese and the foreign journals. Still, taking everything into account, and the rapid changes which have been made, there are no reasons for supposing that in these respects the local government of Japan is much or indeed any worse than many other governments, even of some of those which are held up as examples of efficiency and purity. As the emoluments of the officials are increased, and as public opinion is more influential through the press and otherwise, there is every reason to believe that the standard of excellence of local government in Japan will rise in every department.

In the preceding chapter the Imperial Decree of April 1875, instituting an annual meeting of the provincial governors, has been mentioned. The powers of that meeting were gradually extended and representative methods adopted in the various local bodies. In 1880 the Provincial Assembly Regulations were enacted, followed in 1884 by the Civic Corporation Regulations, and in 1888 the local government system as it exists to-day was in thorough working order.

For purposes of local administration the whole empire is divided into 47 prefectures (*ken*), 653 counties (*gun*), 48 towns (*shi*) and 14,734 districts (*cho* or *son*). The three metropolitan prefectures of Tokyo, Osaka, and Kyoto are called *fu*, and the districts are divided into " urban " *cho* and " rural " *son*, according to the number of houses they contain. In each of these full effect is given to the principle of popular representation, and the local representative bodies have control of the financial and other important matters in the locality. The governor of a prefecture, the mayor of a town, or the head man of a county or district is *ex officio* president of the representative bodies. The system is divided into three grades—prefectural, sub-prefectural, or county and civic corporations. Of these three divisions, the last one, relating to municipal and rural communities, represents the self-government mechanism in its most striking form ; for in the other two higher divisions, owing to the greater part they have to play in administrative affairs, their self-government function does not lie so distinctively on the surface as in the other. Both legislatively and also practically the municipal and rural communities are *bona fide* self-governing bodies ; for they are entitled by law to enjoy the rights of juridical persons, also to incur obligations as such and to arrange all public matters relating to their own communities. The system of local government has now been in operation since

1885 and it has been found to work well. It not only affords a thorough method of political education for the people, but it also gives them the opportunity of assisting directly in promoting their collective, economic, and social welfare. Local and municipal politics in Japan, as in other parts of the world, are now assuming increasing importance. The local governing bodies will have increased functions, without, however, in any way lessening the ultimate power of the central Government, and thus they will obey the general law of evolution by the transformation of a homogeneous into a heterogeneous form of government, with increased coherence between its parts.

BIBLIOGRAPHICAL NOTE

A very good outline of the administrative system of Japan is given in Part I. of H. Yamawaki's *Japan in the Beginning of the Twentieth Century*. Chapter x. of Clement's *Handbook of Modern Japan* has also a well-written digest of the subject. Several papers on the subject are to be found in the *Transactions of the Asiatic Society of Japan*. A systematic history of the subject in all its bearings, however, has still to be written.

CHAPTER XV

FINANCE

THE fall of feudalism left the finances of Japan in a state of chaos, and one of the most pressing problems which con-
Financial position at the time of the Restoration. fronted the new Government was the establishment of a system of national taxation which would secure sufficient resources to carry on the affairs of the nation, and at the same time be on such a basis as would encourage the economic progress of the country and not be unduly burdensome to any section of the community. The difficulty of the problem may be inferred from the fact that during the first year after the Restoration of the Emperor the revenue arising from taxation was little more than one-tenth of the expenditure and that the balance had to be met chiefly by the issue of inconvertible notes. A detailed account of the financial affairs of Japan would require a large volume for itself; all that I can attempt is a short outline dealing with some of the most important points. A study of this, however, will be sufficient to show that the management of the national finances has not been the least noteworthy achievement of Japanese statesmen. The great changes which took place involved many difficult problems, and not infrequently the financial conditions of the country not only caused much uneasiness among those personally interested, but called forth predictions of disaster from outsiders ; but by skilful management all sinister forecasts have been falsified, and while many problems have still to be solved,

there can be no doubt that Japan has sufficient resources to ensure her a stable financial position.

The third of the five guiding principles of the new Government, as proclaimed by the Emperor on his accession to the throne, was that "means shall be found The old and the for the furtherance of the lawful desires of all new taxation. individuals without discrimination as to persons"; which meant that every man, even among the common people, should be allowed to have full scope for his abilities. This principle marked the fundamental distinction between the conditions which were to exist under the new regime and those that had existed under the feudal system, which was in fact a military organisation in which the welfare of the agricultural, industrial, and commercial classes was avowedly and wantonly sacrificed for the maintenance of the warrior class. The daimyos not only governed their respective provinces, but they also held a sort of proprietary right over their respective domains, and there was no clear distinction between administrative powers and proprietary rights. The rice tax was the main source of the revenues of the daimyos, and its rate varied in different provinces, while other miscellaneous duties were imposed according to the industrial conditions of the localities. The burdens on all classes were heavy, and, what was worse, they were uncertain, as the people were liable to arbitrary contributions in the form of money and personal service. The primary conditions for individual and national welfare were therefore wanting, as increased exertion brought no advantage to the persons concerned.

The financial position of the central Government of the Shogun was equally unsatisfactory. While the Shogun exercised a supreme authority over all the clans, the respective daimyos were only to a very limited extent under his authority. They were required, in case of need, to place their military forces at his disposal and to render certain other services. No tax could be directly imposed by the central Government upon the subjects of the various fiefs, although contributions not very great in amount were made by some of the clans to the revenue of the Shogunate. Its ordinary revenue was raised principally from the territories reserved as its own, in distinction from those granted to the clans.

The financial problems before the new Government were peculiar and complicated. After the Restoration, while the central authority was transferred to the Imperial Government, the resources of the country were not under its command. Before anything like a satisfactory social and political organisation was possible, it was absolutely necessary that the methods of the feudal system should be completely changed, and especially that the particularism of the clans and the undue privileges of the warrior class should be abolished and the claims of all classes in the community be placed on a basis about which there could be no dispute and the amounts of which were certain. For some time tentative measures had to be adopted and the deficit in the revenue had to be met by the issue of inconvertible notes. Gradually, as the administration of the country came under the direct control of the Imperial Government and all the feudal privileges were abolished, it was possible to enforce uniform laws before which all sorts and conditions of people were to stand on a footing of equality.

Under the feudal system a great variety of paper notes was circulated in the various districts for purposes of trade, the value of which depended on the credit of those who issued them ; and the first duty of a centralised Government was to reform the currency and bring something like order out of chaos. The paper money of the fiefs amounting to 25,000,000 yen was exchanged for Treasury notes, but the new Government was compelled to adopt the same device as the feudal chiefs ; in five years it had issued fiduciary paper aggregating nearly 60,000,000 yen, and the notes circulated freely throughout the whole empire at par with silver, even commanding. at one time a small premium. As public works developed and the national organisation was improved to meet the requirements of the new conditions, further demands were made on the Government, which thus found itself under the necessity of issuing more paper money, with the consequence that it rapidly decreased in value, until in 1881, fourteen years after the Restoration, notes to the face value of 150,000,000 yen had been put in circulation, and eighteen paper yen could be purchased with ten silver coins of the same denomination.

The Government fully recognised its responsibilities in the matter, and, after various temporary expedients, in 1881 it was resolved that a determined effort should be made to place the currency of the country on a sound basis ; first, by reducing the volume of the fiduciary notes in circulation, and, secondly, by accumulating a specie reserve. Reference must be made to special reports for details of the methods adopted. It is sufficient for our present purpose to note that, by the middle of 1885, the volume of the fiduciary notes had been reduced to 119,000,000 yen, and their depreciation had fallen to three per cent, and the metallic reserve of the Treasury had increased to 45,000,000 yen. The resumption of specie payments was then announced and became in the autumn of that year an accomplished fact. Captain Brinkley, after reviewing the transactions involved, says : " Viewed by the light of results, the above facts constitute a fine economical feat, nor can it be denied that the statesmen who directed Japan's finances at that critical time showed clear insight, good organising capacity, and courageous energy."

As early as 1871 the New Coinage Law was promulgated, with the view of establishing the gold standard, but as in those days silver was the universal medium of exchange in the trade of the Far East, it was difficult for Japan to maintain gold mono-metallism, and for a considerable time the currency system of Japan was on the basis of bi-metallism. It was not until 1st October 1897 that the gold standard system was put in operation. Count

Matsukata, who, as Minister of Finance, was directly responsible for the change, has published a detailed report
on the subject which has been officially translated into
English, and to this reference must be made for further
information.   It may, however, be mentioned that one yen
in gold, which is the new unit of coinage, was made
approximately the same value as the old unit in silver, so
as to avoid an abrupt change in the price of commodities
and a disturbance of the relations between debtor and
creditor.

The economic change which took place when the
daimyos surrendered their "domains and people" to the
The land
tax. Emperor was in a sense a change from the
communism of feudalism to individualism.
The new Government retained the sovereign administrative
power, according to the modern principles of public law,
while proprietary right over land was granted to private
persons.   For giving up their domains the feudal lords and
their retainers were indemnified by the grant of Government
loan bonds on which they drew interest, while all occupiers
of land were at once, and without any transaction of a
personal character, recognised as owners of the respective
lands actually held by them.   Probably as economic ideas
develop in Japan this will be recognised as having been a
very serious mistake, but meantime we are merely recording
the fact.   Under the Shogunate the sale and purchase of
land were forbidden (though various means of evading the
law were not unknown), while the tenants were not at liberty
to use the land as they thought proper.   Each clan aimed
at making itself self-sustaining as far as possible and
insisted upon a certain order of crops, without due regard
to the real capabilities of the soil.   Under the new regime
the proprietors not only had perfect freedom in the cultivation of the soil, but they also had the right of selling it;
which no doubt was an excellent arrangement for those who
happened to be tenants at the time of the change.

The Government, however, claimed a tax on the value

of the land held by the different proprietors. In assessing this value the annual amount of its net produce over an average of five years was first converted into a money value according to its average price for the same period; and then this money value of the produce being considered as interest, the amount of capital necessary for yielding it was taken as the value of the land. A cadastral survey of the whole country was made, the official valuation of the land was completed in 1881, and revised in 1899 with a view to remove certain defects. The land tax was made payable in money and its rate was fixed at a percentage of the legal value of the land. At the initiation of the system it was fixed at three per cent, and in 1877 it was reduced to two and a half per cent, at which rate it remained until the augmentation of taxes that took place as a part of the so-called *post-bellum* financial programme. In 1881, the year in which the land-tax reform was completed, the yield of the land tax amounted to 42,000,000 yen in a total taxation of 60,000,000 yen; so that it was the chief source of the national revenue. Writing on the subject of the land tax, Count Matsukata, after noticing the history of the reform, says: "Land being, after all, the basis of our material life, there can be no question about the great importance of a radical change in the system of land tenure. It may be said, indeed, that the land-tax reform ushered in the social conditions under which a free play of the economic forces of the country became possible. The general principle that the obligation of the people as taxpayers should be regulated by proper laws was also implied in, and exemplified by the land-tax legislation—a principle which was afterwards expressly guaranteed by a provision of the Constitution." These sentences indicate the economic principles which guided the men who moulded present conditions in Japan.

In order to meet the rapidly increasing wants of the country, other sources of revenue besides the comparatively stationary land tax had to be found. In 1887 an income tax, at the rate of from one to three per cent was introduced as a new direct tax. A tax on Other sources of *saké*, the common drink of the Japanese, revenue. brewed from rice, had long been in force, in a somewhat arbitrary fashion, and in 1878 it was placed on a more exact basis, depending on the amount of *saké* brewed from a given quantity of rice. Its amount has been raised several times, and the tax now covers beer and other similar alcoholic liquors, and is the most important not only among the indirect taxes but among all the other sources of revenue, whether indirect or direct, including the land tax.

The war with China gave rise to considerable changes in the financial conditions of Japan, and therefore it will be useful to give here the figures showing the main items of the national revenue in the year before that memorable event :—

THE ORDINARY REVENUE IN 1893.

	Yen.
Land tax	38,808,680
Income tax	1,238,763
Saké tax	16,637,436
Customs duties	5,125,372
Other duties	8,194,512
Total taxation	70,004,763
Revenue from Government industries and property . . .	11,743,268
Miscellaneous receipts	4,135,049
Grand total	85,883,080

The termination of the war with China marked a new epoch in the financial conditions of Japan. The *post-bellum* programme of military and naval development and of engineering and industrial undertakings caused a great increase in the national Budget. Part of that was met by the indemnity paid by China to Japan and part by taxation.

At the same time the opportunity was taken of changing the standard of the currency from silver to gold. As China had in any case to raise a loan in Europe, she was easily induced to pay the indemnity in British instead of Chinese money. Thus the sum of £32,000,000 sterling was put at the disposal of the Japanese Government, and with a portion of it as reserve of the Bank of Japan, the gold standard was put in operation.

The last Budget presented to the Japanese Parliament was that of the year ending March 31, 1903, and the estimated revenue was as follows :—

ORDINARY.

	Yen.
Excise (alcohol and sugar)	69,882,212
Land tax	46,845,971
Customs duties	17,045,611
Income and business taxes	12,713,812
Other taxes	6,942,935
Total taxes	153,430,541
Stamp duties	14,304,951
Receipts from Government undertakings and State property (posts, railways, etc.) . .	50,814,978
Miscellaneous	6,244,570
Total ordinary revenue	224,795,040
Extraordinary revenue	48,835,836
Total estimated revenue	273,630,876

The estimated expenditure was as follows :—

ORDINARY.

	Yen.
Imperial household	3,000,000
Foreign affairs	2,282,785
Carry forward . .	5,282,785

	Yen.
Brought forward . .	5,282,785
Interior	10,583,416
Finance, National Debt charges . .	39,905,495
Finance, other expenses	21,858,183
Communications (post office, telegraphs, etc.), harbour works, lighthouses, etc. . .	21,172,977
Army	38,432,317
Navy	21,349,054
Justice	10,837,646
Public instruction	4,845,708
Agriculture, industry, and commerce . .	2,948,913
Total ordinary expenditure . . .	177,216,494
Extraordinary expenditure . . .	93,208,001
Total estimated expenditure . . .	270,424,495

The extraordinary expenditure included the amount disbursed in connection with the North China expedition and now replaced in State reserves from which it had been previously borrowed, large sums for railways, harbours, and other public works, the development of the army and navy, and of works connected therewith, besides extensions in the Departments of Education, and of Agriculture, Industry, and Commerce. While the *post-bellum* programme caused new taxes to be introduced and old ones to be increased, certain taxes, on the other hand, have been abolished, with a view to simplifying the system of taxation. Since the revision of the treaties which allowed freedom in the imposition of import duties, the rates of duties vary from five to thirty-five per cent *ad valorem*, according to the kinds of commodities, and also on account of the great increase of foreign trade there has been a marked increase in the customs duties. On this subject Count Matsukata has remarked :—
" Henceforth the customs duties may be counted as one of the chief items of the State revenue. Moreover, the Japanese Government has now acquired greater freedom in regulating the general system of taxation, because import duties on certain articles may be raised to degrees corre-

sponding to the internal taxes on similar articles, as has
already been done in the case of alcoholic drinks and
tobacco. We have thus recovered tariff autonomy, so far
as the general principle is concerned. But it is to be
deplored that the import duties on certain commodities are
still limited by our treaties with a few countries, of which I
am happy to say the United States is not one. Not that
the Japanese nation contemplates adopting a policy of
protection, and finds an obstacle to the adoption of such a
policy in the remaining restrictions on tariff autonomy.
Conventional tariffs on the basis of reciprocity may also be
welcome to Japan. All we desire—I think, justly—is the
total abolition of the unilateral obligations imposed upon us
in regard to the tariff that have been allowed to linger in
our existing treaty relations."

Notwithstanding the increase of national income and
expenditure in Japan, the burden of taxation on the people
is small. The direct taxes only come to a little
over three yen (between six and seven shillings) The burden of
per head of population ; which cannot be con- taxation on the
sidered excessive. It is evident from the figures which have people.
been given that the termination of the war with China
marked a most important point in the economic and
financial conditions of Japan. The country was suddenly
called upon to face the new situation which had arisen in
the Far East. Events had shown that a strong army and
navy were absolute necessities for national existence in face
of the aggressive action of some of the European Powers,
and the new position involved an increase of taxation.
Meantime, however, foreign commerce was developing at
a very rapid rate ; Western industries and engineering
undertakings were being introduced and the sources of wealth
were thus being developed, so that the increased taxation was
not very severely felt except by the poorest classes of the
community. The prices of agricultural products had greatly
increased, so that the real value of the land had at least
trebled on the average value which was assessed as the basis

of taxation. When therefore the rate of the land tax was in 1899 raised to 3.3 per cent of the legal value of the land, the real rate was hardly more than one per cent of its actual value ; so that the increase of the land tax is only a partial set-off to the relative reduction of the burden of land-owners that has automatically come about since the date of the land-tax reform. When, moreover, we remember that the farmers entered into absolute possession of the fields they had hitherto cultivated as mere tenants, and that in return for being transformed into owners they were required to pay a rent assessed on a basis of eighty years' purchase, it is evident that the so-called land tax is only a very moderate rent, and strictly speaking the farmers should not include it among their taxes.

The income tax and business tax fall chiefly on those who have benefited by the improved economic conditions of the country. Moreover, a considerable part of the national revenue is independent of taxation and is derived from Government enterprises and properties (as railways, posts, telegraphs, telephones, factories, forests, etc.) ; an item which naturally increases with the country's prosperity. Twelve years ago the income from this source was 8,500,000 yen ; now it is over 50,000,000 yen. This amount is, in fact, the dividend which is paid on the investments made in national undertakings. Further, another considerable part of the national revenue is derived from the taxes on *saké* and tobacco, which, of course, need not be paid by any person desiring to avoid them, as they are of the nature of luxuries, while the customs dues are an indirect impost scarcely felt by the buyers of imported goods. When the whole facts of the case are considered, they do not seem to indicate any excessive addition to the burden of taxation.

The following table shows the relative position, *per head of population*, of revenue, expenditure, taxation, imports and exports for the years 1892-3 and 1902-3 ; in the interval a gold standard had been adopted and the figures for the first-named year are reduced to that standard.

	1892-3	1902-3
	Yen.	Yen.
Total Revenue . . .	3.33	6.16
Total Expenditure . .	2.52	6.15
Ordinary Revenue . .	2.64	5.06
Ordinary Expenditure .	2.09	3.88
Taxation	2.15	3.32
Imports	2.35	5.93
Exports	2.98	5.64

One of the most striking features in the administration of Japan is the fact that the greater part of the developments which have taken place have been brought about without much assistance from foreign National debt. capital, the amounts required being, for the most part, raised in Japan. Reference must be made to the Reports of the Finance Department for details of the various loans. It should, however, be noted that none of them have been used for the purpose of making up any deficit in the ordinary revenue of the State. They have been occasioned by the reorganisation of national institutions, the adjustment of finances, the construction of public works and the development of civil and military affairs generally. The following table shows the amount of interest-bearing debts at intervals of ten years from 1871 :—

Year.	Amount.	Rate of Interest.	Interest per head of Population.
	Yen.	Per cent.	Yen.
1871	4,880,000	9.00	.013
1881	237,349,361	6.45	.417
1891	246,042,374	5.42	.328
1901	547,575,950	5.15	.602

Even with the highest figures the amount of debt per head of population is under twelve yen, or twenty-four shillings, which is very small compared with what we find in European countries. According to the financial scheme which has been fixed, the total amount of the debt will be redeemed in fifty years. Such schemes are seldom carried out as arranged, as national events occur which make some alteration necessary, but unless something very unexpected happens the capacity of Japan to pay off her liabilities is ample, provided her finance be well managed.

When we compare, as is done in the following table, the amount of national debt *per head of population* for some of the chief countries of the world, we find that of Japan is very small indeed.

NATIONAL DEBTS IN 1901 :—

	£	s.	d.
Commonwealth of Australia	51	3	4
France	33	1	0
Argentina	18	14	11
Great Britain	18	9	11
Italy	15	17	11
Egypt	10	12	2
Russia	4	19	8
Sweden	3	15	5
Mexico	3	14	0
Japan	1	6	4

The yearly interest on the British national debt comes to about 10s. per head, whereas that on the Japanese national debt is only about 1s. 2d. per head of population. Moreover, that amount in Japan does not all represent taxation, as a considerable part of the national debt has been invested in productive works which return a very large and increasing revenue. Measured by the standard of wages, the working classes of Japan should find it much easier to pay the interest on her national debt than do those of Great Britain.

With the development of local government the expenditure of the local authorities has been increasing at a rapid rate. Large sums have been devoted to useful public works, the establishment of public institutions of various kinds and the support of education. Less than ten years ago the prefectural and communal

Local finances.

revenue aggregated about 53,680,000 yen and the expenditure about 44,730,000 yen, while the latest published returns give the former as 129,300,000 yen and the latter 112,860,000 yen. The increase may be expected to continue with the progress of the times, and the central Government is exercising strict attention to prevent any undue expansion of the local expenses.

To meet the expenditure a large sum is obtained from property owned by the local administrations, and the central treasury grants a considerable sum. The system of local taxation is complicated, but, speaking generally, two kinds of impost have to be paid : first, a prefectural tax ; and secondly, a town or district tax. Some of the local taxes are levied on the basis of the national tax, in which case the former must not exceed a certain fixed fraction of the latter ; some are levied independently, as taxes on houses, vehicles, and draught animals. The same principle of graduation is observed in the case of the house tax as in the income tax, and in other cases a distinction is made between the taxation of the rich and the poor ; so that the burden decreases rapidly as the poorer classes are reached. Before any new local tax is levied it must receive the approval of the prefectural or city, town or village legislative council, as the case may be. For a tax of importance the sanction of the Ministers of Home Affairs and of Finance must be obtained.

Prior to the Restoration the only organisations which existed for the collective use of capital in business were the guilds or unions and the exchange merchants who undertook the exchange business of the Banking system. feudal princes. The new Government lost no time in devising measures for the promotion of foreign trade, and very soon banks of different kinds were established which took a very important part in the development of the country. In 1872 the Government issued banking regulations, and a number of National Banks were established. They had the privilege of issuing convertible notes under seemingly favourable conditions, and these notes were designed gradually to replace the inconvertible notes issued by the Government. Owing, however, to the great flow of specie from the country, the National Banks soon found it impossible to maintain specie payments, and the Government had to allow them to exchange their notes with Government notes. Thus they failed to be of use as instruments for the gradual withdrawal of inconvertible notes, and with few exceptions their influence was small. It soon became evident that there was need for a central bank, placed in a supreme and commanding position, above all the others, and in 1882 the Bank of Japan was established for the purpose of bringing the other banks nearer together and of facilitating the monetary circulation throughout the country. After several alterations in the regulations regarding the Bank of Japan, the National Banks were ordered to give up their privilege of issue at the expiration of their term or at their option, and to redeem their notes with those issued by the Bank of Japan, which are convertible into gold. The Government then began to work for central and local industrial banks, in order to give facilities to agriculture and industry, as well as to turn the money spent for *post-bellum* enterprises into useful channels by means of the debentures issued by these banks. Most of the National Banks, after the expiration of their charters, have been changed into private banks and are now on the whole efficient organs of monetary circulation. The savings-banks have been an object of particular care to the Government, which, besides establishing the post-office system, has made special regulations for them, so that their business may be carried on with greater security than in the case of ordinary banks. Their number is now 487, with an aggregate capital of 58,000,000 yen. The Yokohama Specie Bank, established in 1880, with a capital of 24,000,000 yen, at present is specially designed to facilitate foreign exchange. The Hypothec Bank (*Credit Foncier*) of Japan was established in 1896 for the purpose of making long-term loans at low rates of interest on the security of real estate. To complete the organisation of the banking system, a loan was arranged in 1900, providing for the establishment of the *Credit Mobilier* of Japan, whose chief and characteristic function will be to make loans on the security of shares and debentures ; but owing to ministerial changes, the state of the money market and various other reasons, it has not yet been put into operation. A fairly complete account of the banking system of Japan is given by Mr. Yamawaki in his book on *Japan in the Beginning of the Twentieth Century*, while Dr. Sakatani, the Vice-Minister of Finance, has published a very elaborate history and description of the financial conditions in Japan, and to these and similar works reference must be made for details.

The wealth of Japan is a subject which has not been sufficiently investigated that it is possible to give an altogether trustworthy statement of its amount. The following has been given as an approximate estimate :— *Present financial conditions.*

		Millions of Yen.
Land	. . . . . .	7000
Mines	. . . . .	500
Live stock	. . . . .	80
Buildings	. . . . . .	1900
Furniture	. . . . .	400
Railroads	. . . . .	350
War and merchant ships	. . .	250
Specie	. . . . . .	200
Miscellaneous	. . . . .	300
Goods, etc.	. . . . .	800
Total	. .	11,080

Some of these items are due entirely to developments which have taken place in recent years ; the amounts of the others have been considerably increased on account of these developments, and when it is remembered that, apart from the Chinese indemnity (a great part of which was spent

on the army and navy), Japan has received little assistance
from foreign capital, the increase is remarkable.   The bulk
of the floating cash of the country has been sunk in various
enterprises, and as a natural consequence Japan now finds
herself, as put by the Tokyo correspondent of the *Times*,
"not only debarred from undertaking numerous other enterprises which would be lucrative, but also compelled to work
many of her existing enterprises with ruinously expensive
working capital.   Investments which sound almost incredible
in English ears go a-begging in Japan.   Railways offer
preferential stock at 10 per cent to complete their construction ; wealthy corporations are willing to sell 6 per
cent bonds at a considerable discount for the building of
waterworks ; and banks of the highest class gladly pay 7 per
cent on fixed deposits for six months."

The real position of a country cannot be estimated
simply by looking at purely financial returns ; due regard
must be had to its general economic and industrial conditions.   The survey which we have made of the progress
of Japan in agriculture, fishing, and mining, and of the
development of her manufacturing industries, her railways,
telegraphs, posts and telephones, her mercantile marine, her
banks and all the organisations connected with finance and
commerce, forces us to the conclusion that her economic
progress has been far more rapid than that of any other
nation.   Moreover, that progress is not by any means
superficial, but has been built on a sound basis of education,
which in some respects affords a lesson to Western nations.
The financial results which have followed from the industries
founded almost entirely by Japanese capital are proofs of
business capacity of a very high order.

Still, it must be admitted that cheap foreign capital,
introduced under proper conditions, would enable Japan to
continue her industrial and commercial development, and
hasten her national evolution.   So long as the currency was
on a silver basis, Japan hesitated to contract gold debts, and
European capitalists would not lend in terms of silver.

Now, however, that a gold standard has been adopted, the conditions are much more favourable. Moreover, both in Europe and in America the Japanese are now better known than formerly, and confidence is being strengthened in their integrity. Foreigners have now opportunities of investigating the conditions attached to any proposed undertaking, and of ascertaining the value of its security and of estimating the trustworthiness of those connected with it, and the success which has attended existing undertakings shows that there is a wide field for the employment of foreign capital, which would not only afford returns advantageous to the lenders, but also increase the wealth of Japan. On this subject Mr. Jiuchi Soyeda, the correspondent for Japan to the British Economic Association, says :—" Japan is just in the growing stage ; therefore if she becomes larger it is by natural growth, and her economic development is not as quick as it might be, because of the deficiency of nourishing capital. When once the due amount of capital is properly supplied, first from the savings of her own people, and then from the far-seeing capitalists, the progress of Japan will be much accelerated, to the mutual advantage of herself and her creditors. It is a great misfortune for Japan that her real strength is not duly known and fully admitted by the world at large. In the art of war she showed it amply, in the China-Japanese War and the Boxers' affair. Now it remains for her to prove that her capacity and ability are not inferior to her fighting power, on which she is now beginning to find out that too much stress was laid. If judgment, prudence, and patience be well exercised hereafter, a bright future lies before her in the peaceful works of commercial and industrial progress, for which she possesses many natural advantages."

BIBLIOGRAPHICAL NOTE

The Japanese Government have always published very complete accounts of the financial conditions of the country, and have thus afforded every opportunity for discussion and fair criticism. The *Financial and Economical Annual,* issued by the Department of

Finance, is a model of clearness and good arrangement, and it contains very complete statistics relating to financial and economic matters. Further details are given in H. Yamawaki's *Japan in the Beginning of the Twentieth Century*, a work which should be carefully studied by all who are specially interested in financial matters in Japan. Very full accounts of the annual Budget of the Government are published in the newspapers, and every opportunity is thus given for detailed criticism. The *Report on the Post-Bellum Financial Administration in Japan*, 1896-1900, by Count Matsukata, the Minister of State for Finance for the period, is a very valuable contribution to the history of the subject during an important period, while his *Report on the Adoption of the Gold Standard in Japan* bears testimony to his ability not only as an administrator, but also to his knowledge of the principles of international finance and trade. His article on the "Financial System of Japan," in the *North American Review* for May 1902, gives an excellent *résumé* of that system and a clear statement of conditions at that date. Chapter i. of vol. v. of Captain Brinkley's large work on *Japan and China* is probably the most useful statement on the subject for general readers. An exhaustive history of the financial administration of Japan has been written (in Japanese) by Dr. Sakatani, Vice-Minister of Finance, and it must be considered the standard work on the subject. During the past year or two many articles on different aspects of the financial conditions of Japan have appeared in British and American magazines, while the daily papers published in Japan (both in Japanese and in English) have fully discussed them ; so that students of the subject have no difficulty in obtaining either facts or opinions regarding them.

CHAPTER XVI

INTERNATIONAL RELATIONS

IN the preceding chapters it has been stated several times that the chief motive which urged the Japanese in their adoption of Western civilisation was neither the desire for increased wealth nor the blind imitation of Western customs; it was the sense of honour which cannot bear to be looked down upon as an inferior Power. The new system of education was adopted in order that men might be trained who were able to guide the destinies of the nation under the altered conditions. The laws and the administration of justice were brought into harmony with Western ideas and practice that foreigners might feel they had security for the safety of their persons and property; a constitutional form of Government was adopted that its action might reflect the ideas of the people; the means of communication were improved that the resources of the country might be developed and that Japan might take her place among the commercial and industrial nations of the world; but in all these changes the underlying motive was that "the status of the Empire of Japan may be raised ever higher and higher." The story of the attempts made by Japan to obtain what she believed to be her due position is a long one, and in some respects does not reflect honour on the representatives of the foreign nations concerned, but still the obstacles which were put in the way were, in a sense, blessings in disguise; for they made the Japanese more determined not only to attain their object, but also to fit themselves more adequately for the new duties and responsibilities which would fall upon them when they had full control of their own affairs.

On March 31, 1854, a treaty was signed by Commodore Perry on behalf of the Government of the United States and the representatives of Japan, by which the ports of Shimoda, in the province of Idzu and of Hakodate, in the island of Yezo, were opened for the reception of American ships, to be supplied with such articles as wood, water, provisions, and coal. There were stipulations with respect to the treatment of shipwrecked sailors, an article giving facilities for trading, a favoured nation's clause and provision for the appointment by the Government of the United States of consuls or agents to reside in Shimoda, provided that either of the two Governments deemed such arrangements necessary. In this year Admiral Sir James Stirling arrived with a squadron and concluded a convention with Japan by which Nagasaki and Hakodate were to be opened to British ships for repairs, supplies, etc.

First treaty with a foreign Power.

On July 29, 1858, Mr. Townsend Harris, after many delays, succeeded in concluding a fresh treaty on behalf of the United States, and shortly after this was followed by similar ones with Great Britain, France, and other nations. The treaty with Great Britain was signed by the Earl of Elgin and Kincardine and the representatives of the Tycoon (Shogun), and after pledging the two countries (in the usual diplomatic fashion) to perpetual peace and friendship and stating the arrangements for the residence of representatives, it stipulated for the opening for purposes of trade of the ports and towns of Hakodate, Kanagawa (Yokohama), and Nagasaki, and later on Niigata, and made arrangements with regard to trade and commerce. According to Article IV. it was agreed that "All questions in regard to rights, whether of property or person, arising between British subjects in the dominions of His Majesty the Tycoon of Japan, shall be subject to the jurisdiction of

New treaties.

the British authorities." Article V. stipulated that " Japanese subjects who may be guilty of any criminal act towards British subjects shall be arrested and punished by the Japanese authorities, according to the laws of Japan. British subjects who may commit any crime against Japanese subjects, or the subjects or citizens of any other country, shall be tried and punished by the Consul, or other public functionary authorised thereto, according to the laws of Great Britain. Justice shall be equitably and impartially administered on both sides." Trade and residence were allowed to foreigners in the treaty ports and they were permitted to travel without passports within a radius of 10 *ri* (about 24½ miles). A very low scale of import dues, at most five per cent, *ad valorem*, was fixed. In 1859 regular diplomatic relations were established between Great Britain and Japan, Mr. Rutherford Alcock arriving in Yedo as Her Majesty's Consul-General, on June 26. Towards the end of the year he was appointed Envoy Extraordinary and Minister Plenipotentiary, and representatives of other nations followed in due course.

On June 25, 1866, a Convention was concluded at Yedo between a Japanese minister of Foreign Affairs and the Representatives of Great Britain, France, the United States of America, and Holland, whereby some modifications were made in the tariff and some new arrangements for the encouragement of trade. By Article IV. the Japanese Government undertook to establish a bonded warehouse system, for the purpose of enabling the foreign merchants to re-export unsaleable goods without the payment of any duty. Article V. was intended to protect all Japanese produce on its way to the markets of the open ports from the payment of transit duties or any other tax, with the exception of such road or navigation tolls as were levied equally upon all native traffic. Article VI. provided for the establishment of a free mint on certain conditions. By Articles IX. and X. restrictions which were formerly placed on foreign trade were removed and all classes of Japanese, whether merchants, daimyos, or people in the employment of daimyos, were given perfect liberty to trade or to hold social intercourse with foreigners at all the open ports, without any interference on the part of the Government. They were also permitted to employ foreign shipping to trade either with the open ports of Japan or with foreign countries, and under the provisions of a passport system they were allowed to go abroad for purposes of study or trade and to accept employment on board foreign ships. By Article XI. the Government agreed to light and buoy the approaches to all the open ports. This Convention was a great step in advance, for, as Sir Harry Parkes states, "if its stipulations were faithfully executed, they would enable Japan and her people to share freely in the commerce of the world, to the complete abandonment of their old exclusive policy."

After the Restoration these treaties were confirmed by the Emperor, but from the very first the Japanese felt that some

Feelings of
Japanese
with regard
to the treaties. of their provisions placed them in a very humiliating position. They were made on the tacit assumption of the unequal status of the two contracting parties, civilised white men on the one hand and on the other Japan, just emerging from Asiatic semi-barbarism. In making treaties with Oriental non-Christian nations, Occidental Christian nations had always insisted that their subjects and citizens should be exempted from the procedure and penalties prescribed by the criminal law of the countries in which they were residing; in short, that they should enjoy within the territories of such countries the privilege of being arraigned before tribunals of their own nationality and tried by judges of their own race. In civil jurisdiction a division of functions was arranged. These principles were applied in the case of Japan, and no doubt, at first, their application was both wise and expedient. It soon, however, became evident that the Japanese were very different from other Eastern peoples in many respects, and that their loyal independent spirit rebelled against even the appearance of being in a subordinate position to Foreign Powers ; from the time the treaties were signed the "extra-territorial" regulations were vehemently condemned by all classes of Japanese, and no doubt it was the hope of being able to remove these that was the immediate cause for the despatch of the embassy mentioned in a previous chapter. As there stated, the date fixed for the revision of the treaties was July 1, 1872, and it was thought at least by some in power that an attempt should be made to have it brought about. Whatever may have been the intention, the treaty revision did not take place till a number of years later ; but although the embassy failed in its immediate object, it was fully justified by its results. It was the means of making Japan known to the Western nations, and the information which was collected on all subjects relating to national life laid the foundations of many of the developments which have brought Japan to its present position.

The foreign consular tribunals were in some cases very unsatisfactory, and, apart altogether from the principle involved in "extra-territoriality," gave just offence Foreign to the Japanese from the nature of their con- consular stitution, their methods of procedure, and their tribunals. judgments. A few of the great Powers, and notably Great Britain and the United States, organised competent tribunals and appointed expert judicial officials to preside over them ; but the majority of the Treaty States were content to entrust their authority to merchant consuls, who were not only unacquainted with the details of the laws they were expected to administer, but might also be interested, financially or otherwise, in some of the business questions which required their decision, and a Japanese subject might occasionally find that the defendant in a case would also be the judge. Still, on the whole, there were not many abuses of power on the part of consuls, and although little could be said in support of the system, it cannot be doubted that during the transition period it saved the Japanese from much trouble in which they would have been involved if they had been entrusted with a jurisdiction which they were not prepared to exercise in an efficient manner from the want of men with the necessary experience.

As I have stated, the existence of the "extra-territorial" system did much to spur on the Japanese to qualify them-

Discussions on extra-territoriality. selves for what is the right of every sovereign State; namely, judicial autonomy. In the two previous chapters we have seen how they developed their system of government, local administration, and legislation, and how they remodelled their law courts and took steps to equip them with a competent judiciary to administer the new codes. During all the time I was in Japan the subject of treaty revision was continually coming up in some form, and strong opinions on the subject were expressed both by Japanese and by foreigners. The impression which was given to those who were anxious to assist the Japanese in their efforts to raise the status of their country, was that they received little sympathy either from the representatives of the foreign Powers or in the foreign press; but as I have indicated, this may have been to the Japanese a blessing in disguise, because it made them more determined to bring their institutions up to a high pitch of efficiency, and ultimately enabled them to obtain better terms than they would have been able to get at an earlier period.

Captain Brinkley, whose long experience in Japan and intimate knowledge of Japanese matters enable him to give

Captain Brinkley's opinions. an opinion which carries authority, has summarised the position during these years in the following paragraphs :—" A portly volume might be filled with the details of the negotiations that followed Japan's proposal. Never before had an Oriental state sought such recognition, and there was extreme reluctance on the part of Western Powers to try the unprecedented experiment of entrusting the lives and property of their subjects and citizens to the keeping of a 'pagan' people. Even the outlines of the story cannot be sketched here, though it abounds with diplomatic curiosities, and though several of its incidents do as much credit to Japan's patience and tact as its issue does to the justice and liberality of Occidental Governments. There is, however, one page of the history that calls for brief notice, since it supplies a key to much which would otherwise be inexplicable. The respect entertained by a nation for its own laws and the confidence it reposes in their administrators are in direct proportion to the efforts it has expended upon the development of the former and the education of the latter. Foreigners residing in Japan naturally clung to consular jurisdiction as a privilege of inestimable value. They saw, indeed, that such a system could not be permanently imposed on a country where the conditions justifying it had nominally disappeared. But they saw also that the legal and judicial reforms effected by Japan had been crowded into an extraordinarily brief period, and that, as tyros experimenting with alien systems, the Japanese might be betrayed into many errors. A struggle then ensued between foreign distrust on the one side and Japanese aspirations on the other—a struggle often developing painful phases. For whereas the case for the foreign resident stood solid and rational so long as it rested on the basis of his proper attachment to the laws and the judiciary which the efforts of his countrymen through long generations had rendered worthy of trust and reverence, and on the equally intelligible and reasonable ground that he wanted convincing proofs of Japan's competence to discharge her novel functions with discretion and impartiality before submitting himself to her jurisdiction, it ceased to be a solid and rational case when its champions undertook, not merely to exaggerate the risk of trusting Japan implicitly, but also to demonstrate her radical unworthiness of any trust whatever, and to depict her under aspects so deterrent that submission to her jurisdiction assumed the character of a catastrophe. The struggle lasted eleven years, but its gist is contained in this brief statement. The foreign resident, whose affection for his own systems was measured by the struggle their evolution had cost, and whose practical instincts forbade him to take anything on trust where security of person and property was concerned, would have stood out a wholesomely conservative and justly cautious figure had not his attitude been disfigured by local journalists who, in order to justify his conservatism, allowed themselves to be betrayed into the constant *rôle* of blackening the character of Japan, and suggesting harshly prejudiced interpretations of her acts and motives. It is one thing to hesitate before entering a new house until its fitness for occupation has been ascertained: it is another thing to condemn it without trial as radically and necessarily deficient in this respect. The latter was in effect the line often taken by the opponents of Japan's claims, and, of course, no little resentment and indignation were aroused on the side of the Japanese, who chafing against the obvious antipathies of their foreign critics, and growing constantly more impatient of the humiliation to which Japan was intentionally condemned, were sometimes prompted to displays of resentment which became new weapons in the hands of their critics. Throughout this struggle the Government and citizens of the United States always showed conspicuous sympathy with Japanese aspirations, and it should also be recorded that, with exceptions so rare as to establish the rule, foreign tourists and publicists discussed the problem liberally and fairly; perhaps because, unlike the foreign communities resident in Japan, they had no direct interest in its solution."[1]

At the same time it must be admitted that the American attempts at treaty-making were not very successful. On July 25, 1878, a treaty was concluded at Washington (and ratified there on April 8, 1879) between the Japanese Minister, Kiyowari Yoshida, and Mr. Evarts, Secretary of State. By this instrument the question of jurisdiction was left as before, except a provision of Article IV., which stipulated that all

Attempts at treaty revision.

[1] *Encyclopædia Britannica*, new vols., article "Japan," p. 699.

criminal cases connected with the customs should be submitted for decision to the American tribunals,—but with the addition that the fines and confiscations in all such matters should fall to the Japanese treasury ; an arrangement which, from the Japanese point of view, made matters worse than before. In Article V., however, a favourable concession was made to Japan by which the right of the Government to regulate the coasting trade was recognised, while Article I. equally acknowledged the Japanese right of customs autonomy. In contradistinction to this right, Article III. stipulated that there should be no export duties on Japanese products consigned to America. This convention created considerable sensation at the time in diplomatic circles, but as Article X. stipulated that its provisions would come into force only after Japan had revised her treaties with the other Powers in a similar sense, it remained a dead letter, as the other Treaty Powers had not the slightest intention of making the desired concessions.

A statement of what may be considered the official British view of treaty revision in Japan will be found in *The Life of Sir Harry Parkes*,[1] and while some of the opinions therein expressed were justified, it illustrates very clearly the difference of the points of view of the Japanese and the foreigners. The former expected recognition of the progress which they had made before arrangements for the administration of justice on Western lines were fairly complete, and they were intensely anxious to get rid of even the appearance of foreign sovereignty. Sir Harry Parkes held that it was a misconception on their part to consider extra-territoriality *per se* as a derogation from national sovereignty. He pointed out to them that " throughout the Middle Ages in Europe different degrees of extra-territoriality were the rule rather than the exception. The Jews were more or less under their own jurisdiction, the clergy were almost wholly independent of territorial laws, the Hanse towns had their

Opinions of Sir Harry Parkes.

[1] Vol. ii. chap. xxxviii. p. 313.

privileges. Exemptions of a similar kind still exist, even in the United Kingdom. The American States are more or less extra-territorial in their system of law and administration, and in Old Japan the *tozama* daimiates enjoyed, in practice, complete home rule. There was no surprise on the one side nor concession on the other when extra-territoriality was established by the treaties of 1858. The extra-territorial system was absolutely necessary, if merely to supplement the deficiencies of Japanese law, which did not in truth exist at all." After further historical illustration of the subject, he added that " in truth, in Japan, as in China and Turkey, it was rather out of contempt—or perhaps indifference—that the foreigner was denied the benefits of territorial laws, of which he was not deemed a proper object." It must have been exceedingly difficult at the time the treaties were made to ascertain the opinions of the Japanese on this subject, but there can be no doubt that from the time of the Restoration their feeling was very strong against the system of extra-territoriality. The foreign commercial population in Japan was almost unanimous against treaty revision on the lines suggested by the Japanese, because they could not bring themselves to believe that either their persons or their property would be safe under Japanese law, and their opposition continued to the very end. Their opinions were reflected for a considerable time by their representatives to the Government of Japan, but ultimately these were convinced that the demands of the Japanese were both just and reasonable, and the majority of foreigners in Japan would now be willing to admit that they had been mistaken in the position which they took.

In 1883 the Japanese Government felt that sufficient progress had been made in the reorganisation of their national institutions and methods of adminis-
Conferences on treaty revision. tration to justify a formal demand that the foreign powers should consider the whole position and agree to the abolition of consular jurisdiction. A conference was held at Tokyo of the representatives of all

the Foreign Powers to determine a basis on which the respective Governments might come to some conclusions as to the modifications to be made in the existing treaties. On this occasion Japan was represented by her Minister of Foreign Affairs, Kaoru Inouyé, one of the most experienced statesmen in the country. He, of course, had come to the conclusion that his country's only chance of procuring international recognition of its claims was to break completely with its old system of isolation, to adopt the principle, practised by all the European States in their relations with one another, of the equal footing of natives and aliens in affairs of trade and commerce. Mr. Inouyé therefore, in return for the abolition of the consular jurisdiction of the Powers hitherto existing, offered to throw open to trade the whole empire and to place foreigners, in their pursuit of commerce and industry, on the same footing as the natives of Japan. The Japanese Government, however, did not demand that its jurisdiction over foreigners should begin at once, but suggested a transition period of five years, during which the Consular Courts should continue to some extent to exercise their authority, which would then be gradually transferred to the native tribunals. During the transition period foreigners were not to enjoy in their entirety all the rights promised to them in the interior later on. As a concession to foreign feelings it was suggested that, for a certain definite period, a number of foreign jurists should be attached as titular judges to the Japanese tribunals. Various other safeguards were suggested in order to guarantee as far as possible to resident foreigners the proper and impartial administration of justice. It was proposed that the new treaties should be valid for twelve years, while the corresponding tariffs, etc., might be subject to revision after the lapse of eight years.

Practically nothing came of this conference. Some of its members were opposed to the concessions asked for by the Japanese, and did not hesitate to express their opinions to their respective Governments, which simply shelved the

voluminous records of the proceedings. There can be no doubt,
however, that these served as a solid foundation for the
subsequent revision of treaties. Even in political circles in
Japan there now arose misgivings as to whether the proposal
to open up the empire to foreigners was not somewhat
premature ; and special objection was taken to the proposal
to appoint foreign lawyers to assist in the native courts, as
this seemed to be only another form of " extra-territorial "
jurisdiction, and not much improvement on the existing
system. On the part of the foreigners it was felt that the
clause giving the Japanese the right of denunciation after a
period of twelve years would enable Japan, after that time,
to claim a free hand simply on the ground of international
law. Even those who sympathised strongly with the claims
of the Japanese felt that the preparations for making and
codifying the laws were not yet in a stage sufficiently
advanced to impress the European Powers with the wisdom
of placing their subjects under their jurisdiction ; so that the
delay which occurred was, as I have indicated, really a
blessing in disguise, as it urged on the improvement of
legislation and administration which enabled more satisfactory arrangements to be made later on.

The subject of treaty revision was allowed practically to
lie in abeyance for a period of four years. On May 1,
Negotiations 1886, a conference of the representatives of
renewed. the Treaty Powers met in Tokyo. Japan was
again represented by Mr. Inouyé (who had meantime been
raised to the rank of Count). The subjects of the tariffs
and of the judicial arrangements were fully discussed, and it
became evident that the representatives of the Foreign
Powers were willing to make several very important concessions on the suggestions of the conference held in 1882.
The British and the German delegates on June 15 tabled a
project which, after expressly acknowledging the progress
made by Japan since the last conference in the field of
legal reform, offered to her Government the assumption of
jurisdiction over aliens, but without the conditions previously

attached to the proposed transition period and which had met with insuperable difficulties. This was decided testimony to the effect that Britain and Germany recognised the progress which had been made in Japan, and that they were willing to acknowledge her claims to equality of treatment with other Powers. Although the representatives of the other Powers gave a general adhesion to this position, they were unable to agree as to the means of carrying out the proposed changes and the guarantees deemed necessary by some of the Powers. The conference continued to sit at intervals till the beginning of July 1887, and meanwhile Japanese popular opinion grew somewhat virulent against some of the proposals, as they were thought to be derogatory to the national sovereignty. On June 19, 1887, Count Inouyé adjourned the conference *sine die*, so that the Japanese Government might be able to show what progress had been made in the codification of the laws and in the improvement of their administration, and thus prove that the guarantees demanded were no longer necessary.

In 1889, after lengthy negotiations at Berlin, a treaty was signed by the representatives of Germany and Japan, by which Japan granted very far-reaching concessions in respect of commerce, industry, and settlement, while Germany agreed to the abolition of her consular jurisdiction and recognised the complete legal sovereignty of Japan ; but only under the condition, which was still regarded as indispensable, that a number of foreign jurists should be attached to the Japanese Court of Appeal. This stipulation caused the treaty to be received with disfavour in Japan, and Count Okuma Shigenobu, who had succeeded Count Inouyé as Minister of Foreign Affairs, was made to feel this disfavour. He was attacked by a would-be assassin and severely wounded, and in consequence of the feeling which was aroused, the coming into force of the obnoxious treaty was suspended by the Government, as well as that of the identical agreements with Russia and the United States, which had meantime also been concluded.

A review of these negotiations shows very distinctly the determination of the Japanese to insist on complete sovereign powers. Foreigners generally ascribed all this to what they were pleased to call conceit, but which after all was only a very keen spirit of patriotism and national loyalty. No doubt that spirit sometimes caused them to make demands before they were in a position to satisfy all the necessary conditions, but it was a spirit of noble discontent which spurred them on to greater efforts to improve these conditions and also showed clearly to the representatives of the Foreign Powers that they were determined to gain their point. Although the conference brought no definite results, still it must be admitted that on each occasion they brought the problems a step nearer solution by causing the foreign representatives to understand the Japanese point of view. Foreign diplomatists, as a rule, look at Eastern problems from the outside only and therefore in a very superficial manner, and this ignorance of the Eastern mind, to a large extent, accounts for all the difficulties which have occurred with Eastern peoples, who are governed more by ideas than by principles and statutes. This fact should be more distinctly remembered than it is in our dealings with our Indian Empire and with that of China. Fortunately for Japan the Foreign Powers had to deal with a people which did not allow them to forget it.

Not by study but through practical experience in their dealings with the Japanese did the representatives of these Powers at last come to recognise that the time had arrived when the demands of the Japanese Government ought to be conceded. Changes had taken place in the personnel of the membership of the diplomatic body in Tokyo, and the newcomers, although for the most part profoundly ignorant of Eastern ways of thought, were free from preconceived ideas and from opinions resulting from unfavourable personal experiences ; they approached the subject of treaty revision with open minds and their common sense led them to a solution of the problems which had baffled their predecessors; and it is satisfactory to find that in these matters the representatives of Great Britain took the lead. Details of the negotiations are to be found in a well-arranged British Blue Book,[1] to which those who wish to study the subject must be referred. That document, to those who know the events of the previous twenty years, contains a great deal of condensed history and diplomacy. The Japanese representatives always seem to have retained their native politeness, which, if report be true, was not always returned by the foreign representatives, but on several occasions their patience seems to have been sorely tried. Mr. Mutsu, the Minister for Foreign Affairs, felt himself compelled on one occasion to say that " the Japanese Government do not consider themselves bound to acquiesce for ever in the present position of the question or to go on maintaining indefinitely a system of relations with Foreign Powers which they consider to be no longer compatible with the progress and changed institutions of the country "; and he added that by meeting with discouragement in London " it might be necessary to resort to other means of asserting what Japan believes to be her rights." Lord Kimberley, the British Minister for Foreign Affairs, retorted that if such language meant that Japan would set aside her treaty obligations, it would retard rather than advance the revision which they desire. In a carefully prepared memorandum, which is an excellent combination of politeness, firmness, and diplomacy, Mr. Mutsu explained that he meant nothing offensive to the British Government, but he insisted on the fact that consular jurisdiction as understood and practised in Japan is incompatible with a constitutional form of Government, and he concluded as follows :—" The conscientious endeavour on the part of the Imperial Government to fulfil, in good faith, their existing conventional obligations, coupled with their recent attitude on the subject of the strict enforcement of Japan's treaties, are in themselves strong

[1] *Correspondence respecting the Revision of the Treaty Arrangements between Great Britain and Japan* (August 1894).

guarantees that the Imperial Government have no thought of resorting to denunciation in order to free the Empire of those treaties. It only remains for the Imperial Government unequivocally, and without any reservation whatever, to declare that the proposals now under consideration of Her Britannic Majesty's Government rest solely upon their own inherent merit. They are not supported by any menace of denunciation, and the Imperial Government have no wish or intention of attempting a modification of their treaties except by the method prescribed in those treaties."

The national feeling in the matter was reflected in a letter from Count (now Marquis) Ito to Prince Nijo, of which the following passages appear in the above-mentioned Blue Book :—" Those national rights which may be asserted by the strict enforcement of the treaties should, of course, be strictly enforced ; and, moreover, should it be necessary to insist upon our national rights, we must labour to abolish and amend the provisions of such treaties. . . . The Government is convinced that it does not lie under the obligation of willingly acquiescing in the sacrifice of Japanese rights by submitting to the present treaties permanently and indefinitely."

If Mr. Mutsu had had the same knowledge of international law as his successors who now represent Japan at their own Foreign Office and in the various countries of the world, he would not have assumed such an apologetic tone. He would, with true Japanese politeness, have simply read his opponents a lesson in international law and reminded them that, as the term for which the treaties had been concluded had expired, they could be renounced by Japan without any question as to her legal right to do so. Moreover while we may give Mr. Mutsu full credit for writing what he believed to be the true facts of the case and with no intention of using a threat, it cannot be doubted that if there had been much longer delay in the revision of the treaties neither the Japanese nor the British Government, nor indeed a combination of all the foreign Governments, could have prevented some other steps than those of diplomacy from being taken, as evidence was abundant that the patience of the Japanese people had almost reached its limit.

Fortunately for all parties, no such steps were necessary, as in March 1894 the question so long at issue found definite solution in the negotiations between Lord Kimberley, represented by the Hon. Francis Bertie, Under Secretary of State on the one part, and the Japanese Minister, Viscount Aoki, on the other. On the 16th July the work was completed by the signature of a Treaty of Commerce and Navigation between Great Britain and Japan. Article XVIII. of this Treaty provides that "the several foreign settlements in Japan, possessing extra-territorial rights, shall be incorporated with the respective Japanese communes"; while by Article XX. it is stipulated that the present treaty, from the date it comes into force, shall be substituted for all previous conventions, "and, in consequence, the jurisdiction then exercised by British Courts in Japan, and all the exceptional privileges, exemptions, and immunities then enjoyed by British subjects as a part of or appurtenant to such jurisdiction shall absolutely and without notice cease and determine, and thereafter all such jurisdiction shall be assumed and exercised by Japanese courts." The Blue Book contains memoranda by Viscount Aoki and the representatives of the British Government explaining the various points in the treaty. The Japanese Minister said: "The treaty opens to Japan a new era in her foreign relations, for it proclaims for the first time its full and legitimate reception into the fellowship of nations. To Great Britain it signifies free access to the whole interior of the Japanese Empire on the usual terms of European international intercourse."

The example given by Great Britain was gradually followed by the other Treaty Powers, and it was agreed, subject to the fulfilment of certain conditions, that from

July 1899 Japanese tribunals should assume jurisdiction over every person, of whatever nationality, within the confines Followed by other Powers. of Japan, and that the whole country should be thrown open to foreigners. The foreign settlers were, as a rule, opposed to the revision of the treaties and to the giving up of the privileges which they had hitherto enjoyed, but when they saw that revision was inevitable they accepted the position and showed their willingness to co-operate with the Japanese authorities. On June 30, 1899, an Imperial Rescript was issued in the following terms :—

"Assisted by the surviving influence of the virtues of Our ancestors, it has been Our good fortune to uphold the Imperial Rescript. reign of sovereign rule and disseminate the benefits of orderly administration, resulting at home in the increased prosperity of the nation, and abroad in the strengthening of Our relations with Foreign Powers. As to the revision of treaties, Our long-cherished aspiration, exhaustive plans and repeated negotiations have, at last, been crowned by a satisfactory settlement with the Treaty Powers. Now that the date assigned for the operation of the revised treaties is drawing near, it is a matter for heartfelt joy and satisfaction that, while, on the one hand, the responsibilities devolving upon the country cannot but increase Our friendship with the Treaty Powers, on the other, it has been placed on a foundation stronger than ever.

"We expect that Our loyal subjects, ever ready to discharge public duties, will in obedience to Our wishes, conform to the national polity of enlightenment and progress, and be united as one man in treating the people of far-off lands with cordiality, and in thereby endeavouring to uphold the character of this nation and enhance the glory of the Empire.

"Further, we command Our Ministers of State to under-take the responsibility of putting the revised treaties into operation in such a manner that, by means of proper supervision over their subordinates, and the exercise of prudence and discretion, both Our born subjects and strangers may be enabled equally to participate in the benefits accruing from the new system, and that the friendly relations with the Treaty Powers may be permanently cemented."

All classes in the country united to carry out the wishes expressed in the Imperial Rescript. The Premier and other Ministers of State issued instructions to the effect that the responsibility now devolved on the Government and the duty on the people of enabling foreigners to reside confidently and contentedly in every part of the country. Probably the most significant sign of the change which had taken place in Japanese opinion was the action of the chief Buddhist prelates in addressing to the priests and parishioners in their dioceses injunctions pointing out that, freedom of conscience being now guaranteed by the Constitution, men professing alien creeds must be treated as courteously as the followers of Buddhism, and must enjoy the same rights and privileges. The confidence which the Foreign Powers placed in the good faith of the Japanese people has been fully justified, and their relations with the Government of Japan have been of a cordial nature. No doubt some questions have arisen about details and some individuals may have thought that they had some grievances, but, on the whole, foreigners in Japan have greater freedom than and as much safety as they would have in any other civilised country in the world.

As Great Britain was the first Foreign Power to recognise the freedom of Japan from foreign jurisdiction, she was also the first to follow that up by a treaty of alliance which bound the Britain of the East to that of the West with more than the ties of diplomatic friendship.[1] The advisability of such an alliance had been gradually impressing itself on the minds both of British and of Japanese statesmen as a very natural result of the political developments which had taken place in the Far East, and among others no one had recognised more clearly

Alliance with Great Britain.

[1] See Appendix B.

than Marquis Ito that the interests of Great Britain and Japan would be served by an alliance which, while actuated solely by a desire to maintain the *status quo* and general peace in the Far East and to secure equal opportunities for the commerce and industry of all nations, would at the same time ensure that the Governments of Great Britain and Japan would co-operate in all matters directly affecting these interests. On January 30, 1902, a treaty of alliance, defensive and offensive, was signed by Lord Lansdowne and Baron Hayashi, representing Great Britain and Japan respectively— a step which may be looked upon as the final stage in the recognition of Japan as one of the Great Powers of the world.

When the true and complete history of the early international relations of Japan comes to be written, it will afford Remarks on many interesting lessons to the psychologist treaty revision. and the moralist. I have touched on some of its main points only. Captain Brinkley, reviewing the subject, has said : " The most tolerant of Europeans has always regarded the Japanese—and let them see that he regarded them—merely as interesting children. Languidly curious at best about the uses to which they would put their imported toys, his curiosity was purely academic, and whenever circumstances required him to be practical, he laid aside all pretence of courtesy and let it be plainly seen that he counted himself master, and intended to be so counted. If the archives of the Japanese Foreign Office were published without expurgation, their early papers would make a remarkable record. Diplomatic euphemisms are the last thing to be sought there ; and in that respect they reflect the demeanour of the ordinary foreigner. When not a harsh critic he was either contemptuously tolerant or loftily patronising. The Japanese chafed under that kind of treatment for many years, and they resent it still, for though a pleasant alteration has gradually been effected in the foreigner's methods, the memory of the evil time survives. Besides, they neither consider the change complete nor regard its causes with unmixed satisfaction. It is not complete because the taint of Orientalism has not yet been removed from the nation, and the causes are unsatisfactory because they suggest a low estimate of Western morality."

Captain Brinkley has thus summarised the privileges conceded to foreigners under the revised treaties :—(1) They may trade, travel, and reside in any part of Japan, enjoying full protection for their persons and property ; (2) they may use the law courts on the same terms as Japanese subjects ; (3) they have full religious freedom ; (4) they are exempt from any taxes except those imposed on Japanese subjects ; (5) they are exempt from military service, military contributions, and forced loans ; (6) they may engage in all legitimate trades and mechanical operations, subject to the provisions of the law ; (7) they may enter into partnership with Japanese or foreigners or become shareholders in joint-stock companies ; (8) their ships and cargoes may come to all ports open to foreign commerce without paying any higher duties or charges than those paid by Japanese subjects ; (9) they are exempt from all transit dues, and they enjoy equality of treatment with Japan in regard to drawbacks, exportation and warehousing facilities, but the coasting trade is reserved to Japanese vessels except in the case of the existing open ports ; (10) they may lease land ; (11) they may take mortgages on land. The conditions relating to the holding of land and other matters affecting industry and commerce have been mentioned in a previous chapter.

Laws specially affecting foreigners.

We have now glanced at the most important international relations of Japan in so far as these are embodied in formal treaties, but nowadays the engineers, manufacturers, and merchants bring about conditions which have great influence in politics. Before we can understand the foreign policy of any country we must study its business relations with other countries, and therefore it is desirable that we should look at the industry and commerce of Japan in their international relations and ascertain their

International business relations.

influence on political action. It has been truly said that the engineer is the real revolutionist. He creates forces against which the efforts of politicians are vain, and even the actions of armies and navies are of little avail, since ultimately economic conditions determine the fate of nations. Legislation and political action may divert for some time the forces which are moulding national affairs, but in the long run they must yield to the economic forces which are at work. In no part of the world has this been so distinctly shown as in the countries in the Far East during the latter half of the nineteenth century.

The opening of the Suez Canal in 1869 was an event which produced immediate and serious economic changes—industrial, commercial, and financial—in the affairs of the Far East. Before that time all the trade of the Western Hemisphere with India and the Far East had been by the Cape of Good Hope, at an expenditure in time of from six to eight months for the round voyage, and the time and risks involved naturally caused a vast system of warehousing, distribution, and banking suited to the conditions. The opening of the Canal rendered the greater number of the sailing ships hitherto in use practically valueless, and an amount of tonnage, estimated by some authorities as high as two million tons, and representing an immense amount of wealth, was virtually destroyed. New steamships specially designed for the passage of the Canal were constructed, and with the improvements which have been made in recent years, the voyage from London to Bombay can now be performed in less than three weeks, while the Far East can be reached in a time varying from a month to six weeks, according to the route selected.

The telegraph communication which has been made between the Far East and all parts of the world has been the cause of great changes in commercial methods and results. The world has been shrunken into small dimensions, and economic conditions tend to a uniform level. Formerly large fortunes could be made by taking advantage of the conditions of local markets, and a good part of the wealth acquired by early British merchants in China was made by keeping swift steamers, which carried goods to markets where there was a great demand, and selling them at prices which were much above those ruling in the places of supply, and from which goods did not arrive until the high-priced stocks were disposed of.

During the past few years still further changes have been made which will have profound effects on the commerce and industry of the Far East. The completion of the Siberian Railway has brought Europe within a month of the ports of China and Japan, and has been the immediate cause of the development of Russian progress in the direction of the Pacific coast. The war between Japan and China in 1894-95 awoke the Powers of Europe to a sense of the military and naval strength of Japan, and led to those political developments which have kept the Far East in a state of unstable equilibrium ever since. In a sense, the war between the United States and Spain was a sequel to that between Japan and China ; for recent industrial and commercial developments in America and the growth of the imperial spirit in politics have made the United States a power in the Pacific, and Hawaii and the Philippine Islands were required as midway naval and military stations. These developments will lead, before long, to the construction of a Trans-Isthmian Canal either at Panama or Nicaragua (possibly ultimately at both places), which will have a profound effect on the commerce, not only of Japan and China, but also of the other countries and colonies in the East, such as Siam, Hong-Kong, Straits Settlements, and even of India. The creation of the Australian Commonwealth, which was rendered possible largely through the work of the engineer, by the construction of lines of swift steamers, of telegraph cables and connecting railways and overland telegraph lines, have all emphasised the fact that the Pacific area is destined to be the scene of the struggle, not only for political but also for commercial and industrial ascendency, by the nations of the world. Meantime we can only consider briefly one aspect of that struggle, namely, the part which Japan is likely to take in it, in order that we may the better understand her foreign policy.

A glance at a map of the world shows us that Japan is placed in a peculiarly advantageous position not only for

Geographical advantages of Japan. purposes of trade but also for military and naval defence or offence. It forms the centre of all the most important trade routes not only of the Pacific area but also of the world, connected as she is on both sides with Europe and America by lines of steamships and railways which must concentrate in her a large amount of trade and give her a great advantage in nearly every market in the world.

Japan is equally well situated for every military or naval operation which is likely to take place in the Far East, and her geographical position would go a long way to ensure her success should matters ever reach the terrible arbitrament of war. The long line of the Japanese Empire from Yezo to Formosa affords safe and convenient stations for both military and naval purposes ; the army and navy would be near their sources of supply and not thousands of miles away as would be the case with the European and American Powers. The coasts of China would thus be commanded, and the passage of any hostile forces made very difficult. Korea is within a few hours' sail of some of the strongest and most convenient ports of Japan, and Hong-Kong is close to the southern point of Formosa, the Philippines are only about seven days' steaming from Nagasaki, while Indo-China, Siam, and even Australasia are all within easy reach. It is evident, therefore, that Japan, by herself, must be a very potent factor in all Far Eastern questions. In alliance with Britain, as she now is, she would be irresistible against any combination which was likely to be formed. Moreover, there is another aspect of the subject which should not be overlooked. While I do not believe that the Japanese have any wish or intention to follow an aggressive policy, it would be well if the Foreign

Powers would recognise not only the strength of her position but also the possibilities of a stupendous military and naval organisation under the leadership of Japan, which would make the peoples of the East all-powerful should the selfish policies of European Powers drive them to an offensive position.

As I have already stated, there are two distinct and essentially different kinds of industries in Japan ; namely, those which are of native or Chinese origin Industrial com-
and which are still carried on to a very large petition with
extent in Japanese style, and those which have foreign nations.
been introduced from Western countries and are carried on on the factory system. With the former of these there is no competition in the markets of the world and they must win their way through their own inherent merits. The production of the keramic and cloisonné ware of the Japanese, of their silk fabrics, their pictures and their carvings, and in short, their art productions of all kinds, must be carried on in what is essentially the domestic system of industry if they are to retain their excellence. Each workman is an artist to a greater or less degree, and he revolts against being converted into a machine or the mere attendant of a machine. He requires work which, in itself, gives him pleasure and on which he can imprint his own personality. There is indeed a danger, as I have already pointed out, that the artistic capabilities of the Japanese may be crushed out by the use of machinery, and that they will be brought face to face with all the problems, industrial, physical, and social, which lie heavily on the hearts of all thoughtful men who have observed the conditions of modern industrial nations. While all that is admitted, it must also be recognised that mechanical and industrial development in the production of goods to satisfy many of the ordinary wants of life is a stage in the necessary evolution through which nations must pass before they arrive at a state of equilibrium in which they will endeavour to live and not simply struggle for the means of life.

The industries in Japan which will have a direct effect on her foreign policy are those conducted on the factory system and the products of which come into direct competition with those of other countries. The one which meantime appeals most to British manufacturers is that of cotton, which, as we have seen, has made great strides in Japan during recent years. Not only are the products of Japanese mills able to supply the greater part of the wants of the people of the country, but the surplus now forms a very important item in the trade with Korea and China. The Statistical Secretary of the Chinese Imperial Maritime Customs in a recent report, writing of manufactured goods, says that Japanese productions, made of cotton, imported in a raw state from China, are able to return to China and compete successfully with the home-made yarns, which are heavily taxed. In short the Japanese mills, though obliged to pay export duty on the raw cotton, together with the cost of two transportations between China and Japan, and finally import duty on the yarns as they re-enter China, can undersell the Chinese yarns in China ; a fact which speaks well of the efficiency of Japanese workers and organisation. It is a remarkable fact that Japan is now a larger importer of Indian raw cotton than all the Continental ports and the United Kingdom together. The consequence of the development of the cotton industry in Japan is that the trade of British yarns is practically at an end. The problem of an increased supply of raw cotton is one which Japan must face, in the same way as British manufacturers are attempting to face it at the present time. What is true of the cotton industry will also be true, before long, of other departments, and therefore the economic relations of Japan to other countries are a matter of great importance, not only for the supply of raw materials, but also for the sale of the manufactured products. China and Korea being the nearest countries to Japan and offering the most convenient markets are naturally those in which the Japanese take the greatest amount of political interest.

Although the development of Japanese industries has in some cases increased the competition with British and other foreign goods, it has at the same time given a great impetus to the manufacture of others, especially the machinery required in industries and in all the accessories of modern Western life. A glance at the list of imports shows that the Japanese are now users to a greater or less extent of almost all classes of foreign goods ; so that an increased demand for these has arisen which counterbalances the loss in special departments in which they now produce not only for themselves but also for their neighbours in the Far East. As the different countries in the world develop their own resources, so must the exports of Britain and other manufacturing countries change their nature. Many of these have had their origin in chance conditions which are rapidly disappearing, and the cheap supply of raw materials and efficient labour must in great part determine the future of any industry. Any attempt to prevent the action of economic forces by tariffs or otherwise must result in the great body of the people being taxed for the benefit of a small number of manufacturers.

The direct economic influence of Japanese industrial development on the countries in the Far East will, no doubt, be to disturb the conditions which have existed for generations ; but by itself it is not likely to be very great for a considerable time, for, after all, the best market will be the home market ; still as a factor in the evolution which is going on it cannot be neglected. Japanese products are finding their way into all the countries in the Far East, are gradually changing the social customs of the people and leading them to the use of Western appliances and methods, and thus again affecting economic conditions in other departments. But probably most important of all is the indirect and the educational influence of the Japanese in China and Korea ; for this is certain to tell before long on large numbers of the people, who will be stirred up to attempt manufactures on their own

Japanese industrial influence in the Far East.

account. If the Chinese were undertaking modern industries with the same energy as the Japanese, they might become the greatest manufacturing nation in the world, but they are slow to move, not because they are either stupid or lazy, but because they have a philosophy of life which keeps them out of the competitive struggle. It will be interesting to note how far they are drawn into that struggle, or whether their philosophy will be sufficient to enable them to take advantage of Western methods without allowing these to dominate social and even political conditions.

The fear has sometimes been expressed that the cheap labour of the Far East will cause a decrease in the wages of the West and a consequent deterioration of the standard of life, but that aspect of the subject has been greatly exaggerated. The tendency will be one of levelling up rather than of levelling down, and already the wages of all skilled workers in Western industries in the Far East have greatly increased. Local economic advantages will, of course, tell, but inherited skill and experience, superior organisation and management will for a considerable time more than balance these advantages. British manufacturers have much more to fear from the competition of America and Europe than from that of Japan. The start which they had in the industrial world gave them a great advantage, but it is now having its disadvantages ; for many manufacturers have kept neither their machinery, their organisation, nor their management up to the standard to be found in many of the works of the United States and the Continent, in which full use has been taken of the latest inventions and the most improved methods. The telegraph and the other means of communication to all parts of the world have to a large extent made the markets of the world one, except where they are hedged in by protective tariffs, which not only allow the local manufacturers to accumulate large profits but also discourage attempts at improvements in machinery and organisation. With the constant change in conditions there must be a constant change in methods and appliances involving not only a temporary loss of capital but also in many cases a loss, or at any rate a change, of employment which will inflict hardships on many of the individuals concerned. Whether these hardships can be met with the present individualistic social organisation is a problem which will require to be considered in the not distant future, and the study of such problems may lead to very important results. Britain especially will require to study her position very carefully and recognise the changing conditions. It was a happy concurrence of circumstances more than any virtue or talents inherent in us that gave us such a predominant position in industry and commerce during the nineteenth century, but now circumstances are tending in the opposite direction. Not only in Japan and China are great economic changes taking place, but in all the countries bounded by the Pacific area we may expect still greater changes in the near future, and these are certain to influence not only the foreign policy of Japan but that of all the great Powers of the world. If we look at the marvellous Pacific coast-line of Asia, stretching from Singapore to Vladivostock, with the vast countries of Siberia, China, and Australia, and then turn to the Pacific coast of America opposite, stretching from Alaska to Patagonia, with the vast countries of Canada, the United States, South America, and the rest, and imagine the population which will be in these countries by the end of this century, we are almost overwhelmed with the thought of the possibilities of the position. Meantime we cannot discuss these possibilities, but we may rest assured that Japan will take a very important part in them. In conjunction with China she might not only revolutionise economic conditions in the Far East, but also have great effect on those of the West. The late Secretary Seward, nearly forty years ago, made a prediction in the Senate of the United States that "the Pacific Ocean, its shores, its islands and the vast regions beyond, will become the chief theatre of events in the world's great Hereafter."

That prophecy is now being fulfilled; but whether these events are to be the outcome of free economic forces, whether they are to be guided by legislation and tariffs or whether the competitive struggle will lead to armed combinations which will upset all calculations and speculations, are secrets that only the future will reveal. The direct as well as the indirect economic influence of Japan on other countries and especially on those which are bounded by the Pacific area, will form a most interesting study during the course of the present century, and attention to that study will be necessary on the part of the men who guide the destinies of the nations concerned, if their policy is to be carried out on rational lines.

BIBLIOGRAPHICAL NOTE

A history of treaty revision in Japan will be possible only when access is given to the archives of the Japanese Foreign Office and to those of the Foreign Powers, or when some of those who took part in the negotiations publish their impressions and observations. An outline has been given in Captain Brinkley's article on Japan in the supplementary volumes of the *Encyclopædia Britannica*, and Baron Alexander von Siebold has given a fuller account of it in his book, *Japan's Accession to the Comity of Nations*, although in some parts it does not seem to be quite impartial. The files of the daily newspapers are almost the only sources of information available to general readers. The British Blue Book containing the correspondence respecting the revision of treaty arrangements between Great Britain and Japan, and the corresponding publications of the other Foreign Powers, are the only official published documents, and from these a good deal can be learned by those who lived in Japan at the time and thus are able to read between the lines. With regard to international business relations, little of a scientific nature has been written, and reference can only be made to current publications, as the conditions are rapidly changing. Stafford Ransome's *Japan in Transition* contains some suggestive matter on the subject, and Alfred Stead's *Japan, Our New Ally*, will be useful to general readers. Interesting chapters on " Japan as a World Power " will be found in the two last-named works, also in Clement's *Handbook of Modern Japan*, and Norman's *Real Japan*. Conditions, however, are changing rapidly, and with them new problems are arising.

CHAPTER XVII

FOREIGN POLITICS

WE are now in a position to understand the foreign politics of Japan. I have endeavoured to indicate the motives and the economic forces which have been at the root of all the great changes which have taken place ; and we cannot doubt that the intense feeling of patriotism among the Japanese and the determination to make their country stand in a position of equality with foreign nations were the most important factors in the movement which has profoundly changed all the conditions of Japan. Such a feeling naturally led to actions which, in many cases, had the appearance of presumption, and no doubt sometimes the appearance had a good deal of reality ; but in times of transition, when old ideals of individual and national conduct are disappearing and new ones have not yet fully taken their place, a certain amount of eccentricity is to be expected. However, after discounting all that even the most severe critics have said about them, it cannot be disputed that, notwithstanding their apparent fickleness, the Japanese have steadily kept to the main ideas with which they started when they decided to adopt Western methods. These, as I have more than once stated, were embodied in the principles proclaimed on oath by the Emperor on the occasion of his accession to the throne.

Behind the patriotic motives there are strong economic and political forces which have influenced the foreign policy of Japan. The rapid increase in population and the necessity for outlets not only for the surplus population but also for the surplus industrial products, has been forcing

Economic forces. Japanese statesmen to consider the problems involved, and like the statesmen of other countries they have sought them in the settlement of numbers of their people in foreign countries and in an extension of their foreign markets. Korea, from her geographical position, her sparsely peopled territory and her undeveloped resources, is the most natural outlet. Moreover, its historical connection with Japan gives the Japanese a first claim among Foreign Powers for close relations and, if necessary, friendly protection. The development of industry in Japan is making the country to a certain extent (although as yet not to a very great extent) dependent on the produce of other countries for the food of its population ; and as Korea is a rich agricultural country, it is important that Japan should be able to control it so far as to ensure a supply of food for those of her people who are engaged in manufacturing industries. Most important of all, however, is the fact that the possession of Korea by a strong Foreign Power would give her a strategetical position which would not only dominate Japan but even threaten her national existence. These considerations have to a large extent displaced the ideal of a self-contained empire, by one whose influence would be felt in the councils of the world, and especially in all that directly affects the countries in the Pacific area.

When I arrived in Japan (in 1873) the highest ambition of all the officials with whom I came into contact, and also

Ambition to become the Britain of the East. of my own students, was that their country might become the Britain of the East, and they not infrequently got laughed at by foreigners for what was considered their concelt. During the thirty years which have elapsed since that time they have kept their ideal steadily in view, and few will deny that they have gone a long way towards its realisation. They have laid a solid foundation for national progress in a system of education which is very complete in every department, and which, in some respects, affords lessons to Britain; they have formed an army and a navy which cause the opinions of Japan to be considered with respect; they have developed their railways, their shipping, their telegraphs and the other appliances of modern life to an astonishing extent; their industry and their commerce have made wonderful developments, and the machinery of legislation and administration has been brought into line with those of European countries.

The geographical position of Japan gives her a maritime advantage relatively to Asia precisely analogous to that occupied by Great Britain to Europe. So far as I have been able to judge from the utterances of her statesmen, from the opinions expressed by the press and the general ideas of the people, the Japanese have no higher ambition than that their country should become the Britain of the East, resting secure in her own strength, but with no wish for territorial expansion in other parts of the world. Whatever influence she exercises on Asia or indeed on any other Continent, they wish that that should be through wise statesmanship and the peaceful methods of commerce and education. A great part of the success of the modern movement in Japan arises from the fact that the impulse came from within and that the people have recognised their own powers and the possibilities of their country. As a thoughtful Japanese writer has said: " It was some small degree of this recognition that remade Japan and enabled her to weather the storm under which so much of the Oriental world went down." No doubt, believing that Asia can be really influenced for good only by those who understand Asiatic modes of thought, the Japanese think that they have a special rôle in the regeneration of the Far East, and this idea may occasionally lead them into what, to Western minds, may seem extravagances; but on the whole, so far as I have been able to judge of those who have any authority in Japan, they will be content to allow their influence to develop in a natural way; that is, through the intercourse of commerce and industry and the results of education. It must, however, have been evident to those who have studied the subject, that Japanese policy, both at home and abroad, has developed through change of conditions, and recent events in the Far East may have enlarged the views and ambitions of the Japanese ; or perhaps, to be more exact, they may compel them to take steps in self-defence which never occurred to them when the subjects were first discussed. The aggressive action of Foreign Powers may indeed compel them to actions which also seem aggressive, but it is to be hoped that whatever happens, they will always be willing to grant to other Eastern nations all the rights which they have claimed for themselves, and chief among these is the right to work out their own national salvation in their own way, without foreign domination.

As we have seen in previous chapters, for a good many years after the advent of foreigners in Japan, diplomatic action was, for the most part, confined to the dis-cussion of the revision of treaties, and especially in so far as these affected tariffs and the question of extra-territoriality, and Japan had practically no foreign politics. Now that she has attained a position of equality with other nations, she asks no favours, but she means to insist on her rights. Her alliance with Great Britain was formed from a desire to maintain the *status quo* and general peace in the Far East, especially the territorial integrity of the Empires of China and Korea, and to secure equal oppor-tunities in these countries for the commerce and industry of all nations. She has in many ways made it clear that she has no wish for territorial aggrandisement, but she may be driven to take steps to protect her interests and reach her ideals which may seem to be opposed to the strict letter of some of her words. If that be so, the Foreign Powers will have themselves to thank. She is not likely to interfere either in European or in American politics if her legitimate rights are respected. Her task lies in the Far East, and whatever influence she exercises in the countries of the West will only be indirect. She may, however, afford those countries many useful object lessons, and it is sincerely to be hoped that their foreign policy will be such as will enable East and West to co-operate in advancing the highest welfare of both.

While it is, of course, impossible to give what may be considered a strictly official view of Japanese foreign policy, the speeches and writings of representative men who hold or have held high positions in the Japanese Government may be taken as indicating fairly well the opinions of those who guide the policy of the Government, and especially when it is found that the diplomatic and political action of the Government agrees with the ideas expressed by those from whom we quote. The following from a paper read to the American Academy of Political and Social Science[1] by Mr. Takahira, the Japanese representative at Washington, on "The Position of Japan in the Far East," may be taken as representing what may be called the intelligent official view of the subject. After dealing with some historical details, Mr. Takahira said: "Japan has never had an intention to take advantage of the misfortunes of her neighbours or to seek for territorial aggrandisement, but the sincere desire of her Government and people is to have all neighbouring countries realise that mutual interests can best be promoted by the maintenance of peace, the promotion of commerce and industry, and the strengthening of the ties of interdependence. It is not meant by this that a race coalition should be formed hostile to the interest of other countries ; such a coalition as has been typified in the expression 'Yellow Peril.' My meaning simply is that a country to be truly prosperous should have peaceful and prosperous neighbours. That naturally leads to interdependence, not political, but social and commercial, and establishes the surest guarantee of peace to all concerned. Some portions of the world have been compared to an armed camp, each country watching the others and each jealously

Japanese ideas on foreign policy.

[1] March 7, 1903.

apprehensive of encroachment. Under such conditions men prosper not because of this policy but in spite of it. It is no part of the ambition of Japan to establish such a state of things in the Far East, least of all to combine with her neighbours for aggression or even for defence. She wishes them to be peaceful and prosperous, because that is the most certain means by which her own peace and prosperity can be assured; and she desires them to appreciate at its full worth the advantage of interdependence, because their relations and their relative positions are such as to render it an indispensable pre-requisite to mutual prosperity. . . . It is not out of place here to call attention to statements which have appeared in different publications expressing the fears of certain over-anxious persons regarding the modernisation of Asiatic peoples. [Here follows a quotation from an article written in 1893.] In this group of wonderful hypotheses may be found the only basis for the fear of a so-called 'Yellow Peril' to which I have already alluded. The usual corollary is that Japan has a desire to control China thus rejuvenated, and to lead her myriads against the rest of the world. So far as China is concerned, the best answer to such arguments is her present condition, ten years after the foregoing article was written. As for Japan, her conduct throughout the Boxer troubles and the course she has pursued since those unfortunate events, have shown the world that she has the same cause to uphold in China and the same interests to protect as other civilised nations. It is therefore self-evident that so long as China maintains a correct position towards the civilised world she will retain Japan's friendship; but that she cannot rely on Japan for support when she assumes a wrong attitude. . . . While we are thus labouring for ourselves, our most earnest desire is that the kindred people who are our neighbours shall labour in the same manner for themselves and endeavour, as we have done, to raise themselves above the hardships and miseries of their present condition. That sums up, in a word, Japan's position among Eastern nations. We are in duty bound and in interest forced to do all that lies in our power to assist our neighbours in the path which we have followed, and in performing this task we esteem peace and the preservation of the kindliest and most cordial relations with all as an essential pre-requisite to success."

Commenting on these opinions, the editor of the *Japan Daily Mail* (Captain Brinkley, a very competent authority) says : " These utterances have, of course, a certain academical sound, but as an exposition of Japan's position, coming from one of her responsible officials, they are undoubtedly valuable. A man's interpretation of his neighbour's mood is generally a reflection of his own. There has not been any period of the world's history since mediæval days when racial prejudice prevailed more strongly among Western peoples than it prevails to-day, and naturally these nations expect to detect the same sentiment on the side of its Oriental victims. It is not an unreasonable expectation. Within easy reach of Japan's hand are materials which might be welded by her into a stupendous military machine. No observer with any experience doubts that the Chinese are capable of being converted into good soldiers, or that well equipped and well led they could stand in any field. Assuming Japan to be ambitious of imperial aggrandisement, and assuming that the racial prejudice of the Orient towards the Occident is as strong and effective as that of the Occident towards the Orient, it is quite within the range of possibilities that the Japanese should be found one day at the head of an almost irresistible hegemony of Eastern peoples. Some such apprehension may fairly be assumed to have influenced Russia and Germany when they combined to expel Japan from Manchuria, and that the same apprehension is almost overwhelming in Russia's case seems to be the only way of explaining her subsequent aggressions in Manchuria, which could scarcely fail to strain Japan's patience to breaking point. A hard task is imposed on Japan to prove herself true to the creed that Mr. Takahira enunciated at Philadelphia. But she is trying."

Many opinions have been given (very often on imperfect knowledge and very scant experience), on the future of Japanese policy, but the following by Lord Curzon, now Viceroy of India, may be taken as representing the intelligent and statesmanlike view of the subject. After criticising some of the opinions expressed by foreign writers, Lord Curzon says : " The critics to whom I allude had lost sight of the part which Japan aspires to play in the Far East, and to which her policy of expenditure and organisation has been strictly subordinated. That part is determined by her geographical situation. Placed at a maritime coign of vantage upon the flank of Asia, precisely analogous to that occupied by Great Britain on the flank of Europe, exercising a powerful influence over the adjoining continent, but not necessarily involved in its responsibilities, she sets before herself the supreme ambition of becoming, on a smaller scale, the Britain of the Far East. By means of an army strong enough to defend our shores, and to render invasion unlikely, and still more of a navy sufficiently powerful to sweep the seas, she sees that England has retained that unique and commanding position in the West which was won for us by the industry and force of character of our people, by the mineral wealth of these islands, by the stability of our Government, and by the colonising genius of our sons. By similar methods Japan hopes to arrive at a more modest edition of the same result in the East. Like the English, her people are stubborn fighters and born sailors. If she can but intimidate any would-be enemy from attempting a landing upon her shores, and can fly an unchallenged flag over the surrounding waters, while from her own resources she provides occupation, sustenance, clothing, and wages for her people, she will fulfil her rôle in the international politics of the future." [1]

The greatest difficulties in the problems connected with China and Korea arise from the fact that the Governments of those countries are not animated by that spirit of

[1] *Problems of the Far East*, p. 393. .

patriotism which made the Japanese so jealous of everything touching their independence. The conduct of European
Governments has been so unscrupulous and Chinese opinions
selfish, and the Chinese officials so untrust- and ideals.
worthy, that it is impossible for outsiders to state any
guiding principles in the foreign affairs of China. At the
same time, even an approximately correct opinion about
Japanese policy in China cannot be formed without a study
of these affairs. All that we can do, meantime, is to give
a general idea of the impression which the policy of the
Foreign Powers has left on the Chinese mind. This has
been expressed by Sir Robert Hart in the following terms :
—" We did not invite you foreigners here," they say ; " you
crossed the seas of your own accord and more or less forced
yourselves on us. We generously permitted the trade you
were at first satisfied with, but what return did you make ?
To the trade we sanctioned you added opium-smuggling,
and when we tried to stop it you made war on us. We do
not deny that Chinese consumers kept alive a demand for
the drug, but both consumption and importation were
illegal and prohibited ; when we found it was ruining our
people and depleting our treasury we vainly attempted to
induce you to abandon the trade, and we then had to take
action against it ourselves. War ensued ; but we were no
warriors, and you won, and then dictated treaties which gave
you Hong-Kong and opened several ports, while opium still
remained contraband. Several years of peaceful intercourse
followed, and then Hong-Kong began to trouble us ; it was
originally ceded to be a careening place for ships simply,
but, situated on the direct route to the new ports, it grew
into an emporium, and also, close to our coast and rivers, it
became a smuggling centre ; in your treaties you had undertaken a certain control of any junk traffic that should spring
up, but when that traffic became considerable you dropped
the promised control and our revenue suffered. Originally
uninhabited, Hong-Kong now became the home of numerous
Chinese settlers, many of them outlaws, who dare not live

on the mainland; these became British subjects, and you gave the British flag to their junks, which were one day British and another Chinese just as it suited their purpose; and out of this came the *Arrow* war, followed by new treaties, additional ports, legalised opium, and fresh stipulations, in their turn the causes of fresh troubles. Whether it was that we granted you privileges or that you exacted concessions, you have treated the slightest mistakes as violations of treaty rights, and instead of showing yourselves friendly and considerate, you insult us by charges of bad faith and demand reparation and indemnities. Your legalised opium has been a curse in every province it penetrated, and your refusal to limit or decrease the import has forced us to attempt a dangerous remedy; we have legalised native opium, not because we approve of it, but to compete with and drive out the foreign drug, and it is expelling it, and when we have only the native production to deal with, and thus have the business in our own hands, we hope to stop the habit in our own way. Your missionaries have everywhere been teaching good lessons, and benevolently opening hospitals and dispensing medicine for the relief of the sick and the afflicted, but wherever they go trouble goes with them, and instead of the welcome their good intentions merit, localities and officials turn against them; when called on to indemnify them for losses, we find to our astonishment that it is the exactions of would-be millionaires we have to satisfy! Your people are everywhere extra-territorialised; but, instead of a grateful return for this ill-advised stipulation, they appear to act as if there were no laws in China, and this encourages native lawlessness and makes constant difficulties for every native official. You have demanded and obtained the privilege of trading from port to port on the coast, and now you want the inland waters thrown open to your steamers. Your newspapers vilify our officials and Government, and translated into Chinese circulate very mischievous reading; but yet they have their uses, for by their threats and suggestions they warn us what you may some day do, and so help us indirectly, although that does not conduce to mutual respect or liking. All these things weaken official authority— therefore the official world is against you ; and they hurt many native traders — therefore the trading classes are indignant. What countries give aliens the extra-territorial status? What countries allow aliens to compete in their coasting trade? What countries throw open their inland waters to other flags? And yet all these things you compel us to grant you ; why can you not treat us as you treat others? Were you to do so you would find us friendly enough, and there would be an end of this everlasting bickering and these continually recurring wars ; really you are too short-sighted, and you are forcing us to arm in self-defence, and giving us grudges to pay off instead of benefits to requite." [1]

Those opinions which Sir Robert Hart puts into the mouth of a Chinaman are becoming public opinion in China, and they have been intensified by the events of recent years. The so-called leases of Kiao-Chow, Port Arthur, Talienwan, and Wei-Hai-Wei, and especially the doings of the Russians in Manchuria, have raised very strong feelings among the educated Chinese. The excesses which are sometimes perpetrated in China are simply the blind, inarticulate reaction against the feelings of injustice which the people have with regard to the action of foreigners. These feelings are the causes of Japanese influ-the increasing influence of Japan in China, as ence in China. the Chinese recognise that the Japanese understand their ways of thought better than Europeans, and it is becoming more and more evident that the idea is taking hold of the Japanese that it is the mission of Japan to bring China, as it were, into the sphere of her intellectual, moral, and social influence. Not only, as we have seen, is the trade with Japan increasing, but Japanese influence is rapidly extending in educational, military, and police affairs in China.

[1] Hart, *These from the Land of Sinim*, pp. 119-122.

Many of the educational institutions throughout the country are superintended by Japanese, and in the training of Chinese troops Japanese have, to a large extent, taken the place of the Europeans who were formerly employed. Gunboats and other vessels are being built in Japan for the Chinese service, and it is understood that arms and ammunition are being purchased in Japan. Hundreds of Chinese students are now in Tokyo and other parts of Japan fitting themselves, in many ways, for their future work in China; so that in a sense Japan is repaying to China the debt she owed to her for her former civilisation. We are safe in assuming that if the foreign policy of Japan ever brings her into collision with a European power, the real (whatever the apparent) *casus belli* will be the control of China, and that not merely on account of the commercial and industrial interests involved (which, of course, are very great and more than sufficient to give the controlling Power a preponderating influence on the Pacific) but probably even to a greater extent because of the special mission which Japan believes herself to have in the rejuvenation of China.[1]

Korea being the nearest part of the Asiatic continent to Japan, is, of course, the part which commands the first atten-
Japan and tion. The earlier relations which existed between
Korea. Japan and Russia have been briefly indicated.[2] The interference of Russia, Germany, and France to prevent the Japanese permanently occupying any part of the mainland of China was evidently prompted by jealousy and selfish ends. Not only did Russia see that such an occupation would prevent her progress towards the Pacific, but probably also the representatives of the three Powers named shared the opinion of the German Emperor that it might lead to a combination of Eastern forces which would threaten the safety of Europe, and

[1] For an excellent and condensed account of the doings of the Foreign Powers in China and their results reference may be made to Brinkley's *China and Japan,* vol. xii., and especially to the last three chapters.

[2] Cf. pp. 69-73.

indeed of the world. Such a thought was entirely unwarranted, and it had never entered the brains of any responsible Japanese ; while the Chinese have shown by their conduct that war will never be of their seeking, not because they are cowards, as is frequently supposed, but because they are philosophers and detest war.

After the war with China (1894-95), Japan was for a time supreme in Korea, and if more prudent counsels had prevailed, that supremacy would not have been disturbed. It was admitted by every one who knew anything about Korea that its Government was in a most corrupt and decrepit condition, and that reform was a necessity before there was any hope of the country. The Japanese ought to have known from their own experience that real reform was only possible when it came from within, and that it could not be impressed from without, and that it was therefore absurd to present the Korean Government with a cut-and-dried scheme of reforms as precise as their military plan of campaign, and to insist on it being carried out as if it were a school exercise. The programme included the reorganisation of the finances, the reform of the civil service and the institution of a national army, as well as educational and judicial reforms. When to all this was added a demand for the compulsory development of Korean resources by mining, railway, and commercial concessions, in which would be found a profitable outlay of Japanese capital, there was raised not only the opposition of the Korean Government but also that of the Foreign Powers. The hatred of the powerful family of the Queen, the members of which found themselves threatened with the loss not only of their offices but also of the opportunities which these gave them of enriching themselves, was found to be a great obstacle to the success of the Japanese, and in 1895 a party of Korean malcontents, accompanied and aided, if not actually led by Japanese soldiers, broke into the palace and murdered the Queen and a great number of her relatives. These unfortunate occurrences had most disastrous effects on Japanese influence. The King took refuge in the Russian Legation, and from that time date the troubles which now seem to be nearing a crisis. The Japanese minister who had served his country so badly was replaced by Baron Komura, the present Japanese Minister of Foreign Affairs, whose diplomatic tact and ability was as conspicuous as was the lack of it in his predecessor.

From that time, Japan's earnest wish has been to come to terms with Russia, and to secure the safety and independence of Korea by diplomacy. She has extensive interests both commercial and industrial in the country, and has large settlements at every port open to foreigners. Three-fourths of all the foreign trade and shipping of Korea are in the hands of Japanese, whereas Russia has practically no commercial interests. Two conventions with regard to Korea were agreed to between Japan and Russia. By the first each Power was allowed to have in Korea a sufficient number of troops, not exceeding 800, for the protection of its legation and settlements, and in addition the Japanese were allowed a certain number of gendarmes for the protection of their telegraph line between Fusan and the capital. By the second, concluded in Tokyo in 1898, between Baron Nishi, the Japanese Minister for Foreign Affairs, and Baron Rosen, the Russian Minister, both Governments "definitely recognised the sovereignty and entire independence of Korea, and mutually pledged themselves to abstain from every direct interference in its internal affairs"; and that of Russia further pledged itself "not to obstruct the development of industrial and commercial relations between Japan and Korea." Mr. Longford (late of the British Consular Service in Japan) remarks that "all these undertakings of both conventions were faithfully observed by Russia, as long as it suited her to do so, and that period only lasted until her military resources in the Far East reached a stage of development which she thought would enable her to meet Japan on equal terms."

The discussion of affairs between Japan and Russia

became very acute during the summer of last year, when it was found that the Russians had taken possession of a concession which was said to have been granted by the King of Korea when he was a refugee in the Russian Legation in 1896, and the usual Russian methods were followed. Forts were erected commanding the Yalu River, and a claim was put forward that the valley of the Yalu was included in the sphere of Russian influence. The Japanese saw that this looked suspiciously like their methods of procedure in Manchuria. There they had commenced with the leasing of a small portion of the Liaotung peninsula, and they gradually extended their military occupation over the whole of Manchuria. They disregarded with cynical effrontery their promises to evacuate the territory by specified dates, and instead they steadily strengthened their military position, giving every indication that they meant to make their occupation permanent. The Japanese took these lessons to heart, and determined to bring the matter to an issue before Russia had time to make herself overwhelmingly strong. We need not follow all the discussions and correspondence which were carried on in the latter half of last year, the following Japanese official *communique* plainly states the case for Japan :—

" It is absolutely indispensable to the safety and welfare of Japan that the independence and territorial integrity of Korea should be maintained, and that Japan's own paramount interests there should be safeguarded.

" Accordingly, the Japanese Government find it impossible to view with indifference an action endangering the position of Korea.

" Russia, despite her solemn treaty with China and her repeated assurances to the Powers, not only continues in occupation of Manchuria, but has even taken aggressive action in Korean territory.

" Should once Manchuria be annexed to Russia, the independence of Korea would naturally be impossible.

" This must, no doubt, be acknowledged by Russia

herself, because in 1895 Russia expressly intimated to Japan that the possession of the Liaotung peninsula by Japan would not only constitute a constant menace to the capital of China, but would render the independence of Korea illusory.

" Under these circumstances, the Japanese Government, being desirous of securing a permanent peace in the Far East by means of direct negotiations with the Russian Government, with a view to arriving at a friendly adjustment of mutual interests, in both Manchuria and Korea, where the interests of Japan and Russia meet, communicated such desire to the Russian Government towards the end of July last, and invited them to meet it. The Russian Government then expressed their willing consent.

" Accordingly, on the 12th August last, the Japanese Government proposed to the Russian Government, through their representative at St. Petersburg, a basis of agreement on the subject, which was substantially as follows :—

" 1. A mutual engagement to respect the independence and territorial integrity of the Chinese and Korean Empires.

" 2. A mutual engagement to maintain the principle of the equal opportunity for the commerce and industry of all nations in those two countries.

" 3. Reciprocal recognition of Japan's preponderating interests in Korea and Russia's special interests in railway enterprises in Manchuria, and mutual recognition of the right of Japan and Russia respectively to take such measures as may be necessary for the protection of the above-mentioned respective interests in so far as the principle set forth in Article 1 is not infringed.

" 4. Recognition by Russia of the exclusive right of Japan to give advice and assistance to Korea in the interest of reform and good government in the Peninsular Empire.

" 5. An engagement on the part of Russia not to impede an eventual extension of the Korean railway into Southern Manchuria, so as to connect with the East China and Shanhai-Kwan and Newchwang lines."

The *communique* then gives a detailed account of the negotiations which took place; it states that "the Japanese Government have throughout the negotiations been actuated by the principles of moderation and impartiality, and have demanded of the Russian Government nothing more than the recognition of a principle which has been repeatedly and voluntarily declared by Russia herself, while the Russian Government have persistently refused to accede thereto. While unduly delaying to hand their reply, whenever they had to make one, they have, on the other hand, eagerly augmented their naval and military preparations in the Far East. In fact, large Russian forces are already on the Korean frontier." Enough has been said to make the question at issue clear from the point of view of Japan.

In order, however, that we may understand the whole position, it is necessary that we should look at it from the point of view of Russia. When we do that we find many of the same forces at work as in the case of Japan. In a previous chapter I have noted some of the early relations of Japan and Russia, which showed that the difficulties between the two countries were of long standing.

The case for Russia.

The history of Russian expansion in its details is, of course, beyond our present scope; it is sufficient for our purpose to notice some of its main features. Since the Crimean war great industrial changes have taken place in Russia, and many parts of the country are being transformed from agricultural to industrial and the population has rapidly increased. As the methods of Russian agriculture are extensive rather than intensive it has become necessary to absorb more and more territory not only for purposes of trade but also for colonisation. These were, no doubt, the causes, in the first instance, which chiefly led to the construction of the Trans-Siberian Railway, not only in order that the vast resources of Asia might be developed, but also that an outlet might be found for the rapidly increasing population. Russian foreign policy is therefore being guided by what are believed to be the overpowering needs of the nation, and the expansion of her territory is now being planned on a truly imperial scale at all the borders of the Empire. In North and South Europe, in Persia, in North Asia, and on the borders of India we find a Russian question which is a sort of nightmare to the countries concerned.

That question is made very difficult by the ambitions of the military leaders of Russia, before which the autocratic Russian ideas. although peacefully inclined Czar is nearly powerless. These ambitions carry the foreign policy of Russia far beyond the national requirements. Internal difficulties are shelved by attracting attention to a spirited foreign policy, and the voices of Liberalism and of Nihilism are smothered in the universal acclamation over the extension of Russian territory and influence. Moreover, it must not be overlooked that the religious feeling of the masses in Russia has always been used as a motive power for political ends. The religious cant which is uttered in connection with tortuous diplomacy or in justification of aggression is sufficient to disgust all thoughtful Easterns, whose conduct, both national and personal, is very often an example which might well be copied by those who think themselves their superiors in civilisation. It cannot be doubted that the enthusiastic Russian believes that his country has a mission in the world, not only to civilise savage tribes but to combat and correct the diseases of Western civilisation by means of the Orthodox Church. He distrusts all liberal institutions as leading to anarchy and the dissolution of society, and he believes that the Russian theocracy, religion, and such social organisations as the village community are the best antidotes to socialistic and nihilistic agitation. It is evident therefore that in discussing Russian as well as Japanese foreign policy we must go below the surface and ascertain the forces which are behind it. Unless we do this all our ideas are of a haphazard and of a generally impotent nature. The opposition between Japan and

Russia arises, at bottom, from the clash of two different ideals of civilisation.

The rapid expansion of Russia across Northern Asia is easily explained when we look at the geographical conditions. The Siberian steppes offer facilities for unlimited Expansion of expansion, and the importance to a country almost Russia. completely landlocked or ice-bound on its European frontiers naturally drove it to the Pacific shores in search of ports which were open to the trade routes of the world. The construction of the Trans-Siberian railway intensified the need for such ports. At first, its terminus was intended to be at Vladivostock, and while it was constructed to that port, it soon became evident that that was only a stepping-stone to one farther south, and which was ice-free all the year round. British statesmen have, indeed, recognised the reasonableness on the part of Russia in taking this step, and probably this accounts for the seeming weakness of British policy and action. Russian diplomacy is an art which requires long study to understand, and it is difficult to describe it. It is not doing it any injustice to call it tortuous, prevaricating, and insincere. This was clearly shown in the events which followed immediately on the termination of the war between Japan and China, which we have briefly mentioned. The more recent doings in Manchuria are further illustrations of the same thing. After obtaining possession of Port Arthur by means of her clever, if somewhat unprincipled diplomacy, Russia always protested that she had no ulterior designs on Manchuria. On that pretext she was allowed to occupy the country during the Boxer rising lest her railway to Port Arthur should be cut up. Since then she has remained in Manchuria, notwithstanding her repeated promises not only to Japan, but also to Britain, the United States, and China, to evacuate the territory long ago. The official despatches of the British Secretary of State for Foreign Affairs must be read in order to understand how difficult it is to teach Russian diplomacy to be honest. That correspondence shows that Britain and the United States are both agreed as to the necessity of preventing Manchuria from becoming a Russian province and preserve, but neither of these Powers seems inclined to take up a position which would put a stop to Russian aggression.

With them, however, the decision on the matter, while affecting their trade, is of comparatively small importance, but with Japan it is a matter of life and death. It is absurd for Russia to hold that Japan has no special interests in Manchuria as distinct from the other Powers, and therefore that she could not enter into a discussion with her on the subject. The Japanese recognise that if Russia is entrenched in Manchuria she could easily collect troops and munitions of war, overwhelm Korea and bring the Russian territory up to the Pacific Ocean. Moreover, the fact that Russia filched the results of Japan's victories in 1894-95 from her, and appropriated them for herself, gave Japan the right to raise the question in a form which will prevent the repetition of such a piece of deception. While willing to recognise the special claims of Russia in Manchuria, and especially those which arise from the construction of the railway connecting the main Siberian line with Port Arthur, the Japanese firmly insist on the political integrity of China as regards Manchuria. While Russia has promised to observe that integrity, she has shown most distinctly by her deeds that she will never give up possession until she is compelled to do so, and further, that she will, as soon as she can, take steps to obtain a firm hold on Korea. Looked at simply from a Russian point of view, and especially when sea power is considered, the possession of Korea, with its good harbours, most of which are open all the year round and capable of easy defence, is of enormous value. As Captain Brinkley puts it : " Korea is a kind of half-way house between Liaotung and Vladivostock. It commands the maritime communications between the two places. Japan, holding Korea as Russia's enemy, could close the Broughton Strait and the Tsugaru Strait to· Russian ships and thus effectually isolate Vladivostock by water. Economically it is equally necessary ; for neither Manchuria nor Siberia possesses a harbour offering first-class mercantile facilities, whereas Korea possesses many such. In fact, to become owner of Korea would secure for Russia the end she has so long sought to compass, free access to open seas in a temperate zone." When we examine the whole case for Russia, we see, as has been stated by a well-informed writer in the *Quarterly Review*,[1] that "not only is there no real difference between the earth appetite of the Muscovite and that of other great colonising nations, but there is also nothing in the policy which has enabled it to achieve such stupendous things that differentiates it in any essential way from the motives and methods of rival empire builders. The enormous expansion of the Russian dominion and the rapidity of its advance have been mainly due, not so much to conscious statesmanship, as to ethnological and geographical conditions. The vast scene of that expansion is a prolongation of the *mère patrie*, generally analogous to it in physical features, and peopled with races with whom the Russian colonists easily establish terms of sociability, if not of assimilation. In these circumstances Russian colonisation was a comparatively natural and rapid process, and the political consolidation of the conquests thus effected was correspondingly accelerated." It can scarcely be doubted that if it had not been for the rise of Japan as a strong Eastern Power, ere this Russia would have extended her territories to the Pacific coast, down to and including the Gulf of Pechili, and she would not have been content until she had obtained possession of Japan. A distinguished Japanese statesman expressed the opinion to me that the work of the students of the College of Engineering had been the chief means of preventing Japan from falling under the domination of Russia.

The gradual aggrandisement of Russia in the remote solitudes of Eastern Asia was regarded with comparative

[1] April 1904, p. 578.

on th
gave
Britisl
and
treatie
tions,
it wa
conce
violat
friend
faith
legali
penet
has f
legali
to co
expel
to de
we h
siona
benev
the r
troub
good
them
to o
milli
wher
for tl
were
ness
You
from
inlan
pape
into
they

ladivostock by water. Econo
for neiher Manchuria nor Sib
g first-lass mercantile facili
nany sch. In fact, to bec
are for Russia the end she ha
free acess to open se-
we examine the whole
n state by a well-infor
that " ot only is the
th appete of the Mu
ising ations, but th
ch has abled it to a
fferenties it in any es
ethods of rival empir
of the Russian dominie
have ben mainly du
smanship as t thno
The va scen at
nère pa ie, ger
peoped wit
ily estalish t
the cir
ratively ature
tion of 1e co
rated." It c
or the rise
Russia o
coast, e
vould n
sion o

indifference by the European Powers, but for fully a century it has given rise to very serious apprehension in Japan.

Reasons which dominate the foreign policy of Japan. Especially since the termination of the war with China in 1895, when through the action of Russia, France, and Germany, Japan was compelled to relinquish a great part of the results of her victories, Japanese statesmen have watched with great solicitude the action of Russia. They have carefully noted the trend of events, and they determined on a simple but clear and decided policy as regards China and Korea, in which while recognising all legitimate international rights of other Powers, they mean to insist on the independence and territorial integrity of these two countries. This policy explains the attention which they have given to the development of their army and navy. The expenditure on these two departments is really the price which Japan has had to pay for her membership of the comity of nations.

With Russia they have shown every wish to be reasonable in their relations ; in fact their self-restraint under very difficult circumstances has been beyond praise. They recognise not only the legitimate ambitions of Russia, but also the economic forces which are compelling her to provide openings for her surplus population and her manufactured products. They mean also, however, to insist on what they believe to be their own rights. The Czar called a conference at the Hague for the purpose of discussing how war was to be prevented. Deeds which lead to the peaceful solution of international problems are far more useful than discussions which have no practical results. If the Czar and his Government made their policy in the Far East quite clear and reasonable, and if they respected the legitimate interests of other Powers, especially of Japan, there are no reasons why there should be a collision. Instead, however, of pursuing a reasonable policy, the Russians have not only broken their engagements, but they have ostentatiously and defiantly collected what they consider to be an invincible fleet, and they are parading that fleet in Korean waters, and while delaying an answer to the demands of Japan, they have almost seemed to invite a conflict. The other Powers interested have not taken a very noble part in the present crisis, but have thrown on Japan the task of defending their rights. If Britain and the United States had taken a firmer position, the crisis with Russia would never have arisen, as that Power never fights until she has exhausted the resources of her peculiar diplomacy ; although it must be admitted that that diplomacy in the Far East and the actions following upon it, since Japan laid bare the impotence of China, have been sufficient to provoke war many times over. The present crisis is likely to awaken China to a sense of her strength, and to the necessity of showing that she means to use it if her territory or her rights are violated, and with the help of Japan she would be able to repel any encroachments by whatever Foreign Power they were made. Moreover, Russia ought to recognise that if her object is to become the absolute and uncontrolled mistress of the Far East, and to secure to herself and her traders a supreme monopoly of commerce, she will have to reckon not only with Japan but also with the other Powers which are interested.

When Russia proposed to Japan that the latter should not oppose Russian action in Manchuria or her acquisition of Masampho—a port in Korea almost opposite Shimonoseki and the dockyard of Saseho (or Sasebo)—Marquis Ito is reported to have said to one of his colleagues : " A free hand in Korea, with Masampho in the power of Russia, would be like a free hand in a bag of gold, with the mouth of the bag drawn tightly round one's wrist." If that were so with a comparatively small concession, we may well ask what would be the position if Korea were dominated by Russia? The national existence of Japan would be at her mercy, or to be more exact, at the mercy of the first ambitious Russian officer who thought he saw an opportunity of winning renown for himself and adding to the already overgrown possessions of the Russian Empire. The aim of Russia is evidently predominance both naval and commercial on the Pacific. That of Japan is not simply for additional markets and openings for her surplus population, and certainly not for territorial aggrandisement, but for the preservation of her life, her national identity, and the exercise of her natural and legitimate influence in the affairs of the Far East. Should she be compelled to defend her rights with her army and navy, she will bring to the contest with Russia's enormous forces a living patriotism and a scientific completeness of preparation which will more than compensate for the comparative smallness of her numbers.

BIBLIOGRAPHICAL NOTE

The foreign politics of a country cannot be understood from books and articles alone. One requires to live in the country to know the mind of the people and to understand existing conditions and the economic and political forces which have produced them. In the preceding chapters I have indicated the more important of these forces, and while not professing to give an official statement of Japanese foreign politics, I have endeavoured to show how the Japanese look at the problems which have arisen. Chapter ii. vol. v. of Captain Brinkley's *Japan and China* contains a clear statement by one who is thoroughly acquainted with all the conditions, and will be found sufficient for the majority of general readers. For more than a year past many articles on the subject have appeared in British and American journals, and as these have generally been written by men who have had special experience, they are worthy of special study, although in some cases the personal equation requires to be taken into account. The subject of economic and political dynamics is beginning to receive attention, and such articles as those by Captain Mahan are very valuable. World politics is gradually becoming a science, and when it is better understood, it will lead to the solution of international difficulties without resort to war. As an introduction to the subject, reference may be made to Professor Reinsch's book on *World Politics, at the end of the Nineteenth Century*, in the "Citizen's Library," published by the Macmillan Company, New York, and to the list of books and papers bearing on the subject which are mentioned by the author.

CHAPTER XVIII

SOCIAL RESULTS

THE sketch I have given of the changes which have taken place during the past half-century or so, enables us to appreciate the economic and political signifi- The funda-
cance of the sudden rise of Japan among the mental question.
nations of the world and to form an estimate of the kind, and even of the amount, of influence which she is likely to exercise in the evolution which is going on not only in what is usually called the Far East, but also in the Pacific area generally, and indeed in the whole world. After all, however, these developments are of small importance to the Japanese compared with the answer to the question, Have they been gainers by the changes? That is to say, Has the great body of the people been made healthier and happier and been enabled to develop their personalities to a higher degree than was possible under the old conditions? All other questions sink into insignificance beside this one, and unless it is kept in mind at every stage of national development, both energy and means are simply wasted, and indeed possibly used to hasten national decay, if not destruction.

Life in Old Japan had much to commend it to the thoughtful student of social conditions. The majority of the people lived their own lives and did not simply Life in Old
struggle for the means of existence or for Japan.
wealth and power, as is too often the case in Western countries. True, measured from the point of view of modern civilisation, the outlook must have been narrow, at least so

far as the affairs of this world were concerned ; but their
religion, or at any rate their philosophy, took them beyond
those affairs and to a large extent made them indifferent to
them and thus caused them to neglect the means which
were necessary to enable them to realise their higher
personalities.   Intellectual activities and material means are
however not necessarily the accompaniments of moral and
spiritual development.   Moreover, Western writers in dealing
with Eastern conditions assume the truth of Western metaphysics and overlook the fact that Eastern civilisation is in
great part built upon the idea of reincarnation (the possibility
of the truth of which was admitted by an agnostic like
Professor Huxley), which, if it be true, upsets all their
estimates, as it indicates a much higher view of the doctrines
of heredity and environment than is held in modern Western
scientific thought.   The discussion of this aspect of the
subject, however, would take us far beyond our present limits,
and it is simply mentioned to show that it has not been
overlooked.

As in all feudal systems, it must of course be admitted
that the military class dominated the rest of the people,
whose welfare was made secondary to theirs.   Life was held
at a low value, no doubt because its existence at any time
was considered insignificant when compared with the cycles
through which it extended.   In addition to this view, there
can be no doubt that mere bravado and a domineering spirit
led to a reckless use of their swords by the samurai class.
Measured by Western standards, the lives of the majority
of the people were empty, as education in the modern sense
of the term was rare.   Many, however, found pleasure in
their work, and they asked for no other blessedness.   Even
the most common craft had something artistic about it which
revealed the personality of the worker.   Outdoor pleasures,
which were taken advantage of by all classes and all ages
of the community, prevented tedium and maintained health ;
the absence of material wealth was not much missed,
as life was simple and wants were few.   .There were no

great fortunes, but there was no degrading poverty ; for the semi-communism which prevailed provided for the wants of all without the machinery of a poor law. Children supported their parents in their old age, and even the poorest classes had friends or relations who supplied their wants. Modern industry, emigration, and war had not upset the provisions of nature, and practically all the women obtained husbands, who were able to provide for them in some way ; so that the woman question, as we know it, did not come to the front.

No doubt, in some respects the position of women was very far from satisfactory, at least when measured from a Western point of view, and they were too much the mere subordinates of the men ; but in the great majority of cases their lives were not unhappy, and they proved themselves model wives and mothers. Any one who knows the conditions of the lives of the poorest class of women in Britain and compares them with what existed and still exists in Japan, would have no hesitation in saying that the lot of the Japanese was to be preferred. They had few who would compare with the best type of Western women, but, on the other hand, they had none who led the lives of the so-called leaders of society, who sacrifice not only themselves but also their families in the hunt for what they call pleasure, nor had they the degradation of extreme poverty and drunkenness.

Men's position and influence were measured by their personal worth and not by their riches. The samurai had their incomes secured from the revenues of the land, and they often supplemented these by a little amateur farming. The tiller of the soil was looked up to with respect, because it was recognised that he, above all others, was an efficient worker, as he produced the necessaries of life. Tradesmen, artists, and workers of all kinds carried on their employments very much at their ease, as they had learned that real happiness was found in giving out to their work the best that was in them. Merchants and speculators occupied the lowest position in the category of vocations. Conse-

quently commerce did not reach a high degree of development, and the obloquy attached to the calling naturally
brought within its pale such as cared little for social repute;
a fact which, as I have already indicated, explains many of
the characteristics which have given Japanese merchants a
bad name among commercial men—a name which is rapidly
disappearing as education develops and as a superior class
of men enter into mercantile life.

The development of commerce and industry has had a
profound effect on social and economic conditions, and that
Modern conditions. development has been hastened by the improvement which has taken place in the roads and
by the introduction and extension of railways, steamboat
services, telegraphs and telephones. These means of communication have had the effect of consolidating the empire
and causing almost the last vestiges of the feudal system to
disappear; they have made intercourse between the people
in all parts of the country not only possible but in
the majority of cases very easy; they have allowed its
natural resources to be developed, have thus added greatly
to its wealth and made it possible to undertake many
national functions, the most important of which we have
mentioned, and which have enabled Japan to take a position
of equality among the nations of the world. On the other
hand, as I have more than once indicated, these changes
have not been without some very serious drawbacks.

In many parts of Japan many of the old customs and
methods of life still survive, but in the neighbourhood of
large towns they are rapidly disappearing before the pressure
of modern commerce and industry and the competition which
they inevitably bring along with them. The results of that
competition, with which we are so well acquainted in Britain,
are beginning to appear, and Japan is now face to face with
many of the social problems which have been the puzzle of
Western social reformers and statesmen for several generations. Large fortunes (comparatively speaking) are being
accumulated at one end of the social scale, while degrading

poverty is appearing at the other, and as yet no effective means have been devised either to alleviate or to prevent it. The increased strain, worry, and anxiety, even among the well-to-do classes, make not a few of the older generation look back with regret on the conditions which existed in the days of their youth. Some of the most distinguished men in Japan indeed have been so impressed with the seriousness of the position that they have given up all their other pursuits in order that they may assist in the solution of the social problems which lie before their country.

We are sometimes told that the Western civilisation of the Japanese is only skin-deep, for the most part confined to outward appearances, and that they are never really comfortable in their foreign clothes and in the use of foreign appliances. It is true that, notwithstanding all the developments which have taken place, in many respects the inner life of the people has not been much changed, and that many of them lead a kind of dual existence, conforming to the requirements of Western methods during the day, but reverting to purely Japanese customs in their own homes. Even those who have handsome houses on Western models always have an annexe where their familiar alcoves, verandahs, matted floors, and paper sliding doors continue to be found, and where family and familiar life is carried on in Japanese style. In my opinion, these characteristics are praiseworthy rather than otherwise. All the time I was resident in Japan I always urged that while the Japanese should take full advantage of Western science and civilisation, in so far as these were necessary to make their country great and their individual lives full and complete, they should retain all the characteristics of Japanese life and character, and maintain their individuality not only nationally but also personally. The seeming reaction of recent years is therefore all in the right direction. A nation which forgets its past and gives up all its special characteristics neither deserves nor indeed is ever likely to attain true greatness.

The richer classes and many of the middle and working

classes have been able to add to the luxuries and conveniences of their lives, but even among the wealthy there
Life of the well- is an utter absence of vulgar display, and the
to-do classes. majority of them continue to live in a quiet,
unostentatious way, just as if they were poor. " Which of
us," asks a well-known writer who has been a long time in
Japan, " which of us knows of even one very wealthy
Japanese who makes a parade of his riches or devotes his
money to purposes of glitter and display." They have not
forgotten the social canon of Old Japan which made osten-
tation a sin. No doubt the increase of wealth has led to
luxurious habits on the part of some who have become
rapidly rich ; but almost without exception those with whom
I have come into contact are very temperate in their manner
of living, and in some cases almost ascetic. Of course, I do
not wish to particularise, but many of the most distinguished
as well as some of the richest men in the country have, for
the most part, retained their simple personal habits, and they
look upon their wealth as a trust which they must use not
simply for their own gratification but for the good of their
country.

Notwithstanding the development of industry and
commerce in Japan, the number of men who would be
considered rich is still comparatively small, and even their
incomes are insignificant compared with those of the
millionaires of America. According to a return recently
published in a Japanese economic journal, there are only
2 men who pay an income tax on over 250,000 yen, and
there are only 13 men in the whole country who pay on
39,000 yen, only 67 who pay on 24,000 yen, 96 who
pay on 17,000 yen, and 140 who pay on 11,000 yen.
Out of every 1000 inhabitants there are only 7 persons
who make 2700 yen a year. Measured therefore by
income, the Japanese cannot be considered rich. According
to Captain Brinkley, careful investigations now show that
the number of men possessing property valued at £50,000
sterling does not exceed 441. Comparing this record with

American statistics, for example, it appears that whereas there are 3828 persons in the United States credited with possessing, at least, £200,000, or in other words 1 for every 20,000 inhabitants, there is in Japan only 1 owner of £50,000 for every 100,000 of the population. The contrast is very striking. The figures which have been quoted show that there is still considerable equality of economic conditions among all classes of the people in Japan.

For the most part, the life of the common people remains simple. Their staple food is rice, with fish—fresh and dried—seaweed, beans and other fruits of the earth. Meat and poultry form but a small part of their dietary. Their houses

Life of the common people.

are plain wooden structures, their furniture is scanty and cheap, and their dress, both of men and women, is inexpensive. In short, the Japanese have solved many of the problems of life by simplifying their wants ; so that we can understand why even those who have the means and the opportunity of indulging in·Western habits and methods prefer, as soon as they can, to return to the simpler life of their own country. Such a procedure is not blameworthy but rather the reverse. They have found that the increase of possessions and the multiplication of complex appliances lead neither to health nor to happiness, and they have recognised, what many foreigners have also recognised, that the simple Japanese life is in many respects to be preferred. While not neglecting the advantages to be derived from Western appliances, they are coming to the Greek ideal of life, and while keeping their personal and family wants simple, they are determined to make their civic and national life as full and complete as possible. We have had sufficient evidence to show that patriotism is the dominant feature in the Japanese character, and the aspiration of every educated Japanese is to keep up with Western nations in the race for progress. The problem, however, which they have to solve is to arrive at a clear understanding as to what constitutes real progress.

In reviewing the general financial position of the country Captain Brinkley comes to the conclusion that the tax-payer is much more favourably circumstanced now than he was ten years ago. People receiving fixed salaries, as administrative and judicial officials, persons engaged in education, etc., have had no increase of income to compensate them for increased taxation or for the sharp appreciation of prices. But such persons form a small fraction of the nation. All the other classes are earning more and possess much larger property. On the other hand, their taxes have not undergone any proportionate increase, and instead of saying that the nation is embarrassed by the payments it has to make to the State, the truth is that it pays relatively less than it did ten years ago.

In a previous chapter [1] figures were given which showed that the wages of workmen, and especially those engaged in Western industries, had in some cases nearly doubled, and that in nearly all cases there had been very considerable increases. We have also seen [2] that the prices of nearly all the necessaries of life have risen, although not so much as the wages ; so that on the whole the economic condition of the majority of the people has improved. On the other hand, their wants have also developed, and it is doubtful if there is a large proportion who find themselves better off than they would have been under the old conditions. Moreover, a considerable number have been unable to fit themselves to the altered circumstances, and as is the case in all competitive communities they have gradually drifted down to the lowest depths of poverty.

Some very dark pictures have been drawn of the conditions of the poorest classes. Probably some of these have been exaggerated, but there can be no doubt that the problem of the " submerged tenth " is becoming as acute in Japan as in other countries. This indeed is the problem which confronts all industrial communities. The following interesting comparison between the cost of living in 1889 and

[1] P. 183.   [2] P. 229.

1899 was given some time ago in the Japanese journal, the
Miyako, and it is calculated to show the monthly expenditure of a family of six members—a married couple, a parent,
two children, and one servant—living with strict economy :—

	1889. Yen.	1899. Yen.
House Rent.	2.50	5.00
Cleaned Rice	4.50	7.00
Soy	0.45	0.75
Salt and *Miso*	0.40	0.70
Oils	0.45	0.69
Sugar	0.60	0.90
Milk	0.90	1.10
Newspaper	0.25	0.35
School Expenses	0.80	0.90
Stationery	0.60	0.90
Hair-dressing	0.34	0.69
Bath	0.90	1.50
Vegetables	0.90	1.50
Fish	1.08	1.80
Beef	0.60	1.20
Auxiliary Foods	0.24	0.42
Tea	0.40	0.50
Fuel	1.00	1.80
Total . . .	17.21	28.20
Security money for Rent . .	7.00	15.00

The above figures represent what may be considered the
necessaries of life for a superior working-class family of six
members, but when other petty expenses are included, the
total will amount to fully thirty-five yen per month.

The economic position of the agricultural classes does
not seem to have improved to any great extent. The steady
increase of population has been an important
factor in keeping rents high, as the competition
for farms has become much greater and the
consequence is that very often the share of
the profits which falls to the tenant-farmers is barely
sufficient to provide them with the means of subsistence and

Economic conditions of farmers and labourers.

with the manure and tools required for their farms. Exact statistics are not available, but there are about one million and a half freeholders, about one million tenant-farmers, and about two million who are partly freeholders and partly lessees ; so that it is evident that the agriculturalists form a very important part of the population, and their economic conditions must be carefully considered when estimating the results of the recent changes in Japan. Mr. Yamawaki, the Private Secretary of the Minister of Agriculture and Commerce, states that " the farmers find it hard to keep up with the progress of the times " ; and he adds, " Something must be done towards ameliorating their condition, for though individually they are comparatively insignificant, their combined interests in the economy of the nation predominate considerably over all the others put together. The farming classes, for instance, constitute 60 per cent of the whole population and are largely sending their surplus population to cities and towns. In view of this circumstance, both the Government and the general public are doing their best to improve the mode of tillage, to encourage the use of labour-saving machines and devices, and also to promote all the important economic contrivances provided for the interests of the farmers ; so that it may safely be expected that the conditions of our farmers will become much better in the near future than they are now."

Some time ago the editor of one of the Japanese journals sent out a form making inquiries regarding the lives and work of the labouring classes ; the following are two of the family budgets which were returned, and they throw much light on the inner life of the Japanese workers :—

No. I

House, 2 rooms ; a family—man, 30 ; wife, 23 ; mother, 53 ; two sisters, 14 and 11 ; occupation, blacksmith.

		Yen.
Working days in a month	. . .	26
Working hours in a day	. . ..	12

	Yen.
Daily Wages	0.52
Monthly Income	13.83
Monthly Expenses	13.65
House Rent	0.96
Rice	5.76
Fuel and Light	1.08
Vegetables	0.87
Fish	0.96
Saké	0.24
Soy	0.73
Tobacco	0.20
Hair-cutting and dressing	0.83
Bath	0.88
Pin Money	0.25
Sundries	0.89

No. 2

House, 2 rooms, with kitchen; a family—man, 27; wife, 25; boy, 6; girl, 2; business, iron-worker.

	Yen.
Daily Wages	0.25
Overtime Income for one month	1.50
Monthly Income	8.28
Monthly Expense	9.44
House Rent	0.75
Rice	3.25
Fuel and Light	0.41
Vegetables	0.60
Fish	0.60
Soy and *Miso*	0.23
Tobacco	0.25
Hair-cutting and dressing	0.18
Bath	0.20
Pin Money	0.60
Sundries, including interest on debt	2.37

The family life of a country and the position occupied by women are probably the best tests of its civilisation. In comparing nation with nation we have no doubt in asserting that one of the most important forces in the progress of society is

Home life and the position of women.

the education which the mothers convey to their children, and no nation can ever be truly great unless women rise to a high plane of thought and life, and kindle and foster similar ideas in the minds of the young.   In the East the focus of civilisation is to be found in the idea which prevails with regard to the home.   Very often that does not lead either to physical or to moral efficiency, and this fact, no doubt, to a large extent accounts for the impotence of Eastern nations.   In some respects Japanese home life affords an example to Western nations.   The love of the Japanese for their children and the happiness of Japanese childhood requires to be seen to be appreciated.   In fact, Japan has been called the paradise of children, and the name is not altogether undeserved.   No such delightful children are to be found anywhere else in the world.   It has been said that "to the beauty and grace of childhood they add the roguishness, the playfulness, and the gentleness of puppies or kittens, and they are just as self-possessed. To describe adequately the children's life in Japan, at least as it existed under purely Japanese conditions, would require a large volume.

When, however, we inquire into the conditions which affect the intellectual and moral life of women, we find much that stands in need of improvement.   Under the old régime women were entirely at the mercy of their husbands in almost every respect, and although great improvements have taken place, much more is to be desired.   A very competent observer has said "the woman of Japan is a charming personage in many ways—gracious, refined, womanly before everything, sweet-tempered, unselfish, virtuous, a splendid mother and an ideal wife, from the point of view of the master.   But she is virtually excluded from the whole intellectual life of the nation.   Politics, art, literature, science are closed books to her.   She cannot think logically about any of these subjects, express herself clearly with reference to them, or take any intellectual part in conversations relating to them.   She is, ·in fact, totally disqualified to be her husband's intellectual companion, and the inevitable result is that he despises her."

A great deal has been written about the sexual morality of the Japanese, into details of which, however, I cannot enter ; but it is very doubtful if in this respect they are any worse than the people of other countries, although they make less effort at concealment. In these matters, however, improvements are taking place, and public opinion is strengthening against some of the customs which formerly prevailed. Women are no longer compelled to follow prostitution against their wills, and many who had entered on such a life have voluntarily given it up. The accounts of this aspect of Japanese life which have been given by foreign writers have often been grossly exaggerated, and give an altogether false impression of the actual conditions. It is a very significant fact that many of the foreign visitors who write about Japan seem to think it their first duty to visit the special districts licensed for these purposes. One thing is certain ; a person may live in Tokyo for years and not see anything to offend his notions of propriety. So long as the most important streets of London, Paris, and other European cities present such scenes as they very often do, the West has no grounds for criticising the East. Too often the pictures which are painted represent the degradation of the open ports, where the morals have been pared down to European requirements. The Geisha of Japan, under good conditions, is by no means the degraded, sensual person she is represented to be, but on the contrary is highly intellectual and accomplished ; her first function is to minister to purely intellectual pleasures, and with many it remains the only function. The accounts of the writers who gloat over the moral deficiencies of the Japanese should be received with a great amount of caution.

A great improvement has in recent years taken place in the position of women. Mr. Gubbins, in the introduction to his translation of the Codes, says : " In no respect has modern progress in Japan made greater strides than in the

improvement of the position of women. Though she still
labours under certain disabilities, a woman can now become
a head of a family, and exercise authority as such ; she can
inherit and own property and manage it herself; she can
exercise parental authority ; if single, or a widow, she
can adopt ; she is one of the parties to adoption effected by
her husband, and her consent, in addition to that of her
husband, is necessary to the adoption of her child by
another person ; she can act as guardian or curator, and
she has a voice in family councils." Meantime, as we have
seen, attention is being paid to the education of women, and
already a considerable number have shown both literary and
artistic ability, and are able to discuss social and political
problems with intelligence. The most thoughtful minds in
Japan recognise that if their country is to be truly great, the
women must be educated and animated with a conscious
moral purpose which will always keep abreast of the highest
level of the existing generation.

Modern industrial conditions threaten to take away the
joy of young life in Japan, and undermine the national
Factory work health by the employment of women and
of women and children in factories of all kinds in which the
children. hours are long and the conditions of employment insanitary. A great deal has been written on the
subject in Japan recently, and although the descriptions
of actual conditions have in some cases been overdrawn,
there can be no doubt that the subject is one demanding
careful attention on the part of the authorities. The
industrial development of Japan will be bought at too
dear a price if it causes the health of the rising generation
to be undermined, and destroys that joyous life which has
been so characteristic of the Japanese.

On the whole, however, it is admitted by competent
medical authorities that the physique of the Japanese
National health. people generally has improved in recent years.
Sanitary conditions have been bettered, the
quality of the food of the majority of the people has

improved, and more attention is now being paid to systematic physical development than was the case under feudal conditions, when it was for the most part confined to the samurai class. During the past few years especially the purely Japanese system of physical training entitled *jiu-jitsu* has been very much extended in its application (and indeed is becoming common both in Europe and America), with the result that wonders can be performed in the way of physical endurance. The soldiers, sailors, police, and others in official positions go through a systematic and thorough training. This training is in fact indicative of a great deal that is done by the Japanese, as their knowledge of scientific principles and their ability to apply them in an efficient manner enable them to surprise their adversaries, even although these surpass them in numbers and size. On the other hand, some of the conditions of modern industrialism tend to lower the state of the national health, and therefore to decrease the amount of the national wealth, in the true sense of that term.

Since the revision of the treaties and the development of the means of communication with the Far East, the intercourse between Japan and foreign countries Intercourse with has been greatly extended. Many Japanese foreigners. go abroad for purposes of study, commerce, and special investigations, and many foreigners now visit Japan, for the most part, however, for purposes of pleasure. Indeed, Japan is becoming somewhat like Switzerland in this respect (for there is no more delightful country in which to spend a holiday), and what may be called the "tourist industry" is increasingly lucrative. It is doubtful, however, whether it does not do more harm than good to the people of Japan. It certainly causes prices to be raised to those who are engaged in more serious researches, and who are of more moderate means. Rich people who make Japan a mere holiday resort are likely to be somewhat extravagant in their habits, and some of them are objectionable from other points of view; so that their influence on the people with whom they come into contact is not likely to be for good. Even when I went to Japan, the manners of the Japanese deteriorated as we approached a foreign settlement ; a fact which was a somewhat sad commentary on Western civilisation. The value of that civilisation will be estimated not by its material advantages or its profession of religion, but by its effects on the lives of those who represent it in the Far East.

It is evident that the development of modern industry in Japan has brought it face to face with those labour Labour and problems which are to be found in Britain and social problems. all other industrial countries, and which are the inevitable results of a transition stage of society, and it will be interesting and no doubt instructive to note how they are met in the Britain of the East. Meantime the same processes are going on as in the Britain of the West. Factory legislation is being proposed with the view of preventing the most apparent evils, and combinations of employers and workers are being formed for the purpose of safeguarding their respective interests. Both, however, are still in a very indefinite position, but the employers have the advantage on account of their capital, and while uniting for their own purposes, they are, as a rule, opposed to unions for the workers, and several of the large organisations refuse to engage union men. The problems of the relations of capital and labour are in Japan, as in other industrial countries, the problems which are certain to attract most attention.

While duly recognising all that has been accomplished in Japan, as I have said, many of the most thoughtful minds in the country look back with something like regret on the old state of affairs, and I must confess that I share in that feeling to a very considerable extent. What we call modern civilisation does not captivate those who have imbibed something of the ideals and the spirit of the East. A writer from whom I have already quoted has truly said : " There are two forms of the cultivation of Self. One leads to the exceptional development of the qualities which are noble, and the other signifies something about which the less said the better. But it is not the former which the New Japan is now beginning to study. I confess to being one of those who believe that the human heart, even in the history of a race, may be worth infinitely more than the human intellect, and that it will sooner or later prove itself infinitely better able to answer all the cruel enigmas of the Sphinx of Life. I still believe that the old Japanese were nearer to the solution of those enigmas than are we, just because they recognised moral beauty as greater than intellectual beauty. And by way of conclusion I may venture to quote from an article on education by Ferdinand Brunetière :—'All our educational measures will prove vain if there be no effort to force into the mind and to deeply impress upon it the sense of these fine words of Lamennais : *" Human society is based upon mutual giving, or upon the sacrifice of man for man, or of each man for all other men ; and sacrifice is the very essence of all true society."* It is this that we have been unlearning for nearly a century ; and if we have to put ourselves to school afresh it will be in order that we may learn it again. Without such knowledge there can be no society and no education—not, at least, if the object of education be to form man for society. Individualism is to-day the enemy of education, as it is also the enemy of social order. It has not been so always, but it has so become. It will not be so for ever, but it is so now. And without striving to destroy it—which would mean to fall from one extreme into another—we must recognise that no matter what we wish to do for the family, for society, for education, and for the country, it is against individualism that the work will have to be done.' "[1] These opinions are being shared to a considerable extent in Japan, and they are certain to influence the future of the nation ; but the transition which is going on is not yet sufficiently advanced to hazard a prediction as to the probable form of social organisation which will be the outcome. I believe that Japan will learn

[1] Hearn, *Kokoro*, p. 38.

a great deal by a careful study of her former conditions, and thus may be able to temper the extreme individualism which is the cause of so many social evils.

BIBLIOGRAPHICAL NOTE

In Japan, as was the case in Britain, the social results of the industrial revolution are being forced on the attention of the people from the observation of actual conditions. These are freely discussed in the Japanese newspapers and also in the foreign papers published in Japan, but as yet nothing systematic has been done either to solve the problems which have arisen or even to record the actual conditions. Many articles have appeared giving details of special cases, and the conscience of the country is being awakened. Actual observation and reference to the files of the daily newspapers are the chief means of obtaining information, although some of the recent books on Japan touch the subject; none of them deals with it thoroughly or in a systematic manner. A few years ago an investigation was undertaken by M. Andre Siegfried and published by the Musée Social (Paris), entitled *Le Developpement Economique et Social du Japon*, which contains a good deal of interesting and important information regarding the working of the factory system in Japan. Chapter VIII. of M. Dumolard's book on Japan treats of *La Question Ouvrière et le Pauperisme*, and may be read with advantage, although some of the statements are one-sided. Alfred Stead, in *Japan, Our New Ally*, also has a chapter on the Labour Problem, and in addition gives a good deal of interesting information on social and economic subjects. It is to be hoped that Japanese students of sociology will deal with social problems in the same thorough manner as scientific problems have been dealt with in Japan, and their efforts will be watched with great interest.

CHAPTER XIX

THE FUTURE

THE past history of Japan and China shows most distinctly how the economic and social conditions of a country may be influenced by the prevailing ideals of National ideals individual and national life. In Japan, under and economics. the feudal system, everything was conditioned by the fact that it had been determined that the country was to be self-contained and self-supporting. The position has thus been stated by a competent writer: "A population of twenty millions at a start—that number nearly doubling before the country was again thrown open—was to be subsisted solely upon the resources which the empire itself could supply, with only one-twelfth of its area susceptible of cultivation. At the same time, in the face of the tendencies to the contrary, which isolation is ordinarily sure to develop, the people were to preserve their self-respect and live in peace, happiness, and content with each other.

"That the policies adopted to secure these seemingly impossible ends were successful, the condition of the people at the present time when, after the centuries of seclusion, the barriers have been broken down and the feudal system abolished, is ample proof. These people are indeed wretchedly poor, but their occupation being held in high esteem, their access of pride is to them and to the nation more than compensation for their poverty ; while the wonderful development of agriculture under the stimulus of that pride has made the arable twelfth of the empire more than

383

sufficient to support its teeming millions. And, again, the pinching and searching economics enforced upon the masses, having not only the law but the fashion, even in the higher ranks of society, have resulted in that simplicity of living and consequent freedom from superfluous cares which have practically made the Japanese, in the best sense of the word, the most independent people of the world."[1] Under these conditions a man's value was not estimated by the amount of his wealth, but by his worth as a soldier, a statesman, an artist, or other useful worker, or as a citizen. The separation between power and riches kept the distribution of the latter fairly equable, as few thought the accumulation of wealth a sufficient object of life. It was true that new developments in science and industry were discouraged and that literature was repressed; still, on the whole, life was simple and free and offered many compensations for what, from a Western point of view, would be considered its imperfections, and many thoughtful Japanese look back on the old days with feelings of regret.

The Japanese theory of life was founded to a large extent on Confucian philosophy, and Japan owed practically Confucian philosophy of life. all the chief features of its civilisation to China, and therefore it is to that country we must look if we wish to understand the Japanese mind. My old friends the first Chinese Ministers to Japan, Their Excellencies Ho Ju-Chang and Chang Sz-Kwei, with whom I very often discussed such matters, were in the habit of saying to me that while they gave Western people great credit for their knowledge of science and its applications to industry, they were of opinion that the steam and the electricity had got into their brains and that the machines were their masters, not their servants. Thoughtful social reformers have long recognised this fact, and have come to the conclusion that political, economic, and social problems are to be solved only by individuals and nations who have realised the object and meaning of life. Eastern people, as

[1] Knapp, *Feudal and Modern Japan*, vol. i. p. 117.

I have already remarked, have as a rule neglected the means necessary to enable them to live the highest life, whereas those of the West exhaust a great part of their energy in the struggle for the means of life and for superfluities which in many cases are of no real value. The Christian conception of life has been lost in the race for individual riches and for personal and national ambitions, and no country has suffered so much as China from those who profess the Gospel of Peace.

It must not be imagined that I am placing the civilisation of Old Japan or of China before that of the West; what I wish to insist upon is, that the peoples of the East should retain all that is characteristically Eastern in so far as it helps the higher life, and adopt only those Western methods which will enable them to live their own lives in their own way and according to their own ideals. The task of Asia. As a Japanese writer from whom I have quoted has put it: "The task of Asia to-day becomes that of protecting and restoring Asiatic modes"; and while keeping in view the *ends* of life, it should also develop the *means* of life in such a manner as to make the highest life possible. Instead of rushing into the competition for cheap production and spending a large part of their national resources on the materials of war, they must recognise that the production of souls of good quality is, after all, the most lucrative one. Ruskin was laughed at when he held up this ideal in Britain, but the necessity for it being kept in mind is being slowly recognised. One of the chief faults of the British people, and to a great extent of all Western peoples generally, is that they are so pleased with the advancement and excellence of their own institutions that they cannot understand why any other nation cannot be content with what contents them, and this tactless, unimaginative charity has been the main cause of their troubles in all parts of the world.

Before ideals can be realised attention must be paid to the foundations on which they are expected to rest, and

therefore economic conditions must receive careful attention. As I have already indicated, there are difficult
Future financial problems before Japan, and each of these must
and fiscal policy be studied in all its aspects. Their solution
of Japan. will depend in great part on the national policy
adopted with regard not only to home but also to foreign
affairs. The problems connected with fiscal policy are now
being very much discussed in all parts of the British Empire,
and it will be interesting to observe how they are dealt with
in Japan. The conditions of the two Empires, are, however, very different, and the arguments which apply to the
one will not apply to the other. The past history of Japan
affords lessons which will not be forgotten by Japanese
statesmen, although they are not likely to return to a
policy of seclusion. While developing their own resources
and taking advantage of the applications of science to
industry, it is to be hoped that they will retain sufficient
of their native philosophy not to allow the struggle for
the means of life to cause them to forget the ends of
national life; namely, the highest welfare of the great body
of the people, physically, intellectually, and morally.

The financial arrangements connected with the developments which have taken place in Japan have been managed
with great skill and with comparatively little help from
foreign countries. Large sums have been spent on the
army and navy, but it is to be hoped that the policy pursued
by European Powers will be such as to render unnecessary
any great increase in that department of national expenditure,
so that the resources of the country may be developed and
prosperity increased. If intercourse with Foreign Powers
brings to Japan the curse of militarism, with all its attendant
evils, the people of the country will pay dearly for their
admission into the comity of nations.

The question of the use of foreign capital is one requiring
great care. As a rule capitalists are too intent on securing
large returns for their money to pay much attention to the
social results of their undertakings, but still, with proper

precautions, it would be possible to employ foreign capital not only to the advantage of those who lent it, but also to that of the people of Japan.

We cannot expect the Japanese to be content with modern manufacturing industries which are just sufficient for use in their own country. They must be able to obtain whatever they require for the develop- Manufacturing industries. ment of their national life, and as imports can be paid for only by exports, they must send to other countries some of their own productions. Not only their economic conditions but also their national ambition impel them to enter the markets of the world, and especially those of the Far East ; but if they are wise they will subordinate their external trade to the welfare of the great masses of their own people and estimate their national wealth, not by the value of their cheap productions, but by the results on the Japanese nation and on the world. The conditions which existed in the early days of the manufacturing system in Britain, and some of the worst of which are being reproduced in Japan, should be a warning against the adoption of any policy that would degrade the conditions of the working population. A thoughtful writer has pointed out that " the industrial reformation for which Western Europe groans and travails, and the advent of which is indicated by so many symptoms (though it will come only as the fruit of faithful and sustained effort), will be no isolated fact, but will form part of an applied art of life, modifying our whole environment, affecting our whole culture, and regulating our whole conduct ; in a word, directing all our resources to the one great end of the conservation and development of humanity." [1]

This may seem too much of an ideal to be of use in practical life, but the Japanese, above all modern nations, have shown themselves most capable of rising to a national ideal, and symptoms are not wanting that such a one as has been indicated would rouse their imagination and stir them

[1] Ingram, *History of Political Economy*, p. 246.

to practical action, and their example would have a powerful influence on the nations of Europe and America.

While that ideal should be kept in mind and approximated to as rapidly as possible, a strong army and navy Effects on will be national necessities for Japan for a very foreign policy. considerable time, and her statesmen recognise that fact. Gradually, however, the attempt to carry out the ideal I have mentioned would have great effect, not only on the home but also on the foreign policy of the country, and would do more to strengthen Japan than doubling her army and navy. The position of Japan in the Far East is a matter which concerns, to a greater or less degree, every nation in the world ; and a policy such as I have indicated would gather allies round her whose friendship would be sufficient to ward off the aggression of any one Power, even if Japan felt herself unequal to the task, which I do not believe she would. The policy of the Britain of the West has often seemed to other nations too self-assertive, and the increase of her naval armaments has led to great expenditure and to a great increase in the navies of the other Powers. Surely, if civilisation has any meaning, it should give us confidence in the good intentions of our neighbours, or at any rate, if these intentions prove bad, it should lead to such action on the part of all the other nations as would bring the troublesome party to its senses. A small international naval force, acting as a police for the Pacific area, and under the orders of a Council representing all the Powers concerned, should be all that was required in the way of naval expenditure, and then the resources of the various countries could be employed in advancing the welfare of the people.

The real and ultimate solution of the problems of the foreign policy of Japan, and indeed of every other country, Ultimate solution is not to be found in the struggle for foreign of the problems markets, but in the development of the home of foreign policy. market and in the improvement of the social, intellectual, and moral conditions of her own people. Colonisation and emigration can only be temporary ameliorations of the population question, as it is evident that when all the industrial nations of the world pursued the same policy, every part of the surface of the globe would soon be overcrowded, and the difficulty would be greater than ever. Poverty, in all its forms, not only in so far as it arises from absence of wealth, but also, much more, in the want of spirit and in a low state of morality, combined with the severe struggle for merely material ends, is the main cause of the rapid increase of population. A general improvement in the standard of comfort and intelligence would tend more than anything else to prevent an undue increase of population, and, there is good reason to believe, would bring about an equilibrium between the birth and death rates. As the world becomes wiser the waste of infant life will be much reduced and longevity extended. In the past, Japan was able to solve her population question, and there can be no doubt that if, with her greater knowledge, she studies all the factors in the problem, she will be quite able to do it in the future, without returning to a policy of seclusion, with all its results, or even resorting to emigration on a large scale, but by raising her people to a high standard of intellectual, moral, and social conditions which would make them not only respected abroad but also prosperous at home. The solution of this problem involves the solution of many other social problems, and it would put an end to all troubles connected with foreign policy.

The sketch which has been given in a previous chapter of the development of constitutional government in Japan, as well as the historical notes on the events of recent years, show that, notwithstanding the introduction of representative institutions into Japan, the old principles of loyalty to the Emperor and of implicit obedience to his will still have a great hold on the people of the country. On several occasions an indication of that will has quelled party spirit and compelled Parliament to look at the questions before it

Future of constitutional government in Japan.

from a patriotic point of view. As we have seen, the Japanese Constitution makes the Ministers independent of Parliament and responsible only to the Emperor ; but while that is so, it cannot be disputed that, indirectly, the decisions of Parliament have had a great deal to do with the making and unmaking of Ministries. The Emperor has adhered faithfully to the terms of the Constitution, and the proofs which he has given of his wisdom and patriotism show that there is no danger of a return to the old state of autocracy. Moreover, popular influence is increasing so rapidly that no Minister of the Crown, however reactionary, dare advise a suspension of the Constitution. As Mr. Tokiwo Yokoi has put it : " How these two principles of the divine right of the sovereign and the divine right of the people, which in Europe have so often waged fierce contests for ascendency, are to be harmonised, is the problem which is at present taxing the efforts of the most thoughtful politicians of the country. These politicians all see that it has been the intense loyalty of the people which, more than anything else, has carried the ship of state through the troubles of recent times, and that it is the Imperial House which to-day gives unity to the nation, notwithstanding the presence of a hundred divisive forces. At the same time these statesmen also see that the rights and liberties of the people are not only to be preserved and guarded intact, so far as they exist already, but that they must be more and more increased in proportion as the people prove themselves capable of a larger exercise of their powers."

The future evolution of government and administration in Japan will form a most interesting study, and there are many difficult problems to be faced. On the one hand, the demand for a popular form of government, directly responsible to the elected representatives of the people, will become stronger, while on the other there will be great opposition to any change which will seem to diminish the glory of the crown and make the government less stable. What form the government will ultimately take it is impossible to say, but there are not likely to be any violent changes. The intense loyalty to the Emperor and the spirit of patriotism which compels all Japanese to lay aside merely personal and party reasons, and probably also the danger arising from the aggressive policies of some of the great Powers of Europe, will cause the ancient "Bushido" of Japan to reappear in a form suited to the new conditions, and solve the difficulties which at present are appearing on the political horizon.

It is sincerely to be hoped that Japan, in her own interests, will continue her present policy, abstain from any attempt at territorial aggrandisement in Asia, and confine herself to commercial and Japan in Asia. industrial intercourse and to guidance in the rejuvenation of that vast continent. There are too many interests involved to allow any one Power to obtain a dominating influence in the Far East, and especially in China. Free intercourse, without any sign of political aggression, is the only bond which will bring about the brotherhood of nations. Unless the Foreign Powers interested in China recognise this fact, they are only transferring to China the problems with which they are confronted in Europe. Their duty is, therefore, to aid in the peaceful development of Asia and to give all assistance to the Chinese and the other peoples to reform their own Government and to take advantage of Western methods, in so far as these are necessary for the purpose of raising the standard of life. Whatever the result of the contest between Japan and Russia may be, both Powers should remember that the peoples of the countries concerned have rights which should not be overlooked, and that their object should be to raise them to a higher state of national life. As I have frequently pointed out, this cannot be done by imposing a civilisation on them from without; the impetus must come from within. Education should be developed in all its departments so that the people of China and Korea may learn what is necessary in order to hold their own in the international struggle for existence.

Probably, as the representatives of the Western Powers become wiser, they may recognise the futility of a great part of that struggle, and decide, as many of the Chinese have done, that the object of life is to live, and not simply to struggle for the means of existence. Intercourse with Western people and with the Japanese will, however, show the slow-moving people of China and Korea that a knowledge of science and of its applications to the development of the national resources is necessary for the fullest individual and national life.

All the Powers interested in the Far East may rest assured that the civilisation of the future demands the maintenance of strong independent nations, fearless of oppression, entering into closer commercial and social intercourse with each other ; that thus by the practice of material aid upon the plane of physical life, they may lay the foundation of a higher spiritual fellowship. Any attempt at military or political domination simply leads to the suppression of all real national life and hinders the cause of true world civilisation, the object of which is, not to extinguish individual nationality, but rather to bring it into strong organic harmony with the life of other nations.

The bogey of the "Yellow Peril" has been raised as a reason why Eastern nations should not be encouraged to strengthen themselves with all the appliances of Western arts, both of peace and war, and the rapid development of Japan has led to the fear that she may place herself at the head of an Asiatic combination which might overwhelm the civilisation of Europe. Mr. Charles H. Pearson has drawn a gloomy picture, not only of the possibilities but also of the probabilities of the future ; and Mr. Meredith Townsend has argued that Asia, which has rejected Christianity and hates the European mind, will one day attempt to shake itself free from the Western world. If that day ever comes, it will have been brought about by the conduct of the European Powers, which have so long taken advantage of the weakness of Asia. It is just possible that the ends of

The so-called "Yellow Peril."

eternal justice require such a retribution, but I believe it is not yet too late to prevent it. To the Eastern nations the "White Peril" is a reality, while to the Western nations the "Yellow Peril" is only a speculation. I am inclined to agree with the opinions of Professor E. G. Browne of Cambridge University, who in a recent lecture said : "The curious thing is that nobody has any idea of whether there would be any 'Yellow Peril' even if the other Asiatic Powers shook off their weakness as Japan has done. For it is to be remembered that while our civilisation has developed very largely on military lines, that of China (which is the dominant factor in the case) has tended away from militarism. The Chinese despise fighting as a propensity of brutes, beasts, or savages, and leave it to the riff-raff of the populace. And even if, under the influence of Japan and the pressure of European rapacity, they should organise themselves to resist the violence of others, it does not follow that they will embark on a career of aggression. On the contrary, it is possible that China may yet give the world a lead in the direction of peace." If that lead be not followed, we are not likely to be far wrong in assuming that, if the unexpected ability of the Japanese and the Chinese to defend themselves against the "White Peril" means a "Yellow Peril," that peril is certain to appear.

Meantime Japan is face to face with some of the problems of a similar nature to those which have appeared in Europe and America. The inevitable result of the developments of industry and commerce and the increase of competition has been, as we have seen, the formation of large combinations of capital which are beginning to have very important effects on the conditions of the people, and one of the most important problems of the future is :—What forms will these combinations ultimately take and to what will they lead? Will they cause a return, in a modified form, to the semi-communistic conditions of the feudal system in which the due maintenance of the lives of the people was considered the first

Future of combinations of capital.

charge, or will they tend to become more and more capitalistic in their nature, and dividends for the fortunate few be ground out of the lives of the workers? Under modern conditions, in all industrial countries, wealth has increased at one end of the social scale and poverty at the other, and already in Japan these two features have given rise to a considerable amount of socialistic writing and speaking. Indeed a prominent Japanese politician has written a book in which he has pictured a socialistic Utopia where poverty will be unknown, but he has copied his picture too closely from Western models and has not sufficiently considered the idiosyncrasies of the Japanese mind. While the philosophy and former social order of the Japanese was, to a very considerable extent, communistic in its nature, still their genius is individualistic, and they are not willing to sacrifice results to a rigid organisation. What ultimate form the combinations will take it is of course impossible to say; but it is to be hoped that the organisation of the future will allow the work which is done to be representative not only of the Japanese ideals of life and art but also embody many of the features of the new civilisation, and in this way Japan would be able to exercise great influence on the life and thought of every country in the world.

The amount and nature of this influence would depend on the moral standard in Japan. At present that is very Future of ethics indefinite. Old ideas have to a large extent in Japan. disappeared, and during the transition nothing very definite has taken their place, although the discussion of ethical problems is now occupying the attention of many thoughtful men in Japan. In a previous chapter I have indicated some of the steps which have been taken in the direction of arriving at an ethical basis for modern Japanese life. Probably the process will be slow, and in the interval many different opinions will be expressed and many experiments be made. Mr. Tokiwo Yokoi, from whom I have already quoted on this subject, says: ·" The Japanese professors of morals cannot appeal to the authority of a religious system. After the failure of the attempt to revive Confucianism, no other similar project can succeed. Education has never been, at least during the last three centuries, in the hands of the Buddhist priests. Their ethical interests are to-day too weak to seek to influence the policy of moral education. Christianity is not to be thought of. It is yet new and untried, and its position, though highly respectable, is not commanding enough to take the lead in this work. The only available course left to the educators of Japan is to appeal to the sentiments of loyalty and patriotism which lie latent in the breast of every Japanese. Such appeals carry immense weight with the young, and go no doubt a great way in solving the problem." He points out, however, that they are apt to become one-sided, and to forget that in order that efficient public service may be performed, there must, in the first place, be men of good personal character, and that the rising generation must not only have impressed upon them that truthfulness, temperance, generosity, and thrift are indispensable to those who would be loyal and patriotic subjects of the Mikado, but that they are so important in themselves, they ought to be freed from the domination of any other class of virtues and given independent positions. He thinks, however, that most likely this one-sided emphasis on the importance of public virtues to the neglect of the private is a momentary phase in the educational development and will gradually pass away, and with the increase of intelligence among the people and the growth of private schools which are conducted on less formal and more liberal lines than the Government institutions, there will be evolved a system of ethics suitable to the new conditions.

There are at present three distinct trends in Japanese ethical thought. In the first, it is argued that the religion and ethics of Old Japan, if maintained in their purity, are sufficient for the wants of the future; in the second, that the materialistic and utilitarian philosophy is all that is necessary;

and in the third, that a higher development is required in the direction of Christianity, although it may be necessary to present it in a form different from that which is common in Western countries.

The ideals of "Bushido" which inculcate right-doing combined with the highest code of honour have still a great hold on the minds of many of the people of Japan. Life without honour is not worth living, and death is faced without fear if either personal or national honour is in question. Buddhism, which permeates the thoughts of the common people ; Shintoism, which makes the bond of personal loyalty to the Emperor so strong ; Confucianism, which guides their practical ethics ; and the influence of Western science, philosophy, and religion must all be reckoned with in considering the possibilities of the future. That future is therefore difficult to forecast.

Future of religion in Japan.

Marquis Ito may be taken as a representative of the spirit of the Revolution. Some years ago when a suggestion was made that national education should be put on a religious basis, a Japanese interviewer reported that Marquis Ito "did not hesitate to dismiss the rumour as a baseless fabrication. That religious votaries should endeavour to push their evangelical efforts in every direction, educational or political, was intelligible enough. But it would be the height of folly for educationists to invoke the aid of religion. . . . The modern progress of Japan was, in his opinion, due, among other things, to the fact that all religious entanglements had been wisely avoided in the domains of education and politics. 'Look,' said he, 'look at those Oriental countries which are still in a state of religious bondage. Do we not observe in those countries that religious prejudice still constitutes a fatal barrier to the introduction of an intelligent system of administration ? Do those among us who would have religion introduced into the field of education desire to follow in the footsteps of the backward countries of the East ?' He did not mean to say that religion should be banished altogether from society ; the people were perfectly free to believe and profess any form of religion, only . . . . with re-affirmation of the drastic and sufficing efficiency of Education, pure and undefiled." He continued : " In the view of the ruling classes, religion is a secondary affair. The important thing is to conserve the national morality, which inculcates love of country, loyalty to the Sovereign, filial piety, family harmony, respect for parents, goodwill among sons and daughters, the worship of ancestors, etc. These are civic and family observances, not religious. This moral system limits its aims to this world, and its practice contemplates no celestial reward." The religion of the Revolution is evidently not a religion in the ordinary sense, but a civic and family morality, and seems to be very similar to that inculcated by Comte.

On the other hand, it cannot be disputed that Christianity, in some of its varied forms, is having considerable influence, both direct and indirect, in Japan, but it will be presented to the people in a form widely differing from that of Western countries. Count Okuma has expressed the opinion that "Civilisation does not depend upon religion. The old characteristic civilisation of Japan has assimilated Christianity, giving birth to something better. Japan's progress for the last thirty years does not depend on Christianity, but upon the peculiar attractiveness of the Japanese character. Japan has her own philosophical system, based on Chinese ethics, and strictly speaking she has no religion ; but she has capacity for Western civilisation, which enables her to assimilate the best that the Western nations possess." Mr. Shimada Saburo, a professed Christian and a well-known journalist and politician, writes : " The Christianity that gains the hearts and minds of the people of Japan will be our own— a Japanese Christianity. It will not be exactly like that of England or of the United States. Just as we have united the Benevolence of Confucius and the Mercy of Buddha, and have made a product peculiar to Japan, so Christianity will be tinged with the national characteristics." Dr. Nitobe (from whom I have so often quoted) believes that the profit and

... further development is required in ... although it may be necessary ... different from that which is common ... which inculcate right-doing ... of human love with a great ... of the people of ... is not worth living, ... without fear if either personal ... question. Buddhism, which ... the common people; Shintoism ... loyalty to the Emperor ... guide their practical ethics; ... philosophy, and religion ... considering the possibilities of ... therefore difficult to forecast. ... as a representative of the ... years ago when a suggestion ... should be put on a ... reported that Marquis ... answer as a baseless ... The religious ... should endeavour to ... efforts in every direction, educational ... But it would be the ... to invoke the aid of religion. ... of Japan was, in his opinion, due, ... that all religious entangle... ... every exerted in the domain of education ... and its, 'look at those Oriental ... to a state of religious bondage. ... in those countries that religious prejudice ... ... know in the introduction of an

loss philosophy of utilitarians and materialists finds favour only among logic-choppers with half a soul; an opinion which is rather hard on the scientific men in Japan, who are for the most part inclined to this way of thinking. He explains his own position (which may be accepted as that of many thoughtful men who have had opportunities of studying Western thought and its results) in the following words : " It is with ecclesiastical methods and with the forms which obscure the teachings of Christ, and not with the teachings themselves, that I have little sympathy. I believe in the religion taught by Him and handed down to us in the New Testament, as well as in the law written in the heart. Further, I believe that God hath made a testament which may be called 'old' with every people and nation—Gentile or Jew, Christian or heathen." He further believes that before Christianity can make much progress in Japan or in the East generally, it must divest itself of its foreign accoutrements and the superstructure of Western metaphysics with which it has been loaded. At a religious conference held in Amsterdam last year, Mr. Z. Toyosaki, of Tokyo, said that " the Japanese are usually said to be indifferent towards religion, but this is not their real attitude. In fact, their dissatisfaction with popular Buddhism and orthodox Christianity has led them to stand aloof from all religions. They have found that popular religious conceptions are incompatible with the scientific and philosophic thought of the present day. Yet they have come to acknowledge the possibility of a higher religion capable of satisfying the intellectual as well as the spiritual cravings of mankind." Any one who keeps himself acquainted with Japanese thought, as that is expressed in their journals and current literature, must admit that moral and religious subjects claim a large share of attention.

   The Japanese, indeed, must find it very difficult to ascertain *what* Christianity really is, as it has been presented to them in so many different forms ranging from the Salvation Army to the Roman Catholic and Greek Churches, and all claiming to spread the true Gospel. They must have a further difficulty in discovering *where* Christianity is, when they observe the results on either the individuals or the nations with whom they come into contact. The former are, as a rule, more intent on the worship of mammon and the pursuit of pleasure than the service of God and their fellow-men, while the latter in their dealings with Eastern peoples constantly deny the religion which they profess. When they visit Europe and America and study the results of Western civilisation they find many things with which they are by no means enamoured. The effects of Christianity in Japan must be measured, not by the number of professing Christians, although that is now considerable, but by the influence of Western civilisation on the national life and thought. Modern Japan has, to a large extent, as Count Okuma has expressed it, assimilated the best that Western nations possess, and to a very considerable degree has justified the opinion that the nation which has from ancient times imbibed and assimilated the elements of Oriental civilisation, may produce a new and strong tissue, and this may be done not by a suddenly professed change of religion, but by a slow process of evolution in which many forces—economic, intellectual, and spiritual—will co-operate. Those who are working in this direction may rest assured that personal and national example will have more effect on Eastern ethics and religion than formal teaching and preaching, especially if these be conducted entirely on the lines of Western thought.

Lafcadio Hearn says: "With the acceptance of the doctrine of evolution old forms of thought crumbled, new ideas arose to take the place of worn-out dogmas, and we have a general intellectual movement in directions strangely parallel with Oriental philosophy." The probability of the doctrine of pre-existence is being admitted not only by theologians but also by scientific men, and even the modern theories of stellar evolution and dissolution seem to confirm the general principles of Eastern cosmogonies. Changes in religious thought as a rule are slow, and are usually more the result of unconscious permeation than of deliberate conviction. This is strikingly illustrated by the developments in religious thought which have taken place in the West during the past quarter of a century. These developments, combined with greater experience of Eastern peoples, have led to great modifications in the methods of presenting to them the fundamental truths of religion. Much of the crude anthropomorphism and many of the materialistic ideas regarding the future life which formerly characterised Christian theology have disappeared, and have been replaced by teaching which commends itself to the intellect and the conscience, and many of the narrow sectarian doctrines formerly preached are now seldom heard. Most important of all, religious toleration has been greatly developed. A great deal, however, still requires to be done before Western theology can appeal to cultivated Eastern minds. It must be admitted by all who know much of the subject that while astronomy is no longer geocentric but heliocentric, Western theology is still largely geocentric, and has not been much affected by the developments of science, although there has been a somewhat indefinite demand for a roomier universe. If they wish their work to prosper, religious teachers must not only take to heart the lessons of science, but they must also free themselves from the fatal distinction and breach between the Church and the world which is the very negation of the central teaching and privilege of Christ. They must not only place the doctrines of their religion on a proper basis, but they must remember that it is not only a creed but a life. No society has a right to call itself Christian which lives by principles that turn the earth into a battlefield, and in the evening summons the ambulances, picks up the wounded and sheds tears of pity over the dead. Intelligent Easterns will be inclined to judge of a religion, not so much by its dogmas as by its results on the lives of the individuals who profess it, and on the social conditions of the people. On the other hand, we may rest assured that they will not be content with the cast-off theological garments of the West. The work of doctrinal reconstruction is only beginning, but already some of the most repulsive beliefs have been replaced by others of a more rational nature. The old material Hell of the theologian has practically disappeared, and a new Heaven is being imagined which shall have at least its foundations laid on this earth and its superstructure in similar parts of the universe ; while Buddhism, that wondrous creed by which every human life is the Heaven or Hell of a life which preceded it, is insensibly permeating the best thought of our modern preachers and scientific men. If its fundamental principles were clearly understood and acted upon, they would have most important results not only on individual conduct but also on social conditions.

It is gradually being recognised that if religion has any meaning, science, industry, and commerce must not be used as ends in themselves, but as means to raise the standard of life of the people, not only materially but also intellectually, morally, and spiritually. The Easterns, as a rule, in contemplating eternity forget terrestrial realisation of individual and social life, and consequently fall into a degraded condition. The civilisation of the West is in danger of extinction through social upheavals and moral decomposition, and faith is disappearing before the most dangerous form of scepticism ; namely, that which arises from the doubt of the possibility of regenerating society and making the Kingdom of God stretch over the earth. For the highest culture we require a combination of Eastern with Western thoughts and methods, so that in this way may be reconciled the forces which on the one hand make for the renunciation of the world, and on the other for the accumulation of wealth. Science must become religious, and religion must become scientific, and both must be applied to the solution of social and political problems. The most thoughtful men in the West are beginning to recognise that these problems are most likely to be solved by calling in the old world to redress the balance of the new. One of them recently wrote: "England, as the member of the Anglo-Saxon family least possessed by the passion of industrial progress, may then discover in her imperial position a historic signifi- cance as yet unrealised, and having still her share of Anglo- Saxon energy and virility, but with a more mellowed temperament, and perhaps a more rooted hold in the past, she will find that the fortunate accident of conquest has called her to mediate between East and West, ancient and modern, and so in due time to contribute no mean illumina- tion to lessen the obscurity in which we now find ourselves. For only a race of the highest virility can learn from the East with profit—a race possessing the implicit faith of the West that the Wheel of Being does not merely revolve but moves forward. It is only some such expansion of thought beyond racial limits that will save modern philosophy from self-stultification."[1] We may rest assured that there is no peace for the intellect and heart until science, philosophy, and religion are not merely reconciled but are seen to be one, as root, stem, and leaves are organic expressions of the same living tree. Then the highest truth of reason will be one with the highest object of faith, for only the thought which trusts can truly indicate faith in the God which gave it. Then, and then only, will national welfare be laid on a solid foundation.

A new Power has arisen in the Far East which has not only a large share of Anglo-Saxon virility, but is also deeply imbued with Eastern thought, and it may have very im- portant functions to perform not only in the domains of industry, commerce, and politics, but also in the realms of thought. The tendencies of the present day seem to show that Eastern philosophy streaming back to the West will produce a fundamental change in our thought and know- ledge, and profoundly affect social and political conditions. It has been argued with no little force that "to reconcile the East with the West; to be the advocate of the East

[1] W. F. Alexander, *Contemporary Review*, April 1904, p. 531.

and the harbinger of the West; this we believe to be the mission which Japan is called upon to fulfil." It will be interesting to watch how far the Britain of the East is in alliance with the Britain of the West, not only for political purposes, but also how far the two Powers are able to co-operate in the solution of the most important problems which lie in the future, and thus promote the highest welfare of the human race.

CHAPTER XX

(*Supplementary*)

RECENT EVENTS

IN the original plan of this book it was intended to conclude with the preceding chapter, but early in the present year, The methods of war broke out between Japan and Russia, and history. as it will mark a most important epoch in the history of the Japanese Empire, and probably of the world, I propose in this supplementary chapter to indicate how far recent events have justified the opinions expressed in the preceding chapters, and at the same time to mention some of the chief lessons which the Britain of the West may learn from the experience of the Britain of the East.

As I have stated in my preface, my object is not to give a history of modern Japan, but rather to indicate the forces which have been at work in bringing about what is admitted to be the wonder of the latter half of the nineteenth century, and to note some of the chief results. Political conditions are considered up to the end of last year, when the question of war with Russia still hung in the balance. A systematic history of modern Japan, and indeed of any other part of the world, would be a sort of dramatic poem in which every scene and person is determined not by imagination or accident but by conditions which all lead up to the purposeful plan of the whole. All that I have attempted to supply are some materials for such a history by a preliminary study of the dynamics of the subject. What Ranke designates as the "art" of writing history consists, not simply in the narration of facts, but in the arrangement of these facts in such a manner as to show their relations in the causal and teleological connection of an organic whole which is developed by individuals or nations acting as the conscious organs of the general tendencies dominating their times.

For some years past the Japanese have been consciously making history with very definite objects in view. The events of the Restoration gave them many   The making of difficult problems to solve. The feudal system   Japanese history. had disappeared and the whole machinery of government had to be erected on a new basis. Administration and education received their first attention ; but contact with Foreign Powers soon showed that these, in themselves, were not sufficient to enable them to attain a position of equality with the other nations of the world. The long negotiations in connection with treaty revision awoke within them the consciousness of the need of a national policy which would make them strong and cause their just claims to be considered with respect. The fear of aggression from European Powers, especially from Russia, developed that consciousness ; and the action of that Power, along with France and Germany, after the conclusion of the war with China, almost turned it into a passion. Without rest, but also without haste, they strengthened their army and navy and developed their means of communication and other appliances, and thus made themselves a strong military Power. They disclaimed all intention of aggression, but at the same time they studied carefully the trend of events and determined to resist to the death any action by outsiders which injuriously affected their welfare or threatened their national existence. The doings of Russia had long been a cause of anxiety to them, and especially those in Manchuria after the war with China filled them with grave apprehension. They were anxious to come to an understanding with Russia on the subject, and their self-restraint has been admired by all disinterested parties.

Negotiations were commenced in August of last year

with regard to affairs in Manchuria and Korea, and the Japanese Cabinet drafted a treaty embodying its proposals on the lines which I have indicated in a previous chapter. They proposed to place Manchuria and Korea on approximately the same basis, and assimilated the position of Russia in the one country and Japan in the other, and thus afforded a clear proof of their wish to arrive at an understanding on the subject. In order to safeguard the supposed rights of Russia, Japan expressed her readiness to define the interests accruing to Russia, through her railway in Manchuria, as comprising the administration, military and civil, of a strip of territory measuring thirty miles on each side of the line and including the town of Harbin, situated at the junction of the Manchurian railway with the main Trans-Siberian line to Vladivostock. These proposals did not satisfy Russia, and believing that Japan would not dare to go to war, she put forward counter-proposals which clearly indicated her ambitions. They limited the treaty to Korea, and even for that, restrictions were placed on Japan, while Russia was to be allowed to do as she pleased in China. Russia declined to pledge herself to the policy of the "open door," or indeed to anything which in any way restricted her freedom of action in Manchuria. On the other hand, she made three further and uncompensated demands stipulating for (1) no fortifications on the Straits; (2) a neutral zone exclusively Korean; and (3) the abandonment by Japan of all political interest in Manchuria. These demands clearly showed that Russia did not wish a reasonable settlement.

Negotiations dragged on till the end of last year, and on 21st December Japan presented what she called her "last amendments," the object of which was to guarantee the independence and integrity of China by defining strictly the position of Russia in Manchuria. About the middle of January of the present year the Japanese Minister in St. Petersburg was instructed to ask for an "early reply." Meantime Russia was busily employed in strengthening her naval and military position. Every ship that could be spared was being sent out to the Far East, evidently for the purpose of overawing the Japanese. On 26th January the Japanese Minister at St. Petersburg was informed that the Russian Government had resolved not to yield on the Manchurian question, but to make substantial concessions to Japan on other points. Still no formal reply had been sent to the proposals of Japan, and it was evident that the whole object of Russia was to gain time. On 5th February, and not until after Russian troops had already invaded Northern Korea, Mr. Kurino, the Minister for Japan in St. Petersburg, was instructed to break off negotiations.

The Japanese were at once ready to strike a determined blow, as they were well aware that the first blow counts much. On 9th February, Admiral Togo made a successful attack on Port Arthur, disabling seven Russian warships. The Russian Government issued a memorandum to their representatives abroad giving their version of the negotiations, and complaining that Japan had not waited for their reply and had commenced war without a formal declaration. I shall deal with that complaint further on, but it is evident that the object of Russia was to gain time so that she might have a sufficient naval force in Eastern seas to settle the matter without any operations on land. At the outbreak of the war the naval forces of Japan and Russia in the Far East were so nearly equal that a very slight superiority in skill might have been sufficient to have decided the struggle in favour of Russia, but the Japanese showed such brilliant qualities of strategy and such bravery that they soon obtained a practical command of the sea.

War begins.

The Russian military authorities must have recognised the difficult position a large army would be in, at a distance of 4000 miles from its base, and supplied only by a single line of railway. Some time ago an eminent Russian professor of the art of war solemnly declared that it was "historically and philosophically impossible for Japan to prevent Russia from fulfilling her manifest destiny in Asia."

To this it has been answered that such a saying reminds us of Huxley's definition of Herbert Spencer's conception of a tragedy as "a syllogism strangled by a fact." The Russian officials, despite all their bluff, must have seen that they were placed on the horns of a dilemma which is this:— "The army which can be fed by the Trans-Siberian Railway will not be strong enough to beat the Japanese; the army that is strong enough to beat the Japanese cannot be fed by the Trans-Siberian Railway." It is therefore easy to understand why the Russians were anxious, if possible, to confine their operations to sea.

The position of Japan was clearly shown in the Imperial Proclamation of War, which was as follows:—"We, by the Grace of Heaven, Emperor of Japan, seated on the Throne occupied by the same Dynasty from time immemorial, do hereby make Proclamation to all Our loyal and brave subjects as follows:—

Japanese Proclamation of War.

"We hereby declare war against Russia, and we command Our Army and Navy to carry on hostilities against that Empire with all their strength, and We also command all Our competent authorities to make every effort, in pursuance of their duties and in accordance with their powers, to attain the national aim with all the means within the limits of the law of nations.

"We have always deemed it essential to Our international relations and made it Our constant aim to promote the pacific progress of Our Empire in civilisation, to strengthen Our friendly ties with other States, and to establish a state of things which would maintain enduring peace in the Extreme East, and assure the future security of Our Dominion without injury to the rights and interests of other Powers. Our competent authorities have also performed their duties in obedience to Our will, so that Our relations with the Powers have been steadily growing in cordiality. It was thus entirely against Our expectation that We have unhappily come to open hostilities against Russia.

"The integrity of Korea is a matter of constant concern to this Empire, not only because of Our traditional relations with that country, but because the separate existence of Korea is essential to the safety of Our Realm. Nevertheless Russia, in disregard of solemn treaty pledges to China and her repeated assurances to other Powers, is still in occupation of Manchuria, and has consolidated and strengthened her hold upon those provinces and is bent upon their final annexation. And since the absorption of Manchuria by Russia would render it impossible to maintain the integrity of Korea and would in addition compel the abandonment of all hope of peace in the Extreme East, We determined, in these circumstances, to settle the questions by negotiation and to secure thereby permanent peace. With that object in view, Our competent authorities, by Our order, made proposals to Russia, and frequent conferences were held during the course of six months. Russia, however, never met such proposals in a spirit of conciliation, but by her wanton delays put off the settlement of the question, and by ostensibly advocating peace on the one hand, while she was, on the other, extending her naval and military preparations, sought to accomplish her own selfish designs.

"We cannot in the least admit that Russia had from the first any serious or genuine desire for peace. She had rejected the proposals of Our Government ; the safety of Korea is in danger ; the vital interests of Our Empire are menaced. The guarantees for the future which we have failed to secure by peaceful negotiations, We can now only seek by an appeal to arms.

"It is Our earnest wish that by the loyalty and valour of Our faithful subjects, peace may soon be permanently restored and the glory of Our Empire preserved."

The rapid action of the Japanese in attacking Port Arthur immediately after the negotiations were broken off, caused the Russians to bring against them the Justification of charge of treachery. I cannot, of course, dis- Japanese action. cuss all the *pros* and *cons* of this subject, but the following are the conclusions of Dr. T. J. Lawrence, Lecturer on International Law in the Royal Naval College, Greenwich. After sketching the course of events which preceded the outbreak of the war, Dr. Lawrence states that "the accusation of treachery rests entirely upon the assumption that International Law imposes upon belligerents the duty of making to one another a formal declaration of war before commencing hostilities. Never was assumption more groundless. Nearly every war of the last two centuries has been commenced without a declaration. Sometimes one has been issued, as in the present case, a greater or less time after the forces of the combatants have begun their work of conflict. Sometimes there has been none from the beginning to the end of a war. Occasionally a manifesto by a State to its own subjects, or a diplomatic circular sent to foreign Governments, has taken the place of a formal notice delivered to the enemy. The constant practice has been for the better-prepared State to strike a sudden blow at her unready adversary, whatever form or absence of form seemed advisable at the moment. Nor is there in this anything that necessarily involves bad faith. A period of negotiation precedes a period of hostility. As relations grow more and more strained, a prudent State prepares for eventualities. Very often an *ultimatum* is presented ; that is to say, a demand, the refusal of which will be followed by war. The rupture of diplomatic relations is the constant precursor of armed conflict. Unless the first blow falls, like a bolt from the blue, in a period of profound peace, without previous complaint and demand for redress, there is nothing in it which savours of treachery." Dr. Lawrence illustrates his conclusions by historical precedents and proceeds to say :— " Unless we are prepared to maintain the ridiculous proposition that the law of nations, instead of being deduced from the practice of nations, has no connection whatever with it, we must acquit Japan of the charge made against her. Instead of being guilty of a breach of International Law, she went beyond it by giving her adversary ample notice of what he might expect. Relations between the two Powers had been strained for a long time. There would have been no treachery in a sudden attack. But the note delivered on 6th February by the Japanese representative at St. Petersburg not only broke off diplomatic intercourse—an act which is constantly followed by immediate war—but also expressly stated that Japan must take such measures as she thought fit for her own safety. Its exact words were : ' The Imperial Government reserve to themselves the right to take such independent action as they may deem best to consolidate and defend their menaced position, as well as to protect their established rights and legitimate interests.' The merest tyro in diplomacy knows what this meant. It was a distinct warning that hostilities might be expected at any moment, and the first blow was not struck till about sixty hours after it had been given. As a matter of fact, Russia was not taken unawares. She had expected war for some time, and had prepared for it, though her preparations were ill-conceived and badly carried out." [1]

On the other hand, Sir John Macdonell, C.B., LL.D., has some doubts on the subject. He says : " On the night of the 8th or 9th Admiral Togo torpedoed the Russian vessels at Port Arthur. It was an attack of surprise. Was it a treacherous and disloyal act ? The question must be put with the knowledge that a nation which is patient may be duped ; that the first blow counts much ; and that under cover of continuing negotiations a country unprepared might deprive another better equipped of its advantages. But it is a nice question whether the negotiations had reached, on the 8th or 9th of February, a point at which discussion had been abandoned, and both sides had accepted the arbitrament of battle. I will only say that the recent precedent is of evil omen, and that it is to be feared that, in future, we may see blows struck, not merely without formal notice, but while diplomatists are still debating. I am not expressing an opinion on the particular act in saying that there has been

[1] *War and Neutrality in the Far East*, pp. 27-32.

an unfortunate—perhaps inevitable—retrogression. Since 1870 there has been a tendency to abide by the old rule, which regarded a war without a declaration or ultimatum as disloyal." [1] Baron Suyematsu, a high Japanese authority, while appreciating Sir John Macdonell's contention that no blows should be struck without adequate warning or while diplomatists are still debating the matters in dispute, undertakes to prove that Japan, so far from taking her enemy unawares, did actually do precisely as Sir John Macdonell is anxious to show she ought to have done, and that, in the sense of his comment on the operations, there was no room for the Russians to be surprised in any degree whatever. I can only give a brief résumé of Baron Suyematsu's facts and arguments ; for details the original article must be consulted.[2] He gives an outline of the negotiations which were carried on at the end of last and the beginning of this year, and makes it quite clear that the Japanese Government pressed on the Russian Government the urgent necessity of accelerating the despatch of an answer to the proposals of the Japanese Government as much as possible, because further prolongation of the existing conditions was not only undesirable but dangerous. On the evening of the 31st of January Count Lamsdorff admitted to Mr. Kurino, the Japanese representative at St. Petersburg, that he fully appreciated the gravity of the situation. Notwithstanding this admission, the delay continued, and it was not until the *fifth* day after this interview which Mr. Kurino had with Count Lamsdorff, and the *third* day after the reply had been promised to be given, namely, on the 5th of February 1904, at 2.15 P.M., that Baron Komura (the Secretary of State for Foreign Affairs in Japan) telegraphed to Mr. Kurino that further prolongation of the existing situation being inadmissible, the Imperial Government had decided to terminate the pending negotiations. After a statement of the position of the Japanese Government on the subject under dispute (and

---

[1] *The Nineteenth Century*, July 1904, p. 147.
[2] *Ibid.*, August 1904, p. 174.

which was for the most part embodied in the Declaration of War already quoted) Baron Komura's communication concluded with the sentence mentioned by Dr. Lawrence, reserving the right of the Japanese Government to take such independent action as they may deem best to consolidate and defend their menaced position, as well as to protect their established rights and legitimate interests.

Simultaneously with the presentation of Baron Komura's note, Mr. Kurino was instructed to write to Count Lamsdorff and inform him that as the efforts of the Japanese Government to arrive at an honourable understanding with the Russian Government had been unsuccessful, it was his intention to take his departure from St. Petersburg, with the Staff of the Imperial Legation. These notes were presented to Count Lamsdorff by Mr. Kurino on the 6th of February, at 4 P.M., and on the same day Baron Komura conveyed a formal intimation to Baron Rosen, the Russian Minister in Tokyo, in the sense that:—" Whereas the Japanese Government had made every effort to arrive at an amicable settlement of the Manchurian question with Russia, the latter had not evinced any disposition to reciprocate this peaceful purpose. Therefore Japan could not continue the diplomatic conferences. She was regretfully compelled to take independent action for the protection of her rights and interests, and she must decline to accept the responsibility of any incidents that might occur in consequence."

A perusal of these despatches should have left no doubt on the minds of the Russian statesmen that Japan had finally, though reluctantly, arrived at the conclusion that war was inevitable. As Baron Suyematsu puts it: " The wording is polite, but who can doubt that it was a clear notice of war?"

Those in command of the Russian fleet were evidently quite aware that their Government were determined on war, for as Baron Suyematsu points out :—" At the moment when Admiral Togo actually made his attack *the Russian ships lay outside the harbour in a perfect battle array*, in front of the shore forts and batteries of the fortress, a position that they had taken up on their return from their cruise to the south-eastward. Wherein was the unpreparedness? If the officers of the Russian ships were caught in an unguarded moment, blame must not be imputed to the Japanese. The cause must rather be sought in a misconception on the part of the Russians of the watchful strategy which the situation demanded. The facts are, moreover, that the Russian ships had lain under a full head of steam for days off the Port Arthur entrance, had been continually using their search-lights as though they apprehended an attack, the battleships had their decks cleared for action, and the instant that the first torpedo was launched the Russians opened fire on the Japanese boats."

The best proof of the determination of the Russian Government to settle the matter in dispute by the arbitrament of war is to be found in its actions for a year previous to the close of the negotiations. It had promised to complete the evacuation of Manchuria in April 1903, but instead of doing so, it strengthened its position as rapidly as possible. During that year, it despatched to Far Eastern waters

	Combined Tonnage
Three battleships	38,488
One armoured cruiser	7,727
Five other cruisers	26,417
Seven destroyers	2,450
One gunboat	1,344
Two mine-laying craft	6,000

Seven other destroyers were sent by rail to Port Arthur and there put together, while two vessels of the "Volunteer" Fleet were armed and hoisted the Russian naval ensign at Vladivostock. Considerable numbers of troops were sent to Manchuria; but as I have already remarked it was evidently the intention of the Russian Government to have a sufficient naval force in Eastern waters to settle the conflict without any operations in Manchuria or Korea. How in the face of all these facts the Russian Government could complain of having been taken unawares is incomprehensible, and the charge of treachery seems to have been made for the purpose of covering the want of attention and skill on the part of those in command of the fleet. If it had not been for the self-restraint of the Japanese Government, war might have broken out some months before it actually did, when the Russians were still more unprepared than they were on the 9th of February.

The operations carried on by the Japanese in the war, both by land and sea, have fully justified the opinions which I have expressed in the preceding chapters. Events of the war. Their intense patriotism has caused them to perform deeds of daring which have won for them the admiration of the world, their skill in strategy and in the application of the latest scientific methods in all they have done, has made them almost uniformly successful in their operations. They have demonstrated the importance of the work of the engineer. The railways which have been built in Japan have been fully utilised to convey men and materials and the ships to transport them oversea. The telegraphs have been used to communicate instructions and to keep the authorities informed regarding movements and requirements. The dockyards and shipbuilding yards have been ready to undertake repairs, and the arsenals and machine shops to turn out war material of all kinds as well as appliances which aid operations in the field. Light railways have been laid down on the way to battlefields and wireless telegraphy and telephones to convey instructions to the soldiers ; in short, all the latest applications of mechanical, electrical, and chemical science have been freely and intelligently employed.

The barest notice of the events of the war is all that, meantime, I can give, not only on account of want of space, but also because the war has, to a large extent, been fought *in camera* and the circumstances attending it are only imperfectly known to outsiders. The Japanese have shown that they look upon war as a serious matter and not simply as a game which is useful for the supply of interesting copy for the newspapers. Their strategy has been most skilful, but they did not think it part of their duty to allow correspondents to communicate their plans to the world and to the enemy, and it is probable that they have established a precedent which will become of universal application. If this be the case, the occupation of war correspondents is gone for ever. It would be well if those responsible for newspapers exercised some of the self-control of the Japanese and were more careful about the news they publish. In the absence of anything authentic, the reports of coolies or of other equally untrustworthy persons have been telegraphed round the world and announced on flaring bills, only to be contradicted or ignored in the next issue of the papers. It almost seems as if an extension of Japanese methods were required in order to prevent the newspapers becoming public nuisances if not public dangers.

The assaults by the Japanese forces on Port Arthur, both by land and by sea, when accurately described will rank among the most heroic struggles in the history of the world. The sending of men to sink themselves and their ships in the fairway of Port Arthur, and the storming of the heights of Nanshan show that the Japanese military and naval commanders are able to reckon on a national instinct which Western peoples are scarcely able to appreciate in its full significance. The advance on the strong position of the Russians at Kinchau proves that Japanese soldiers do not hesitate to sacrifice themselves in order to gain the object they have in view. Wasteful self-immolation, however, is no part of their programme. It is stated that the Emperor has kept back the final assault on Port Arthur so that lives might not be uselessly sacrificed. He has at the same time shown a great regard for his enemies and has given orders that non-combatants may have an opportunity of leaving Port Arthur. The strategy of General Kuroki and the other Japanese leaders has been carried out with all the deliberation and skill of a game of chess. Military discipline and scientific training, of course, account for a good deal of the success which has attended the arms of the Japanese, but they do not give a complete explanation. A national consciousness of unprecedented intensity has enabled the Japanese army and navy to achieve ends of incommensurable magnitude.

At the date of writing this, events of great importance are proceeding rapidly. The Port Arthur fleet of the Russians has been dispersed, the Vladivostock fleet has been in part destroyed and the remainder badly damaged. The final assault on Port Arthur is impending and the operations in other parts of Manchuria are rapidly bringing matters to a crisis. For our present purpose it is not necessary to follow them further. Enough has been said to demonstrate the truth of the opinions expressed in the preceding chapters, and to show the results of the training to which Japan has subjected itself. The sequel must be left to another opportunity.

One of the most interesting revelations to the peoples of the West regarding the Japanese character has been the behaviour of the troops during war-time. Behaviour of After referring to the absence of all attempts Japanese troops. to intensify racial hatred, Sir John Macdonell remarks that :—" Not more remarkable is the swift assimilation by Japan of the resources of military science than the assimilation, rapid and complete, of the best traditions, the courtesies and amenities of European warfare. Experience shows that if hostilities are long continued, passions kept in check at last break loose ; the vanquished are irritated and desperate ; the victors become impatient at resistance unreasonably continued. But, so far as things have gone, one may say that a non-Christian State has set an example to Christian nations in the conduct of war (as far as it is possible) on the lines of civilisation. The superior prestige of the West for humanity is gone. Touches of humanity and sympathy, never wanting in war, have abounded. The Japanese have tended their wounded adversaries and have resorted to no shabby subterfuges; and on the death of Admiral Makaroff they paid the tribute of brave men to a fallen foe. They have paid for what they have taken. They have made friends of the population in which they have moved. Already the ring of European nations whose consent has made International Law is broken in upon by the admission of Turkey and Japan. International Law cannot be quite what it was if it henceforth expresses the consent of powerful Asiatic non-Christian States as well as of European nations."[1] It is a remarkable fact that although the International Arbitration Tribunal was formed on the suggestion of the Czar, the Japanese have adhered more scrupulously to the rules of the Hague Convention than the Russians. In a recent interview Count Katsura, the Prime Minister of Japan, said that he did not think that any Government in the world at the outbreak of war ever took such pains as the Government of Japan has taken to emphasise to all the duty of conducting the war in strict accordance with the principles of humanity and the usages of International Law. Immediately upon the opening of hostilities, communications were sent to all the Governors of Prefectures reminding them of their responsibilities and especially with regard to any Russians that might be residing within their jurisdiction. Under the authority of the Minister of Education, directions were issued by which all the students in the empire, from the young men in the higher institutions of learning down to the children in the primary schools, have been instructed as to the principles and duties to be observed. In addition to this, communications were sent to the recognised representatives of all the religious bodies in the country—Buddhists, Shintoists, and Christians alike—asking them to take pains to discountenance any wrong tendencies among the more ignorant of the people. Among the points emphasised by the Government

[1] *The Nineteenth Century*, July 1904; p. 145.

are these :—That the war is one between the State of Japan and the State of Russia ; that it is not waged against individuals ; that individuals of all nationalities, peacefully attending to their business, are to suffer no molestation or annoyance whatever ; and that questions of religion do not enter into the war at all.

Perhaps the best proof of the power of self-restraint of the Japanese is to be found in the conduct of the great body of the people during war - time. I lived in Japan during the Satsuma rebellion, and al- _{Japan in war-time.} though affairs were sometimes in a very critical condition, there were no signs of alarm or even much to show an ordinary observer that there was anything serious going on. The arrangements which were made to meet the crisis were carried out quietly. When victory at last came to the Imperial Government there was no exultation, simply an official announcement that the war was at an end. Similarly in the war with China in 1894-5, there was little to show to visitors that the country was at war, everything being done in a quiet systematic manner.

In the present war with Russia the same calm has been preserved. In a circular which has been issued by the chief Chambers of Commerce in Japan, it is pointed out that none of the arrangements for the convenience of visitors who wish to enjoy the attractions of the country have been dislocated, but that " on the contrary, to the many objects of interest which invite inspection in normal years, there was added the remarkable spectacle of an insular people preserving a demeanour of absolute calm and imperturbability while engaged in a struggle for life or death with the greatest of continental military Powers. Since the outbreak of this war, as well as during the period of suspense that preceded it, the quiet self-possessed attitude of the Japanese people has been a theme of constant admiration and surprise to foreign onlookers, and has been described in eulogistic terms by foreign journalists. In truth, the country is just as it has always been. The Japanese people are not swayed by any frenzy of revenge or fired by any heat of territorial ambition. They are fighting for what they believe to be the minimum of their just right ; for the cause of free institutions ; the cause of security against the spread of military despotism ; the cause of a commercial field untrammelled for all, and the cause of lasting peace : causes which they have fervently embraced and for which they are ready to make any sacrifice. Under such circumstances this war has not impaired in the slightest degree the friendly feeling entertained by the Japanese nation for the peoples of Europe and America. On the contrary, it has greatly intensified that feeling, inasmuch as the crisis has elicited throughout nearly the whole of the Occident expressions of sympathy with Japan, which she welcomes with profound gratitude and satisfaction. She appreciates that the purpose for which she is shedding blood and treasure have the full endorsement of the enlightened nations of the West, and she sees that by lending her whole strength to the promotion of those purposes, she has drawn greatly closer the bonds of amity between herself and the Occident." All this goes to prove that Japan will not use the results of the war, however victorious she may be, for purposes of merely national aggrandisement, but that while safeguarding her own interests and keeping in mind her mission in the Far East, she will do nothing which will forfeit the goodwill of Europe and America.

The most remarkable feature in the domestic situation in Japan at the present time is the admirable reticence observed by the influential political parties and their organs. In view of the momentous issues at stake, all are agreed in refraining from saying or writing anything calculated to cause disunion or the appearance of it, and are united in giving the Government their support in bringing the war to a successful issue. That they are able to do this they are perfectly confident, and the events of the war justify their confidence. Its cost, so far, has proved to be less than was expected, it having been carried on at an expenditure equivalent to only two-thirds of the original estimate. They appreciate perfectly that the war may be a protracted one ; but if Russia is prepared to resort to the last extreme in order to maintain her national honour, Japan will not hesitate to sacrifice her last farthing in order to come out victorious from a struggle involving her very existence.

The question has often been asked during the past few months—What is the secret of the weakness which has been shown by Russia since the beginning of The secret of the war with Japan ? The complete answer to Russia's failure. that question would involve a disquisition on the educational, economical, social, and religious conditions of the Land of the Czar. Dr. Emil Reich has pointed out that, " Every one of the great Western nations has had to stand the test of a triple trial before it could reach its actual condition. It has had to pass through an intellectual Renaissance, a religious Reformation, and a political Revolution. And we may suppose that Russia will not escape the necessity of passing through a like series of stages." Russia dare not educate her people, and the consequence is that three out of every four are illiterate. Hierarchy and bureaucracy alike discourage the schools of the local councils. The universities are being more and more dominated by stupid officialism, and freedom of thought and teaching is impossible. An attempt has been made to build up modern industries under a system of protection which fosters artificial conditions and perpetuates antiquated methods, and thus throws a great burden on the agricultural classes. These latter are very often drunken and barbarous, and their methods of work entirely wanting in the applications of modern science. The bureaucracy is corrupt and brutal, and there is no intelligent public opinion to correct abuses. The most hopeless barrier to Russian progress, however, is the Greek Church, which has sterilised and paralysed both the intellectual and the moral powers of the people. The Russians are, for the most part, patriotic, for their religion is also a patriotism ; but it is not to be compared to the burning patriotism of the Japanese, which causes them to look upon death for their country as the highest honour for which they can compete. The Russian soldiers are no doubt brave when put in a position of danger, but for the most part it is mere brute courage, without that intellectual activity and scientific knowledge which are the most important factors in modern warfare. Many of them have been forced into the army against their wills and have little enthusiasm for the work, a considerable proportion indeed have a strong aversion to it. From men like these little is to be expected. The Russian Government has still to learn that the most powerful means either of offence or defence in a modern State is a well-educated enthusiastic people.

Another cause of the failure of Russia is the contempt in which they have held the Japanese. Those responsible for the negotiations preceding the outbreak of war seem to have had a very inadequate idea of the developments which had taken place in Japan and of the forces which had produced these developments. On this subject Baron Suyematsu has remarked : " In the eyes of the Russians there was no such Japan as they have, or rather the world has, begun to see since the opening of the war. They trusted, no doubt, either to be able to bluff through or crush at a blow if necessary. Even in the battle of the Yalu, nay, even in the battle of Kinchow, or Wafangu, they were unable to believe that the Japanese were not after all 'monkeys with the brain of birds'! Only a little time ago an eminent French statesman told me that France understood Japan little ; Russia still less. It was the sole cause of the present unfortunate war. ' In that respect,' he continued, ' England was sharper, for she understood the Far East, and, consequently, the changing circumstances of the world, before any other Occidental nation.' "

While the Japanese owe much to their utilisation of Western science, appliances, and methods, the secret of their

The secret of phenomenal success in every department of
Japan's success. national life lies in the spirit with which they have been animated. In a previous chapter I have given a

sketch of what is involved in that spirit, but a study of the doings in Japan of the past thirty years is its best illustration, if not explanation. I may, however, repeat a sentence or two of what I have quoted from Dr. Nitobe : " Needless to repeat," he says, " what has grown a trite saying, that it is the spirit that quickeneth, without which the best of implements profiteth but little. The most improved guns and cannon do not shoot of their own accord ; the most modern educational system does not make a coward a hero. No! What won the battles on the Yalu, in Korea and Manchuria, was the ghosts of our fathers, guiding our hands and beating in our hearts. They are not dead those ghosts, the spirits of our warlike ancestors. To those who have eyes to see, they are clearly visible." These are not simply the opinions of a philosopher (some might be inclined to call him a mystic) like Dr. Nitobe ; they are held even more strongly by the practical and by the fighting men. A few months ago Engineer-Captain Matsuo, one of my Kobu-Daigakko students, came to Glasgow to bid me good-bye before returning to Japan after he had despatched the cruisers *Kasuga* and *Nisshin*, and in the course of my conversation I showed him the chapter of this book which dealt with the army and navy, and he asked me to make it quite clear that while he valued Western ships and appliances he attached far more importance to the spirit which animated the men in charge of them.

The present war has shown most distinctly that the spirit of Old Japan still lives in its modern army and navy. I can only give one or two illustrations. When volunteers were asked to undertake the blocking of Port Arthur, over 2000 offered themselves for the dangerous task, and some of the applications were written with the blood of the men who sent them in. Seventy-seven officers and men were selected, and the farewell ceremonies which were held were of a striking and touching nature. On board the battleship *Asama* Captain Yashiro took a large silver cup presented to him by H.I.H. the Crown Prince, and filling it with water (it being an old Japanese custom to drink water on the occasion of permanent parting between near relatives), thus addressed the volunteers: "In sending you now on the duty of blocking the harbour entrance of Port Arthur, which affords you one chance out of thousands to return alive, I feel as if I were sending my beloved sons. But if I had one hundred sons, I would send them all on such a bold adventure as this, and had I only one son I should wish to do the same with him. In performing your duty, if you happen to lose your left hand, work with your right; if you lose both hands, work with both feet; if you lose both feet, work with your head, and faithfully carry out the orders of your commander. I send you to the place of death, and I have no doubt that you are quite ready to die. However, I do not mean to advise you to despise your life nor to run needless risks in trying to establish a great name. What I ask you all is to perform your duty regardless of your life. The cup of water I give you now is not meant to give you encouragement but to constitute you as representatives of the bravery of the *Asama*. A great shame it would be if our men needed Dutch courage to go to the place of death! I look forward to a joyous day when I see you again coming back with success. Submit your life to the will of Heaven and calmly perform your onerous duty."

Among the volunteers was Commander Takeo Hirose, who will always be remembered as one of the heroes of the war. Before the first attempt on Port Arthur he wrote: "How can I refuse to die as a patriotic sacrifice for my country? It will be a glorious death to go down with the ship at the entrance to Port Arthur." Before the second attempt, in which he perished, he wrote: "Knowing that the souls of the brave return seven times to this world to serve their country, I sacrifice with confidence this life, and expecting now to achieve final success I will go on board the ship cheerfully." These and similar words are now printed on picture post-cards and sent all over Japan and indeed to Japanese in all parts of the world. Their enthusiasm is thus raised to the highest pitch, and all merely personal considerations are put aside for what is believed to be the welfare or need of the country. This enthusiasm is the main cause of the success of Japan, in the arts both of peace and war, and her experience proves that a nation becomes whatever she believes herself to be. Without attempting to discuss all the transcendental effects of the beliefs of the Japanese, there can be no doubt that the practical results are embodied in the rule which every one from the highest to the lowest unflinchingly obeys, namely, that " it is the imperative duty of man in his capacity of a subject, to sacrifice his private interests to the public good. Egoism forbids co-operation, and without co-operation there cannot be any great achievement." The application of this rule to its logical conclusion will take the Japanese a long way and will enable them to solve many of the social problems of the present time, the true meanings of which are only beginning to be dimly perceived by the statesmen of the West. The war with Russia is still in progress, and its immediate results are uncertain, but whatever they may be, we cannot doubt that it has opened a new chapter in the history, not only of Japan, but of the world, and when that is adequately written, the debt which is due to the Britain of the East will be fully recognised.

Meantime, Great Britain should not be above learning a few lessons from Japan. I do not propose to enter into the lessons in military and naval administration and strategy, which no doubt will be taken to Lessons for Great Britain. heart by the proper authorities, but there are matters of more general interest on which a few remarks may be made. Already, indeed, Lord Selborne, the First Lord of the Admiralty, has in Parliament been directing attention to various lessons which may be learned from Japanese experience. He attached the greatest importance to the quality of the personnel, and he insisted that the officers and men were of more importance than the ships. This, as I have tried to make clear, has long been recognised by the

d Japanese custom ı drink water on the occasion of
inent parting betwec near relatives), thus addressed the
teers : " In sending ou now on the duty of blocking
arbour entrance of bıt Arthur, which affords you one
e out of thousands ı return alive, I feel as if I were
ıg my beloved son: But if I had one hundred sons'
Id send the'n a'l on uch a bold adventure as this, and
only one son I sh.d wish to do the same with him.
rforming your duty if you happen to lose your left
work with your rı t : if you lose both hands, work
ıth feet ; if you los b.th feet, work with your head,
a'thfully carry out ıe orders of your commander. I
you to the place of death, and I have no doubt that
ıe quite ready to do. However, I do not mean to
you to despise you lıfe nor to run needless risks in
ın establish a grɛt name. What I ask you all is
rf ım y ur duty reaıdless of your life. The cup of
I give you now is ct meant to give you encourage-
but to constitute vo as representatives of the bravery
Aırmı A greı shame it would be if our men
! Dutch courage to o to the place of death! I look
d ın a joyous day wen I see you again coming back
across. Submit ver lıfe to the will of Heaven, and
' perf ım your oneras duty."

mong the volunteer was Commander Takeo Hirose,
ıll always be remnbered as one of the heroes of
ar Before the fıt attempt on Port Arthur he
"How can I refus to die as a patriotic sacrifice for
untry ? It will be gıcrious death to go down with
.p at the entrance tı Port Arthur." Before the second
k. ın which he peshed. he wrote : "Knowing that
u!ı of the brave reim seven times to this world to
their country, I sacfice wıth confidence this life, an
ıng now to achievefinal success I will go on bo
ıp cheerfully." Tese and similar words are
l on picture post-cars and sent all over Japan
to Japanese in al parts of the world. Thei

thusiasm is thus raised to the highest pitch, and all mood personal considerations are put aside for what is believed to be the welfare or need of the country. This enthusiasm is the main cause of the success of Japan, in the arts both of peace and war, and her experience proves that a nation becomes whatever she believes herself to be. Without attempting to discuss all the transcendental effects of the beliefs of the Japanese, there can be no doubt that the practical results are embodied in the rule which every one from the highest to the lowest unflinchingly obeys, namely, that "it is the imperative duty o man in his capacity of a subject, to sacrifice his private interests to the public good. Egoism forbids co-operation, and without co-operation there cannot be any great achievemet." The application of this rule to its logical conclusion will take the Japanese a long way and will enable them to solve many of the social problems of the present time, he true meanings of which are only beginning to be dimly perceived by the statesmen of the West. The war with Rssia is still in progress, and its immediate results are uncertain, but whatever they may be, we cannot doubt that it has opened a new chapter in the history, not only of Japan, but of the world, and when this is adequately written, the debt which is due to the Britain of the East will be fully recogised.

Meantime, Great Britain should not be above learning a few lessons from Japan. I do ot propose to enter into the lessons in military and naval administration and strategy, which no doubt will be taken to heart by the proper authorities, but there are more general interest on which. few remarks may be made Already, indeed, Lord Selboie, the Admiralty, has in Parliament been various lessons which may be learne experience. He attached the greatest quality of the personnel, and he insisted that men were of more importance than the sh have tried to make clear, has ng been rec

Japanese. What is true of the army and navy is true of every department of national life. The real measure of the importance and even of the power of a nation is to be found ultimately in the quality of its people.

The evolution in this country has been comparatively slow, and many of our industrial developments are due to conditions which are rapidly disappearing. Our supplies of raw materials in our most important manufactures, especially those connected with iron and steel, are becoming scarce and therefore expensive, and many of our manufacturers continue to use methods and appliances which are out of date on account of recent advances of science. Other countries, notably France, Germany, the United States, and above all Japan, have developed their educational arrangements and applied the results to national affairs in such a way as to affect profoundly economic and social conditions at home and trade abroad. We have seen that the educational arrangements of Japan are very complete, and that those who have had the advantage of them have been fitted to take an active and intelligent part in the great developments which have taken place.

Five years after my arrival in Japan I drew up a somewhat exhaustive report on the work which we had accomplished, and indicated some of the aims which ought to be kept in view. I took occasion to point out that in many respects engineering education in Great Britain was very defective, and for this I was criticised by some of the foreign residents and even by some of my colleagues. Since that time, practically all the improvements which we had adopted in the Imperial College of Engineering, Japan, are to be found in almost all the colleges in this country. Engineering is no longer taught as a single subject but as a group of allied subjects, and the field which was formerly supposed to be taken up by one professor or lecturer is now divided among several, and engineering laboratories are parts of the equipment of every well-organised college. Two or three years ago, when Lord

Kelvin was inaugurating the James Watt engineering laboratory in Glasgow University, he reminded his audience that the Imperial College of Engineering, Japan, was the first educational institution which had a laboratory of this kind. The experimental and graphical methods introduced into every department of its course are now common in all the colleges of this country. The method of combining theory and practice in the training of engineers which I introduced into Japan is now being strongly recommended under the name of the " sandwich " system of apprenticeship. I am not, however, so sure that the spirit which animated the professors and students in Japan is yet very common in Britain. The distinction between instruction—the mere collection of facts and figures—and real education is not sufficiently kept in mind. The Japanese students were not crammed ; they were trained to think and to act for themselves, and their subsequent careers have fully proved the success of the methods adopted. We have seen that in the arts of peace and war they have applied their knowledge in a manner which has surprised the world.

Probably, however, the chief lesson to be learned from Japan is the need for a truly national spirit for the accomplishment of great ends. The present war has shown most distinctly that Japanese soldiers and sailors are careless of personal survival if they feel that they are taking part in the accomplishment of a national aim. It is, of course, in war that this spirit is most distinctly shown, because in industry, trade, and political life merely personal interests are apt to interfere, but even in these the Japanese have shown that considerations of national welfare come before everything else. The guiding principles enunciated by the Emperor when he ascended the throne have always been kept in mind, not only by himself and the Government but also by the people, and the national policy has been directed to the attainment of the objects in view. Education, industry, the army and navy, foreign politics ; in short, the national life was subordinated to the attainment of these objects. Plans were carefully drawn out in every department, and were carried out with great deliberation. The national life was conscious.

Can we say that this is the case in Britain? Is it not rather true that we have no real national policy, and that our statesmen drift according to their own whims or to what may be called accidental circumstances? Our greatest need is a conscious national aim to which all our efforts would be constantly directed, and to which the latest developments of science would be efficiently applied. In this connection, however, science must not be used in its limited sense, but include all that is essential to individual and national welfare.

In one of his last addresses on technical education the late Professor Huxley pointed out the dangers of a one-sided treatment of the subject, and urged the necessity of keeping an anxious eye upon those measures which are necessary for the preservation of that stable and sound condition of the whole social organism which is the essential condition of real progress, and a chief end of all education. He added: "You will recollect that some time ago there was a scandal and a great outcry about certain cutlasses and bayonets which had been supplied to our troops and sailors. These warlike implements were polished as bright as rubbing could make them; they were very well sharpened; they looked lovely. But when they were applied to the test of the work of war they broke and they bent, and proved more likely to hurt the hand of him that used them than to do any harm to the enemy. Let me apply that analogy to the effect of education, which is a sharpening and polishing of the mind. You may develop the intellectual side of people as far as you like, and you may confer on them all the skill that training and instruction can give; but if there is not, underneath all that outside form and superficial polish, the firm fibre of healthy manhood and earnest desire to do well, your labour is absolutely in vain." Much of the time, money, and energy at present spent on education is spent in vain because this advice is overlooked. The applications of physical and natural science by themselves may simply sharpen the tools which may drive us to destruction. The scientific method must be applied to ethics, sociology, and politics, and above all to the training of men and women, healthy in body, acute in mind, and animated with high ideals of individual, civic, and national duty. A writer in a daily paper says with a great amount of truth, " What makes Japan particularly valuable as an exemplar for us is, that the virtues in which it specially excels are precisely those we most need and lack. Among our most unpleasant traits are the worship and display of wealth, the lack of general courtesy, the insensibility to the charms of art, the feverish absorption in needless work, and the consequent inability to enjoy elegant leisure."

These remarks apply to a greater or less extent to all the nations of the world, but there are a few lessons in what may be called world politics to which Lessons for attention may be drawn. the nations of the world.

The first indeed should be evident to all who have taken any interest in Eastern peoples, and it is the profoundly significant phenomena of history, that the West, *by itself*, is impotent to exert directly a real and vital influence upon the East. Japan, which seems a striking proof to the contrary, is its strongest confirmation. As a Japanese writer from whom I have quoted insists : " It was some small degree of self-recognition that re-made Japan, and enabled her to weather the storm under which so much of the Oriental world went down," and he generalises that " it must be a renewal of the same self-consciousness that shall build up Asia again into her ancient steadfastness and strength." Probably it will be replied that it is no part of the plan (so far as they have any plan) of the Western Powers to help Asia to attain this object. If this be so, they are simply using the East for selfish purposes, and their efforts are doomed to failure.

The second lesson which it is hoped the nations of the

education is ....
The application of physical and ....
selves may simply .... them-
to destruction. The ....
ethics, sociology, and politics, and ....
of men and women, healthy in body ....
animated with high ideas of ....
duty. A writer in a daily paper says ....
of truth, "What makes Japan .... to
exemplar for us is, that the .... which it
excels are precisely those we most ....
our most important ideals are the safety, ...
wealth, the lack of .... necessary, but
the charms of art, the foremost also
and the consequent inability to ...

These remarks apply to ....
the nations of the world. But ....
what may be called ....
attention may be drawn.

The first .... should be ......
have taken any interest in the ....
profoundly significant phenomenon ....
by itself, is important in some ....
influence upon the East. ....
proof to the contrary, in the character
Japanese writer from whom I have
some small degree of ....
and enabled her to weather the storm ...
of the Oriental world went down," ....
"it must be a renewal of the cause ......
shall build up Asia again ....
strength." Probably it will be ....
of the plan (so far as they have ....
Powers to help Asia to ....
they are simply using the West for .....
their efforts are doomed to failure.

The second lesson which it is ....

world will take to heart is that, in so far at least as Japan, China, and Korea are concerned, there must be a profound change in the methods of dealing with these nations. The days of crooked diplomacy, gunboat policy, veiled threats and monstrous indemnities must be looked upon as past, and all questions must be discussed and settled on a basis of international equity. I have already expressed the opinion that if the bogey of the "Yellow Peril" ever becomes a reality, it will be on account of the conduct of some of the Western Powers, whose aggressions will drive the peoples of the Far East into militarism. Neither Japan nor China has shown the slightest signs of aggression, they simply ask to be treated with justice and to be allowed to develop on their own lines. I believe Count Okuma when he says: "The China-Japan war was the outcome of the feeling that Korea under the suzerainty of China was a constant menace to the future prosperity of our Empire. The same feeling is the cause of the present war, for Korea in the possession of Russia means the loss of our national independence. How patient we were during the protracted and tedious negotiations with Russia all the world knows. The war is not the result of any racial hatred, or of the spirit of revenge, or of aggressive designs. Having been forced upon us, it is purely defensive. When the war is concluded the whole world will be surprised to see, as after the war with China, that not a trace of enmity or any ill-feeling exists towards our temporary enemy. Not even towards the Russians shall we cease to possess the feeling of amity, which comes from confidence in our own strength, and from the fact that through 2500 years of our history we have never known defeat; and as in the past, so in the future, it will be our sole guide in our efforts to attain a high stage of Western civilisation."

This is not merely a personal opinion on the part of Count Okuma, it is a national sentiment which was clearly reflected in an Imperial proclamation of 21st April 1895, in which the following passages occur:—"We deem it that the development of the prestige of the country could be obtained only by peace. It is Our mission which We inherited from Our ancestors that peace should be maintained in an effectual way. The foundations of the great policy of Our ancestors have been made more stable. We desire that, together with Our people, We be specially guarded against arrogance or relaxation. It is what We highly object to, that the people should become arrogant by being puffed up with triumph, and despise others rashly, which would go towards losing the respect of Foreign Powers. Since the development of the nation can be obtained by peace, it is a divine duty imposed upon us by Our ancestors, and it has been Our intention and endeavour since Our accession to the Throne to maintain peace, so as to enjoy it constantly. . . . We are positively against insulting others and falling into idle pride by being elated by victories, and against losing the confidence of Our friendly States."

The action of Russia in seizing and in some cases destroying neutral merchant vessels because they were supposed to be carrying contraband of war has raised some difficult questions of International Law, which will require very careful consideration. It is impossible to say whether the difficulties which have arisen are due to deliberate Russian diplomacy or to the indiscretion of Russian naval officers ; but it is evident that the Russian Government's declaration as to what it proposes to treat as contraband, and therefore, subject to seizure is unprecedently wide in its terms, and attempts to carry it out are certain to bring Russia at once into hostility with the established law of nations. Articles which are the common exchange of peaceful life and commerce are by the precedents of that law not legally attachable, unless it can be shown that they are intended for the use of the military forces of the country of their destination. It has been laid down as unchallengeable by a great jurist that " to divert food from a large population where no immediate military end is in view would be to stop all neutral trading during a war." The action of

Russia has been further complicated by the use to which the "Volunteer" Fleet has been put, not only when its position is considered from a general legal point of view, but also because of the special treaty obligations of Russia in connection with the Black Sea. If the doings of Russia be allowed to pass unchallenged, an end would be put to all peaceful commerce when any two Powers happened to be at war. Evidently the nations of the world must come to a distinct understanding on these points, not only on account of their bearings on the present war, but also in view of future possibilities. Russia cannot be allowed to become a law unto herself.

Meantime I shall only mention another lesson which ought to be learned by the nations of the world in their dealings with Eastern peoples, and that is the necessity of looking from an international point of view at the political questions which arise. As ethical philosophy is no longer purely individualistic, so in like manner practical politics can no longer be purely national. The engineer has shrunk the world into small dimensions, and the social and economic conditions of the various countries are closely connected. Statesmen must therefore study what may be called the dynamics of politics if they wish to carry on their work in a rational manner. We have been told very often recently that we must think " Imperially." I would rather put it that we must think " Internationally," and I am convinced that the greatest real successes will fall to those statesmen who are international in their conceptions and not insular and individual. In this respect the statesmen of Japan have given an example to the nations of the world, as in all their actions they have dealt with the other Powers with perfect frankness. This has been the case for years past, but it has been strikingly shown since the outbreak of war with Russia. The British Secretary of State for Foreign Affairs when he concluded the alliance with Japan showed that he recognised the international nature of many of the problems in the Far East, and that alliance was the first definite, public and

Recent Events   433

intelligible measure taken to prevent chaos in that part of the world. As a well-known American statesman put it: "The immediate effect of the announcement of this treaty was to bring the world to its senses. Contemporaneously with its publication, our State Department sent a memorandum both to Pekin and St. Petersburg, asserting in plain terms that the situation in Manchuria was a distinct breach of the stipulations of treaties between China and Foreign Powers, not only damaging the rights of American citizens by exposing them to discriminations, but tending also to cripple the Chinese Empire in the discharge of its international obligations. The terms of this memorandum indicate that it was written with the text of the Anglo-Japanese treaty within easy reach." Even the Governments of Russia, France, and Germany approved of the treaty, and the Russian official press said that it contained exactly the idea they had long cherished, a statement which may be taken as an index of the sincerity of Russian professions. If Britain and the other Powers named had shown a little more distinctly than they did that they really meant what they said, the war would not have broken out. Russia's diplomats are too shrewd men of the world to have allowed a conflict not simply with Japan but also with the other most powerful nations. Meantime Japan is fighting not only her own battle for freedom, it might almost be said for existence; she is also fighting the battle of Europe and America for liberty to develop international trade and intercourse, and to bring about a closer union of East and West.

August 16, 1904.

(B 207)   2 F

APPENDICES

APPENDIX A

Japanese Weights, Measures, and Moneys, with English and French Equivalents

Japan.	Great Britain.	France.
Ri	2.4403382 miles.	3.9272727 kilomètres.
Ri (Marine) . . .	1.1506873 miles.	1.8518182 kilomètres.
Square *Ri* . . .	5.9552506 square miles.	15.4234711 kilomètres carrés.
Square *Chō* = 10 *Tan* .	2.4507204 acres.	99.1735537 ares.
Tsubo	3.9538290 square yards.	3.3057851 mètres carrés.
Koku = 10 *To* = 100 *Shō* (Liquid).	39.7033130 gallons. ⎱	1.8039068 hectolitres.
Koku = 10 *To* = 100 *Shō* (Dry).	4.9629141 bushels. ⎰	
Koku (capacity of vessel).	$\frac{1}{10}$ of ton.	$\frac{1}{10}$ de tonne.
Kwan = 1000 *Momme* .	8.2673297 ℔s. (Avoir.) ⎱ 10.0471021 ,, (Troy.) ⎰	3.7500000 kilogrammes.
Kin	1.3227727 ℔s. (Avoir.) ⎱ 1.6075363 ,, (Troy.) ⎰	6.0000000 hectogrammes.
Momme	2.1164364 drams (Avoir.) ⎱ 2.4113045 dwts. (Troy.) ⎰	3.7500000 grams.
Yen = 100 *Sen* = 1000 *Rin* = 10,000 *Mō*.	2.582 shillings.	2.583 francs.

APPENDIX B

TREATY OF ALLIANCE WITH GREAT BRITAIN

Agreement between Great Britain and Japan, signed at London, January 30, 1902.

THE Governments of Great Britain and Japan, actuated solely by a desire to maintain the *status quo* and general peace in the Extreme East, being, moreover, specially interested in maintaining the independence and territorial integrity of the Empire of China and the Empire of Korea and in securing equal opportunities in those countries for the commerce and industry of all nations, hereby agree as follows :—

ARTICLE I

The High Contracting Parties having mutually recognised the independence of China and of Korea, declare themselves to be entirely uninfluenced by any aggressive tendencies in either country. Having in view, however, their special interests, of which those of Great Britain relate principally to China, while Japan in addition to the interests which she possesses in China is interested in a peculiar degree politically, as well as commercially and industrially, in Korea, the High Contracting Parties recognise that it will be admissible for either of them to take such measures as may be indispensable in order to safeguard those interests if threatened either by the aggressive action of any other Power, or by disturbances arising in China or Korea, and

438

necessitating the intervention of either of the High Contracting Parties for the protection of the lives and property of its
subjects.

Artilce II

If either Great Britain or Japan, in the defence of their
respective interests as above described, should become
involved in war with another Power, the other High
Contracting Party will maintain a strict neutrality, and use
its efforts to prevent other Powers from joining in hostilities
against its ally.

Article III

If in the above event any other Power or Powers should
join in hostilities against that ally, the other High Contracting Party will come to its assistance, and will conduct the
war in common, and make peace in mutual agreement with it.

Article IV

The High Contracting Parties agree that neither of
them will, without consulting the other, enter into separate
arrangements with another Power to the prejudice of the
interests above described.

Article V

Whenever, in the opinion of either Great Britain or
Japan, the above-mentioned interests are in jeopardy, the
two Governments will communicate with one another fully
and frankly.

Article VI

The present agreement shall come into effect immediately after the date of its signature, and remain in force for
five years from that date. In case neither of the High
Contracting Parties should have notified twelve months
before the expiration of the said five years the intention of

terminating it, it shall remain binding until the expiration of one year from the day on which either of the High Contracting Parties shall have denounced it. But if, when the date fixed for its expiration arrives, either ally is actually engaged in war, the alliance shall, *ipso facto*, continue until peace is concluded.

In faith whereof, the Undersigned, duly authorised by their respective Governments, have signed this Agreement, and have affixed hereto their seals.

Done in duplicate at London the 30th January 1902.

(L. S.) (Signed) LANSDOWNE,
His Britannic Majesty's Principal Secretary of State for Foreign Affairs.

(L. S.) (Signed) HAYASHI,
Envoy Extraordinary and Minister Plenipotentiary of His Majesty the Emperor of Japan at the Court of St. James.

With this treaty as published (Japan, November 1902) appeared the following explanatory letter from Lord Lansdowne to Sir Claude Macdonald, British Minister in Tokyo :—

THE MARQUIS OF LANSDOWNE TO SIR C. MACDONALD

FOREIGN OFFICE, 30*th January* 1902.

SIR—I have signed to-day with the Japanese Minister an Agreement between Great Britain and Japan, of which a copy is enclosed in this despatch.

This Agreement may be regarded as the outcome of the events which have taken place in the Far East, and of the part taken by Great Britain and Japan in dealing with them.

Throughout the troubles and complications which arose in China consequent upon the Boxer outbreak and the attack upon the Peking Legations, the two Powers have been in close and uninterrupted communication, and have been actuated by similar views.

We have each of us desired that the integrity and independence of the Chinese Empire should be preserved, that there should be no disturbance of the territorial *status quo* either in China or in the adjoining regions, that all nations should, within those regions, as well as within the limits of the Chinese Empire, be afforded equal opportunities for the development of their commerce and industry, and that peace should not only be restored, but should, for the future, be maintained.

From the frequent exchanges of views which have taken place between the two Governments, and from the discovery that their Far Eastern policy was identical, it has resulted that each side has expressed the desire that their common policy should find expression in an international contract of binding validity.

We have thought it desirable to record in the Preamble of that instrument the main objects of our common policy in the Far East, to which I have already referred, and in the first Article we join in entirely disclaiming any aggressive tendencies either in China or Korea. We have, however, thought it necessary also to place on record the view entertained by both the High Contracting Parties that, should their interests as above described be endangered, it will be admissible for either of them to take such measures as may be indispensable in order to safeguard those interests, and words have been added which will render it clear that such precautionary measures might become necessary and might be legitimately taken, not only in the case of aggressive action or of an actual attack by some other Power, but in the event of disturbances arising of a character to necessitate the intervention of either of the High Contracting Parties for the protection of the lives and property of its subjects.

The principal obligations undertaken mutually by the High Contracting Parties are those of maintaining a strict neutrality in the event of either of them becoming involved in war, and of coming to one another's assistance in the event of either of them being confronted by the opposition of more than one hostile Power. Under the remaining provisions of the Agreement, the High Contracting Parties undertake that neither of them will, without consultation with the other, enter into separate arrangements with another Power to the prejudice of the interests described in the Agreement, and that whenever those interests are in jeopardy they will communicate with one another fully and frankly.

The concluding Article has reference to the duration of the Agreement, which, after five years, is terminable by either of the High Contracting Parties at one year's notice.

His Majesty's Government have been largely influenced in their decision to enter into this important contract by the conviction that it contains no provisions which can be regarded as an indication of aggressive or self-seeking tendencies in the regions to which it applies.

It has been concluded purely as a measure of precaution to be invoked, should occasion arise, in the defence of important British interests. It in no way threatens the present position or the legitimate interests of other Powers. On the contrary, that part of it which renders either of the High Contracting Parties liable to be called upon by the other for assistance can operate only when one of the allies has found himself obliged to go to war in defence of interests which are common to both, when the circumstances in which he has taken this step are such as to establish that the quarrel has not been of his own seeking, and when, being engaged in his own defence, he finds himself threatened, not by a single Power, but by a hostile coalition.

His Majesty's Government trust that the Agreement may be found of mutual advantage to the two countries, that it will make for the preservation of peace, and that, should peace unfortunately be broken, it will have the effect of restricting the area of hostilities.—I am, etc.

LANSDOWNE.

APPENDIX C

Japanese Government Reports issued by the various Departments.
British and American Consular Reports.
Transactions of the Asiatic Society of Japan.
Transactions of the Japan Society, London.
Murray's Handbook of Japan, by Chamberlain and Mason. Latest edition.
CHAMBERLAIN, Professor B. H.—Things Japanese. London, 1902.
YAMAWAKI, H.—Japan in the Beginning of the Twentieth Century. Tokyo, 1903.
STEAD, ALFRED (Editor).—Japan by the Japanese; a Survey by its highest Authorities. London, 1904.
This is a valuable collection of papers written by distinguished Japanese statesmen and administrators. It was published after my book was printed.
BRINKLEY, Captain F.—Japan and China, 12 vols. London, 1903.
——, Article on " Japan " in supplementary volumes of *Encyclopædia Britannica.*
VON WENCKSTEIN.—Bibliography of the Japanese Empire. London, 1895.
OLIPHANT, L.—Narrative of the Earl of Elgin's Mission to China and Japan. Edinburgh and London, 1859.
ALCOCK, Sir R.—The Capital of the Tycoon. London, 1863.
BLACK, J. R.—Young Japan. Yokohama, 1880.
ADAMS, F. D.—History of Japan. London, 1875.
GRIFFIS, W. E.—The Mikado's Empire. New York, 1876.
——, Townsend Harris, First American Envoy. London, 1895.
MOUNSEY, A. H.—The Satsuma Rebellion. London, 1879.
MURRAY, D.—The Story of Japan. New edition. London, 1904.

REED, Sir E. J.—Japan : its History, Traditions, and Religions. London, 1880.

DICKENS and LANE-POOLE.—Life of Sir Harry Parkes. London, 1894.

BIRD, Miss (Mrs. Bishop).—Unbeaten Tracks in Japan. London, 1888.

DIOSY, A.—The New Far East. London, 1904.

VON SIEBOLD, A.—Japan's Accession to the Comity of Nations. London, 1901.

KNAPP, A. M.—Feudal and Modern Japan. London, 1898.

NORMAN, H.—The Real Japan. London and New York, 1892.

——, Peoples and Politics in the Far East. London and New York, 1896.

STEAD, A.—Japan, our Ally. London, 1902.

CURZON, G. N. (now Lord).—Problems of the Far East. London, 1896.

DAVIDSON, J. W.—The Island of Formosa, Past and Present. Yokohama and London, 1903.

BROWNELL, C. L.—The Heart of Japan. London, 1903.

FRASER, Mrs. H.—A Diplomatist's Wife in Japan. London, 1899.

RITTNER, G. H.—Impressions of Japan. London, 1904.

MORRIS, J.—Advance, Japan. London, 1895.

——, Japan and its Trade. London, 1902.

WATSON, W. P.—Japan, Aspects and Destinies. London, 1904

DAVIDSON, A. M. C.—Present Day Japan. London, 1904.

HARTSHORNE, A. C.—Japan and her People. London, 1904.

DEL MAR, W.—Around the World through Japan. London, 1903.

RANSOME, S.—Japan in Transition. London, 1899.

LEROY-BEAULIEU, P.—The Awakening of the East. London, 1900.

CLEMENT, E. W.—Handbook of Modern Japan. Chicago and London, 1904.

SCHERER, J. A. B.—Japan To-day. London, 1904.

WESTON, W.—The Japanese Alps. London, 1896.

DICKSON, W. G.—Gleanings from Japan. Edinburgh, 1889.

DIXON, W. G.—The Land of the Morning. Edinburgh, 1882.

PEERY, R. B.—The Gist of Japan. Edinburgh, 1896.

VLADIMIR.—The China-Japan War. London, 1896.

EASTLAKE and YAMADA.—Heroic Japan. Yokohama, 1896.

JANE, F. J.—The Imperial Japanese Navy. London, 1904.

NITOBE, I.—Bushido, the Soul of Japan. Tokyo, 1901.

HEARN, L.—Kokoro and other Works. London, 1896, etc.

LOWELL, P.—The Soul of the Far East. Boston, 1896.

GULICK, S. L.—Evolution of the Japanese. New York and London, 1903.

OKAKURA, K.—The Ideals of the East. London, 1903.

GRIFFIS, W. E.—The Religions of Japan. London, 1895.

MITFORD, A. B.—Tales of Old Japan. London, 1876.

HAYASHI, VISCOUNT.—For his People. London, 1903.

WATANNA, O.—The Wooing of Wistaria. London, 1902.

ASTON, W. G.—History of Japanese Literature. London, 1899.

CHAMBERLAIN, PROF. B. H.—The Classical Poetry of the Japanese. London, 1880.

RIORDAN and TAKAYANAGI.—Sunrise Stories. London, 1896.

LEWIS, R. E.—The Educational Conquest of the Far East. New York and London, 1903.

MIYAMORI, A.—Life of Yukichi Fukazawa. Tokyo, 1902.

GRIFFIS, W. E.—Verbeck of Japan. Edinburgh and London, 1901.

BACON, A. M.—Japanese Girls and Women. Boston and London, 1891.

REIN, J. J.—Japan, Travels and Researches. London, 1884.

——, The Industries of Japan. London, 1889.

ANDERSON, W.—Pictorial Arts of Japan. Boston, 1886.

GONSE, L.—L'Art Japonaise. Paris, 1883.

AUDSLEY and BOWES.—Ceramic Art of Japan. Liverpool, 1875.

HUISH, M. B.—Japan and its Art. London, 1889.

HARTMAN, S.—Japanese Art. Boston and London, 1904.

MORSE, E. S.—Japanese Homes and their Surroundings. New York, 1903.

PIGGOTT, F. T.—Music and Musical Instruments in Japan. London, 1903.

CONDER, J.—Landscape Gardening in Japan. Tokyo, 1893.

Reference should also be made to the bibliographical notes at the end of each chapter of this book, and also, when possible, to files of the daily newspapers published in English in Japan, especially the *Japan Daily Mail* and the *Japan Times.*

INDEX

Administration, problems of, 280
Administrative bodies, functions of, 284
Agriculture : in Old Japan, 238 ; new
  conditions, 240 ; improvements in,
  ·241 ; means for encouraging, 245 ;
  legislation on, 246
Alliance with Great Britain, 76, 329, 438
Army and navy, 109 ; development of,
  111
Art, characteristics of Japanese, 205
Art and music education, 95
Art industries : art in Old Japan 204 ;
  Western influences, 206 ; Japanese
  Art Society, 207 ; criticism of foreign
  art, 208 ; modern conditions, 209 ;
  Eastern ideals, 210 ; art and economic
  conditions, 211 ; present conditions in
  Japan, 212 ; comparison with India,
  214 ; future of Japanese art industries,
  216
Asia, Japan in, 391
Asia, task of, 385
Assembly, deliberative, 53
Associations, technical, 185

Balance of trade against Japan, 227
Banking system, 304
Books on Japan, 443
Brinkley Captain, opinions on : Japanese
  religion, 38 ; men of the Revolution,
  52 ; Japanese officers, 113 ; Japanese
  press, 175 ; foreign advisers, 193 ;
  Japanese art, 213 ; foreign treaties,
  316, 330
Britain, Great : alliance with, 329, 438 ;
  lessons for, 425
Britain of the East, ambition to become,
  342 ; geographical advantages of
  Japan, 334
Budgets, family, 373-75
Budgets, national, in 1893 and 1903,
  298, 299
Building industry, 177

"Bushido," 32
Business relations, international, 331

Cabinet, functions of, 283
Capital in Japan, future of, 394
Chemical industries, 176
China : war with, 71 ; results of war
  with, 73 ; aggression of Russia and
  Germany in, 74 ; results of, 75 ; re-
  sults on Japanese policy, 74 ; Japanese
  influence in, 349
Chinese opinions and ideals, 349
Code of Education in Japan, 82
College of Engineering (Imperial). *See*
  Kobu-Daigakko
Colonies, military, 254
Combinations of employers and workers,
  191, 393
Commerce : in Old Japan, 219 ; results
  of new conditions, 220 ; development
  of foreign trade, 222 ; exports and
  imports, 222 ; distribution of foreign
  trade, 224 ; balance of trade against
  Japan, 227 ; current prices, 228 ;
  provisions for encouraging commerce,
  229 ; commercial and industrial
  guilds, 231 ; tariffs, 231 ; commercial
  morality of Japanese merchants, 43,
  232 ; position of foreign merchants,
  234
Confucian philosophy of life, 384
Consular (foreign) tribunals, 315
Cotton spinning, 171

Debt, national, 303
Deliberative assembly, 53
Development on Western lines, 68
Diplomacy, future of, 429, 432
Distribution of Japan's foreign trade,
  224
Dockyards and shipbuilding yards, 122,
  165
Duty to State, 39

447

2 G